On Anthologies

Edited and with
an introduction by
Jeffrey R. Di Leo

On Anthologies

Politics and Pedagogy

University of Nebraska Press
Lincoln and London

Copyright © 2004 by the University of Nebraska Press
All rights reserved. Manufactured in the United States of America

∞

Essays by Laurie Finke, Barbara Johnson, Vincent B. Leitch, John McGowan, and Jeffrey J. Williams originate from "Symposium: Editing a Norton Anthology," published in *College English* 66.2 (November 2003): 173–206, copyright 2003 by the National Council of Teachers of English, and used with permission. Finke, Johnson, and McGowan are reprinted; Leitch and Williams are adapted. Cary Nelson's essay is adapted from "Murder in the Cathedral: Editing a Comprehensive Anthology of Modern American Poetry," in *American Literary History* 14.2 (2002): 311–27, and is used with the permission of Oxford University Press. The essays by Lynn Z. Bloom, Terry Caesar, David Damrosch, David B. Downing, Gerald Graff and Jeffrey R. Di Leo, Karen L. Kilcup, Cris Mazza, Robert L. McLaughlin, Richard S. Pressman, Alan D. Schrift, and Simon Morgan Wortham originally appeared in *symplokē* 8.1–2 (2000), a special issue devoted to anthologies.
Each of these essays is also used by kind permission of the authors.

Set in Quadraat by Tseng Information Systems, Inc.
Book design: Richard Eckersley.

Library of Congress Cataloging-in-Publication Data
On anthologies : politics and pedagogy / edited and with an introduction by Jeffrey R. Di Leo.
p. cm. Includes bibliographical references and index.
ISBN 0-8032-6644-8 (paperback : alkaline paper)
1. Anthologies – History and criticism. 2. Anthologies – Editing. 3. Literature publishing. 4. Canon (Literature) I. Di Leo, Jeffrey R.
PN4397.O5 2004   080—dc22   2004006379

The term is unfairly regarded with some disdain, as if the anthology were in itself a middlebrow enterprise, crafted to eliminate the difficult or the provocative. – William Germano, *Getting It Published: A Guide for Scholars and Anyone Else Serious about Serious Books*

One must resist the notion of treating an anthology as the last word on its subject. It is no more than a first word, a threshold opening on to a new space. – Paul Auster, preface to *The Random House Book of Twentieth-Century French Poetry*

Textbooks are the apparatuses of orthodoxy. And orthodox textbooks are the principle means by which institutions control their subjects. – James Sosnoski, *Token Professionals and Master Critics: A Critique of Orthodoxy in Literary Studies*

I prefer to see anthologies as a theoretically interesting form whose potential for opening up discourse has yet to be sufficiently explored. – Sarah Lawall, "Anthologizing 'World Literature'"

Contents

	ix	Acknowledgments
Jeffrey R. Di Leo	1	Analyzing Anthologies

PART 1
From Anthologizing to Canonizing

David Damrosch	31	From the Old World to the Whole World
Sarah Lawall	47	Anthologizing "World Literature"
Lynn Z. Bloom	90	Once More to the Essay Canon
Karen L. Kilcup	112	The Poetry and Prose of Recovery Work

PART 2
Innovations and Challenges

Robert L. McLaughlin	141	Anthologizing Contemporary Literature
Cris Mazza	155	Finding the Chic in Lit
Cary Nelson	170	The Economic Challenges to Anthologies
Alan D. Schrift	186	Confessions of an Anthology Editor

PART 3
Attitudes and Responses

Jeffrey J. Williams	207	Anthology Disdain
Nancy Cirillo	222	Anthologizing the Caribbean, or, Squaring Beaches, Bananas, and Nobel Laureates
Angeline O'Neill	247	Distinguishing the Map from the Territory
Richard S. Pressman	264	Is There a Future for the *Heath Anthology* in the Neoliberal State?

Contents

PART 4
Theory, Pedagogy, and Practice

Gerald Graff and Jeffrey R. Di Leo	279	Anthologies, Literary Theory, and the Teaching of Literature
Terry Caesar	298	Anthologies, Literature, and Theory in Japan
Simon Morgan Wortham	326	Anthologizing Derrida
David B. Downing	342	Theorizing the Discipline and the Disciplining of Theory

PART 5
Notes on Headnotes

Vincent B. Leitch	373	Ideology of Headnotes
Barbara Johnson	384	Headnotes
Laurie Finke	395	The Hidden Curriculum
John McGowan	405	Headnotes, Headmasters, and the Pedagogical Imaginary
	411	List of Contributors
	415	Index

Acknowledgments

My primary debt of gratitude goes out to the contributors to this volume for sharing their thoughts on anthologies. It is my hope that their experiences as both producers and users of anthologies will help to demystify the process of anthologization as well as assist in making the next generation of anthologies more finely attuned to the needs of their audiences.

I would also like to single out a number of individuals whose insightful suggestions and timely support were of particular assistance in bringing this volume together, namely, Vincent B. Leitch, Elaine Martin, Candice Chovanec Melzow, Christian Moraru, Joseph Ricapito, Carol Schanche, Pete Simon, James Sosnoski, and Jeffrey J. Williams. Furthermore, my own knowledge of anthologization has deepened greatly by my having had the good fortune of working closely with a number of very fine editors, especially Ken King and Jon-David Hague of McGraw-Hill. Finally, I would like to thank my wife, Nina, for her unfailing encouragement, support, and patience.

On Anthologies

JEFFREY R. DI LEO

Analyzing Anthologies

Anthologies and Atlases

Scholars and students alike rely on anthologies for accurate topologies of their disciplines. Initiates generally receive a contemporary anthology as if they had been handed a recently published atlas of the world: just as one does not question the atlas's placement of cities and countries, one does not question the anthology's mapping of authors and writings. Terry Caesar's comments on his first academic job corroborate this attitude.

Newly arrived at the university, Caesar was handed an anthology and assigned to teach two sections of a course entitled World Masterpieces, which he had never taught before. Caesar reflects that the anthology "was given unto me in the same spirit that God gave Moses the Ten Commandments" (160). To be sure, Caesar's experience as a young scholar and teacher is one shared by many – teachers *and* students alike.

Anthologies are considered to be reflective of the laws of their domain. Both students and teachers can be humbled and intimidated by their inventories of readings. The formative power of anthologies is often magical to students and regulative to teachers. While titles, contents, and authors may blur into oblivion over time, the name of the anthology does not.

"Textbooks are the apparatuses of orthodoxy," writes James J. Sosnoski, "and orthodox textbooks are the principle means by which institutions control their subjects" (75). The various forms of orthodoxy and authority that anthologies take on resonate through the essays in this collection. The contributors provide a critical examination of this authority and orthodoxy through the pedagogical, political, and economic implications of using and publishing anthologies.

Anthologies are shaped by pedagogies, and pedagogies are shaped by anthologies. A good anthology can be the difference between a positive educational experience and a pedagogical nightmare. Teachers' attitudes toward their courses are often directly related to the textbooks that they use. Departments and institutions often fall into habits of uncritical acceptance of particular anthologies as the benchmark for what should be taught in courses. Anthology critics call us to question that trust or at least to understand better the conditions upon which it can be accepted. They remind us that while anthologies are in certain ways analogous to world atlases, their construction is vastly different.

In addition to shaping our teaching experience, anthologies have a key role in canon formation and are always already implicated in various political and cultural agendas. Whereas a previous generation of scholars was more inclined to consider the contents of anthologies published by well-respected and revered publishers like Oxford, Longman, and Norton to be necessary and immutable, an emerging generation of scholars is challenging such notions. Contemporary critical theory and cultural studies have revealed the radically contingent nature of the contents of anthologies and the conditions upon which those contents have been determined. "One must resist the notion of treating an anthology as the last word on its subject," writes the novelist Paul Auster. "It is no more than a first word, a threshold opening on to a new space" (211).

Today anthologies are discussed by progressive thinkers in terms of the canonical formations that they propose and the possible political and cultural directions in which they implicate their subject matter. Just as anthologies can empower subjects, ideologies, and canons, making them relevant to students and faculty, they can also disempower them and make them irrelevant. Anthologies have consequences and are grounded in commitments: striving to articulate these consequences and commitments is a priority in higher education today.

What Is an Anthology?

Anthologies can be traced back at least as far as Ancient Greece. In Greek the word *anthologia* (ἀνθολογία), or "bouquet," means a collection of poems. Even though *anthologia* did not acquire this meaning until the Byzantine period, there were many collections of poetic epigrams – large and small – prior to this time. Starting from the fourth century BCE, the Greeks produced collections of poetic epigrams by single poets or on special topics. Unfortunately, most of these early "anthologies" are now lost. The earliest known large critical anthology is the *Garland*, in which Meleager collected the work of some fifty Greek poets. This work dates from about 80 BCE and spans the work of the eighth-century BCE iambic and elegiac poet Archilochus to that of Meleager himself and his contemporaries (Highet 67).

While the subject matter of anthologies now includes much more than merely poetry, the basic notion of an anthology as a *collection of writings* remains the same. Today an anthology is a collection of connected or interrelated writings that center around a topic. Organizing topics may include themes, disciplines, persons, and historical periods. Needless to say, a staggering number of books fit this description. Some titles include collections of previously published contemporary fiction such as Larry McCaffery's *Avant-Pop: Fiction for a Daydreaming Nation* (Black Ice, 1993); collections of new fiction such as Cris Mazza and Jeffrey DeShell's *Chick-Lit: Postfeminist Fiction* (FC2, 1995); world literature collections such as Brian Wilkie and James Hurt's *Literature of the Western World* (Macmillan, 1988); collections of previously published articles such as Simon During's *The Cultural Studies Reader* (Routledge, 1993); collections of newly commissioned essays such as Simon Critchley and Robert Bernasconi's *The Cambridge Companion to Levinas* (Cambridge, 2002); collections of texts by historical figures such as Peter Bondanella and Mark Musa's *The Portable Machiavelli* (Penguin, 1979); and collections of classic and contemporary theory and criticism such as Vincent Leitch's *The Norton Anthology of Theory and Criticism* (Norton, 2001) and Gerald Graff and James Phelan's edition of *The Adventures of Huckleberry Finn* (Bedford/St. Martin's, 1995), which includes critical responses. How might we usefully distinguish among the aims of these differing volumes?

In his insightful book *Getting It Published: A Guide for Scholars and Anyone Else Serious about Serious Books*, William Germano makes a distinction between "collections" and "anthologies." In Germano's formulation a collection is "a gathering of new or mostly new writing," whereas an anthology is "a gathering of previously published, or mostly previously published, work" (121). "A collection," writes Germano, "aims to present the newest research or thought; an anthology aims to present the best of what has been thought and said – and already published" (121). Consequently, Germano's distinction clearly demarcates publications of new writings such as *Chick-Lit* and the *Companion to Levinas* as *collections*, not anthologies.

Germano, vice president and publishing director of Routledge, is approaching these distinctions as a member of the book publishing industry. From the industry's perspective these classifications are important. As essential new material a collection is forward-looking, whereas an anthology, a republication of a group of writings, is preserving valued texts. Each has different markets, production costs, and cachet.

The list above might be further subdivided into *readers* (combinations of unpublished and previously published materials), *casebooks* (major primary texts with secondary sources), and *textbooks* (combinations of previously published materials with newly written pedagogical support materials). However, potential readers of Germano's "gatherings" are less concerned with industry classifications than they are interested in the use and appeal of the publications. In the classroom the term *anthology* tends to be conflated with *collection*, as well as *reader*, *casebook*, and even *textbook*. This volume, entitled On Anthologies, considers all of these different types of collected and edited works.

Anthologies, Academic Culture, and the Public Sphere

Over the course of the past twenty-five years anthologies have shifted from playing a relatively minor role in academic culture to achieving a position of dominance. Anthologies have significant intellectual, economic, political, pedagogical, and creative resonance through all levels of academic life. They announce new and emerging areas of inquiry, are illustrative of ideological currents, and help us to organize and understand the past. They offer students an array of support materials ranging from abridged readings and informative headnotes to study guides and glossaries, all in a single volume. They constitute major sources of income for publishers and editors as well as a source of royalties for the anthologized writers. The confluence of these economic, practical, pedagogical, and intellectual considerations affords anthologies a continuing presence on the academic market.

The power of anthologies in shaping the university is widely recognized. Even outside of academe anthologies are in the news. For example, the *New York Times* recently ran an article on the production and publication of *The Norton Anthology of Theory and Criticism*. The article, "How Lit Crit Finally Won Out over Lit," by Sarah Boxer, opens by informing us that "300 pages of last-minute snips . . . left Goethe, Rousseau, George Eliot, I. A. Richards, Richard Rorty and Elaine Showalter on the cutting room floor." Why would late cuts due to space constraints – a mundane and commonplace occurrence in the production of anthologies – be deemed newsworthy by the *Times*? The popular fascination with anthologies could be linked to the trend toward drawing the academy into the public sphere.

In 1990, when the first edition of *The Heath Anthology of American Literature* appeared under the general editorship of Paul Lauter, the "PC Wars" were in full force. "Political correctness" was the new buzzword, and the popular media were searching for news bites. The *Heath* became the poster child of an anthology whose editing and conceptualization were precipitated by the dual waves of multiculturalism and political correctness. Only in a culture that had come to value public access to academia and its machinations would a new anthology be a newsworthy event.

The engagement of anthologies with the public sphere will only rise in the years to come, though not for the reasons stated above. While it may be fashionable to reveal the inner mechanisms of academia or to cite books that are indebted to multiculturalism and political correctness, the ultimate point of entry into the public sphere will come from publishing: print-on-demand publication and on-line access to anthologizable materials.

Already there are numerous publishers offering lengthy lists of materials that can be selected by the instructor. These sources not only afford instructors the freedom to choose *what* readings they want to assign to their students but also allow them to determine *how many*. On-demand publication literally puts the onus of anthologizing into the public sphere. While there may be suggested tables of contents, the instructor becomes the editor and anthologizer.

On-line publication further lowers the cost of access to materials. Public domain writings could be available on-line through a central database or Web site. Computer programs could be written to allow instructors to anthologize book and journal materials by designing Web sites that provide links to the books and journal articles already in their libraries' collections. The variations on these themes are numerous. New technologies offer the potential to change the business of anthologies and to draw anthologizing more squarely into the public sphere. Once this technology becomes widely available, it will also radically alter the relationship between anthologies and academic culture.

Anthology Studies

Cultural studies dominate the academic landscape in the humanities today. In the age of cultural studies critical discussion of anthologies will ideally intermingle concern with their production, their ideological identity, their use by students and faculty, and the mechanisms that regulate their distribution and usage. Studying anthologies and their role in university publishing and education will not only make us more informed users but also help us to become more knowledgeable members of the academy. Yet while anthologies are a pervasive and dominant part of academic culture, they have not yet been given sustained analysis by cultural theorists.

While some excellent articles have been published on the subject of anthologizing, no single-author monograph or edited collection of essays has been devoted to critically exploring humanities anthologies and anthologizing. Moreover, there has been no general critical study of the process of anthologizing. Until recently, no single volume was solely devoted to exploring any *aspect* of the editing and history of anthologies. This lacuna in the literature was broken by the publication of two excellent pioneering works: Leah Price's *The Anthology and the Rise of the Novel: From Richardson to George Eliot* (2000) and Anne Ferry's *Tradition and the Individual Poem: An Inquiry into Anthologies* (2001).

Still, the bibliography of works on anthologies is scattered and piecemeal. Anthologies are most frequently the objects of scholarly comment either merely in passing or as a subspecies of a more fundamental topic (e.g., book publishing, college teaching, the canon wars, or the nature of discourse). Other contributors to the analysis of anthologies include Friedrich A. Kittler, who argues in *Discourse Networks 1800/1900* (1990) that anthologies in late eighteenth-century Germany replaced the Bible as the book that unified a culture (144, 149), and scholars reviewing the canon, such as John Guillory in *Cultural Capital: The Problem of Literary Canon Formation* (1993) and Paul Lauter in *Canons and Contexts* (1991). Relevant sociological studies of the book publishing industry include Lewis A. Coser, Charles Kadushin, and Walter W. Powell's *Books: The Culture and Commerce of Publishing* (1982) and guidebooks such as William Germano's *Getting It Published: A Guide for Scholars and Anyone Else Serious about Serious Books* (2001).

Beyond these publications, the single most important venue for critically understanding anthologies has been book reviews – the most compressed, underrated, and misunderstood of all the critical venues. Interestingly, on the whole, anthology reviews are more likely to be negative than reviews of single-author volumes. "The term [anthology] is unfairly regarded with some disdain," writes Germano, "as if the anthology were in itself a middlebrow enterprise, crafted to eliminate the difficult or the provocative" (136). Perhaps it is this perception that anthologies are second-class citizens in the book world that empowers their reviewers to vituperate. Alternatively, the disdain of anthologies may stem from their links to publishing corporations and commercial gains. Whatever the reason, anthology reviews tend to be tougher than reviews of other books.

The concerns of anthology reviewers tend to cluster around three sets of three issues. The first triad involves *coverage* (viz., Are all the texts that should be in the anthology in it?), *introductions* (viz., Are the article and general introductions acceptable?), and *comparison* (viz., How does this anthology compare with other anthologies on the market?). The second triad involves *textual editing* (viz., Is the way in which the texts are edited acceptable?), *organization* (viz., Does the organization of the texts make sense?), and *paraphernalia* (viz., Is the teacher's guide and/or study guide acceptable?). Finally, the third triad evaluates *distribution* (viz., How will this anthology be distributed and why?), *production* (viz., Is the paper on which the book is printed adequate and why?), and *costs* (viz., Is the cost of this anthology in any way prohibitive and why?).

The point of entry into the first grouping of issues tends to be *politics*. The issues of *coverage, introductions,* and *comparison* are considered through critical ideologies. When competing anthologies are compared, the ideologies that inform the composition of the anthology are of vital concern. This first group is by far the dominant form of anthology book review today. It is also the locus of much heated debate and contestation between proponents of competing ideologies.

The second triad, *textual editing, organization,* and *paraphernalia,* tends to center around *pedagogical* interests. Reviewers with this set of concerns deal with anthologies as sites of pedagogy. The student/teacher relationship as refracted through the anthology is of prime concern to the reviewer. Given the increased emphasis on understanding and improving pedagogy, this type of approach to anthologies is quite popular. While this approach includes an important political element, political concerns are always secondary to pedagogical concerns. Whereas the primary question of the first triad might be stated as, "What is the politics of this anthology?," the primary question of the second triad might be stated as, "What student identities does this anthology best serve?" or, "What idea of textual consumption does this anthology presuppose?"

The third triad – *distribution, production,* and *costs* – centers around *economic* and *material* concerns. It deals with anthologies as commodities and material objects in the world. Compared to the previous two triads, this one is by far the least dominant type of investigation into anthologies. Its primary question is, "What are the conditions of production and distribution of this anthology?" Of the three triads, however, investigation into the third holds the greatest potential for increasing our critical understanding of the world of anthologies. Far less has been written about the material and economic conditions of anthologies than about their political and pedagogical conditions.

Undeniably, the best point of entry into anthologies and the anthologization process will draw on elements from all three triads: political, pedagogical, and economic/material.

The Value of Anthologies and Anthologizers

Contributor Sarah Lawall prefers "to see anthologies as a theoretically interesting form whose potential for opening up discourse has yet to be sufficiently explored." Her position is not widely shared. Why not? If anthologies are theoretically interesting, used regularly in classrooms, and have a powerful role in canon formation, why the dearth in studies of anthologies? Anthologies, though popular, are generally thought to have little value.

Jason Epstein, editorial director of Random House and recipient of the National Book Award for Distinguished Service to American Letters, presents arguments in this direction. "Topical anthologies, unlike hospital wards and reading rooms," says Epstein, "are of little value in themselves.... They serve no literary purpose, usually find few readers and quickly go out of print" (139–40). Is this a fair assessment of the value of anthologies and, by extension, of anthologizers?

Anthologies, says Epstein, "serve no literary purpose." In other words, anthologies are not creative or aesthetic acts in the same way that novels and poems are. Novels and poems serve a literary purpose, according to Epstein, whereas their repackaging into anthologies does not. The logic here is hard to follow, but Epstein's point is not to be logical. Rather it is to reveal a widely held bias against anthologies: their second-class status in the book world.

Anthologies represent a repackaging of primary sources, and it is this repackaging that is so offensive to scholars – not the anthology readings themselves. The medium presents the problem, not the contents. As for the readership of anthologies, Epstein is right that many anthologies do not find a readership – and quickly go out of print. However, some anthologies find strong readership and stay in print for years. Some, particularly of the textbook variety, even go on into new editions. Nonetheless, the generally received opinion on anthologies in the book world is still negative. Much the same condition holds in academia.

Anthologies are second-class citizens of the academic world. In the academic publishing race anthologizing is not considered as valuable as monograph authorship. But consider what is in itself more valuable to an academic community: a single-author monograph meticulously researched, densely written, and virtually unread by the community, or an anthology that assumes a comprehensive knowledge of the field, stakes out a sense of what is important, and is read and used by countless individuals? Twenty-five years ago there would have been much more support within the academy for an unread monograph as inherently more valuable than a highly regarded and used anthology. Today the situation is changing.

Anthologies and anthologizing are becoming more and more valuable as the academy shifts from a solipsistic model of research value to a model based more strongly in pragmatic ideals. The solipsistic model maintains that a book written on a narrow topic for a specific professional audience maintains a higher value. The pragmatic model of research bases a book's value on its potential usefulness to the academic community as a whole. Does this book further our knowledge in some area? Does it build community and bridges among its members? Does it provide access for more individuals into the community? Through the use of these criteria, all academic publications are judged on their ability to engage in productive and progressive scholarship, not merely on their *form*. Single-author monographs and anthologies both have the potential for achieving these goals.

It is becoming increasingly evident that our notion of research value in the humanities is rapidly changing. This is partly out of necessity and partly out of practicality. The necessity comes from a number of different fronts, including the pressures placed on tenured and nontenured academics to publish single-author monographs. As the number of professors increases and library budgets around the country decrease, the result is tremendous pressure on publishers to publish books that will hasten their economic woes. Out of necessity, members of the academy are actively pursuing ways to relieve the glut of books that are left in the wake of tenure and post-tenure pursuits. We must find ways to assess research and scholarly abilities that do not place severe strains on individuals and institutions.

A model of research value based on pragmatic ideals offers a way out of this bind. Scholarly merit and utility in terms of community building serve as criteria that will promote meaningful publications. Research value based on pragmatic ideals will also increase the perceived value of anthologies and anthologizing in academic culture. No more will anthologies solely be judged on their genre. Single-author monographs, anthologies, and other forms of publication will be judged in terms of what they bring to the community.

Canons and Consequences

The first section of essays in *On Anthologies* is entitled "From Anthologizing to Canonizing." Its contributors are experienced anthologists. Their essays broadly address questions of canonicity with respect to the anthologizing process. The anthology editors in this section are deeply tempered by a strong knowledge of the rich dialogue that has taken place concerning canons and canonization in the humanities over the past twenty years.

The study of canons and canon formation became prominent in the humanities with the publication of a group of papers from the English Institute in 1981. Leslie Fiedler and Houston Baker's edited volume, *English Literature: Opening Up the Canon*, incited a flurry of work on the topic that peaked in the early 1990s with the appearance of a number of major studies, including Carey Kaplan and Ellen Cronan Rose's *The Canon and the Common Reader* (1990), Charles Altieri's *Canons and Consequences: Reflections on the Ethical Force of Imaginative Ideals* (1990), Henry Louis Gates's *Loose Canons: Notes on the Culture Wars* (1992), and John Guillory's *Cultural Capital: The Problem of Literary Canon Formation* (1993).

The latter work speculates that "it was only in the wake of liberalism's apparent defeat in American political culture that such agendas as 'representation in the canon' could come to occupy so central a place in the liberal academy" (5). While the accuracy of Guillory's charge is debatable, it is undeniable that canon issues should be continually evaluated against the backdrop of political culture.

Some of the tangible consequences of the "canon wars" of the 1980s were the emergence in the 1990s of new anthologies based on principles established by the canon debate as well as the reorganization of a number of major anthologies. Equal *representation* came to overshadow the aim of publishing "the best which has been thought and said in the world" (Arnold 6). This latter phrase, famously coined in 1869 by Matthew Arnold in *Culture and Anarchy* as the central aspect of culture, came to be derided for obstructing cultural diversity and politically correct anthologizing.

The essays in this section all address, in part, the delicate issue of how one balances the desire to represent "the best which has been thought and said" with the contemporary mandate toward equality of representation. As each of the contributors is an experienced and respected anthologist, their work serves as an antidote to the often sterile writings of those who have never attempted to put their principles on anthologizing and canonization into practice. As these essays show, editing an anthology in the wake of the canon wars is both a daunting challenge and a pioneering affair.

In "From the Old World to the Whole World" David Damrosch comments that "no shift in literary studies over the past generation has been greater than the opening up of the canon from a focus on a relatively restricted core of masterpieces to the expansive multicultural landscape so evident today." Damrosch believes that while this expansion is in principle praiseworthy, it "poses exceptional difficulties in practice." His essay surveys the ways in which numerous world literature anthologies encounter and contend with these difficulties. He finds that anthologies of world literature offer either "a self-centered construction of the world" or "a highly decentered one" – a choice with which he believes we should no longer be contented.

Instead Damrosch, editor of *The Longman Anthology of British Literature* (2003), contributing editor to *The HarperCollins World Reader* (1994), consultant to the Mesoamerican additions to *The Norton Anthology of World Masterpieces*, and general editor of *The Longman Anthology of World Literature* (2004), believes that a more elliptical approach is needed. This geometrical figure is intended to conjure the image of a world literature anthology "generated from two foci at once." He closes his essay by saying that "future anthologies of world literature must find new and better ways to manage the tensions between the reader's world and the worlds we read about. We will need to draw closer connections between here and there, then and now, while at the same time providing the historical and cultural information to hold ourselves off from an unthinking assimilation of the foreign work to our own norms, whether political or aesthetic." It should be noted that Damrosch's hermeneutical challenge is not unique to merely the latest generation of anthologies seeking to widen the canon: it is a challenge to all anthologies that bring readers into contact with materials from cultures and time periods other than their own.

The next essay, Sarah Lawall's "Anthologizing 'World Literature,'" continues the discussion of world literature. Whereas the perspective of Damrosch's essay is primarily one of viewing the progress of world literature anthologies from *outside* the anthologizing process (even though Damrosch himself is an anthology editor), Lawall's examines them from *inside* the editorial process. Lawall is coeditor of *The Norton Anthology of World Masterpieces: The Western Tradition* (1999), as well as its revised edition, *The Norton Anthology of World Literature* (2002). Since 1977, when she became editor of the twentieth-century section, she has worked on the Norton. In his essay Damrosch calls *The Norton Anthology of World Masterpieces* "probably the most widely used anthology in courses around the country from its first edition in 1956 to the present." Lawall's essay takes us deeply into the genesis and evolution of the Norton. It is a seldom offered opportunity to view the growth of a major anthology from within. However, the scope and subject of Lawall's essay are much broader.

"Although I am best acquainted with the workings of the Norton anthology," says Lawall, "my subject throughout has been the specific enterprise of the academic world literature anthology with its various antecedents and special position in American educational history." She is right in reminding us that many critical discussions of anthologies and anthologizing fail to show an awareness of "the dynamic interrelationships among teachers, editors, publishers, and institutional practice that go into the creation of an academic anthology." Providing insight into these relationships is – perhaps more than anything else – the major contribution of her essay. Lawall shows us that any analysis of an anthology must take into account a complex web of relationships. Her essay stands out for its strong situating of the economic, political, pedagogical, and aesthetic dimensions of anthologies.

The third piece in this section, Lynn Z. Bloom's "Once More to the Essay Canon," uses "contemporary canon theory and an extensive analysis of textbooks" to "explain how the essay, a belletristic genre in the eighteenth and nineteenth centuries, became critically undermined in the twentieth century as a consequence of pedagogy that emphasized its utilitarian rather than aesthetic and intellectual functions." In addition, Bloom offers comprehensive analyses of the evolution of the twentieth-century essay canon and speculates on changes that may occur in the twenty-first century as print-on-demand becomes more widely used. Print-on-demand, as noted previously, is one of the frontiers for anthologies, and Bloom's comments are particularly prescient given her extensive knowledge of the essay canon. By Bloom's estimation some 2.2 million students each year use essay readers. This makes essay collections like her own, *The Essay Connection: Readings for Writers*, now in its sixth edition, one of the most widely used types of anthologies today. The formative role that these readers have in the composition classroom will make them the continuing object of critical attention well into the twenty-first century.

The final contributor to this section is Karen L. Kilcup, editor of *Nineteenth-Century American Women Writers: An Anthology* (1997) and *Native American Women's Writing, c. 1800–1924* (2000). In her article, "The Poetry and Prose of Recovery Work," Kilcup discusses the role of anthologies in "recovering" writers that for various reasons have been lost to print.

Such work has not gone unrecognized by contemporary anthologists. Henry Louis Gates notes in his *Norton Anthology of African American Literature*, "If this anthology does nothing more than recover the works of Melvin B. Tolson to a wider audience, that alone will justify its existence" (1328). For Gates, then, the recovery work of anthologies is one of their primary values.

Drawing largely from her work in anthologizing nineteenth-century women's writing, Kilcup reminds us of "a number of nontrivial, nonintellectual realities [that] help determine what can or cannot be accomplished in today's corporatized academy and its affiliated publishing culture." Beyond the sheer satisfaction of recovering lost writers such as Martha Wolfenstein and Onoto Watanna, Kilcup discusses "the role of power and privilege of varying sorts in recovery work and in the anthologizing and criticism that complement it." Her essay reveals the formative role of anthologies in shaping canons: how recovery into a canon is many times strongly determined by anthologies and anthologizers.

Innovations and Challenges

As noted in the previous section, one of the more exciting consequences of the canon wars is the way they have fostered the exploration and anthologization of ignored texts. Kilcup's essay on the important role of anthologies in recovering ignored texts is seminal in this regard. However, there is a related issue concerning the ways in which the softening of canons has brought about an increasing interest in surveying ignored and emergent *bodies* of texts. Today, more than ever, there is a greater receptivity and interest in non- or uncanonical bodies of writing. Anthologies play a great role in mapping out these spaces. The essays in the section entitled "Innovations and Challenges" might be viewed in this light.

Robert L. McLaughlin's "Anthologizing Contemporary Literature" lays out the writer's experiences in thinking through and editing an anthology of innovative prose fiction. Through this essay one can follow the anthologizing process from conception to inception. McLaughlin, like many anthology editors, began with a very ambitious project.

He then shows how practical, economic, and pedagogical considerations led to a reformulation of this project. The challenges confronting McLaughlin and the innovations that allowed him to overcome them are instructive to anyone editing an anthology.

"Now I certainly don't mean to compare my experiences editing *Innovations: An Anthology of Modern and Contemporary Fiction* to Wallace's writing *Infinite Jest*," writes McLaughlin, "but I do think [David Foster] Wallace articulates wonderfully the conflicting feelings any writer (or editor) can have, feelings about the distance between conception and actualization, about the combination of self-critical awareness of the piece's flaws and the desire that others will love it, about the pride in one's accomplishment subverted by the knowledge of how much of the accomplishment was really out of one's control." McLaughlin's comment reminds us that while the experience of editing an anthology is not equivalent to that of writing a novel or a manuscript, the process can be no less demanding. This is particularly true in cases such as McLaughlin's, where one is undertaking pioneering anthologizing work: if there is no existing compatible anthology, the anthologizer is left without a benchmark.

Whereas McLaughlin's editing experiences involved the challenges of editing an innovative but extant body of texts, our next contributor, Cris Mazza, shares her experiences editing an innovative and *nonextant* body of texts. In "Finding the Chic in Lit," Mazza recounts her work in creating and coediting the two innovative *Chick-Lit* anthologies. Both anthologies were based on calls for manuscripts – the aim of which was to "unearth *more* women writers," not to "compete with a Norton anthology or be an antidote to similar mass-market projects." In this respect her work on *Chick-Lit* stands in stark contrast to the other projects in this volume. The *Chick-Lit* volumes reveal the generative power of anthologies to not only reveal and organize preexisting bodies of texts but also to *create* them. In response to queries from male students – "Why don't you do an anthology for *men* only?" – Mazza responds, "You mean there haven't been any yet? . . . How about most of the anthologies since the beginning of time?" Mazza's efforts remind us that progressive cultural contributions are always within the grasp of the anthologist.

The next essay, Cary Nelson's "The Economic Challenges to Anthologies," puts in stark relief one of the most serious challenges facing anthologists today: economics. Whereas the previous contributions touch on the economic aspects of editing a major anthology, Nelson shares precise figures associated with his editing of the *Anthology of Modern American Poetry* for Oxford University Press. His essay provides a rare peek into the myriad financial considerations that go into editing an anthology. Such considerations are vital to understanding and analyzing anthologies because often they explain why certain texts are included in or excluded from a particular anthology. Permissions fees often deeply influence the contents of anthologies. Nelson's essay reveals how and why this is the case.

Whereas articles by McLaughlin, Mazza, and Nelson take up some of the challenges and innovations associated with editing prose fiction and poetry, the final essay in this section takes up the editing of philosophy anthologies. In "Confessions of an Anthology Editor" Alan D. Schrift, editor of numerous anthologies, shares his intentions with regard to each of his projects. "In so doing," says Schrift, "I hope to expose some of the functions that an anthology might serve and some of the factors that a good anthologizer must consider." Schrift's essay offers a unique opportunity to look into the challenges associated with editing philosophy anthologies (the discourse on editing philosophy anthologies as compared to editing prose fiction and poetry anthologies is almost nonexistent) and offers a view of the intentions underlying his many innovative anthologies. Schrift's essay is also valuable for its review of the work of one editor on numerous anthologies (not just different or revised editions).

Attitudes and Responses

Part 3, entitled "Attitudes and Responses," contains four essays focusing attention on the ways in which our attitudes and responses toward anthologies reveal and reinforce our political values. In "Anthology

Disdain" Jeffrey J. Williams traces the various ways in which anthologies are denigrated and the sources of these positions within the academy. "In formal evaluations of our work – yearly reports, salary documents, and so on – they [anthologies] are not credited in the same blue-chip category as scholarly books or articles, and often not even credited as research, but consigned to the prestige-deprived category of teaching or the default category of service," writes Williams. "In general conversation they are usually mentioned with a long-suffering nod or dismissed with disdain." If scholarly prestige is one's aim, then editing an anthology is not an astute move in the politics of the academic world.

However, Williams asks, "if we think so poorly of anthologies, why do so many of us still use them? And if we use them, why do we feel compelled to speak ill of them?" For Williams our disdain toward anthologies "reveals as much about how we fashion ourselves as academic professionals as it does about their [anthologies'] objective qualities." Williams connects negative attitudes toward anthologies *in toto* to "academic affect." The better we are able to decode the value hierarchy that contributes to making us "the professional subjects we are, constituting or 'performing' our social position," as Williams says, the better we will be able to separate the substantive criticisms of anthologies from those based merely on how we fashion ourselves as academics.

Nancy Cirillo's "Anthologizing the Caribbean, or, Squaring Beaches, Bananas, and Nobel Laureates" continues the discussion of the politics of response to anthologies by American audiences. Cirillo, unlike Williams, is primarily concerned with the response of American readers to works that anthologize writings from a region to which Americans are at best "indifferent" – the Caribbean. After carefully laying out the complex politics and pedagogy of anthologizing the Caribbean for an American audience, she surveys the relative virtues and vices of a number of anthologies of Caribbean literature. One of the overarching aims of her essay is to offer a vision of future anthologies of the Caribbean, a region that V. S. Naipaul has called "the third world's third world."

"Distinguishing the Map from the Territory," by Angeline O'Neill, takes us from the anthologization of the "third world's third world" to the "fourth world" – the work of Native North American and Aboriginal Australian writers and orators. Her reflections on the uncommon topic of responses toward anthologizing indigenous literature bring her to the more common subject of how our attitudes toward the nature of literature and literary value temper our beliefs about anthologization. "In many respects," writes O'Neill, "the process of anthologizing Indigenous literature and orature requires a reconsideration of 'literature' and of the acts of writing and reading, speaking and listening." Her survey of some recent anthologies of Native North American and Aboriginal Australian writers reveals the "tremendous social, political, and philosophical implications" of anthologizing Indigenous literature and orature. O'Neill is herself a coeditor of an anthology of Indigenous literature entitled *Those Who Remain Will Always Remember* (2000).

The final essay in this section is Richard S. Pressman's "Is There a Future for the *Heath Anthology* in the Neoliberal State?" Pressman comments that while "one might see the *Heath* as a kind of literary affirmative action, creating more equal opportunity in a society traditionally racist and sexist," this is not the only way to view the anthology. Pressman remarks, "For all its progressive intent the *Heath* can also be seen as a function of neoliberalism and hence in its way also conservative. While minority advancements are due in large part to painful political struggles, they are also due to the changing needs of capital. In this the *Heath* seems typically liberal, even idealist, for it all but ignores class – whereas capital, which poses as classless, is generally conscious of its class needs." Pressman's comments on the *Heath* will be surprising to readers who regard it as a politically progressive anthology.

Pressman's contribution is important not only for its unpacking of the political complexities of the *Heath* but also for its review of the various responses to it. These responses have been at the center of a continuing debate in academia concerning the politics of representation – not only in anthologies but also in the curriculum, the faculty, the student body, and elsewhere. In this regard, attempts at multiculturalization and representativeness such as the *Heath Anthology* must be viewed as part of the larger debate in the academy over educational reform and what has been described as "the politics of a liberal education."[1]

Theory and the Pedagogical Pact

Earlier it was mentioned that anthologies are shaped by pedagogies, and pedagogies are shaped by anthologies. Thus far in this overview, Sarah Lawall's essay has been the most direct intervention on this topic. Lawall reminds us that the experience of teachers using anthologies in their classes often is used in the revision process. Readings that teachers approve are kept, whereas others are dropped. New readings are often included on the basis of teacher demand. Lawall's essay counters the perception that anthologists are not receptive to the pedagogical demands of their users. One should also remember that the reviewer of an anthology prospectus is usually asked by the publishing house whether he or she would use all of the readings proposed by the anthologist. This is yet another safeguard to ensure that anthologies reflect current pedagogical interests.

Lawall's essay addresses the issue of how anthologies are shaped by pedagogies. The selections in the fourth section, "Theory, Pedagogy, and Practice," examine the relationship from the other side: how pedagogies are shaped by anthologies. Each article shows the ways in which the theoretical assumptions that inform anthology construction find their way into our pedagogical practice via classroom use of anthologies.

The first piece, "Anthologies, Literary Theory, and the Teaching of Literature," is a dialogue between Gerald Graff and myself. Early in our exchange Graff comments that "anthologies tend to efface the mediating intervention of criticism in literary study by reducing criticism to its dullest common denominator – informational headnotes and footnotes, arbitrary questions for study, and so on – thereby propping up the illusion that responding vividly to a literary work is fundamentally a stripped-down encounter of the student up close to the text, with the critical conversation about the text factored out or even seen as an unwelcome form of professional interference." Graff and I go on to discuss the dangers of this reduction of criticism and the ways in which it might be avoided. In the process we address the question of how the Bedford "critical controversy" editions of Twain's *Adventures of Huckleberry Finn* (1995) and Shakespeare's *The Tempest* (2000), which Graff coedited, aim to avoid these problems.

In "Anthologies, Literature, and Theory in Japan" Terry Caesar reflects on his experiences using anthologies to teach English in Japan. "The burden of an anthology is different in a foreign country," writes Caesar, "where the teaching of literature is far more inseparable from the teaching of language and where consideration of another country's literary canon has less to do with intervening in the issues responsible for its very constitution than with providing for students some fundamental cultural literacy, if only in the form of names and dates." Caesar's comment on the role of anthologies in providing students with cultural literacy in Japan holds for many U.S. students as well: anthologies are a primary vehicle of cultural literacy, not just a case study in canon formation. This role is only increasing for the emerging generation of students more versed in visual and auditory culture than in verbal.

Simon Morgan Wortham's "Anthologizing Derrida" discusses various efforts to anthologize the theory of Jacques Derrida. Wortham asks, "Via the work of anthologization, does Derrida's relationship to other thinkers and to various traditions of thought become far too malleable, with the frequent result that Derrida is presented rather abstractly, vaguely, and sloppily as some sort of 'postmodernist,' rather than as a particular thinker emerging out of a more clearly determined or locatable intellectual milieu?" He goes on to speculate on how the anthologization of Derrida affects the teaching of his texts in particular and deconstruction in general. Wortham's comments on the teaching of Derrida via anthologies complement Schrift's comments on the anthologization of continental philosophy. Together, they provide a rich and unique commentary on continental philosophy and anthologization.

The final essay in this section is "Theorizing the Discipline and the Disciplining of Theory" by David B. Downing. Whereas Wortham's essay is concerned with the anthologization of one theorist, Downing's essay widens the field to generalized theory anthologies. "Every contemporary anthology of theory," writes Downing, "confronts an institutional double bind: they must inevitably do two things at once, both of which are mutually contradictory. On the one hand, many of the theoretical essays included in the anthology tend to challenge, cross, or disrupt disciplinary borders; on the other, anthologizing itself cannot avoid its essentially disciplinary function." Downing's essay goes on to examine in detail the pedagogical, professional, and disciplinary implications of this "double bind." He concludes that because "nondisciplinary and postdisciplinary practices often already comprise the larger part of our working lives," theory anthologies need to represent this work more fully. If "disciplinary work" continues to be "valorized as inherently superior to postdisciplinary kinds of teaching and learning" in theory anthologies, "we may not always be preparing students for the culture and the profession they will enter." Downing's essay establishes anthologies as a primary site for positive, practical, and progressive change in graduate education. The pedagogical pact of anthologies with their users, Downing entreats, should be forward-looking, not backward-looking.

Headnote Disdain

The textual apparatus of anthologies includes the chapter introductions, article headnotes, lists for further reading, study and review questions, student study guides, footnotes, instructor's manuals, and glossaries. For many the textual apparatus of an anthology is of secondary importance. Whereas there is a very good chance that an anthology with excellent textual apparatus might be rejected for class adoption by a potential user because the selection of readings is considered inadequate, there is only a small chance that an anthology with a poor selection of readings but excellent textual apparatus will be chosen for class adoption. The received opinion on textual apparatus is that it is of secondary importance to the selection of readings.

The final section of essays focuses on one of the most important and controversial elements of textual apparatus: the headnote. "Notes on Headnotes" features reflections on headnotes from the editors of *The Norton Anthology of Theory and Criticism*. The contributors – Vincent B. Leitch, Barbara Johnson, Laurie Finke, and John McGowan – reflect on the experience of writing headnotes.[2] The essays in this section are compact and practical, in the spirit of headnotes themselves. Anyone who has faced the daunting task of composing these introductory notes will appreciate the writers' candor regarding the role of headnotes in the production of anthologies.

As the contributors to this section indicate, headnotes engage all of the issues of production, politics, and pedagogy discussed thus far. With regard to pedagogical impact, many instructors are wary of the value of headnotes. Some believe that if the headnote outlines the main point(s) and/or argument(s) of the reading, then it will "give away" the reading to the student. According to this account, headnotes are viewed as pedagogically and intellectually pernicious. From the production side the comments are many times not much better.

Some editors advise anthologists to write their headnotes as quickly as possible because instructors do not read or care much about headnotes. These editors believe that the instructors who adopt their anthologies for course use are concerned with the quality of the readings, not the quality of the headnotes. However, even if it is true that instructors do not care about the quality of headnotes, this view is not shared by students.

Students rely heavily on headnotes and other interpretive materials. While many instructors would like to ignore the true reading practices of their students, many students consistently seek out secondary survey literature on the assigned materials. Cliffs Notes and Monarch notes have built an empire on this real need. "Handbooks" and "dictionaries" like *The Columbia Dictionary of Modern Literary and Cultural Criticism* (1995), edited by Joseph Childers and Gary Hentzi, and *The Johns Hop-*

kins *Guide to Literary Theory and Criticism* (1994), edited by Michael Groden and Martin Kreiswirth – to take two examples from a list that can be multiplied many times over – have become the Cliffs Notes for the critical theory generation. Detractors of headnotes fail to recognize the value of this textual apparatus to the group who appreciates it most: students.

The fact that the editors featured in this volume took the task of writing these headnotes so seriously is in itself noteworthy in a book and academic culture that is all too ready to dismiss them. Headnotes open up a host of deep pedagogical questions. The essays in this section critically discuss the technical and intellectual challenges confronting the writers of headnotes and honestly engage the pedagogical politics of instructional aids and textual apparatus: a task that one only hopes will be taken up by more educators in the near future.

Future Inquiry

Most of the contributors to this volume are themselves the editors of anthologies. By drawing upon personal experiences in their essays, these professionals provide a rare glimpse into the economics and logic of anthology publication. Their insights on the material and economic culture of publishing complement the pedagogical, canonical, and political theses regarding anthologies developed throughout the volume. After reading these essays we understand better the ways in which editing an anthology involves negotiation and compromise between intellectual ideal and realistic practice. They leave no question that anthologies are indeed a theoretically interesting genre that calls for more extensive inquiry.

It should be mentioned that a conscious effort has been made to include discussion of a wide range of anthologies used and produced by teachers and scholars of literature and theory. The result is a representative slice of one area of academic life. Anthologies, however, are utilized and produced in most, if not all, disciplines. The insights in this volume on anthologies and anthologizing cross over and speak to those in other areas of academic life. Collectively, the essays in *On*

Anthologies pave the way for continuing critical analysis of anthology production and consumption in all disciplines.

Notes

1. See particularly Darryl J. Gless and Barbara Herrnstein Smith's *The Politics of Liberal Education*.
2. Contributor Jeffrey J. Williams is also one of the coeditors of *The Norton Anthology of Theory and Criticism*. His comments, like those of his coeditors, are drawn greatly from his editing experiences with this anthology. However, his essay, "Anthology Disdain," works better in the "Attitudes and Responses" section than in the "Notes on Headnotes" section, where the focus of the essays is more explicitly on headnotes in themselves.

Bibliography

Altieri, Charles. *Canons and Consequences: Reflections on the Ethical Force of Imaginative Ideals*. Evanston IL: Northwestern University Press, 1990.

Arnold, Matthew. *Culture and Anarchy*. 1869. London: Cambridge University Press, 1960.

Auster, Paul. Preface. *The Random House Book of Twentieth-Century French Poetry*. 1981. Rpt. in *The Art of Hunger: Essays, Prefaces, and Interviews and The Red Notebook, Expanded Edition*. New York: Penguin Books, 1997. 199–237.

Bloom, Lynn Z. *The Essay Connection: Readings for Writers*. 6th ed. Boston: Houghton Mifflin, 2001.

Boxer, Sarah. "How Lit Crit Finally Won Out over Lit." *New York Times*. May 19, 2001. Available at http://www.nytimes.com/2001/05/19/arts/. Accessed August 23, 2003.

Brewster, Anne, Angeline O'Neill, and Rosemary van den Berg, eds. *Those Who Remain Will Always Remember*. Fremantle: Fremantle Arts Centre Press, 2000.

Caesar, Terry. "Affiliation and Mourning in a Career of Specialization." *Affiliations: Identity in Academic Culture*. Ed. Jeffrey R. Di Leo. Lincoln: University of Nebraska Press, 2003. 156–74.

Caws, Mary Ann, et al., eds. *The HarperCollins World Reader*. 2 vols. New York: HarperCollins, 1994.

Childers, Joseph, and Gary Hentzi, eds. *The Columbia Dictionary of Modern Literary and Cultural Criticism*. New York: Columbia University Press, 1995.

Coser, Lewis A., Charles Kadushin, and Walter W. Powell. *Books: The Culture and Commerce of Publishing*. New York: Basic Books, 1982.

Damrosch, David, ed. *The Longman Anthology of British Literature*. 2 vols. 1999. 2nd ed. New York: Longman, 2003.

———, ed. *The Longman Anthology of World Literature*. 6 vols. New York: Longman, 2004.

Epstein, Jason. *Book Business: Publishing Past, Present, and Future*. New York: W. W. Norton, 2001.

Ferry, Anne. *Tradition and the Individual Poem: An Inquiry into Anthologies*. Stanford: Stanford University Press, 2001.

Fiedler, Leslie, and Houston Baker, eds. *English Literature: Opening Up the Canon*. Baltimore: Johns Hopkins University Press, 1981.

Gates, Henry Louis, Jr. *Loose Canons: Notes on the Culture Wars*. New York: Oxford University Press, 1992.

Gates, Henry Louis, Jr., and Nellie Y. McKay, eds. *The Norton Anthology of African American Literature*. New York: W. W. Norton, 1996.

Germano, William. *Getting It Published: A Guide for Scholars and Anyone Else Serious about Serious Books*. Chicago: University of Chicago Press, 2001.

Gless, Darryl J., and Barbara Herrnstein Smith, eds. *The Politics of Liberal Education*. Durham: Duke University Press, 1992.

Groden, Michael, and Martin Kreiswirth, eds. *The Johns Hopkins Guide to Literary Theory and Criticism*. Baltimore: Johns Hopkins University Press, 1994.

Guillory, John. *Cultural Capital: The Problem of Literary Canon Formation*. Chicago: University of Chicago Press, 1993.

Highet, Gilbert. "Anthology." *The Oxford Classical Dictionary*. Ed. N. G. L. Hammond and H. H. Scullard. 2nd ed. Oxford: Oxford University Press, 1970. 67–68.

Kaplan, Carey, and Ellen Cronan Rose. *The Canon and the Common Reader*. Knoxville: University of Tennessee Press, 1990.

Kilcup, Karen L., ed. *Native American Women's Writing, c. 1800–1924: An Anthology*. Cambridge MA: Blackwell Publishers, 2000.

———, ed. *Nineteenth-Century American Women Writers: An Anthology*. Cambridge MA: Blackwell Publishers, 1997.

Kittler, Friedrich A. *Discourse Networks 1800/1900*. Trans. Michael Metteer. Stanford: Stanford University Press, 1990.

Lauter, Paul. *Canons and Contexts*. New York: Oxford University Press, 1991.

———, ed. *The Heath Anthology of American Literature*. 2 vols. 1st ed. Lexington MA: D. C. Heath, 1990.

Lawall, Sarah N., et al., eds. *The Norton Anthology of World Literature*. 2nd ed. 6 vols. New York: W. W. Norton, 2002.

———, et al., eds. *The Norton Anthology of World Masterpieces: The Western Tradition*. 7th ed. 2 vols. New York: W. W. Norton, 1999.

Leitch, Vincent B., gen. ed. *The Norton Anthology of Theory and Criticism*. Ed. William E. Cain, et al. New York: W. W. Norton, 2001.

Mazza, Cris, and Jeffrey DeShell, eds. *Chick-Lit: Postfeminist Fiction*. Normal IL: FC2, 1995.

Mazza, Cris, Jeffrey DeShell, and Elisabeth Sheffield, eds. *Chick-Lit 2 (No Chick-Vics)*. Normal IL: FC2, 1996.

McLaughlin, Robert L. *Innovations: An Anthology of Modern and Contemporary Fiction*. Normal IL: Dalkey Archive Press, 1998.

Nelson, Cary, ed. *Anthology of Modern American Poetry*. New York: Oxford University Press, 2000.

Price, Leah. *The Anthology and the Rise of the Novel: From Richardson to George Eliot*. Cambridge: Cambridge University Press, 2000.

Shakespeare, William. *The Tempest*. Ed. Gerald Graff and James Phelan. Case Studies in Critical Controversy. New York: Bedford/St. Martin's, 2000.

Sosnoski, James J. *Token Professionals and Master Critics: A Critique of Orthodoxy in Literary Studies*. Buffalo: State University of New York Press, 1994.

Twain, Mark. *Adventures of Huckleberry Finn*. Ed. Gerald Graff and James Phelan. Case Studies in Critical Controversy. New York: Bedford/St. Martin's, 1995.

PART ONE

From Anthologizing to Canonizing

DAVID DAMROSCH

From the Old World to the Whole World

No shift in literary studies over the past generation has been greater than the opening up of the canon from a focus on a relatively restricted core of masterpieces to the expansive multicultural landscape so evident today. The tremendous widening of our literary horizons, in turn, is nowhere more evident than in the field of world literature, which until recently usually meant "Western European" literature but which now seems to encompass everything from the earliest Sumerian poetry to the most recent fictional experiments of the Tibetan postmodernists Zhaxi Dawa and Jamyang Norbu. Wholly laudable in principle, this rapid expansion poses exceptional difficulties in practice. Just how is this great wealth of material to be made accessible to readers? What classic texts will have to be dropped in order to make room for the new arrivals within the physical and temporal boundaries of courses and anthologies? What cultural context needs to be provided – and what cultural context *can* feasibly be provided – for nonspecialists to have meaningful encounters with African orature, Japanese *renga*, and Mozarabic *kharjas*? How are all these works to be read alongside Petrarch and Wallace Stevens, always assuming that both of these latter authors still remain on the syllabus?

The fact is that these questions have yet to be answered in any satisfactory way, as a look at several recent world literature anthologies will show. These problems are not actually new: the expansion of the canon only brings into sharp relief a number of tensions that have long existed within the idea of "world literature" as it has been formulated over the course of the past century. We won't do better in presenting the newly expansive world of world literature until we do a better job of clarifying just what we mean to accomplish by presenting "the literature" of "the world" for a contemporary American audience. I will begin, then, by discussing some earlier efforts to create anthologies of world literature, in order to show some of the fundamental issues anthologists had to face even when the scope of "the world" was chiefly European and North American, as these early anthologies raise issues that persist today.

I begin with a pair of ambitious multivolume anthologies that were prepared in the first decade of the twentieth century: *The Best of the World's Classics*, in ten volumes, published in 1909 by Funk and Wagnalls under the editorship of Senator Henry Cabot Lodge; and the still more ambitious fifty-volume series *The Harvard Classics*, published just a year later by P. F. Collier and Son, under the general editorship of Harvard's president, Charles W. Eliot. In many ways these anthologies are similar in intent: both were designed for a general-interest market and appear to have been projects developed by their publishers, who then sought out a prominent figure to serve as the – fairly nominal – overall editor, with the actual work in each case done by a subordinate associate editor. Both anthologies reflect the shift of higher education away from classical studies toward modern culture and the rapid expansion in the system then under way. The publishers clearly saw an opportunity to market the works now being taught on campuses to a wider public, who had heard of these changes but had not had the opportunity to experience them: the romance of higher education was taking hold in America, yet few people could afford to go to college. As Eliot puts it, Colliers invited him "to make such a selection as any intellectually ambitious American family might use to advantage, even if their early opportunities of education had been scanty" (50: 1). Similarly, Henry Cabot Lodge affirms that his series will offer his readers both intellectual and moral benefits:

> To that larger public whose lives are not spent among books and libraries, and for whose delectation such a collection as this is primarily intended, these volumes rightly read at odd times, in idle moments, in out-of-the-way places, on the ship or the train, offer much. They will bring the reader in contact with many of the greatest intellects of all time. . . . There is no man who will not be the better,

for the moment at least, by reading what Cicero says about old age, Seneca about death, and Socrates about love, to go no further for examples than to

"The glory that was Greece,
And the grandeur that was Rome." (1: xiv–xv)

For all these similarities, the two anthologies show a fundamental difference in orientation, already signaled by the publishers' differing choices for their general editors, and this difference well illustrates John Guillory's point in *Cultural Capital* that *who* reads, and why people read, matter as much as the specifics of *what* is read as canonical (18). Both Eliot and Lodge intend their anthologies to assist in the formation of a new and better American citizen – more refined, thoughtful, self-aware, and self-controlled; better able to participate intelligently in public debate – and yet the two editors differ dramatically in the ways they intend to orient their reader toward the world. Eliot takes a cosmopolitan, Arnoldian view, that the purpose of world literature is to broaden the reader's horizons through the encounter with cultural difference: "The sentiments and opinions these authors express are frequently not acceptable to present-day readers, who have to be often saying to themselves: 'This is not true, or not correct, or not in accordance with our beliefs.' It is, however, precisely this encounter with the mental states of other generations which enlarges the outlook and sympathies of the cultivated man, and persuades him of the upward tendency of the human race" (50: 5). If this formulation leaves unquestioned the superiority of present perspectives, Eliot goes a step further in a preface to the second edition of the series, in 1917: "From these volumes, the thorough reader may learn valuable lessons in comparative literature. He can see how various the contributions of the different languages and epochs have been; and he will inevitably come to the conclusion that striking national difference in this respect ought in the interest of mankind to be perpetuated and developed, and not obliterated, averaged, or harrowed down" (50: 14).

Henry Cabot Lodge's perspective is dramatically different. One of the leading members of the U.S. Senate at the time he wrote his preface, he was deeply concerned that the United States not overextend itself on the world stage. Though he supported American involvement in the First World War, he bitterly opposed Woodrow Wilson's proposal for the League of Nations, a body that Lodge saw as compromising America's sovereignty. Lodge organized and led the opposition that doomed American acceptance of the League and, in turn, destroyed Wilson's presidency. The attitudes that would underlie Lodge's actions after 1916 are already evident in his introduction to *The Best of the World's Classics* in 1909. Though the bulk of the anthology's contents are classical and Continental, Lodge places great weight in his introduction on the value of the English-language readings contained in the series:

> The most important part of the collection is that which gives selections from those writers whose native tongue is English. No translation even of prose can ever quite reproduce its original, and as a rule can not hope to equal it. . . . It may safely be said that the soul of a language and the beauties of style which it is capable of exhibiting can only be found and studied in the productions of writers who not only think in the language in which they write, but to whom that speech is native, the inalienable birthright and heritage of their race or country. (1: xvi–xvii)

Lodge's jingoism allows him to move seamlessly from discussing the limitations of translation to denouncing the pretensions of immigrants ever to be full participants in their adopted culture. Where Eliot's collection is meant to inspire a cosmopolitan and even relativistic regard for the variety of the world's cultures, Lodge hopes to foster a nativist public discourse, for which an elevated English style will serve as emblem and reinforcement of a native racial and cultural heritage. "No one," he says in conclusion, "can read the masterpieces of English prose and not have both lesson and responsibility brought home . . . and thus make them more mindful of the ineffable value to them and their children of the great language which is at once their birthright and their inheritance" (1: xxviii–xxix).

Lodge's forthright statement of his views is worth keeping in mind, as it is far from certain that we have yet cast off the nativist teleology that can organize the world's literature into a progression up through history to a comforting conclusion on our own doorstep. Indeed, Charles Eliot's contrasting cosmopolitanism itself admitted a pronounced nativist emphasis. Lodge's series at least begins at a remove from America, with volumes on Greece and Rome; the first volume of *The Harvard Classics*, by contrast, is devoted to the writings of American "Founding Fathers" – Benjamin Franklin, John Woolman, and William Penn. Volume 2 then doubles back, giving Greco-Roman philosophy (Plato, Epictetus, and Marcus Aurelius), before coming forward to Milton, Bacon, and Browne (volumes 3 and 4), before coming home again with Emerson (volume 5) and then going back to Britain for Robert Burns (volume 6). Burns and Milton themselves are given such early prominence, Eliot tells us, just for their value to a student of democracy: "The poems of John Milton and Robert Burns are given in full; because the works of these two very unlike poets contain social, religious, and governmental teachings of vital concern for modern democracies. Milton was the great poet of civil and religious liberty, and Burns was the great poet of democracy. The two together cover the fundamental principles of free government, education, and democratic social structure, and will serve as guides to much good reading on those subjects provided in the collection" (50: 7). As "world literature" began to be defined at the start of the twentieth century, then, cosmopolitanism itself may only have been a higher form of nativism.

By the middle decades of the twentieth century, however, the map of the world was beginning to change, and America's place on the map was newly open for reconsideration. A good index of the shape of world literature in midcentury America can be found in a widely used reference work, Frank Magill's *Masterpieces of World Literature in Digest Form* (also known as *Masterplots*). Written by a team of experts under Magill's direction, this work was first published in 1949, giving summaries and brief analyses of 510 major works (the editors had intended to summarize 500 key works but couldn't quite decide on the final cut). Well-aware that there were more works worth including, in 1955 they produced a second series with a further 500 titles; a third volume gave 500 more summaries in 1960, and a final volume, with another 500 works, appeared in 1969.

From the outset the collection defined "the world" unhesitatingly as the Western world: "The array of literature represented in this book," Magill notes in his preface, "is drawn from the vast reservoir of literary achievements which has been accumulating since the legendary beginnings of Western civilization. All the great literature is not here; perhaps all that is here is not great. But these stories are representative of the places and the times from which they sprang and they have helped to tint the fabric which makes up the composite imprint of our culture" (1: v). The first two volumes focus resolutely on European and American works; of the 1,010 works discussed in those volumes, only 3 are non-Western – the *Thousand and One Nights*, the *Shakuntala* of Kalidasa (beloved of Goethe and introduced as "the Shakespeare of England" [2: 931]), and, somewhat surprisingly, *The Tale of Genji*. The third volume of 1960 finally makes a modest attempt to include "a few titles from the vast reservoir of Oriental literature, an area of world culture long neglected by Western readers" (3: v), and a handful of non-Western works are added in the fourth volume. In the end a total of 1,008 authors are treated in the four volumes of the series; 97.3 percent are Western, 2.7 percent (28 in all) are non-Western.

Magill's collection of summaries was intended for general readers, or more precisely for a combination of *former* and *would-be* general readers. The extensive plot summaries would help you if you wanted to remember who a character was, or what really happened, in a book you'd read some time ago; they would also be useful if you'd heard of a book and wanted to learn more about it so as to decide whether to read it.[1] Whereas both Charles Eliot and Henry Cabot Lodge had focused exclusively on established major authors, Magill freely mixed popular work in with established classics: Arthur Conan Doyle and Pearl Buck appear as early as volume 1, along with Homer and Shakespeare – taking places that might otherwise have been used for Ovid's *Metamorphoses* or for Goethe's *Wilhelm Meister*, both of which appear only in volume 3.

If Magill's preface sounds a little defensive in allowing that "perhaps all that is here is not great," he may be reacting to the gentle mockery provided in an introduction to the volume written by Clifton Fadiman. In soliciting this introduction from Fadiman, guiding spirit of the Book of the Month Club's editorial committee, Magill presumably anticipated a warm introduction from a kindred spirit. This isn't quite what arrived. Fadiman does at least approve of the project overall and stresses its crossover appeal to a wide range of users: "It should make its way at once to the shelf of the writer, publisher, editor, teacher, lecturer, after-dinner speaker, literary agent, bookseller, librarian, radio and television director or editor or producer, motion picture ditto, and of many students and general readers" (1: ix). So far, so good; but Fadiman then spends the bulk of his introduction belittling Magill's choices of popular authors: "One finds, as is natural, titles the grounds for whose inclusion appear incomprehensible. . . . Thus Rex Beach lies down with Aristophanes and Dickens with Lloyd Douglas. Grandiose trumpery (*Ben Hur, Quo Vadis*) is here, and so is *The Magic Mountain*. . . . The editors have not tried to limit their titles to the 'best,' whatever that may be. The aim is not to elevate taste, nor even to instruct . . . but simply to furnish the interested reader with a useful reference tool" (1: x). Fadiman is not being fair here. It is, admittedly, a little disorienting to find *The Sound and the Fury* followed directly by Rex Beach's 1906 Yukon tale *The Spoilers* ("a lusty book about a raw new land filled with adventures and gamblers of all kinds. Blood and thunder leap forth from every page" [1: 919]). Yet Magill and his contributors are constantly instructing their readers in what to look for, showing them how to get into works that are unfamiliar to them – to broaden their world beyond that of current bestsellers and the standard classics taught in school. Here is their pitch for a little-read nineteenth-century French novelist, Edmond About: "Practically unknown in this country, About's novel deserves to be more widely read, for it is ingenious, clever, and witty. Edmond About, who was well-known and honored in his own country, is the equal of many French writers whom we consider great" (2: 534).

This argument is interesting: it tries to extend the bounds of what "we consider great" by recourse to About's standing in his own culture in his own era, suggesting that world literature needs to reflect the values of the originary culture as well as the values of those who receive the work.[2] Even though he stops short of really describing About's novel *as* a "great book" – "ingenious, clever, and witty" are rather modest superlatives, after all – the writer of this entry has apparently been moved to include About because he was both "well-known" *and* "honored" by his countrymen: both a commercial success and a respected figure, his novel appropriate to read among the ranks of elite books even if not a towering masterpiece itself.

This crossover evangelism in turn informs the collection's advocacy on behalf of the difficult, elite works it presents side by side with the work of Conan Doyle and C. S. Forester. *The Sound and the Fury*, for example, is introduced as though it were a worthy companion to Beach's Yukon potboiler: "Beneath its involved and difficult techniques, *The Sound and the Fury* is a compelling study of an old Southern family gone to seed. The members of the Compson family are victims of lust, incest, suicide" (1: 916). Yet once it has drawn the reader in, the Faulkner entry gives a lucid exposition that devotes as much attention to the novel's difficult techniques as to its melodramatic plot, and it closes by encouraging the reader to persevere to the end, for "only in the last two parts does the story fall into a clear pattern. Then the pieces of the puzzle begin to fit into place and the reader finds that he is experiencing stark tragedy and horrible reality" (1: 917).

Encompassing both popular and elite literature from the start, Magill's collection shows in its later series the steady expansion of the category of "literature" as the century progressed. While the first two volumes focus almost exclusively on novels, drama, and narrative poetry, the third series in 1960 acknowledges "the broadening of categories" then under way (3: v). The first two volumes had included a few memoirs and autobiographies, such as Dana's *Two Years Before the Mast* and *The Travels of Marco Polo*, but volume 3 gives a considerably wider range of literary nonfiction: Caesar's *Commentaries*, Abelard's *Historia Calamitatum*, Darwin's *Origin of Species*. The fourth volume goes further still in 1969, including anthropological and psychological writers – Boas, Freud – and even literary criticism (I. A. Richards).

Magill's collection gives a good picture of the shape of world literature in postwar America: a largely Euro-American world, opened a little to some "major" non-Western cultures by the 1960s, and increasingly open to a range of literary works that would not have been classified as literature a few decades earlier. Intended for a general readership, this account of world literature encompassed popular as well as elite work, even as it presented a populist vision of the ideal accessibility of elite masterpieces.

As modest as were Magill's non-Western ventures in the 1950s and 1960s, his 2.7 percent went beyond what was typically found in college "World Lit" courses. With academic literary study sharply divided by language and especially by region, most world literature courses continued to have an exclusively European or Euro-American focus through the 1980s. Consider *The Norton Anthology of World Masterpieces*, probably the most widely used anthology in courses around the country from its first edition in 1956 to the present. As recently as the fifth edition of 1985, the *Norton*'s "World" consisted exclusively of Western Europe and the United States. Finally, the sixth edition of 1992 added a handful of non-Western authors in a newly expanded concluding section called "Contemporary Explorations."

In contrast to Magill's collection, the *Norton* focused from the start on masterworks. As late as 1985 the field of world literature was represented by a only a few dozen authors (rather than Magill's 1,008), and within this group a much smaller number held a pronounced pride of place: much of the anthology's space was taken up with complete works by Homer, Aeschylus, Sophocles, Euripides, Chaucer, Dante, Shakespeare, Voltaire, Goethe, and Dostoevsky. The selections, moreover, were almost entirely literature in the strict sense of poetry, plays, and fiction, with the usual inclusion of some examples of autobiography (Augustine's and Rousseau's *Confessions*) and Montaigne's *Essais*. A similar focus and balance were found in the other most often assigned anthology, Brian Wilkie and James Hurt's *Literature of the Western World* (1984) – whose title at least has the good grace to admit its focus openly.

The picture has changed dramatically in the past decade. Anthologies now typically show a far wider geographical and literary range, usually with extensive selections from non-Western literatures, and some have jettisoned the "masterpiece" approach as well, with briefer selections from a wider range of writers. Thus *The HarperCollins World*

Reader (1994) attempted to give something approaching proportionate representation to all the world's major literary traditions and even some serious attention to many less extensive traditions as well. This resulted in greatly shortened selections from Homer and Dante, making room for the inclusion of work not only from China, Japan, and India but also from Vietnam, Singapore, and Micronesia, among many other areas. Literature itself has become an increasingly fluid category: the HarperCollins text includes Confucius, Boethius, and the journal of Christopher Columbus, and it has extensive and very interesting sections on African oral epic and on Native American orature, works that are not even literature in the root sense of a written text.

At the same time that the HarperCollins anthology was in preparation, the Norton anthology awoke from its European slumber and came out in an expanded edition in 1995, adding two thousand pages of non-Western material to its four thousand Western pages. While the *Norton* retains its core of "Masterpieces" – the entire texts of the *Odyssey*, the *Inferno*, *Candide*, and *Faust I*, for instance – it now includes works that don't fit the older masterpiece model at all. In this new edition the twentieth century begins with "Zuni Night Chants," followed by selections from Sigmund Freud (another example of the opening up of "literature" beyond its traditional boundaries), before finally coming to canonical authors like Yeats, Rilke, and Woolf. Even Wilkie and Hurt's explicitly Western two-volume anthology has expanded its "West" to include a number of Arabic selections (the Koran, the *Thousand and One Nights*), and their publisher, Prentice-Hall, has now introduced a "companion volume" edited by Willis Barnstone and Toby Barnstone called *Literatures of Asia, Africa, and Latin America*.[3]

All these new developments testify to the excitement surrounding the widening of the literary field, as the focus of world literature enlarges from the old world to the whole world and from literature in itself to the literary in general; yet all of these anthologies reveal the perplexities involved in our rapidly shifting situation. What, really, does belong in such a collection, and how should all these new materials be ordered and presented? The anthologies just mentioned have taken very different approaches to the problem, and while each gives a wealth of fascinating new material, none of them has found a really effective presentation for all these riches. The Barnstones' *Literatures of Asia, Africa, and Latin America* works rather awkwardly as a supplement to Wilkie and Hurt's *Literature of the Western World*, edited as it is by different people, with a different organizational structure, and with the Western volumes unchanged to take account of their new companion volume. *The HarperCollins World Reader* proceeds essentially by exploding the "old world," making room for a vivid gallery of snapshots of the "whole world," yet the result is fragmentary, inconsistent, a disorienting series of abrupt leaps from one brief selection to another. By contrast, in its pre-twentieth-century sections the *Norton* layers its "expanded" non-Western material onto a largely unchanged European core in ways that often seem tokenistic and incoherent. Two large sections on European Romanticism and on European naturalism and realism, several hundred pages each, are now interrupted by a new section, "The Ottoman Empire," which consists of a single thirty-page set of selections from Celebi's *Book of Travels*. The five-hundred-page section on the European Renaissance is now followed by an ambitiously titled section, "Native America and Europe in the New World" – but this section is only thirty-two pages long, consisting of a few Aztec poems and selections from the Mayan *Popol Vuh*; no texts at all are given from the Spanish explorers or from direct native responses to the Europeans. The twentieth-century section, on the other hand, gives up regional divisions altogether and goes global, but its only organizing principle is chronological. This arrangement places Inuit poetry in between Kafka and D. H. Lawrence – giving a new meaning, perhaps, to the term "Eskimo Pie" but offering little foothold for reader or teacher.

If the house of world literature has become a little unstable now that its walls are falling away, a new set of problems has emerged as the floor has begun to drop out as well. Western literature traditionally relied on a well-defined double origin, in Athens and Jerusalem, synthesized in Rome and passed along north and west thereafter. Homer and Plato, Genesis and Isaiah could reasonably be taken as starting points when next to nothing was known of the cultures that preceded them. The explosion of knowledge of the ancient Near East during the past century and a half, however, has given us a very different landscape. The Norton *World Masterpieces* had traditionally begun with a little Bible before getting down to business in a five-hundred-page section grandly entitled "Ancient Greece and the Formation of the Western Mind," but in the expanded edition of 1995 a new opening section was introduced, "The Invention of Writing and the Earliest Literatures." This section begins with the *Epic of Gilgamesh* and a judicious selection of ancient Egyptian poetry before going on to selections from Genesis, Job, the Psalms, and the prophets. This section now reaches a millennium and a half further back in time than previously, as well as a good deal farther east than ever before.

A laudable expansion; yet the editors don't quite know what to do with all this new antiquity. Introducing the *Epic of Gilgamesh*, they confess that

> a great lost work like *Gilgamesh* poses particular problems of understanding beyond those posed by the discovery of a lost masterpiece by a known author or of a known time. The meaning of a work of literature is partly contextual – it is established by the culture that produced that work. Yet the whole context of Gilgamesh was lost along with the text. The names of the gods and humans who people the epic, the cities and lands in which they lived, and the whole of their history vanished for thousands of years from common memory. . . . That strangeness has diminished each year as more tablets have been discovered and translated and as our understanding of the languages and cultures of the ancient Middle East has increased, but what we know is still relatively slight compared with what we know of the cultures that succeeded them. Today the names of Ulysses and Achilles and the gods and goddesses of Mount Olympus are familiar even to many who have not read Homer. The names of Gilgamesh, Enkidu, Utnapishtim, Enlil, and Eanna are virtually unknown outside the poem itself. (1: 10)

The end of this paragraph forgets what the middle knows: we now have a wealth of information about the culture that produced the epic, and great gods like Enlil and Ishtar are attested in many recovered texts outside the epic.⁴ The general reader may know little of them, but then again the average college freshman, the anthology's most common reader, probably comes to Homer with little specific knowledge of Hera, say, or even Achilles: the anthology's extensive introductions and notes are designed to supply the cultural context in a way that general readers can absorb. Further, it is simply not true that the ancient Near East is an entirely separate world, unconnected to classical culture and the Olympian gods. As comparative mythology has long demonstrated, the major Near Eastern gods all have direct analogues on Olympus. Moreover, Near Eastern literary forms like the epic show significant continuities with later epic traditions, and though the oldest stories of Gilgamesh antedate Homer, what we now call "the standard form" of *Gilgamesh* was created by a Babylonian priest named Sîn-liqe-unninni in around 1200, at just the time when Homeric oral epic was beginning to develop among the Greek-speaking communities of Asia Minor and the Peloponnesus. *Gilgamesh* then circulated around the Near East – including into the Hittite Empire in Asia Minor – and the story was retold in Greek in the fourth century by the Babylonian historian Berossus. The epic continued to circulate in the original as well, at least as late as the second century BCE: a copy was made in around 130 by a temple trainee named Bel-ahhe-usur.

The *Norton* editors sever this temporal continuity throughout their introduction. They begin by incorrectly dating the epic to "ca. 2500–1500 BC," a range that takes us from early Sumerian Gilgamesh poems up through the Old Babylonian period but leaves off before the actual period in which the epic as we know it was created. Describing *Gilgamesh* as "a poem of unparalleled antiquity," they claim that it "vanished from memory" "at a time when the civilizations of the Hebrews, Greeks, and Romans had only just developed beyond their infancy" (1: 10). Having themselves performed this vanishing act on the epic, the editors are freed from any necessity to set *Gilgamesh* into an active relation with its own cultural traditions or with the classical texts that follow in "Ancient Greece and the Formation of the Western Mind." Instead they head for the high ground of universal truth. On this plane the poem's antiquity can remain unexamined because it turns into a magical protomodernity: "The story of Gilgamesh and his companion, Enkidu, speaks to contemporary readers with astonishing immediacy. . . . It is both humbling and thrilling to hear so familiar a voice from so vast a distance" (1: 10, 12). At once amazingly ancient and astonishingly immediate, *Gilgamesh* is notably unconnected to anything in between.

The account I've just given of problems in presenting an expanded world literature is less a polemic than a confession: I was a contributing editor to the HarperCollins anthology and a consultant on the Mesoamerican additions to the *Norton*. This may have been the best we could do in the early 1990s, but we are going to have to do better in future. We can in fact do better if we can find more varied and flexible ways of placing ourselves, and the works we study, on the maps we draw of the world. From Lodge and Eliot to the HarperCollins and Norton anthologies, world literature has oscillated between extremes of assimilation and discontinuity: either the earlier and distant works we read are really *just like us,* or they are unutterably foreign, curiosities whose foreignness finally tells us nothing and can only reinforce our sense of separate identity. We should no longer rest content with a choice between a self-centered construction of the world and a highly decentered one. Instead we need more of an *elliptical* approach, to use the image of the geometric figure that is generated from two foci at once. Contemporary America will logically be one focus of the ellipse for the contemporary American reader, but the literature of other times and eras always presents us with another focus as well, and we read in the field of force generated between these two foci.

Future anthologies of world literature must find new and better ways to manage the tensions between the reader's world and the worlds we read about. We will need to draw closer connections between here and there, then and now, while at the same time providing the historical and cultural information to hold ourselves off from an unthinking assimilation of the foreign work to our own norms, whether political or aesthetic. If we can plot a series of partially overlapping ellipses on our literary globe, we can create a new and dynamic understanding of the world's multiform literatures and of our own multivalent place among them.

Notes

1. Nowhere does Magill allow that his book might also be used by a third group: *nonreaders*, who could use the summaries to get through a quiz on material they were supposed to have read for a class.

2. A subsequent entry notes the converse, that a work may have greater appeal abroad than at home: "*The Little Clay Pot* is more like Western drama than any other Sanskrit play, in structure, characterization, and tone. This similarity to Occidental drama may account for the fact that its Indian critics have been less enthusiastic than those of the Western world" (3: 586) – an evenhanded formulation that encourages the American reader to expect the play to be approachable, while admitting that this very approachability arises from qualities that make it uncharacteristic of Sanskrit drama in general.

3. On the back cover, apparently wishing to reassure us that this collection of regions can be read as a coherent whole, the publisher somewhat oxymoronically describes the collection as presenting "an enormous province of literature" (Barnstone and Barnstone).

4. It is a little puzzling that the *Norton* editors cite Eanna as an example of a vanished name, as this is not a major figure whose Greek equivalent would be known to readers of Homer today: it is simply the name of a temple in Uruk, as is clear in any event in context in the poem. We no more need a prior knowledge of this name to read the poem than we would need to come to Homer knowing the name of Achilles' horse. Possibly the editors were conflating Ea, god of the ocean, and Inanna, Sumerian goddess of love?

Bibliography

Barnstone, Willis, and Tony Barnstone, eds. *Literatures of Asia, Africa, and Latin America*. Upper Saddle River NJ: Prentice-Hall, 1999.

Caws, Mary Ann, et al., eds. *The HarperCollins World Reader*. 2 vols. New York: HarperCollins, 1994.

Eliot, Charles W., ed. *The Harvard Classics*. 50 vols. 1910. 2nd ed. New York: P. F. Collier and Son, 1917.

Guillory, John. *Cultural Capital: The Problem of Literary Canon Formation*. Chicago: University of Chicago Press, 1993.

Lodge, Henry Cabot, ed. *The Best of the World's Classics*. 10 vols. New York: Funk and Wagnalls, 1909.

Mack, Maynard, et al., eds. *The Norton Anthology of World Masterpieces: Expanded Edition*. 2 vols. New York: W. W. Norton, 1995.

Magill, Frank, ed. *Masterpieces of World Literature in Digest Form*. 4 vols. Pasadena CA: Salem Press, 1949–69.

Wilkie, Brian, and James Hurt, eds. *The Literature of the Western World*. 2 vols. 5th ed. Upper Saddle River NJ: Prentice-Hall, 1997.

SARAH LAWALL

Anthologizing "World Literature"

I seek a form . . . – Rubén Darío

It's difficult to imagine a form to fit such a content. – Richard S. Pressman

Anthologizing "world literature" is a unique editorial challenge with its own special history. First, it is burdened by pedagogical associations with a narrowly Western canon and by a critical history that runs from Goethe's national stereotypes engaged in privileged conversation to the idealist implications of Great Books. Second, theoretical attempts to define the anthologist's task run into the extraordinary ambiguity of the terms *world* and *literature* (Lawall, "Reading World Literature"). More objective terms have been proposed: *globe* for *world* and *global literary studies* for a newly scientific approach based on cultural data. Yet the subject matter is still unclear, and globalization – as Ian Baucom notes – tends to impose static paradigms and a methodology that does not allow for relational dynamics. The inevitable selectivity of the anthology format draws attention to gaps in both global and "world literature" coverage, and the anthology's table of contents is also scrutinized for its relevance to "literary" standards vis-à-vis various forms of cultural production. Finally, world literature anthologies are still *anthologies*: they extract individual texts from their original settings and reassemble them as a collectivity produced for a contemporary audience. The result is often seen not as the passionate exchange of eager voices that Goethe envisaged but as an academic construction with a manual-like facade of authority that chills inquiry and critical speculation.

So much for the bad news. In contrast, I prefer to see anthologies as a theoretically interesting form whose potential for opening up discourse has yet to be sufficiently explored; moreover, I believe that the academic anthology, situated at the intersection of public and private readings, of tradition and cultural change, best embodies this potential. Such an anthology's various constitutive parts – its visibly constructed table of contents, preface, and editorial apparatus (footnotes, headnotes, extended essays, ancillary materials); its self-reflexive identity (always aware of its situation vis-à-vis the audience); and finally its virtual reality as a paradigm enacted differently in each classroom – bring to the surface a web of communicative relationships that might otherwise remain obscure. The academic anthology is the anthology at its most *typical*, to adapt Shklovsky's term for a form that lays bare its own devices, and the world literature anthology is its most typical example. The very diversity of world literature materials raises issues of sameness and difference and of the relationship between different modes of understanding. Readers require new information – and categories of information – as they encounter unfamiliar settings and perspectives and pursue questions of social and personal identity. Taking advantage of that initial curiosity, editors can explore formats that will encourage inquiry, investigate the various uses of contextual information, and open up routes for speculation and critical analysis.

The question is how to do it, and how to find a format that illuminates and raises questions without proposing hidden and limited answers: what materials to choose, where and how to juxtapose them, what systematic relationships to bring to the fore to encourage critical perspectives, and how to avoid both the comfort of traditional arrangements and the lure of a format that promises diversity but instead narrows avenues of inquiry. I don't mean that there is only one formula, but rather that there are pitfalls and possibilities to consider in any proposed structure, and they are worth exploring in both historical and theoretical context. My own experience in editing an academic anthology comes chiefly, but not entirely, from working with Norton's world literature series; I joined the anthology in 1977, after responding to a request to critique the current volume (more on that later). While I am convinced of the actual openness and effectiveness of a work-centered collection (that is, a collection of texts in which the aesthetic function is predominant) in communicating cultural as well as aesthetic patterns, I am well-aware of the critiques directed against such a focus. Other anthologies, ranging from late nineteenth-century to contemporary multicultural collections, have chosen to foreground cultural voices, often making greater use of excerpts in order to sample a larger variety of texts. The aims are not exclusive – we do need to find ways to bring out the cultural embedding of a text, to read it as part of a broad continuum of texts and contexts, and constantly to seek "new questions and new ways in which the literary and nonliterary texts alike can be made to read and rework each other" (Johnson 15). The challenge for a work-centered anthology is to make sure that the analytic focus on individual works also recognizes, in theory and in practice, their relationship to contexts and patterns of reference. The challenge for a representational anthology is not only to validate its categories ("As the years pass we discover more categories of human beings demanding to be heard" [see Pressman's contribution to this volume]) and to interrogate the presumed transparency of each cultural "voice" but also to organize material without resorting to static paradigms and broad historical generalizations. A brief look at some early collections that foreshadow the contemporary world literature anthology shows the extent to which historical perspectives, aesthetic assumptions, changing cultural values, and a strong tradition of autodidacticism intertwine. It may also illuminate changes taking place in literary anthologies around the middle of the twentieth century.

These early examples are not academic anthologies in the modern sense – that is, constructed for use in the classroom during a conventional academic year – but they already have a place in educational history. They date from 1885 to 1901, before the era of mass education, and are part of a proliferation of collected works made possible by the lifting of perpetual copyright in Britain. Jonathan Rose has described the broadly educational role played by such volumes in *The Intellectual Life of the British Working Classes*, noting that the author of the infamous 1886 list of the "Hundred Best Books," Sir John Lubbock, was an adult educator and president of the Working Men's College and that the books on his list inspired and radicalized generations of British autodidacts (128–31). In the United States the populist publisher John B.

Alden claimed to "inaugurate a Literary Revolution" by selling low-cost editions directly to buyers (Korey 3). The American anthologies edited by Alden, Charles D. Warner, and Harry Thurston Peck are quasi-educational multivolume editions of selections aimed at a broad commercial audience: that is, "the great body of the reading public" reading at home (Alden 1: 9). In their prefaces the editors discuss principles of selection and arrangement, the status of literature vis-à-vis other forms, the anthology's cultural aims, and the editors' belief that such anthologies are a new phenomenon important for modern society. The volumes are not organized to develop these principles, however, and the editors differ in the importance attributed to such a project. As might be expected, the very lack of organization and the editors' sense that certain issues do not need to be addressed reveal the power of unspoken assumptions.

Diversity is important in these collections, and it is apparently easy to come by. Alden's *Cyclopedia of Universal Literature* (1885–91) is subtitled *Presenting Biographical and Critical Notices, and Specimens from the Writings of Eminent Authors of All Ages and All Nations*; as the editor reassures us, it provides "a complete survey of the literature of all ages and of all peoples" (1: 7). (Non-Western writers are almost completely missing.) Charles D. Warner's *A Library of the World's Best Literature, Ancient and Modern* (1897) "draws upon all literatures of all time and of every race, and thus becomes a conspectus of the thought and intellectual evolution of man from the beginning" (iii). Harry Thurston Peck further defines the scope of his *Masterpieces of The World's Literature, Ancient and Modern* (1898) in 1901 by changing the title: he drops the word literature (while keeping masterpieces) and expands the title to *The World's Great Masterpieces; History, Biography, Science, Philosophy, Poetry, The Drama, Travel, Adventure, Fiction, etc. A Record of the Great Things That Have Been Said and Thought and Done from the Beginning of History*. The interchangeable titles – universal literature, world's best literature, masterpieces of the world's literature, the world's great masterpieces (but not of literature) – demonstrate not only that literature is a cover term but that the real anchor point is the "history of human culture and progress" (Alden 1: 7) conveyed by representative human voices.

The notion of representative voices – or of cultural ideas embodied in such voices – continues to be a recurrent theme in world literature and in culturally oriented anthologies. It evokes Goethe's 1827 description of world literature as a conversation between representative national figures, Lionel Trilling's assertion that the best subject matter for freshmen is "the great, resounding ideas of the ages" from Homer to Dostoevsky (373), and the "Great Conversation" that is Robert Hutchins's organizing principle for *Great Books of the Western World* (1952). Contemporary authors often use the personalized overtones of "voice" to designate various cultural groups inside the larger global heteroglossia: *Voices from Afar: Modern Chinese Writers on Oppressed Peoples and Their Literature* (1980); *Voices: Canadian Writers of African Descent* (1992); *Voices from an Empire: A History of Afro-Portuguese Literature* (1975). "Voices" constitute a slippery editorial concept, however, insofar as they obscure the editorial process and suggest unmediated cultural expression – transparent speech replacing textual ambiguity. Representing authoritative speech, they recall Harry Levin's description of the early canon's reliance on "*auctores*: authors designated as authorities . . . and collectively accepted to constitute the authorized body of knowledge" (354). In such anthologies the voice you hear is the one the editor hears: an effect particularly visible in these early anthologies that focus not on *texts* but on the presumedly direct expression of numerous authors. It has sometimes been noted that the earlier anthologies include more women and people of color than their mid-twentieth-century counterparts. Despite this apparent openness, the selections usually echo each other and social stereotypes as well: the passages by women in Warner and Peck, for example, run to themes of piety, domesticity, and patriotism.

The two most ambitious editors, John B. Alden and Charles D. Warner, have different editorial missions and approach their tasks differently. The former wishes to edit a volume from a historical or objectively cultural point of view; the latter limits his selections to those with "distinct literary quality." Alden selects a greater variety of forms while stressing an author's personality and social history; Warner explores editorial strategies to make his more traditionally literary list accessible to the reader.

Alden's *Cyclopedia of Universal Literature* is an interesting attempt to combine canonical and noncanonical authors inside a neutral format that avoids editorial bias but leaves room for a picture of cultural evolution. Alden aims to avoid the triviality of collections of "'Elegant Extracts' or 'Gems of Thought' culled from writings which have come to be classics in their various languages." Instead his authors are included because they "have made a distinctive mark in the history of human culture and progress," and he offers biographical sketches followed by extracts "sufficient to give an adequate representation of the characteristics of the authors" (1: 7). This swerve from a belles-lettres convention (the "elegant extracts" he derides) toward cultural history is evident from the beginning, when the title's "universal literature" is followed by more neutral or scientific terms (*specimens, writings, extracts*) set in historical context. At times Alden adopts the language of historical relativism. "Greatness," for example, that staple of anthologies of the "best literature" and of "masterpieces," is for him a relative concept that can be measured by context and historical influence: "The names of some men will appear who were great, not absolutely, but only relatively. Such men, for example, as Diderot, Erasmus, and Paine, whose works exerted a powerful influence in their own day, and thus upon aftertimes, although had they appeared in an earlier or a later century they would soon have been forgotten" (1: 7). Such promising theoretical issues are unfortunately not explored. Alden never explains any of his evaluations, which range from literary-historical judgments like the previous to expressions of moral sympathy that contradict his historical principles. The first volume of his anthology (*Abbott to Arnold*) ends with four passages from Thomas Arnold (1795–1842), an English educator and historian, of whom Alden concludes that "Thomas Arnold was beyond doubt a man much greater than any or all of his published works" (1: 478).

Alden intended to do more than to compile writings from all ages and all peoples; he is an unabashed progressive with no nostalgia for the glorious past. The *Cyclopedia* includes a great many contemporary

American authors because he wishes his readers to study "this current Nineteenth Century" as fully as "any preceding century of human culture and progress." Whether or not we agree with his assumption that British and American writing represents the pinnacle of cultural progress, it is a pity – from an anthologizer's point of view – that he did not take more interest in the editorial process and use it to clarify his intended history of human culture. Some entries – like a traveler's vivid description in 1847 of the expulsion of the Acadians from their homeland – clearly resonate with other selections and would gain interest and significance if those comparisons were made. Yet the headnotes for each entry are limited to summarizing the author's life, positions, and publications with all the charm of a curriculum vitae (except for the canonical authors, where conventional judgments are reproduced). The table of contents marches in alphabetical order throughout all twenty volumes because, Alden explains, that arrangement "after mature consideration . . . presents more advantages and fewer disadvantages than any other" (1: 8). Indeed, any organization of entries has its disadvantages, and Alden is not the only editor to choose the apparently neutral format of alphabetical order – Warner and Peck do the same. Nonetheless, he is turning his back on an opportunity to clarify relationships as he sees them and as he wishes his audience to see them. By refusing to project any organizational structure, Alden neglects to set these authorial voices in a broader context or to display them as a conversation – in short, to create his desired cultural *history* instead of a series of random extracts. Looking at it from another angle, the effect of this refusal to imagine relationships allows him to avoid rethinking his own premises and preserves his view of cultural evolution unchallenged by contradictions or inconsistencies. It is probably clear that I consider such rethinking and projecting of tentative structures part of an academic anthologist's responsibility, if only because it establishes the idea of critical perspective and provides readers with avenues for discussion.

Unlike Alden, Charles D. Warner confronts many of these editorial issues in his *Library of the World's Best Literature, Ancient and Modern*. Warner has a somewhat easier task, in that he has unified his list by restricting it to "literature" and to other writers ("philosophers, theologians, publicists, or scientists") who have "distinct literary quality" or profound influence on literature. He does not ask "What is literature?" or question his global coverage ("all literatures of all time and of every race" [iii]) but relies on a consensus of European and American "writers and scholars, specialists and literary critics" to decide what is best and to edit appropriate entries. The collection thus becomes "in a way representative of the scholarship and judgment of our own time" (v), a new editorial dimension made clear by the exceptionally long signed introductions to individual authors (some with a reproduction of the critic's signature). These scholarly and interpretive essays constitute a good portion of the anthology: in the first volume twenty-one pages are devoted to Abigail Adams's letters, with six pages of introduction; Accadian-Babylonian and Assyrian literature receive ten pages of introduction for twenty-three pages of text; eight and a half pages of Aeschylus are accompanied by over nine pages of introduction. Warner insists on the novelty of this arrangement, whose emphasis on critical perspectives enables his forty-five volumes to fulfill their cultural mission as a "conspectus of the thought and intellectual evolution of man" (iii). It contrasts sharply with the conservative format of Harry Thurston Peck's *The World's Great Masterpieces*, in which each entry is preceded by a short biographical paragraph whose ending sentence assesses the writer's complete work.

Warner was a prolific and popular writer with a strong interest in the relationship of text and audience. Author of *The People for Whom Shakespeare Wrote* (1897), he also cowrote *The Gilded Age* (1873) with Mark Twain and was editor of the *Hartford Courant* for thirty-three years. The preface to *A Library of the World's Best Literature, Ancient and Modern* is the work of a popularizer: he introduces his collection as a "household companion" intended for "American households," including "persons who have not access to large libraries" (iii–iv), and mentions its educational value. The latter claim is certainly advertising, but it also reflects the recently flourishing extension movement in adult education: indeed, the scholarly and explanatory tone of the editorial apparatus goes far toward making Warner's series a forerunner of contemporary academic anthologies. Unlike Alden and Peck, he discusses inclusions and exclusions, explains his principles of organization, and describes at length the means that he has devised to make the lengthy series of works accessible. Like Alden, he retreats to the safety of alphabetical order – "Alcman, Alcott, Alcuin" – for which he makes the best argument that he can: in each volume "the reader obtains a sense of the varieties and contrasts of different periods." Warner is more flexible than Alden, however, and he ventures into the sticky (and revealing) business of grouping entries when he feels that to do otherwise would confuse his audience. If the names of individual writers "would have no significance to the reader," he says, a context is established by grouping "certain nationalities, periods, and special topics" (iv). He explains the weight given to the proportion of classics and moderns and apologizes for the omission of favorite authors by pleading the constraints of space.

Warner echoes other editors of the period by describing his anthology's mission in terms of cultural evolution and the "contemporary achievement and tendencies in all civilized countries." In practice, however, he differs by consistently focusing on "literary qualities" rather than on vague ideas about cultural progress. A writer himself, he insists that the anthology's "general purpose is to give only literature" (v) and concludes that the comparative study of "the older and the greater literatures of other nations" will give the American public "a just view of its own literature, and of its possible mission in the world of letters" (vi). Given this aim, it is not surprising that the various headnotes are so full and interpretive or that Warner chooses sizable or complete entries rather than a greater number of smaller excerpts. "The attempt to quote from all would destroy the Work for reading purposes, and reduce it to a herbarium of specimens" (iv), he says, explaining that a list and "comprehensive information as to all writers of importance" (nowadays, "coverage") will be relegated to later volumes (in fact, volumes 42–43). Contemporary readers may not agree with all of Warner's choices, but they will recognize his unusual willingness to lay out for discussion basic editorial issues of organization, selection, the scope and nature of editorial apparatus, and intended audience. These topics continue to be factors in the creation of the contemporary academic anthology and generate, in each instance, its unique editorial presence.

Such an editorial presence is veiled in the *Harvard Classics: Dr. Eliot's Five-Foot Shelf of Books*, which was produced by a singular team of President Charles W. Eliot of Harvard, an eminent educator and scientist; the publisher P. F. Collier and Son, which proposed the project (and was, incidentally, the first to sell books to the public by monthly subscription); and the scholar who did the real work of editing: William A. Neilson, a professor of English at Harvard and future president of Smith College. Collier's was in no hurry to recognize Professor Neilson's hand; his name is omitted from the title page and from their publicity booklet, which advertises opportunities for ambitious readers to acquire a Harvard education under the "personal guidance of Dr. Eliot" (Eliot, *Analysis* 17) and to read the texts along with Eliot's own "intimate personal comment" (25).[1] Eliot himself was more forthright in his introduction to the series, when he explained that Collier's had promised him "a competent assistant of my own choice" and that he had "secured the services of Dr. William A. Neilson, Professor of English in Harvard University"; "I decided what should be included, and what should be excluded. Professor Neilson wrote all the introductions and notes, made the choice among different editions of the same work, and offered many suggestions concerning available material. It also fell to him to make all the computations needed to decide the question whether a work desired was too long to be included. The most arduous part of his work was the final making up of the composite volumes from available material which had commended itself to us both" (Introduction 11).

The *Harvard Classics* are a mixed phenomenon. They are generally considered a conservative canonical relapse on the part of President Eliot, a liberal educator and scientist who had pushed through an elective curriculum at Harvard (Levin 357). Certainly Collier's, when it proposed to implement Eliot's public statements that a five-foot shelf would hold enough books to give "a good substitute for a liberal education" to anyone reading "but fifteen minutes a day" (Eliot, Introduction 10), intended a commercial rather than a canonical revolution. Eliot's introduction also echoes the vaguely phrased cultural optimism of earlier anthologies, with tributes to "the upward tendency of the human race" (7) and the evolution "from barbarism to civilization" (3). On a practical level, however, his educational beliefs lead him to propose a variable reading model that works – at least potentially – *against* any single or hegemonic interpretation. The all-important last volume, with its *Reader's Guide*, lists, indices, and Eliot's general introduction, foreshadows modern instructor's manuals or even a database search by computer in its care for the integrated use of material throughout the series. Eliot sets forth a reading program whose different options emulate his elective curriculum and encourage self-directed learning: two themes that permeate his many lectures on university education (Eliot, *Harvard Memories* 53–57). Nor does he shy away from discussing editorial problems and solutions: he explains principles of selection in some detail and outlines diverse routes into the material (by chronology or reverse chronology, by subject, by comparison and contrast, by an individual search that uses the index to explore issues raised by any one work). All selections are to be complete and, however diverse, must possess "good literary form." Eliot reserves his greatest enthusiasm for the "encounter with the mental states of other generations" (Introduction 7) and recommends, at one point, a comparative approach that contrasts "different social states at the same epoch in nations not far apart geographically, but distinct as regards their history, traditions, and habits" (8). This belief in the intellectual power of comparison and contrast is supported by a range of interdisciplinary readings (works by Darwin, Faraday, Kelvin, and Pasteur, for example, and a volume of American historical documents) and is governed by the system of selected paths. Collier's publicity, touting the novelty of this pedagogical organization in contrast with previous alphabetically ordered anthologies, asserts that this orderly reading makes the fifty-volume set effectively "one great book" and leaves the mind "with a well-defined impression instead of merely a jumble of facts" (Eliot, *Analysis* 32–33).

It was left to Professor Neilson to execute this grand design and, incidentally, to demonstrate the difficulty of translating inspiring principles into effective editorial practice. Eliot had defined the "principal subjects" of the series: "history, biography, philosophy, religion, voyages and travels, natural science, government and politics, education, criticism, the drama, epic and lyric poetry, and prose fiction – in short, all the main subdivisions of literature" (Introduction 5). Neilson divided the *Reader's Guide* into two classes: the first "subject matter . . . History, Philosophy, or Science"; and the second "literary form, as the Drama or Essay" (50: 17). Drawing on numerous specialists and a staff of assistants, Neilson wrote notes and introductions, created the syllabus-like reading lists, and compiled an enormous index of seventy-six thousand names to let readers thread their way through extended cross references and comparisons. Overall, it is a strange mixture of innovation (exploratory reading facilitated by index and syllabi) and tradition (short conventional introductions and almost no notes). As in previous anthologies, the history of ideas is paramount: in the *Reader's Guide* the topic introduction for the section entitled "History of Civilization" takes eight pages, and for "Religion and Philosophy" six, as compared to two paragraphs for all of "Narrative Poetry and Prose Fiction." Lyric poetry is simply the contents of Palgrave's *Golden Treasury* (1861), printed complete with a few additions chosen by Neilson. Literary criticism is social or personal: readers learn that the *Arabian Nights* represents the social life of the East (50: 22 ["History of Civilization"]), that Pascal's *Thoughts* "suffer from lack of sequence; but their fragmentary nature cannot disguise from the careful reader the astounding keenness of the intellect behind them" (50: 34 ["Religion and Philosophy"]), and that the editor refuses to take responsibility for much in Calderón's *Life Is a Dream* "that defies sober sense" (26: 5 ["Continental Drama"]). Clearly, literariness is not an issue, although "good literary form" is stated as a prerequisite – a theoretical disconnect that reinforces, by default, the series' conventional focus on civilization.

Yet it is a narrow focus. Despite Eliot's stated intention to present "ample and characteristic record of the stream of the world's thought" (Introduction 4), the geographic scope of his selections is much more limited than that of other anthologies: for example, Warner's anthology or even (since Eliot consciously addresses an English-speaking American audience) Chicago educator Richard Moulton's 1911 description of "world literature from the English point of view." Eliot is not really interested in a broader "world" literature, however, but wishes to explain to his American audience the European tradition from which they presumably came; he intentionally includes "a somewhat disproportionate amount of English and American literature" (about half) and emphasizes issues important for American social history (Introduction 5). The true innovation of this otherwise local and conservative series lies in the way it focuses attention on the reader's active participation and organizes different ways to make the masses of reading material accessible. The organization of Hutchins's *Great Books of the Western World* is closely modeled on the *Harvard Classics*: billed similarly as a way to acquire a liberal education, volume 1, *The Great Conversation*, includes an outline entitled "Possible Approaches to This Set" (85–89); suggests assignments in "Ten Years of Reading" (111–31); and recommends pursuing individual interests via a large index of cross-referenced terms and "great ideas" called the *Syntopicon* (volumes 2–3), produced by associate editor Mortimer J. Adler and his staff. The contrast between Eliot's exploratory reading program and the *Harvard Classics'* editorial tendency toward closure exemplifies a familiar tension between objective and interactive approaches: between texts viewed as units positioned inside a cultural canon or the same texts seen as part of a communicative paradigm emphasizing the reader. It is a tension that continues throughout the twentieth century, from early multivolume collections aimed at a large commercial audience whose image is diversified only through a few social stereotypes to smaller anthologies created for use in the classroom and shaped by changing curricular and demographic expectations.

For a long time there was no shortage of anthologies through which English departments could offer a survey of Western literature – a course that was considered "world literature" in that it crossed national boundaries and extended beyond the English literature survey. The first single-volume academic anthology to attempt global scope was Philo M. Buck's *Anthology of World Literature*, published in 1934 and based on his classes at the University of Wisconsin. Buck (whose childhood was spent in India) included Indian, Chinese, and Japanese literature in his classes (Alberson 50), a pattern he hoped to reproduce in book form. His preface summarizes a struggle between various perspectives: a desire to go beyond European tradition, the difficulty of deciding on principles of inclusion and exclusion, a dislike of extracts, a critical and pedagogic intention to focus on great works, and – latent but decisive – the anthology's mission to illuminate the history of Western ideas. This last principle corresponds not only to the book's need to fill its curricular niche (as a literary counterpart to courses in Western civilization) but also to the editor's wish "to discover, not the author's manner, but the matter of his thought – his philosophy of life, and its significance to life today" (Buck [1934] v). Wryly, Buck reviews the usual reasons for including a non-European author: "Shall it be his 'human interest,' or shall it be any of the supposed 'influences' upon our present day thought? Really these are practical questions and difficult to answer." Rejecting extracts on the grounds that they are "fragments only from which to reconstruct the idea" of a whole work (Buck [1934] vi), he must make space by other means. He decides to exclude British and American literature because it is already well-represented in high school and college: a pragmatic choice that unfortunately isolates the one tradition and obscures any more integrative concept of "world" literature. It persists in many curricular patterns today. Translations, especially the translation of lyric poetry, are a "pestilent difficulty." As to literary types, they are "more or less of an accident" and of secondary importance: Shakespeare would be a novelist today, and Buck provides an index of types at the end for those who wish such a grouping.

Buck focuses on works, but works as ideas. He minimizes notes and biographical information to an extraordinary degree: Dante "lived in the Middle Ages – that period of saints and chivalry" (330), and Dante's vision is compared to that of Petrarch and Boccaccio. More factual historical background is relegated to the end of the volume, to a "Chronological Chart" that categorizes each entry under "Author or

Work," "Date," "Nationality," and "Historical Background" in a single row across four columns. Unable to include Asian literature as much as he would like, Buck uses the chart to evoke the missing global context: "Asoka Emperor of India" appears on the same line with Plautus ("250–184 BC, Roman") and "Constantinople Captured by the Turks" along with François Villon. Ultimately, Buck's principle of selection limits his non-Western entries to those that have had a "vital influence" on European tradition: to one section out of fifteen groupings of texts. His concluding pages reinforce the Western perspective by extending "the great tradition" down to present-day European authors – Proust, Joyce, and Pirandello – and to the effects of modern science on Western representations of character and consciousness. The anthology's 1940 revision shows how contemporary historical pressures influence both anthology construction and editorial statements of belief. This revision (reprinted in 1951 and 1961) extends its global scope by adding a great deal of lyric poetry in translation. Conversely, it narrows the volume's intellectual and analytic horizons by eliminating the last section on literary criticism and by reverting to a conservative image of "the symphony of Western culture" (Buck [1951] vi). The classroom mission is clear: Buck's prefatory "confession of faith" states that "it is well that in at least one college course, open to all, there be a reassessment of the ideas that have made human civilization" (v). His revised conclusion (newly subtitled "Some Problems Today" and following nineteenth-century European lyrics instead of literary criticism) no longer emphasizes Pirandello as an example of stylistic ambiguities mirroring "a new age of realistic experiment" with its "current of consciousness – any consciousness" (Buck [1934] 1005). Instead the rewritten second half presents Thomas Mann's *The Magic Mountain* as a moral response from a revitalized humanistic tradition that preserves "the moral world of man's conscience" and rejects "the treason of the intellectual . . . exhibited in an allegory of a sanatorium inhabited by painters, musicians, writers, and theorists – all shut off from the world of life and action" (Buck [1951] 1101). Yet Buck's work overall modifies the Western anthology format in several ways: first, by insisting that world literature should include works from around the globe; and second, by displacing biography as an interpretive tool and moving closer to the interpretation (if not the analysis) of texts.

By the middle of the twentieth century a consistent set of beliefs and practices had emerged that would shape – and continue to shape – anthologies of "world literature." These midcentury beliefs are quite specific when it comes to exploring a work's status in cultural terms but have otherwise little to say: there is certainly no literary analysis or interest in pedagogy. The projected audience is generic-American (of presumed European background) and, for a classroom anthology, is the generic-American English-speaking student taking common-core courses in "Great Texts of Literature" and "Western Thought and Institutions." Stith Thompson's *Our Heritage of World Literature* (1938), for example, addresses readers of "our native English" and excludes foreign authors "felt to be exotic" in favor of "those really significant to us of the English-speaking world" (5). (The eminent folklorist also includes several essays of cultural analysis, notably Matthew Arnold's "Hebraism and Hellenism.") The anthology's educational mission is to give this generic student a perspective on human evolution from barbarism to civilization, with special emphasis on Western tradition as the foundation of twentieth-century America. Global representation is preempted by the community's need to display a common Western heritage, and the role of the editor is prescriptive, framing and conveying that heritage in terms of a history of ideas. It is understood that the writers are male and, for the most part, European. Texts themselves are transparent and have no separate identity to require annotation or analysis (which Robert Hutchins rejected as "vicious specialization" in his preface to *Great Books of the Western World* [1: xxiv]). Selected to illustrate the editor's vision, these texts are more usefully extracts, which have the added advantage of leaving room for more entries. A reader has no way to emerge from the editor's grand design without leaving the anthology, for all facets are subsumed under a single and prescriptive interpretation of culture. When Dagobert D. Runes writes, in his *Treasury of World Literature* (1956), that he would like to include more Asian works but must exclude certain ones because "some of our Eastern friends write with a decidedly Oriental mannerism" (vii), he clearly does not intend to discuss those (literary) mannerisms or that (cultural) Orientalism with the reader. This lack of attention to a work's formal identity, or to the way its structures embed and convey layers of meaning, leaves the way clear for superimposed opinions – opinions with nothing to challenge them so long as they coincide with the reader's expectations.

If I have emphasized the prehistory of contemporary world literature anthologies, my excuse must be that many critics (especially those connected with new anthologies) seem to believe that the world literature anthology began in 1956 with the first edition of *The Norton Anthology of World Masterpieces* and that the future consists solely in reacting to this presumed Origin. It will be more productive, I believe, to examine the way that the Norton anthology itself responded to contemporary cultural and literary-critical practice and the way it has continued to evolve along with the rest of modern intellectual history. There is a tendency to mystify "the *Norton*" that is ultimately not very useful when examining theoretical and practical issues of anthology making or the persistent shaping power of certain historical and analytical habits; moreover, such mystification obscures the way that many of these habits persevere – if in more sophisticated form – today.

When the editors of the first Norton anthology of world literature proposed their manuscript to two large publishing houses in the 1950s, the table of contents displayed a familiar emphasis on Western tradition, and the works included were well-known as literary "masterpieces." The editorial approach did not stress the rise of Western culture, however, and shifted attention to the examination of works. After a preliminary acceptance, Prentice-Hall and Harcourt Brace became worried that the anthology would not be marketable unless sizable changes were made to bring it in line with current practice. The differences were fundamental and could not be negotiated: the encouragement of critical thinking and literary analysis instead of prescribed outlines of cultural history; a focus on imaginative literature instead of the transmission of Great Books; a preference for complete works instead of myriad extracts; and – aimed specifically at classroom teaching – an unprecedented amount of information about the texts: analyses of works, textual annotations, and individual bibliographies. The preface to the first edition (reprinted in the following three) reveals the editors' impatience with current practice: "We have not tried to cover the entire history of the West in print, and have avoided filling our pages with philosophy, political theory, theology, historiography, and the like" (Mack et al. [1956] 1: ix); "In every instance, we seek to go beneath the usual generalizations about periods and philosophies" (1: x). It is, in other words, a rebellion *against* the vague cultural generalizations of preceding anthologies and a revisionary discussion of Western literary tradition (as it was then conceived) *by means of literary criticism*. A similar rebellion occurred in the pedagogical format, for the editors drew on their experience as practicing teachers to accompany the texts with factual, explanatory (and intentionally noninterpretive) footnotes. Control of interpretation thus passed from the unexplained pronouncements of an oracular editor to the classroom interaction of teacher and student, who discussed a single text and body of information. Unwilling to compromise, the editors (Maynard Mack, Bernard Knox, John McGalliard, Pier Pasinetti, Howard Hugo, René Wellek, Kenneth Douglas) looked further and found a small, employee-owned company, W. W. Norton and Co., that was willing to take the gamble. Oddly enough, it appears that one factor in the anthology's acceptance was an innovative format that the publisher, George Brockway, wished to try: instead of the conventional double-column format characteristic of current anthologies of literature – and the Bible – he proposed that the literary texts appear in more readable single columns (Kenney). The first edition of *World Masterpieces* (with the limiting subtitle *Literature of Western Culture*) came out in 1956.

Although there are visible connections between the new anthology's literary-critical approach and New Criticism's focus on texts, distinctions must be made between a critical revolution with bases in English and the separate disciplinary focus of world literature. Theoretical issues peculiar to world literature (for example, the principles of selection for an *international* book list, the accuracy and readability of *translations*, the contextual information necessary for teaching texts from *other* cultural and linguistic traditions) were not important for

English studies. In addition, the editors came from various disciplines – English, classics, Italian, French, and Slavics and comparative literature, most of which had little to do with New Criticism. The only editor who had visible connections with New Critical theory was René Wellek, whose coauthorship of *Theory of Literature* (1949) has obscured the fact that he was primarily an intellectual historiographer with a background in phenomenological aesthetics and Prague structuralism. Wellek's literary-theoretical principles were established (and published) before he came to this country; he was not a literary critic, and – although sympathetic with the work-centered approach – he criticized New Criticism when it ignored a work's dialectical connections with history (Lawall, "René Wellek").

Instead the anthology's editorial principles broadly reflect the Kantian tradition of the work's autonomy as an aesthetic structure. Articulating that tradition inside the current curriculum, and devising a format that would illustrate the principle of literary autonomy, were the main tasks of the first edition: "Our introductions – in consonance with the scheme of the book – emphasize criticism rather than history. While providing all that seems to us necessary in the way of historical background (and supplying biographical summaries in the appendix following each introduction), we aim to give the student primarily a critical and analytical discussion of the works themselves" (Mack et al. [1956] 1: x). History was to be separated from criticism, so that historical perspectives did not become, imperceptibly, evaluation, and the critical introductions for each period were collected in a separate section. The table of contents' conventional division by centuries was replaced by literary-historical terms: section introductions used and explained concepts like Renaissance, Neoclassicism, Romanticism, Realism, and Naturalism. Literary-critical analyses considered the author's life and thought only insofar as they were (broadly) relevant to the selected work, and each concluded with a brief introductory discussion of the text. Relegated to the end was a short section titled "Lives, Writings, and Criticism": brief paragraphs in very small print that outlined basic facts of biography, dates and titles of works, and a recommended critical bibliography. Immediately thereafter, the literary selections appeared in sequence without further comment. This striking separation of literary-critical perspective and biographical data is clearly a device calculated to rebalance habits of interpretation that had been heavily weighted in favor of historical explanation. Occasionally awkward (especially the small print), it disappears later when the need to draw attention to the text is less urgent.

The preface to the first edition (reprinted as a statement of principles along with later prefaces through the fourth edition) addresses issues of "world" coverage with visible discomfort. The anthology does not include the literatures of the Far East because it would not be pedagogically possible, given the current curriculum: "the principal aim of a course in world literature" (presumably, the common-core literature or humanities course) is to "bring American students into living contact with their own Western tradition." To include a different tradition – especially one requiring "extended treatment" to be comprehensible – would defeat that aim and confuse the student. Thus the editors must content themselves with providing unusual variety under the subtitle's "Literature of Western Culture": "English, Irish, American, Russian, German, Scandinavian, French, Italian, Spanish, Portuguese, Latin, Hebrew, and Greek" (Mack et al. [1956] 1: ix). In fact, given the prevailing emphasis on the Big Four of modern European languages – English, French, German, and Russian (languages that were also favored in contemporary comparative literature studies) – this catalog is already a step toward curricular diversity. It clearly does not satisfy the editors' ambitions and thus echoes and prefigures similar struggles to represent global traditions.

It may seem odd that the preface to *The Norton Anthology of World Masterpieces* does not stress the concept of *masterpieces*, either as T. S. Eliot's "ideal order" or as a list of culturally approved Great Books. Not that the concept is missing, but it appears only as a conventional backdrop for the study of autonomous works. Thus the preface discusses how *works* of imaginative literature are to be approached, how such *works* mediate historical experience, and how the range of selected *readings* was decided. The emphasis is technical or procedural: "masterpieces" appears only as a title and in a single reference to the fact that it is difficult to find good translations of "the great masterpieces of the classical and modern foreign languages" (Mack et al. [1956] 1: x). This is not to say that the selections are not also considered (master)works from the traditional Western canon, whose relation to cultural hierarchies has repeatedly been demonstrated. Yet, in the history of world literature anthologizing, the preface marks an important shift away from editorial approaches that define works as signs of cultural progress "from barbarism to civilization." These works are presented as aesthetic objects whose structures of meaning merit critical examination, and the anthology's editorial apparatus is organized to carry out that critical principle. In practice, individual editors differ in the degree to which they examine literary structures or situate works inside intellectual and cultural history. (Compare the adjacent section introductions by René Wellek and Kenneth Douglas.)

The editors themselves were a group of seven friends from a variety of disciplines, with a shared interest in literature and in teaching: four taught at Yale, and the others at Berkeley, UCLA, and the University of Iowa. This editorial group structure was itself unusual. The conventional pattern for world literature anthologies was (and, to a certain extent, still is) to have one or two academics – often with a preponderantly English training – preside over a collection and, when necessary, farm out individual assignments to specialists who subsequently had no connection with the anthology. The Norton editors already represented a broad range of expertise, and they undertook the anthology as an ongoing responsibility. They included a classicist, a prize-winning fiction writer from Italy, a literary historian and theorist from Prague who taught Slavic and comparative literature, a specialist in French literature, and three specialists in different periods of English literature. Many had previously published translations, and all were interested in issues of language use. Except for general editor Maynard M. Mack (whose "Note on Translation" appeared at the end of each volume), each was responsible for a section of the anthology. The editors wrote the period introductions as well as headnotes, footnotes, and bibliographies for individual works, and they compared available translations with an eye to accuracy, literary quality, accessibility, and likelihood of success in the classroom. It is hard to overestimate the importance of their role as teachers, for it gave them a practical sense of the linguistic and cultural information needed to approach foreign works and of questions likely to be raised in class. This combination of broad scholarly expertise and pedagogical experience made the anthology an immediate success in the classroom – it *worked* – and its success was measured by a rapid rise in adoptions and by the closeness with which later anthologies modeled their offerings on the Norton's table of contents.

How and why does an anthology change? "Market forces" is an answer frequently given, and of course the market (another word for *teachers*, perhaps) is part of the continued vitality of any classroom text. In my own experience with the Norton world literature anthologies, change has come partly from teachers' suggestions and reactions to existing volumes and partly from the editors' own sense of developments in their field or of works they have found interesting to teach. It is a lively interaction, and the prefaces to individual editions often give a glimpse into debates behind the scene. Thus in the preface to the third edition Maynard Mack makes the case for the "radical change" of including more lyric poetry in translation, despite his own obvious doubts (which are expressed not only in the preface to the first edition but also in his "Note on Translation"): "There are readers for whom lyric poetry, even when seriously impaired by translation, offers a more satisfying glimpse of the selfhood of an age than any other genre. This, at any rate, is the firm opinion of the teachers who have advised us, and we have taken their words to heart, subject only to the condition that acceptable English versions be available" (2: xi). The issue is not resolved, however, and recurs in succeeding volumes: the fourth edition announces that it has "excluded from this volume most lyric poetry in translation" (1: xiv) because the poems were not widely taught. Translated lyrics gradually reappear in the fifth and sixth editions, along with sample original texts, and they take a more prominent role in the seventh edition.

My personal knowledge of Norton editorial practice dates only from the mid-1970s, when I was one of a number of people asked to review the third edition and recommend improvements. Teaching French,

Francophone, and comparative literature in a curricular framework that did not include "world literature" – the course was "owned" by the English department – I had never seen the anthology. As a Comparatist and inveterate tinkerer with course syllabi and handouts, I was fascinated with the scale of the project and delighted with its focus on complete works: it contrasted with the only teaching anthology I had used, which was a popular survey of French literature that contained myriad short excerpts and, at one point, asked muddled students to choose between the philosophical attitudes of Voltaire and Rousseau. Reviewing the Norton anthology as something of an outsider, I made various suggestions and also objected to the frequently personalized discussion of twentieth-century authors, which seemed at odds with the editors' principles. I could not, for example, agree that André Gide should be introduced with references to a serpent and a statement that "even those favorably disposed to Gide will be ready to admit that the quality of deviousness distinguishes his character" (Mack et al. [1973] 2: 1359). (Rereading the introduction, I still disagree but now recognize a carefully composed "teacherly" essay designed to elicit student interest in "The Return of the Prodigal Son" as a human document.) In 1977 I was invited to become editor of the twentieth-century section and, before long, was working on other aspects of the anthology, meeting regularly with Maynard Mack and the Norton editor in charge of the series. I became general editor with the seventh edition of 1999.

I have described my initial contact not for its intrinsic interest but because it is an example of the relative openness through which the anthology has evolved. Each new editor – including myself – brings different critical and pedagogical expectations, creating an ongoing dialogue with current practice that achieves its own dynamics and helps define the way the anthology will move. From the first edition of *The Norton Anthology of World Masterpieces: Literature of Western Culture* in 1956 to the second edition of the "global" anthology (now called simply *The Norton Anthology of World Literature*) in 2002, these editorial dynamics have articulated changing concepts of "world" literature in ways that relate, more or less openly, to contemporary developments in literary theory, criticism, and cultural history. In 1985 the feminist scholar

Patricia Meyer Spacks replaced the late Howard Hugo as editor of the Enlightenment and Romanticism sections. In 1998 three new editors versed in cultural criticism – William G. Thalmann, Lee Patterson, and Heather James – took charge of the Ancient World, Middle Ages, and Renaissance sections. Throughout, shifts in something as obvious as the anthology's table of contents, and as semivisible as its format and critical framework, have marked stages in an evolving debate over the shape and scope of pedagogical world literature. The competing claims of "world" and "Western" texts, the proportions of innovation and tradition, the search for better translations, the style and substance of editorial introductions, and the best way to implement user suggestions are all issues included inside the larger topic of the anthology's dual role as both a transmitter of the "common heritage" and an introduction to the larger world in which that heritage is situated. The image of an "unchanging masterpieces anthology" may be useful as an oppositional debate tactic, but it is unreal and ahistorical in fact. A materialist critic might indeed profit by examining the publishing history of world literature anthologies: in this conglomerate-bound age, Norton is still, and uniquely, a small employee-owned company with its own evolving tradition of world literature; more typically, a large multinational corporation like Pearson, which owns two large publishing houses (Prentice-Hall and Longman) can make the market choice to package both a conservative anthology of Western world literature and a "multicultural" global textbook arranged along opposite lines. World literature anthologies, individually and jointly, also experience the dynamics of institutional change.

The fifth edition eliminated the previous anthologies' division of parts and began to reunite literary analysis with its cultural matrix. Individual works did not appear in unbroken sequence, evoking Eliot's ideal order, but were presented separately and prefaced by extended headnotes that newly included biographical and cultural information and were followed by the relevant (now annotated) bibliographies. Section introductions were reserved for a general intellectual-historical survey of the period that was organized to suggest social, philosophical, and thematic contexts for the coming selections. These changes did not mean that the emphasis on literary analysis had lessened, but rather that a format had been devised to incorporate historical information insofar as it illuminates literary analysis – which always concluded the headnote. The hermeneutic circle was clear, but expanded.

Changes in the fifth edition entailed further consequences. The new headnote format made it easier to point out different dimensions of the text, but, by focusing on individual selections, it also diminished the notion of an overarching cultural framework – whether "Western" or "world" – and remained open to different ways of viewing intertextual relations. This was a period of complex change in the teaching of literature: over fifteen years critics had demonstrated the cultural narrowness of current literary education, for which they blamed New Criticism, political conservatism, and T. S. Eliot's image of an ideal order of masterworks. Their attacks referred almost exclusively to the teaching of English and American literature and were exemplified in books like Louis Kampf and Paul Lauter's *The Politics of Literature: Dissenting Essays on the Teaching of English* (1972), Lauter's *Reconstructing American Literature: Courses, Syllabi, Issues* (1983), and Judith Fetterley's *The Resisting Reader: A Feminist Approach to American Fiction* (1983). The multiplicity of world literature, or even the linguistic diversity of American literature (discussed later, in Werner Sollors's *Multilingual America*), was not a topic, and issues raised by world literature were not addressed. The world literature anthology, built around the critical analysis of works from various linguistic and cultural traditions, would need to find its own route. In what follows I minimize discussion of ongoing and fairly obvious changes in the *Norton* table of contents – more works by women, more types of writing, more works that focus on cultural issues and implied attitudes – not because they are not important (and imitated) but in order to consider another aspect of construction that involves both the idea of masterworks and the function of different frameworks in representing the horizons of world literature.

When the fifth edition separated the twentieth-century section (hitherto "The Modern World") into "Varieties of Modernism" and "Contemporary Explorations," it ventured into new and contested areas of definition. "Modernism" was an established term in several languages, and the early twentieth century has its Modernist canon – but after that? This pragmatic division of the modern period, caused by the disproportionate length of the twentieth-century list, raised the question of contemporary texts inside a tradition of masterpieces that had always been measured by the "test of time." The "test of time" is not a new educational standard, although how much time remains unresolved: Charles Eliot cited Emerson's view that one should not read a book until it is at least one year old (Thorp 127). The preface to the fourth edition (1979) had already seen this as a potential problem for a canonical anthology, commenting that there was more change in the twentieth-century list because "the canon of authentic masters is better established for earlier periods" (1: xiii). As a section title the fifth edition's "Contemporary Explorations" undoubtedly reflected a cautious approach – to the twentieth-century editor Borges and Beckett were just as established as Brecht and Camus – but "Explorations" also indicated the anthology's openness to different kinds of writing and its desire to represent, without prescriptive labels, "works which so far are less assimilable to any generally recognized cultural pattern" (Mack et al. [1985] 1: xxii). The separate introduction to "Contemporary Explorations" noted current disagreements over what could be called a masterpiece and moved on (typically) to ways of approaching the text, encouraging readers to become acquainted with "new subject matters, new angles of vision, and new techniques of expression" (2: 1907) that teased out contradictory layers of reality and explored areas "beyond the more homogeneous world view of prewar Western society – areas that were earlier seen as marginal" (2: 1910). The selections (still complete works by major authors) encompassed contemporary cultural issues of race, gender, class, economic status, national identity, cultural conflict, and the writing of history; the editorial treatment was consistent with Norton's work-centered approach in that it did not stop with defining these issues but aimed to clarify the verbal and structural elements that made them come alive.

"Contemporary Explorations" also marked the first step in Norton's move to create a global anthology. It was not an inevitable move: most teachers were happy with the current volume, which met the needs of an existing course, and there was plenty of room to explore relationships and representation inside Western culture. Yet many others had asked for more works from other traditions. Several factors come into play at this point: Maynard Mack's regret, stated in the preface to the first edition, that the volume could not include works outside the Western tradition; the enthusiasm of Norton's widely read editor Barry Wade, who made the case to the publisher and considered it his special project until he died in 1993; and probably my own eagerness as a Comparatist who already included non-Western texts in class. One might consider "Contemporary Explorations" a (very limited) pilot project for the larger volume to come. The anthology was still defined as a survey of Western literature, and thus the general preface described works by Mishima, Narayan, and Soyinka (all focused on cultural identity) as "windows opening on experiences and ways of life which are not part of the cultural tradition students brought up on the American continent usually know best" (Mack et al. [1985] 1: xxi). These "windows" opening outward also looked inward: the play by Soyinka, and the next edition's fiction by Naguib Mahfouz and Chinua Achebe, were chosen partly because they probed a *conflict* of Western and non-Western cultural views. Their inclusion in the anthology supplied refracted images of Western tradition: corrective lenses, if you will. It was also a reminder to the editors that an appropriate global framework was needed for the planned *Expanded* edition: one that viewed other cultural traditions in terms of their own development and interactions and devised coherent pedagogical packages for classroom instruction.

Expanded was, in hindsight, an awkward and certainly temporary title. There are now two separate anthologies: one, the global or properly "world" literature anthology; and the other, the classic anthology of the Western literary tradition. The *Expanded* was an "expanded" sixth edition in a literal, bookish sense, inasmuch as it contained (thanks to a different format and new paper) the earlier edition's Western texts together with an equal number of pages of non-Western works. Here function drives form: the book was designed to be usable for either the "Western" or "world" literature class, since no one knew how many teachers would move to a broader syllabus or how many were committed to teaching the Western tradition (which remained, in many institutions, a mandated part of the curriculum). It was a very chunky two-volume set: I once suggested that it be packaged with optional wheels, and certainly the increased weight of our increasing contents pointed the way to the next edition's separation into six smaller and handier volumes. In another sense, however, the book was not "expanded," for it was not produced by the same group of editors. New permanent editors came from various non-Western disciplines (if we except Native American literature, also included in the current Western anthology), so that their scholarly and pedagogical perspectives would bring to the global edition a certain critical distance from the "literature of Western culture." They were John Bierhorst (Native American literature), Jerome Clinton (Near Eastern), Robert Danly (Japanese), Abiola Irele (African and Caribbean), Stephen Owen (Chinese), and Barbara Stoler Miller (Asian literatures, followed after her death by Indira Viswanathan Peterson). Like the first editors, they would assume ongoing responsibility for different sections of the new anthology: in this case for major non-Western literary-cultural traditions.

The word *major* implies both format (a simpler, broader, and perhaps more coherent organization) and point of view. It is clearly only one option among many: other anthologies, especially those emphasizing varieties of cultural experience, have selected excerpts from numerous sources (much as did early, culturally oriented anthologies) as a more equitable representation of global experience. The format is a spatial necessity for Norton, however, given the anthology's commitment to whole works or large coherent units; it also echoes the critical principle stated in the first preface, that only complete works give adequate representation of aesthetic *and* cultural content. Finally, the "major" format reflects a pedagogical conviction that too much fragmentation is confusing in class. As the preface puts it, "Students of all dispositions and capacities retain more of value from an acquaintance of some depth with a few literatures than from a shrapnel burst of many" (Mack et al. [1995] 1: xxi). Yet this was only the first of several format decisions that had to be made, each with potential impact on the reader's understanding of world literature.

The most obvious challenge was to find an organization of materials that would be comprehensible for the reader (teachable in class) without merely imitating Western chronological and generic models. At first this turned out to be less difficult than expected, since the various section editors came to the table with cluster sequences that reflected canons established inside their own non-Western areas. (Anyone teaching "foreign" literature in the United States has firsthand experience of its discrepancies with English literary history and terminology.) These clusters, eventually called "sweeps" to express movement through history, intersected throughout the volumes in broadly chronological order, thus preserving the self-awareness of different cultural traditions while offering readers the broad chronological perspective of "world" literature. They were, in the words of the preface, "continuities from a single cultural tradition enabling students to reach at least a modest familiarity with its characteristic forms of expression before moving on to the next" (1: xxx). The dates of the first and last entries determined the chronology for each cluster, and the cluster dates determined the anthology's material division. No attempt was made to provide an overarching cultural interpretation, whether the early anthologies' "intellectual evolution of man" or modern socioecononomic patterns echoing globalization theory. Yet that very separation of sweeps raised other pedagogical issues: how to avoid an atomistic approach, which puts a great burden on the teacher and easily leads to confusion in the classroom; how to suggest coherent structures without prescribing critical perspectives; and how to mediate inevitable conceptual differences between world-views that derive from different cultural and linguistic traditions. I do not claim that we have resolved all these questions, nor am I sure that they can be resolved, but the attempts to resolve them have a certain pragmatic as well as intellectual interest.

Tables of contents are usually examined for the presence or absence of certain texts, as the minicanons they inevitably are, rather than for their general construction. One reason for the alphabetical ordering of early anthologies was that any further divisions offered guidelines revealing editorial judgments and perspectives that might have to be justified. A primary challenge for postalphabetical anthologies, therefore – whether work-centered or cultural – consists in finding a viable organizational model whose principles are neither hidden nor prescriptive. The overall structure of the *Expanded* edition is visibly determined by a focus on literature (written and oral) and on the artistic imagination. That priority is introduced with the heading for the first section, "The Invention of Writing and the Earliest Literatures," and reinforced by the fact that the following group of texts does not follow the general "sweep" model but extends across three cultural traditions. All of the Western sections retain the same titles, and the non-Western sweeps, where the negotiation of different cultural assumptions is more complex, show a range from historical to mildly interpretive titles. Some, like "Poetry and Thought in Early China" or "The Rise of Popular Arts in Premodern Japan," are descriptive and noncommittal. In general the non-Western titles favor the comparative neutrality of historical definition and avoid Western period or genre terms – *except* when such terms are widely used in the society, in which case they may also be borrowed terms standing for separate realities that must then be explained in the headnote. The classicism discussed in "India's Classical Age," for example, involves the specific historical situation of "classical" Sanskrit as a refined and codified literary language whose development absorbed a more "natural" (changing and dialect-based) Prakrit literature. *Classical* is widely used by Indian scholars to describe this literature, which in itself reveals the widespread influence of Western culture and critical terminology: there is no non-Western equivalent. It was an awkward interlinguistic situation, resolved in this instance by a desire to use a term current among Indian scholars and also familiar to American students.

Simple reference tools like maps and timelines also contextualize works across a larger spectrum that suggests its own priorities and mode of understanding. A reader trying to locate the Ireland of James Joyce or the Japan of Lady Murasaki on a map will receive different impressions of the center and margins of the world according to whether the map projection is centered in Europe or Asia. (The *Expanded* edition gave both, in addition to regional "sweep" maps and, for the modern period, political maps showing the reach of colonial empires.) The timeline's diachronic perspective suggests different views of progress not merely through the relative number of entries but through what they contain. A chronology, "Historical Contexts," which consists of single-line references to battles, conquests, and the rise and fall of dynasties (Buck); or that adds to those events invasions, plagues, state religions, and the rise and fall of cities; or that parcels out human history into the preceding phenomena as well as additional categories of literature and philosophy, and art and music, suggests the importance of certain classifications and the marginality of others. No timeline will be entirely satisfactory: as they creep toward the detail that reproduces historical texture, they become impossibly long, with internal divisions that still need to be justified. Moreover, it is difficult to obtain relevant information on a global scale, inasmuch as current timelines and reference books tend to offer increasingly detailed information about Western history and have much less to say about other parts of the world. A review of a recent timeline of the arts and literature notes the preponderance of Western and more specifically American entries: "The whole is flavored with artist endeavors from all cultures, but the bias is definitely Western Europe/US and, particularly in the 20th century, American popular culture" (*Timelines* 911). We used a single column of "Contexts" after "Texts," and – with a limited number of entries – tried to sketch out a multidimensional perspective that also included women's history, advances in science and medicine, population shifts and ethnic rivalries, economic developments, and environmental concerns as suggested by individual editors (Lawall, "Canons").

The Western and the global anthologies were formally separated with the seventh edition of 1999, which was specifically rededicated to exploring the internal variety of the Western literary tradition. Three new editors – William G. Thalmann, Lee Patterson, and Heather James – added works from diverse literary and cultural traditions to the Ancient World, Middle Ages, and Renaissance sections or revised the presentation of current selections. Their introductions, headnotes, and analyses drew new attention to the interrelationships of aesthetic and cultural history and to interwoven and often competing structures of cultural meaning. Missing or additional passages were inserted into excerpted long works to restore their realistic representation of contemporary life and issues (Rousseau); a group of narrative poems was organized to bring out its underlying examination of diverse images of love and gender (Ovid); new genres such as fantasy (Lucian, Ariosto) and intimate journals (Dorothy Wordsworth) were represented; and pronunciation glossaries were provided, at once an aid to classroom discussion and a reminder of linguistic and cultural difference. Four clusters of poems from medieval, Romantic, Symbolist, and Dada-Surrealist periods reestablished a missing element in literary and cultural history, from the diverse picture of medieval society given by poems written in Arabic, Judaic, Welsh, Spanish, French, Provençal, Italian, English, and German, to the shaping influence of Romantic, Symbolist, and Dada-Surrealist world-views and experimental forms. Such changes are for the most part invisible, but – like the process of excerpting and arranging in the first place – they open or close the horizons of world literature for the anthology's readers.

The seventh edition's complementary global anthology appeared in 2001–02. Based on a thorough revision of the *Expanded* edition, it introduced two relatively simple format changes that had further implications: the metamorphosis of two chunky books into six slimmer volumes and the change in title from *The Norton Anthology of World Masterpieces: Expanded Edition* to *The Norton Anthology of World Literature*. The six smaller volumes have many practical advantages: they are more easily handled and lighter in the backpack; separately available, individual books can supplement other courses; and the separation itself responds to many teachers' desire to spend more time with selected sweeps. Yet the format of smaller individual volumes may also direct attention away from broader literary interaction and the global premise of "world" literature. Partly for continuity, and partly with this fragmentation in mind, the six volumes are initially packaged in two boxed sets. The new title simplifies and clarifies by eliminating two words: *expanded* and *masterpieces*. *World* is a more logical descriptor than *expanded*, which it replaces; *masterpieces* was dropped because the term's accumulated cultural baggage fits neither the anthology's original statement of its mission nor contemporary users' (and editors') perceptions of what they are doing. *Masterpieces* suffers from overlapping methodological and cultural connotations: on the one hand, it refers to a model of technical or artistic excellence (proof, in the guild system, of having mastered the techniques of one's trade), and on the other, it indicates cultural approval or – in recent political criticism – complicity in a system of master-slave power relationships permeating European patriarchal and colonialist history. The traditional Western canon of masterpieces is further implicated in such critiques as part of a campaign to export Eurocentric literary, linguistic, and educational capital throughout the world and thus to dominate cultural imaginations (Guillory). As a consequence the term *masterpiece* has become so tied to disputes over the cultural significance of the Arnoldian tradition that it is a hindrance to approaching any text included in that canon.

Proselytizing for the cultural connotations of *masterpiece* has never been the Norton anthology's mission, however, unlike earlier anthologies devoted to describing "the thought and intellectual evolution of man" in his progress "from barbarism to civilization" or accentuating, as in Philo Buck's revision of his conclusion, important moral truths. It is not that the first editors did not attribute special insights and humanistic value to these works: clearly they did, as demonstrated by the casual references to "great literature" and universal situations ("our common human nature, our common hopes, lusts, ideals, and fears, our common vulnerability to time and change" [Mack et al. (1995) 1: xxxii]). Such valuations are not part of the methodology, however, and references to masterpieces throughout use the word merely as a general marker: *The Princess of Cleves* "is a pioneering psychological novel of great depth and subtlety, genuinely a world masterpiece" (Mack et al. [1985] 1: xx), and "So far as our collective life in this country has roots, these are to be found in . . . recognized masterpieces of drama, poetry, and fiction" (Mack et al. [1995] 1: xxxii). The sixth edition announces plans to create a global edition, "a collection of 'world' masterpieces in the fullest contemporary sense," and these works are later defined culturally as "outstanding literary landmarks" from around the world (Mack et al. [1992] 1: xviii). The *Expanded* edition explains its principles of selection in terms of the separate authority of *other* canons ("The basic principle of this anthology from its beginnings has been to offer works having recognized authority in their own languages and cultures" [1: xxix]) and also of the works' appeal across many cultures ("in the judgment of a larger world"). Nor will you find cultural guidelines prescribed in the introductions or apparatus: the anthology's impulse throughout has been to present works as objects of study and to expand, if anything, the varieties of reading brought to bear. The preface to the latest edition suggests that reading "for the work" and reading "for the world" are two points along the same critical continuum: "In shortening the current title to *The Norton Anthology of World Literature*, we do not abandon the anthology's focus on major works of literature or a belief that these works especially repay close study. It is their consummate artistry, their ability to express complex signifying structures, that gives access to multiple dimensions of meaning, meanings that are always rooted in a specific setting and cultural tradition but that further constitute, upon comparison, a thought-provoking set of perspectives on the varieties of human experience" (Lawall et al. [2002] A: xv).

Although I am best acquainted with the workings of the Norton anthology, my subject throughout has been the specific enterprise of the academic world literature anthology with its various antecedents and special position in American educational history. As Jeffrey R. Di Leo remarks in his prefatory note to the 2000 *symplokē* issue on anthologies, *The Norton Anthology of World Masterpieces* has become a standard reference point – a foil – for recent discussions that situate anthology practice in cultural and ideological context (5). Often, like many foils, it takes on a separate and mystified life of its own, so that it has seemed useful to historicize its position in relation to previous attempts and to speculate on common challenges that any anthology – including those oriented differently – encounters as part of anthology construction.

One element that seems often missing from critical discussions is an awareness of the dynamic interrelationships among teachers, editors, publishers, and institutional practice that go into the creation of an academic anthology. A consistently successful anthology (and I do not mean merely the Norton anthology) is the result of a check-and-balance system in which critical principles are matched with workable format choices, keeping in mind curricular niches; teacher demand; classroom viability (whose classroom? what students? with what needs? in what institutions?); and, of course, such mundane but crucial factors as publishing costs (permissions, paper, volume, advertising, distribution) and availability of texts: some are simply not available, some are not translated or translated poorly, some are impossibly expensive, some allow only a limited number of lines to be anthologized. Often the most inspiring proposals await practical execution, or so it seems when the theoretical arguments are presented in great detail but other parts of the discourse remain undeveloped. Despite the many new publications on pedagogy, the least developed aspect – and certainly the one most difficult to predict – is the world literature anthology's interaction with the diverse and changing world of student readers. They remain for the most part a rhetorical abstraction in discussions of anthology reform. Those who will use the anthology, for example, are "the student," "the American student," "today's students" (possessing "the naiveté of students"), "the teacher," and "the contemporary American audience" – all oddly universalized figures, blind partners defined by their role as either consumers or transmitters of critical principles: "The student can gain entry into this conversation only by acknowledging the scholarship of its members. His or her questions should concern the terms of the discussion, its assumptions and its conclusions" (Graff and Di Leo 114). The theorist is usually "we": "We won't do better in presenting the newly expansive world of world literature until we do a better job of clarifying just what we mean to accomplish by presenting 'the literature' of 'the world' for a contemporary American audience" (Damrosch, "World Literature Today" 7). Karen L. Kilcup is right to ask, "Who are 'our students' and . . . who are 'we'?" (Kilcup 43).[2]

Global world literature raises particular problems for anthologists, starting with the scope of its selections and including the need to present the material in an informative way that proposes structures of understanding but does not prescribe them. This is always a balancing act. Most anthologies move immediately to limit the field: by period, by theme, by language, by region, by excerpts. One anthology of literature by women has global scope but is limited to the modern period; another has chronological depth but is limited to the tradition in English; both are limited by gender. *One World of Literature* is restricted to the world of the twentieth century; *Global Voices* to contemporary literature of the non-Western world (both are interesting volumes, mentioned only to illustrate the practical difficulties of "world" coverage). Anthologies aiming for historical and global coverage often expand their scope by using numerous excerpts and minimizing editorial discussion. Excerpts, however, are always chosen for the way they fit into a selected anthology theme. Shaped by the editorial principles that selected them, they can only bear partial witness and lack even the intertextual openness of true fragments (Susini-Anastopoulos 194). It is always worth asking how such excerpts are chosen, how they are related to their parent texts, what exactly they represent, and whether we should accept the passages as transparent – as "voices" speaking directly across cultures. In the same vein: if the anthology includes guideline questions and topics for use in class, what critical perspectives do they reveal? (In my own quick survey these topics are almost always universal themes: but surely examples of "resisting" discourse are needed to preclude the overquick resolution of diverse materials.)

More ambitious attempts to reproduce cultural texture will need to find an appropriate organizational strategy that does not merely reproduce the categories of existing anthologies "with a difference" or relabel the relationships of familiar texts. In principle there would be fewer major (hegemonic) works, and traditional period and genre divisions (from any culture) would disappear. A modern *Alden's Cyclopedia*, constructed to reflect theories of cultural production, would truly be a fascinating enterprise. It is likely, however, that the other dimensions of anthology construction – the existing curricular niche for world literature, the publisher's requirements, and audience expectations – will give the new anthology a more traditional shape. Assuming that neither Alden's alphabetical order nor simple chronology will return (both would be far too confusing in class), what sets and subsets of titles convey cultural diversity without packaging history in neatly labeled groups? An interesting organization appears in the recent *Bedford Anthology of World Literature* (2003–), whose material is selected, arranged, and annotated to emphasize cultural themes. Each volume contains alternating sections of texts representing different traditions (for example, China, Japan, Europe, India) and smaller thematic units – printed on distinctive blue paper and collectively titled "In the World" – that group excerpts from a range of international texts. Imaginatively edited and produced, with a variety of illustrations and ancillary materials, this anthology has a mission to represent cultural themes on an international scale; it also exemplifies the tradeoff between a large proportion of representative excerpts and concomitant limits on the number of complete texts. A similar, although much more complicated and less colorful organization appears to govern the new *Longman Anthology of World Literature* (2004). Here, a series of differently thematized divisions groups texts to "build links within and between regions and periods." "Cross-Currents" are intended to "illuminate important transitions," "Perspectives" to "focus on literary and cultural issues," and "Resonances" to "provide responses or analogues to a work" (publicity letter from the editor). Both anthologies seek to provide viable approaches to cultural complexity and include a wide range of valuable material. The relevant questions have to do with the implications of the anthology form. If there are a great many excerpts used to gain breadth, then we have shifted attention to a higher, combinatory level while minimizing the time spent on rereading individual texts. Organizational implications become all the more important in this situation: What routes (going back to Charles Eliot) does the format open up for the user – and how easy is it to envisage thematic clusters other than those described? How prescriptive are the inset thematic sections: to what extent do they flatten the image of included works? If there is comparison and contrast, what cultural patterns do they imply? Who is compared to whom, and in what proportions: do the comparisons move outward around the globe, or are global references brought "home" to Western familiarity? Is binary comparison encouraged, or are multiple points of view concurrently brought to bear? David Damrosch has proposed to organize comparisons as "ellipses" between two poles, remarking that "contemporary America will logically be one focus of the ellipses for the contemporary American reader" ("World Literature Today" 10). While the strategy is indeed logical in relation to American curricular patterns, it also projects a mapping of the world in terms of two unified and stable subjects: *we* and *they*, bringing diversity once more under control. Damrosch's recent book *What Is World Literature?* develops more fully his image of an elliptical space – a force field of reading relationships – that defines world literature; he pictures a series of overlapping ellipses in which three or more foreign works are juxtaposed. At that point, "we triangulate between our own present situation and the enormous variety of other cultures around and before us" (300). These are thought-provoking metaphors for the geometry of reading, but as practical advice they recommend only the juxtaposition of multiple of texts. Issues of selection, coordination, and ideological implication recede into the background.

Anne Ferry has pointed out, in reference to English poetry, that anthologists are aware of shaping their readers' impressions and that "self-consciousness is another distinguishing feature of the anthology" (2). The self-consciousness required of a world literature anthology extends in many directions, of which the most obscure is surely the way that format and editorial apparatus reveal the anthologist's literary and cultural principles. Constructing a world literature anthology to express the diversity of global experience requires a rethinking of all editorial levels if we are to avoid unconsciously reinforcing local habits of mind and repeating the early anthologists' static paradigms. Not that anthologists have the final say: the choices they make will be further defined – altered and extended – when the book is used in class and becomes part of an institutional, pedagogical, and demographic matrix adapting the text to its own needs. As teacher and editor, I am wary of organizational systems that propose fixed models of history or culture, because their subset clusters – historical comparisons, cultural resonances, ethnic or gendered groupings – no matter how thought provoking in themselves, potentially limit the way that readers are invited to think about the material. Perhaps I have simply not yet encountered the right one. In any case, I am most comfortable with an approach that foregrounds its bias, if you will, and thus makes it available for deconstruction: in this case, with a work-centered approach using a wide variety of texts and with the study of aesthetic structures as a way to elucidate the intersecting paths of meaning (Baucom's "heteroglossic, heterochronic language" [170]) that situate a text.

"Aesthetic," of course, has a bad press these days; it is associated with "free-floating aestheticism" and contrasted with "cultural concerns." Yet "aesthetic" in that sense is rather like "liberal" in contemporary political discourse: a rhetorical tool, meant here to suggest the insularity of "art for art's sake" and by extension a critical realm of ideal orders, codified beauty, and timeless universal truths. It has little to do with aesthetics as a theoretical and critical principle that relates *work* and *world* – self-reflexive structures to a larger and dynamic cultural continuum. The aesthetic function, according to Jan Mukařovský, is "broadly distributed over the entire area of human affairs" (96), and aesthetic criticism examines both "literary" and "nonliterary" texts. It is not as though this does not already happen: Bakhtin, for example, has been used more than once to study the play of dialogic voices in African American literature. Literary-critical studies of the late twentieth century overflow with cultural analyses of texts. Anthologies like *The Norton Anthology of World Literature* foreground literary works because the works are, in practical terms, exceptionally accessible owing to the routes provided by aesthetic structure and because they can serve as anchor points for an analysis that extends in as many directions as the critic (teacher, student) has knowledge, persistence, and imagination to pursue. This approach does single out texts that support multiple readings and that have therefore found readers in diverse times and places; it also tends to put cultural and historical documents in relation to those texts rather than vice versa. Whether the point of departure be cultural or aesthetic, the range of reference is potentially the same, as is the task of exploring and coordinating perspectives. In the meantime the anthologist's self-consciousness will undoubtedly compel frequent reevaluations and revisions, and different contours for the academic presentation of world literature.

Notes

1. Although the book is listed under Eliot's name, it consists of a series of marketing pamphlets including "Contents of the Five-Foot Shelf Arranged by Volumes," "The Five-Foot Shelf of Books," "Dr. Eliot Tells Why He Undertook the Work," "The World's Civilization on a Bookshelf," and "The Making of the Five-Foot Shelf."

2. David Damrosch, "World Literature Today," Gerald Graff and Jeffrey R. Di Leo, "Anthologies, Literary Theory, and the Teaching of Literature," Karen L. Kilcup, "Anthologizing Matters," and Richard S. Pressman, "Is There a Future for the *Heath Anthology* in the Neo-Liberal State" all appear, with slight modifications, in the current volume.

Bibliography

Alberson, Hazel. "Non-Western Literatures in the World Literature Program." *The Teaching of World Literature (Proceedings of the Conference on the Teaching of World Literature at the University of Wisconsin, April 24-25, 1959).* Ed. Haskell M. Block. University of North Carolina Studies in Comparative Literature 28. Chapel Hill: University of North Carolina Press, 1960. 45-52.

Alden, John B., ed. *Alden's Cyclopedia of Universal Literature, Presenting Biographical and Critical Notices and Specimens from the Writings of Eminent Authors of All Ages and All Nations.* 20 vols. New York: J. B. Alden, 1885-91.

Baucom, Ian. "Globalit, Inc,; Or, The Cultural Logic of Global Literary Studies." *Globalizing Literary Studies.* Spec. issue of PMLA 116.1 (2001): 158-72.

Biddle, Arthur W., ed. *Global Voices: Contemporary Literature from the Non-Western World.* Englewood Cliffs NJ: Prentice-Hall, 1995.

Black, Ayanna, ed. *Voices: Canadian Writers of African Descent.* Toronto: HarperCollins, 1992.

Buck, Philo M., ed. *An Anthology of World Literature.* New York: Macmillan, 1934.

———, ed. *An Anthology of World Literature.* 3rd ed. 1940. New York: Macmillan, 1951.

Damrosch, David, ed. *The Longman Anthology of World Literature*. 6 vols. New York: Longman, 2004.

———. *What Is World Literature?* Princeton and Oxford: Princeton University Press, 2003.

———. "World Literature Today: From the Old World to the Whole World." *symplokē* 8.1–2 (2000): 7–19. Rpt. in this volume, 31–46.

Davis, Paul, et al., eds. *The Bedford Anthology of World Literature: The Eighteenth Century, 1650–1800*. Boston and New York: Bedford/St. Martins, 2003.

Di Leo, Jeffrey R. "Editor's Note." *symplokē* 8.1–2 (2000): 5–6.

Eber, Irene. *Voices from Afar: Modern Chinese Writers on Oppressed People and Their Literature*. Ann Arbor: Center for Chinese Studies, University of Michigan Press, 1980.

Eliot, Charles W. *Analysis of The Harvard Classics: Dr. Eliot's Five-Foot Shelf of Books*. New York: P. F. Collier and Son, n.d.

———, ed. *The Harvard Classics*. 50 vols. New York: P. F. Collier and Son, 1910.

———, ed. *The Harvard Classics*. Vol. 50, *The Editor's Introduction: Reader's Guide; Index to the First Lines of Poems, Songs & Choruses, Hymns & Psalms; General Index; Chronological Index*. New York: P. F. Collier and Son, 1910.

———. *Harvard Memories*. Cambridge: Harvard University Press, 1923.

———. Introduction. *The Harvard Classics*. 50 vols. Ed. Charles W. Eliot. New York: P. F. Collier and Son, 1910. 50: 3–14.

Ferry, Anne. *Tradition and the Individual Poem: An Inquiry into Anthologies*. Stanford: Stanford University Press, 2001.

Fetterley, Judith. *The Resisting Reader: A Feminist Approach to American Fiction*. Bloomington: Indiana University Press, 1978.

Graff, Gerald, and Jeffrey R. Di Leo. "Anthologies, Literary Theory, and the Teaching of Literature: An Exchange." *symplokē* 8.1–2 (2000): 113–28. Rpt. in this volume, 279–97.

Guillory, John. *Cultural Capital: The Problem of Literary Canon Formation*. Chicago: University of Chicago Press, 1993.

Hamilton, Russell G. *Voices from Empire: A History of Afro-Portuguese Literature*. Minneapolis: University of Minnesota Press, 1975.

Hassan, Waïl S. "World Literature in the Age of Globalization: Reflections on an Anthology." *College English* 63.1 (2000): 38–47.

Hutchins, Robert M., ed. *Great Books of the Western World*. 54 vols. Chicago: Encyclopaedia Britannica, 1952.

Johnson, Barbara. *A World of Difference*. Baltimore: Johns Hopkins University Press, 1987.

Kampf, Louis, and Paul Lauter, eds. *The Politics of Literature: Dissenting Essays on the Teaching of English*. New York: Pantheon, 1972.

Kenney, Michael. "Norton Conquest with Nine Anthologies and More to Come, It's Still the 'Canon' for College Literature Courses." *Boston Globe*. January 12, 1997.

Kilcup, Karen L. "Anthologizing Matters: The Poetry and Prose of Recovery Work." *symplokē* 8.1–2 (2000): 38–53. Rpt. in this volume, 112–38.

Korey, Marie E. "John B. Alden." *Publishers for Mass Entertainment in Nineteenth Century America*. Ed. Madeleine B. Stern. Boston: G. K. Hall, 1980. 1–7.

Lauter, Paul, ed. *Reconstructing American Literature: Courses, Syllabi, Issues*. Old Westbury CT: Feminist Press, 1983.

Lawall, Sarah N. "Canons, Contexts, and Pedagogy: The Place of World Literature." *Comparatist* 24 (2000): 39–56.

———. "Reading World Literature." *Reading World Literature: Theory, History, Practice*. Ed. Sarah N. Lawall. Austin: University of Texas Press, 1994. 1–64.

———. "René Wellek and Modern Literary Criticism." *Comparative Literature* 40.1 (1988): 3–24.

Lawall, Sarah N., et al., eds. *The Norton Anthology of World Literature*. 2nd ed. 6 vols. W. W. Norton, 2002.

———, eds. *The Norton Anthology of World Masterpieces: The Western Tradition*. 7th ed. 2 vols. New York: W. W. Norton, 1999.

Levin, Harry. "Core, Canon, Curriculum." *College English* 43.4 (1981): 352–62.

Lim, Shirley, and Norman Spencer, eds. *One World of Literature*. Boston: Houghton Mifflin, 1993.

Mack, Maynard M., et al., eds. *The Norton Anthology of World Masterpieces: Literature of Western Culture*. 4th ed. 2 vols. New York: W. W. Norton, 1979.

———, eds. *The Norton Anthology of World Masterpieces*. 5th ed. 2 vols. New York: W. W. Norton, 1985.

———, eds. *The Norton Anthology of World Masterpieces*. 6th ed. 2 vols. New York: W. W. Norton, 1992.

———, eds. *The Norton Anthology of World Masterpieces, Expanded Edition*. 2 vols. New York: W. W. Norton, 1995.

———, eds. *World Masterpieces: Literature of Western Culture*. 2 vols. New York: W. W. Norton, 1956.

———, eds. *World Masterpieces: Literature of Western Culture*. 3rd ed. 2 vols. New York: W. W. Norton, 1973.

Moulton, Richard. "World Literature from the English Point of View." *World Literature and Its Place in General Culture*. Norwood MA: Macmillan, 1911.

Mukařovský, Jan. *Aesthetic Function, Norm, and Value as Social Facts.* [1936]. Trans. Mark E. Suino. Michigan Slavic Contributions 3. Ann Arbor: University of Michigan Press, 1979.

Peck, Harry Thurston, ed. *The World's Great Masterpieces; History, Biography, Science, Philosophy, Poetry, The Drama, Travel, Adventure, Fiction, etc. A Record of The Great Things That Have Been Said and Thought and Done from The Beginning of History.* 30 vols. New York: American Literary Society, [c.1901].

Pressman, Richard S. "Is There a Future for the Heath Anthology in the Neo-Liberal State?" *symplokē* 8.1–2 (2000): 65–67. Rpt. in this volume, 264–76.

Rose, Jonathan. *The Intellectual Life of the British Working Classes.* New Haven: Yale University Press, 2001.

Runes, Dagobert D. Preface. *Treasury of World Literature.* Ed. Dagobert D. Runes. New York: Greenwood Press [1969, c.1956]. vii–ix.

Sollors, Werner, ed. *Multilingual America: Transnationalism, Ethnicity, and the Languages of American Literature.* New York: New York University Press, 1998.

Susini-Anastopoulos, Françoise. *L'Écriture fragmentaire: Définitions et enjeux.* Paris: Presses universitaires de France, 1997.

Thompson, Stith. Preface. *Our Heritage of World Literature.* Comp. Stith Thompson. New York: Dryden Press, 1938. 5–6.

Thorp, Margaret Farrand. *Neilson of Smith.* New York: Oxford University Press, 1956.

Rev. of *Timelines of the Arts and Literature.* By David M. Brownstone and Irene Franck. *Choice* 32.6 (1995): 911.

Trilling, Lionel. "English Literature and American Education." *Sewanee Review* 66 (1958): 364–81.

Warner, Charles Dudley. Preface. *A Library of the World's Best Literature, Ancient And Modern.* 45 vols. Ed. Charles Dudley Warner. New York: International Society, 1897 [c.1896]. 1: iii–vi.

LYNN Z. BLOOM

Once More to the Essay Canon

Essays live – and die – in freshman English, read annually by some 2.2 million American students. Indeed, composition textbook anthologies (Readers), purveyors of the academy's humanistic and ideological values, are the only places where essays are widely reprinted. Thus the essay canon, enduring essays by 175 authors, is the only literary canon that is determined by teachers' choice and classroom use. Using contemporary canon theory and an extensive analysis of textbooks, this chapter will explain how the essay, a belletristic genre in the eighteenth and nineteenth centuries, became critically undermined in the twentieth century as a consequence of pedagogy that emphasized its utilitarian rather than aesthetic and intellectual functions. I will then analyze the way in which the twentieth-century essay canon has evolved and identify the possible changes that may occur in the twenty-first century as individual teachers compile their own anthologies from print-on-demand lists of essays.

Contingencies of Canonicity

A canon may be seen as a map of the territory it encompasses. In *Contingencies of Value* Barbara Herrnstein Smith explains canon formation as an orderly process influenced by and embedded in a broad context of various cultural norms (see also Harris, "Canonicity"). Smith anatomizes the "diverse forms of evaluation" of literature performed by those who publish, "purchase, preserve, display, quote, cite, translate, perform," imitate, and judge a given work – or, I would add, a genre. One canonical type is the critical canon, which may be further subdivided into *historical*, *national*, and *cultural* canons, often presented as if they were universal, as in Harold Bloom's *The Western Canon*. Critics create this canon by publishing reviews and criticism, rank-orderings, evaluations and reevaluations, awarding prizes. Another type is the teaching canon, sometimes labeled *pedagogical* or *institutional*; a teaching canon – the subject of this article – is invented and reinvented in anthologies, curricula, syllabi, and reading lists (Smith 42–53; Golding 70–113; Rasula 415–69). Frank Kermode sees critical canons as "strategic constructs by which societies maintain their own interests, since the canon allows control over the texts a culture takes seriously and the methods of interpretation that establish the meaning of 'serious'" (qtd. in Altieri 42). Because, as Alan C. Golding observes, "any given period has its canonical genres; its canonical critical paradigms, or ways of seeing and reading" (59), the reinterpretations or advocacy of any powerful group–or even a single influential person – can produce a revisionist canon such as that presented by the multiethnic *Heath Anthology of American Literature*. Its editors, spearheaded by Paul Lauter, deliberately set out to remap a brave new world of American literature, using as their guide not "previous anthologies or our graduate school training" but a survey of "a new literary world . . . the vast range of the literary output of this country" (Lauter, "Preface" xxxv), reflective of women writers, "colonization and decolonization, urbanization, and the color line" (Lauter, *Canons* 39), and including a great deal of nonfiction prose.

Thus canons, it would seem, are more deliberate than casual readers might realize. Collectively, teachers have more influence over the pedagogical canon than might be apparent to the single individual or department that constructs a curriculum; prepares a syllabus or reading list; adopts a textbook; and holds students accountable for reading – as Matthew Arnold says – "the best which has been thought and said in the world," or works by women, or by ethnic minorities, or that fit any other desired criteria. A work gains pedagogical value through "repeated inclusion" in anthologies (Smith 46) and frequent assignment to many students over extended periods of time – even if it is ignored by critics, as essays are.

As I explain in "The Essay Canon" (from which some parts of this essay are adapted), I am currently engaged in analyzing 20 percent of all the Readers published in the United States for the past half-century, 1946–96, with ongoing updates. This means every Reader published in four or more editions, fifty-eight titles in 325 volumes. These canonical Readers contain approximately twenty-one thousand reprintings of some eight thousand different essay titles by 4,246 authors; this information is compiled in a database that can be sorted by authors, titles, and years of publication. I've used viability – rather than, say, supreme quality – as the major criterion for determining who the canonical essayists are, those whose works have been reprinted one hundred or more times during the past fifty years. That only 175 authors have emerged as canonical may seem a surprisingly small number, but it's on par with the theoretical explanation of canon formation in, for example, poetry (see Rasula, *The American Poetry Wax Museum*; and Golding, *From Outlaw to Classic*); evidently nobody has had the fortitude to count novels.[1] The appended table (appendix 1) identifies the top 25 essayists and works most widely reprinted in best-selling freshman Readers from 1946 to 1996; multiply the numbers of this 20 percent sample by five to get a more precise estimate of the actual number of reprints – which is how twenty citations in the table actually represent one hundred reprintings. After defining essays (in the next section) the rest of this chapter will explain how the process of essay canon formation has worked in American colleges for the past 150 years – the evolution, devolution, and potential revolution of the genre that owes its perpetuation to academia.

On Essays: Definitions of a Dubious and Disputed Genre

Twentieth-century essayists, unlike their nineteenth-century predecessors, particularly in America, are lonely travelers in an indifferent universe of belles-lettres, lurking on the edges of the mainstream territories mapped out and claimed by writers of fiction, poetry, and drama. Indeed, essays are less likely to be published initially in whole books than in less easily mapped locales – big and little magazines (*Harper's*, the *Michigan Quarterly Review*); organizational publications (the Audubon Society's *Audubon*, the *New England Journal of Medicine*); newspaper op-ed and feature sections. Yet we seldom regard the authors primarily as essayists or even as article writers, but as novelists, poets, or other professionals working at their day jobs in medicine, economics, politics, science, and other fields. In the absence of the European tradition of public intellectuals, even North American writers who distinguish themselves as essayists are also novelists, such as Cynthia Ozick and Susan Sontag; or editors, such as the *American Scholar*'s Joseph Epstein and Anne Fadiman, his successor; or college professors. My colleague Sam Pickering, a well-published and widely respected writer of essays (*Living to Prowl*, *The Blue Caterpillar*), whooped – he does that a lot – with laughter as he opened his royalty check of $2.37 for his most recent essay collection, noting as he did so the disparity between the notice accorded his chosen genre and that given our novelist colleague whose first novel had been selected for the book club of America's premier canon maker, Oprah Winfrey.

Another form of obscurity for the genre is the scant attention critics and researchers pay to essays outside of writing done for school, kindergarten through college. The scarcity of the term *essay* in both critical and composition studies literature – the two areas of academic studies most likely to be concerned with this genre – indicates the absence of common terminology even when the genre itself is under study. For example, *essay* does not appear in the index to Stephen North's *The Making of Knowledge in Composition* (1987), even though the writing of essays (which he usually calls "texts") is the subject of much of the research North surveys. Even a decade later, by which time *creative nonfiction* and its prime constituent, *essays*, have become familiar literary terminology in college curricula, research studies still use the term *essays* interchangeably with *expository writing, themes, compositions, papers*.

As a consequence of such fragmentation and neglect, physical and linguistic, the essay as a genre has had a furtive if not fugitive status in twentieth-century American belletristic writing. There are very few single-authored collections of essays relative to the numbers of other types of nonfiction published in the same time period; many types of nonfiction are known by subject (history, philosophy, science, food, travel, politics, sports) rather than by form. At this turn of the millennium, despite the distinctive literary presence of essayistic critics, Americans have no tradition of buying and reading collections of what they regard as *essays* as they might have done in the nineteenth century with the works of Ralph Waldo Emerson or Oliver Wendell Holmes. Holmes could style himself "the autocrat of the breakfast table"; no essayist today claims such authority, even if one were to substitute *Internet* for the arbiter's venue.

Despite their Cinderella status, essays – broadly conceived – are the lingua franca of the American academy, the mainstay of first-year college composition courses, which are devoted to the reading and writing of this genre. Composition textbook anthologies (to which I refer as *Readers*, as opposed to *readers* – those who do the reading) in hard copy, and recently on CD-ROM, are virtually the only contemporary collections of reprinted essays on a variety of general topics.[2] For many students these essay collections may constitute their only exposure to great ideas, liberal thinking, providing a briefly humanistic education in an otherwise vocationally or technologically oriented program. Even if students call their assigned reading *stories* and their assigned writing *papers*, it is *essays* that they read in any of the two hundred composition anthologies on the market in any given year, which collectively publish about thirteen thousand essays. And it is *essays* that they write. Except for Robert Atwan's *Best American Essays*, an annual series begun in 1985, there has been no predictable, widely accessible gathering place for essays in twentieth-century America other than the textbook anthologies on which this chapter focuses. What is in these books is what we understand to be *essays*.

Textbooks define the genre pragmatically, by a myriad of diverse examples, but rarely in terms of either form or substance. If we were as comfortable with *essay* as with, say, *novel* or *poem*, definitions would be unnecessary; we'd know an essay when we saw it and could agree on what we were asking our students to read – and to write. But, as O. B. Hardison notes, *essay* is a protean term, playing "the same role in literary criticism that the term 'miscellaneous' does in budgeting." He explains: "If there is no genre more widespread in modern letters than the essay, there is also no genre that takes so many shapes and that refuses so successfully to resolve itself, finally, into its own shape" (12–13).

One major reason that discussions of essays cry out for definitions is the fact that *essays* and *articles* are often lumped together and treated as interchangeable. All Readers do this, without exception – and I will do so here, for my definition is empirically based on the works contained in these Readers. In "Reflections on the Peculiar Status of the Personal Essay" Wendell V. Harris makes useful distinctions among three types of essays, the *personal*, characterized by a sense of "presence" – "an authorial personality, character . . . an undeniable persona"; and two other types often found in textbooks: the "*informational*, which includes the instructional, technical, analytical, and advisory; and the *programmatic*, which includes the didactic, admonitory, and hortatory" and is deductive in form (934–37, italics mine).

Indeed, textbook editors choose this variety because of the particular types of thinking and writing each type encourages. Personal essays – George Orwell's "Shooting an Elephant," E. B. White's "Once More to the Lake," Alice Walker's "Beauty: When the Other Dancer Is the Self" – capture readers' hearts, minds, and memories, encouraging students to respond to the common humanity they represent. As Scott Russell Sanders says, "It is the singularity of the first person – its warts and crotchets and turn of voice – that lures many of us into reading essays and that lingers with us after we finish" (37). Montaigne earns pride of place in being the first to use *essay*, derived from the Old French *essai*, "a trial, an attempt," to mean a literary composition of limited length and range and variable style. His essays were first published in 1580; Francis Bacon adopted the term, publishing his own *Essayes* in 1597 (Hardison 16). The essays of Montaigne – personal sounding, discursive, Bacon-brisk (almost brusque), and to the point – model the two pervasive types of personal essays that have prevailed from the inception of the form to the present time. Personal essays and excerpts from autobiographies (such as various portions of Frederick Douglass's *Narrative*, Maya Angelou's *I Know Why the Caged Bird Sings*, and Richard Rodriguez's *Hunger of Memory*) dominate the canon and occupy about 35–50 percent of the space in most Readers, serving both as models for narration and as telling examples of individual and ethnic history and cultural practices.

Informational and programmatic essays share the remaining space about equally in twentieth-century Readers. In language and form informational essays (even if they are excerpts from book chapters) provide models of various types of academic discourse and research practices in diverse academic disciplines, as well as discipline-specific content. Every humanistically oriented Reader (over 90 percent of the total) has to make space for informational writings on the following topics (illustrated in each case by the work of a canonical author): education (Jonathan Kozol, "The Human Cost of an Illiterate Society"), linguistics (S. I. Hayakawa, "How Dictionaries Are Made"), history (Bruce Catton, "Grant and Lee"), science (Stephen Jay Gould, "Evolution as Fact and Theory"), religion (Bertrand Russell, "A Free Man's Worship"), anthropology (Margaret Mead, "The Gift of Autonomy"), psychology (Stanley Milgram, "The Perils of Obedience"), medicine (Lewis Thomas, "The Technology of Medicine") – and, more recently, business and technology. Programmatic writings include works such as satires (Swift's "Modest Proposal"), political manifestos ("The Declaration of Independence"), speeches (Lincoln's "Gettysburg Address"), letters (Martin Luther King Jr.'s "Letter from Birmingham Jail"), and newspaper editorials and columns (Martin Gansberg's "38 Who Saw Murder Didn't Call the Police"). If I were adopting a strict belletristic definition, many of these works would not be considered essays. But for the operational purposes of this study – and the wide range of textbooks it comprehends – an essay is whatever appears in essay anthologies that isn't poetry or fiction – even material that would be labeled differently in a context other than a Reader.

Shooting a Canon: The Essay's Fall from Canonical Status to a School Genre

The essay's problematic and contested status is a twentieth-century phenomenon. Numerous nineteenth-century essayists, such as Coleridge, Lamb, Hazlitt, De Quincey, Irving, Carlyle, Emerson, Macaulay,

Newman, Holmes, Pater, Ruskin, and Arnold, had canonical status, as did their Augustan predecessors, such as Pope, Swift, and Johnson. (These authors appear in period anthologies and are staples of doctoral reading lists in English departments nationwide, as revealed, for example, in the University of Michigan's 1960 doctoral reading list and echoed in the University of Connecticut's 1998 list.) Nevertheless, the twentieth-century chasm between belles-lettres (read fiction, drama, and poetry) and utilitarian prose of the workaday world began as a modest but philosophically significant fracture in the eighteenth century, says Donald M. McQuade. He observes that Scottish rhetoricians George Campbell (Philosophy of Rhetoric [1776]) and Hugh Blair (Lectures on Rhetoric and Belles-Lettres [1783]) shifted the grounds of rhetoric as it was taught in the schools "from the study of persuasion, the strategies used to express thought, to the study of thought itself . . . and to the moral qualities of the taste associated with it." By the nineteenth century this shift, coupled with education extended to women and the working classes, and vernacular composition substituted for Latin drills, gradually undermined "the primacy of the classical rhetorical tradition" as the basis of education in Europe and the United States. Thus "as education became less the intellectual property of the elite and more a practical and political tool to train an increasingly industrialized work force," the historic alliance among rhetoric, literature, and literary criticism "began to weaken" (McQuade 486–87).

Patricia Bizzell and Bruce Herzberg attribute the separation of rhetoric from belles-lettres, as exemplified by the Readers' pragmatic orientation, to the distinction made by Coleridge and others between "the *active* concerns of rhetoric and the contemplative ones of literature" (639). Mid-nineteenth-century British universities formalized this difference by separating instruction in rhetoric from that in belles-lettres, and American universities followed suit by the end of the nineteenth century. Composition, including nonfiction prose, eventually appeared as a branch of rhetoric, conceived by such works as Henry Day's *Elements of the Art of Rhetoric* (1858) as "the art of discourse" or "the faculty of communicating thoughts." Composition thereby acquired a derivative identity, assuming a "connective rather than a creative" function

(Bizzell and Herzberg 864, 663). As McQuade notes, "The opposition between 'connective' and 'creative' is similar to the distinctions Coleridge draws between 'active' and 'contemplative' and between 'imagination' and 'reason'" (486). Rhetoricians and their pedagogical successors from the late nineteenth century to the present time have compiled collections of essays to serve students as models for clear thinking and utilitarian writing.

In *Composition-Rhetoric: Backgrounds, Theory, and Pedagogy* Robert J. Connors explains why these school collections of essays arose in the 1890s and continued to flourish throughout the twentieth century. At the turn of the last century, at universities such as Harvard, seasoned composition professors with a knowledge of rhetorical theory and the classics were being replaced by TAs, lecturers, and junior faculty – the very cadres of the temporary and disenfranchised who continue to teach first-year composition to this day. These "underprepared" teachers needed textbooks that spelled out the basics and included "apparatus and classroom exercises." In 1900 the Reader was published that became the prototype for textbooks from that day to this, Edwin H. Lewis's *Specimens of the Forms of Discourse*, which promulgated the four modes of discourse – narration, description, exposition, argument – as forms for students to emulate (Connors 85, 87). Lewis claimed that these "specimens" were not meant to be "models, in the [mechanical and thus] enslaving sense of that word," but illustrations of "living organisms" intended to inspire students to write original literary compositions (iii–iv).

But mechanical models they became. The Readers that proliferated after 1900, says Connors, small and cheap, were used throughout the twentieth century to structure class discussion, to illustrate rhetorical principles, and to provide rhetorical models for the students' own writing (88). Lewis calls these *compositions*, and his successor of long duration, Maurice Garland Fulton, calls them *expository writing*. These anthologists established the century-long pattern of including short prose passages – essays, speeches, newspaper and periodical articles, criticism, book chapters, and brief segments of novels – that not only would serve as models to imitate but would provide examples of, as

Fulton explains, "the kind of writing that is most directly serviceable in practical life," prose that exemplifies "accuracy, logicalness, and economy of presentation" (v). Fulton also sees the *selections* (Fulton's word, used by virtually all subsequent editors, is a debasing term that substitutes a process for a genre) on science as affording "training in the power to think straight, which is so little a part of the rising generation. It is the duty of the modern college not to truckle to this weakness, but to cure it" (vii).

As a consequence of the dubious company essays kept – other essays in the composition textbooks to which they were relegated – essays emerged in twentieth-century education at the bottom of a loaded deck, buried under a load of hierarchical metaphors with heavily negative connotations that denigrated the pedagogical uses to which the essays were put. "Composition," the course in which students were required to write essays, was – and still is, a century later – a lower-division, required, "service course," teaching the practical "basic skills" necessary for the students to succeed throughout the academy in higher-level courses of greater intellectual substance and complexity. As McQuade observes, these terms imply that composition – as a course and also as a form of writing – "functions at a lower level of ability, purpose, and seriousness" than either rhetoric, as conceived by Blair, or belles-lettres. The ultimate degradation of school themes is their devolution into what Robert Scholes calls "pseudo non-literature" (7), the ubiquitous but unreal five-paragraph theme (consisting of an introduction, three "body paragraphs," and a conclusion). In the binary categorization scheme later reified by countless literary textbooks such as Brooks and Warren's *Understanding Poetry* "composition is characterized as concrete and practical rather than abstract and theoretical, as operational rather than speculative, as circumspect rather than imaginative." "Practical," in turn, emphasizes prudence, efficiency, "and the economy of an act, an agent, or a solution," its workability depending on proper management (McQuade 487–88).

Consequently, concludes McQuade, "in practice and effect, composition remains a matter of work, of training and managing labor-intensive skills." Because even today composition is still "often described in terms of the service or the product it provides, rather than the process or the production it involves, composition remains distinct from either rhetoric or belles lettres in the capacity, rank, and authority associated with – and permitted to – it." In twentieth-century English departments the essay was quickly adopted as the major mode of academic writing, but in handmaiden capacity, reduced from its nineteenth-century status as "a *primary* form of literature" to "*secondary*" status as a "commentary on literature." McQuade finds that contemporary academicians, whether theorists, critics, teachers, or researchers of any persuasion, discuss "literature" "in terms of talent, composition in terms of skill." Within the conventional curriculum hierarchy, literature "remains elegant and elite, composition commonplace and declassé" (488, 491; see also Scholes chapter 1). That freshman composition functions throughout our nation's colleges and universities as an agent of middle-class socialization – teaching students to write with correctness, efficiency, economy, order, and decorum – reinforces the extraliterary status of the essay (L. Bloom, "Freshman Composition"), I note here with regret.

Where Essays (Still) Live and What They Live For: Distinguishing Features of Canonical Essays

To have a shot at canonicity an essay must be reasonably well-written; it must reinforce the book's cultural, political, and social orientation and/or contribute to the balance among disciplines. Its reprint price must be right – costly contemporary pieces must be balanced by classics in the public domain. Above all an essay must be teachable. Concepts of what is teachable reflect both the aesthetics and the politics of the times. Thus for the past half-century essays have either had to be short enough (say, under five thousand words) to be discussed in one or two class periods or else capable of being excerpted in short, self-contained sections that fit the course's time frame. Essays must be accessible in intellectual concepts, cultural references, and vocabulary, so students can understand them without a great deal of class discussion – and so teachers can teach works from a wide variety of fields without a great deal of background knowledge. They may represent a controversial political stance, preferably slightly left of center – writers can be liberal but not outrageous – as if student awareness should be raised but not aroused. (The essays of political conservatives rarely become canonical, except for ethnic minorities such as Richard Rodriguez, high on the canonical list with his opposition to tokenism and bilingual education, largely derived from his autobiography, *Hunger of Memory*.) Contemporary dissension must as a rule be treated with politeness, irony, or humor, as in Patricia Williams's "On Being the Object of Property" or Jamaica Kincaid's "A Small Place." Outright anger is reserved for issues on which there is considerable consensus among teachers, if not their students. Thus editors select topics they deem more suitable to abstract discussions of ethics and social justice than political activism, such as slavery (Frederick Douglass, "Resurrection"), the status and treatment of minorities (Brent Staples, "Black Men and Public Space") and the poor (Jonathan Kozol, "Are the Homeless Crazy?"), and equal rights for women (Sojourner Truth's "Ain't I a Woman?"). Readers often include essays on current social and political issues, such as global warming, AIDS, bilingual education, Internet use and abuse, genetic engineering. However, their stance and their topicality render them quickly outdated (and thus not canonical) unless distinguished writing transcends the immediate issue – as it does in Swift's "Modest Proposal," Lincoln's "Gettysburg Address," and King's "I Have a Dream." To be anthologized repeatedly an essay must also, as a rule, illustrate some rhetorical concepts – definition, narration, argumentative strategies. That these criteria are pragmatic, not aesthetic, helps to explain why Bacon remained canonical throughout the twentieth century, but not Carlyle, Ruskin, or Pater; and why an excerpt from a 1952 article in *Scientific American* by biologist Alexander Petrunkevich, "The Spider and the Wasp" – an excellent example of comparison and contrast – is reprinted year after year after year.

Despite the presence of a few authors unknown to English teachers, such as the entomologist Petrunkevich and Judy Brady (whose only published work is the often reprinted "I Want a Wife"), the felt sense of who belongs in essay textbooks reflects the sense of who the movers and shapers of the culture are at any given moment – whether or not they are its most distinguished writers. The author's literary or professional prominence matters, but in different ways at different times. From the 1890s through the 1960s the essay canon's liberal arts orientation was shaped by scholars in various disciplines (see the earlier list) whose writing is clear and accessible to general readers, irrespective of their academic specialty, and by professional writers: journalists (William Zinsser, Norman Cousins), belletristic essayists (E. B. White, George Orwell), novelists (Mark Twain, E. M. Forster), poets (John Donne, John Ciardi), satirists and humorists (James Thurber, Jonathan Swift), critics (Gilbert Highet, Joseph Wood Krutch) – almost entirely white men. (Their dominance is true in other literary canons, as well, as Harold Bloom's *The Western Canon* and Paul Lauter's *Canons and Contexts*, Part I, demonstrate.)

Textbook Readers are permeated with American culture and the prevailing values of their time of publication. Beginning in the 1960s and reflecting the civil rights movement, textbook editors took pains to make students aware of the history and current practices of racial and social injustice by including more writings by black belletristic writers (Richard Wright, James Baldwin) and political activists (Stokely Carmichael, Malcolm X). For comparable reasons, as a consequence of the women's movement, women writers arrived in significant numbers in the 1980s. Their heightened visibility led publishers to establish guidelines for nonsexist writing (and to reprint Casey Miller and Kate Swift's "One Small Step for Gen Kind") and editors to include essays by equal numbers of women and men authors. The only canonical women authors before 1980 were Rachel Carson (with excerpts from *The Sea Around Us* and *Silent Spring*), Susanne Langer ("The Lord of Creation"), Margaret Mead ("Every Family in a Home of Its Own"), and Virginia Woolf ("How Should One Read a Book?"). After 1980 they were joined by Joan Didion, Annie Dillard, Maya Angelou, Ellen Goodman, Maxine Hong Kingston, Robin Lakoff, Alice Walker, and Eudora Welty, among others; excerpts from Woolf's feminist *A Room of One's Own* now supplanted her familiar essays from *The Common Reader*. Textbook anthologies from 1995 to 2001 reflect the country's increasingly multiethnic composition and give prominence to ethnic minorities' writings and concerns – many of which are comparable to those of women and blacks, if not people in general: Chinese (Gish Jen, Amy Tan), Hispanic (Sandra Cisneros, Gary Soto), Indian (Bharati Mukherjee, Abraham Verghese), Japanese (Garrett Hongo, Michiko Kakutani), Native American (Louise Erdrich, Linda Hogan), Vietnamese (Lê Thi Diem Thúy). Although as of this writing none has yet attained canonical status, the frequency of their reprints makes them good bets for canonicity within this decade. Turn-of-the-twenty-first-century Readers have quickly shaken off the white male dominance of the previous 125 years, though they still maintain their liberal arts orientation. Indeed, the only writers to leave the canon after 1995 – because their works have not been reprinted for a decade or longer – are white men – Jacques Barzun, X. J. Kennedy, Lewis Mumford, George Bernard Shaw, John Steinbeck, with James Agee, Norman Mailer, and Leo Rosten following soon thereafter.

Common Readers: The Death – or Democratization – of the Essay Canon?

The existence of a canon implies a hierarchy of works chosen for election by the canon makers. Because the essay canon is a pedagogical canon rather than a critical one, who determines the pedagogy determines the canon. Historically, as this chapter has shown, the electors in the essay canon are not the initial publishers of the works but those who determine which essays get reprinted in widely used Readers with long lives. It would be easy to say that the editors of textbook anthologies, themselves composition teachers, determine the existence of the essay canon and its changes over time. But that would be too simple. Some textbooks are more equal than others. The longest-lived textbooks – particularly *The Norton Reader* (currently in its eleventh edition) and *Patterns of Exposition* (currently in its sixteenth edition; the first edition introduced readers to Petrunkevitch) – have priority of influence, especially because other anthologists copy their selections. Editors of Readers also mine each new volume of Atwan's *Best American Essays*, invaluable not only for the two dozen essays selected by the guest editor but for Atwan's list of 150 additional "Notable Essays," winnowed from hundreds of essays published in magazines big and little, professional journals, and a host of specialized locations. Atwan, in effect, along with the Norton editors (originally spearheaded by Arthur Eastman; since the ninth edition by Linda Peterson), does the preliminary searching and screening for anthologists who study his list – a gatekeeping function analogous to a newspaper's book review editor who funnels to reviewers 1 or 2 percent of the published books received.

Publishers, too, have a significant but more subtle influence on the essay canon. A review of the annual textbook bibliographies (since 1981) in *Writing Program Administration* reveals that 90 percent of Readers are published only in a single edition. Of the 10 percent that survive, eight out of ten are published by Bedford/St. Martin's. Bedford Books began in 1982 with a commitment to Readers unusual among publishers. Bedford (and its affiliate, St. Martin's) expends a great deal of editorial time developing and promoting first editions that reflect individual features and distinctive personalities and do not look like clones of competitors' books; not all publishers do this. Defying other publishers' common practice of killing off books that lose money in the first edition, Bedford gives virtually every Reader a second edition with nearly as much promotion as the first, sometimes more. Thus the Bedford editorial and marketing practices help to create the canonical Readers that reprint the canonical essays (Christensen).

As of 1999 the process of the creation of the essay canon seemed stable and fairly predictable. But with the new millennium customized print-on-demand Readers have become available. Here's how the process works, as indicated in the marketing of such works as Kathleen Shine Cain et al.'s *The Mercury Reader* (Pearson Custom Publishing, 2000) and my own (with Louise Z. Smith) *St. Martin's Custom Reader*, consisting of my updated canon research list (Bedford/St. Martin's, 2001). Classroom teachers receive an annotated list of 250 to 400 essays and a CD-ROM that lets them read the complete text. From this they can choose whatever essays and accompanying apparatus (biographical headnotes, study questions, teaching aids) they want. Teachers can custom-order these printed and bound, along with supplementary material from their own classes – such as syllabi and sample student papers. Best of all, the teacher's name goes on the book's cover; the list's editors get second billing. If print-on-demand is not the ultimate in democratic pedagogy, it comes close, for control over the content has passed from the editors to individual teachers – indeed, to the very composition teachers generally marginalized in the academy.

What will teachers choose to do? Will they switch to print-on-demand books and thus drive out the classroom staple, the large hard-copy Readers that have dominated composition classrooms and consequently have determined the exposure of our nation's millions of first-year students to the essays and authors that may comprise their sole humanistic experience in college? With a wealth of essays to choose among, will teachers download compilations of canonical favorites – say, George Orwell's "Shooting an Elephant," E. B. White's "Once More to the Lake," Virginia Woolf's "The Death of the Moth," Martin Luther King Jr.'s "Letter from Birmingham Jail," and Swift's "Modest Proposal"? Will they choose only contemporary works? Or a mix? Will they select only essays by women? Minorities? On a particular theme? Representatives of a given mode – say, argument or narration? Or some other combinations? Will there be a few favorites amid a horde of wallflowers, never chosen and therefore doomed to essay oblivion? Or will all three hundred possibilities be chosen equally? Will teachers' choices be driven by costs to the students?[3] What will happen if the skinny print-on-demand Readers of tomorrow supplant the fat books of yesteryear? The jury is still out.

Anecdotal evidence from bookstore personnel and teachers around the country says that even as textbooks are getting longer, students are reading less. So short compilations may accommodate (I would say pander to) student sloth. Nevertheless, the amount of work required to put together a meaningful essay collection and to use it well in the classroom is deceptive – as I know from my own experience of having edited three Readers, including *The Essay Connection*, currently in its seventh edition. Editors do a great deal of work in finding new and teachable essays, interpreting the essays they select, providing a meaningful intellectual and pedagogical context. Hard-copy works offer material that print-on-demand users can request or dismiss: interpretive introductions to topics and authors, study questions that analyze the text at hand and make connections with other readings in the book (impossible with on-demand compilations), rhetorical commentary, and other apparatus. Print-on-demand, by decontextualizing and re-contextualizing each essay the teacher chooses, abrogates the textbook editor's responsibility and the hard copy's intellectual and aesthetic resonance, perhaps even its social and political concerns, and puts most of the burden of how to teach these essays on the teacher who compiles the book. Teachers can certainly rise to the opportunity. If, harassed and burdened by mountains of papers to grade, they choose not to do so, they may in time find it easier to return to familiar textbooks where the editor has done much of the work for them.

In the absence of evidence the answers to these questions are imponderable, as is the longevity of print-on-demand publication. Canon theory does not yet allow for free agency. On the one hand, the current canonical figures may hold their ground, supplemented by new faces as canon formation and re-formation proceeds in its usual fashion. On the other hand, the essay canon as we know it today may disappear, buried in an on-line free-for-all. My guess is that if this happens, a new or newly configured essay canon will emerge, phoenixlike, as it always has done and will continue to do as long as essays and the academy in which they are embedded contain the breath and pulse of life.

Appendix 1
Canonical Essayists and Most Frequently Reprinted Titles

Name	No. of Reprints	No. of Titles	No. of Anthologies	No. of Editors	Date Begun	Date Ended
George Orwell	357	19	45	221	1952	1996
"Politics and the English Language"	118					
"Shooting an Elephant"	113					

Appendix 1
Continued

Name	No. of Reprints	No. of Titles	No. of Anthologies	No. of Editors	Date Begun	Date Ended
E. B. White	268	37	40	177	1946	1996
"Once More to the Lake"	88					
Joan Didion	219	30	43	151	1971	1996
"On Keeping a Notebook"	44					
Lewis Thomas	205	50	41	141	1976	1996
"Notes on Punctuation"	21					
H. D. Thoreau	180	29	35	139	1948	1996
"Civil Disobedience"	48					
Virginia Woolf	177	26	37	122	1946	1996
"The Death of the Moth"	44					
Jonathan Swift	173	7	38	163	1957	1996
"A Modest Proposal"	151					
Martin Luther King Jr.	165	14	35	145	1967	1996
"Letter from a Birmingham Jail"	50					
"I Have a Dream"	68					
James Thurber	158	35	31	116	1946	1996
"University Days"	35					
Samuel L. Clemens	143	30	32	131	1946	1996
"Two Views . . ."	25					
Annie Dillard	136	39	37	109	1974	1996
"Sight into Insight"	21					
Thomas Jefferson	132	9	28	110	1952	1996
"The Declaration of Independence"	96					
Russell Baker	126	45	37	99	1967	1996
"The Plot against the People"	21					

Appendix 1
Continued

Name	No. of Reprints	No. of Titles	No. of Anthologies	No. of Editors	Date Begun	Date Ended
Loren Eiseley	121	31	28	108	1960	1996
"The Brown Wasp"	25					
E. M. Forster	118	11	22	86	1957	1996
"My Wood"	47					
Maya Angelou	113	16	26	105	1973	1996
"Graduation"	44					
Ellen Goodman	112	45	33	95	1979	1996
"The Company Man"	11					
James Baldwin	102	15	25	82	1962	1996
"Strangers in the Village"	37					
Richard Rodriguez	99	21	34	94	1977	1996
"Aria"	23					
Plato	96	8	23	80	1948	1996
"The Allegory of the Cave"	45					
William Zinsser	87	14	21	78	1968	1996
"College Pressures"	18					
Alice Walker	86	15	30	70	1976	1996
"Beauty: When the Other Dancer Is the Self"	24					
Stephen Jay Gould	85	28	25	61	1980	1996
"Evolution as Fact and Theory"	8					
Bertrand Russell	84	27	23	67	1948	1996
"A Free Man's Worship"	14					
Bruce Catton	81	8	19	80	1959	1996
"Grant and Lee: A Study in Contrasts"	70					

Note: Compiled by Valerie M. Smith and Lori Corsini-Nelson

Notes

1. However, comparable research I have done, which appears in "American Autobiography: The Changing Critical Canon," reinforces my suspicion that the proportion of novelists attaining canonicity would be about the same – less than half of 1 percent of the works published by mainstream presses.

2. Except for canonical nineteenth-century essayists (Emerson, Thoreau, Lamb, Arnold), essays are largely absent from literature textbooks designated for courses beyond first-year composition. Single-volume American literature anthologies largely ignore the genre ("I wanted to put in a whole section on essays," says a colleague of his recent twenty-five-hundred-page literature compilation, "but there wasn't room"). Two-volume anthologies use excerpts from autobiographies and histories, such as Mary Rowlandson's *Narrative of the Captivity and Restoration* and Olaudah Equiano's *Interesting Narrative of the Life* – works not written as essays per se – primarily to incorporate the perspectives of women and minorities, rather than as exemplary models of nonfiction prose.

3. Current figures indicate that the per-copy cost of print-on-demand Readers will be about five dollars base price plus seven cents a page. The pricing structure thus dictates a short book, of say 20 selections maximum, as opposed to the 65 to 120 pieces in hard-copy Readers. The break-even point comes between 275 and 300 pages, after which it is cheaper to buy a hard-copy book than a print-on-demand Reader.

Bibliography

Altieri, Charles. "An Idea and Ideal of a Literary Canon." *Canons.* Ed. Robert von Hallberg. Chicago: University of Chicago Press, 1984. 41–64.

Atwan, Robert, ed. *The Best American Essays of 1986–.* New York: Ticknor, 1986–93. Boston: Houghton Mifflin, 1994–.

"Bibliography of Writing Textbooks." *Writing Program Administration* 5– (Spring 1981–).

Bizzell, Patricia, and Bruce Herzberg, eds. *The Rhetorical Tradition: Readings from Classical Times to the Present.* Boston: Bedford, 1990.

Bloom, Harold. *The Western Canon: The Books and School of the Ages.* New York: Harcourt, 1994.

Bloom, Lynn Z. "The Essay Canon." *College English* 61.4 (1999): 401–30.

———. "Freshman Composition as a Middle Class Enterprise." *College English* 58.6 (1996): 654–75.

Bloom, Lynn Z., and Louise Z. Smith, eds. *The St. Martin's Custom Reader*. Boston: Bedford/St. Martin's, 2001.

Bloom, Lynn Z., with Ning Yu. "American Autobiography: The Changing Critical Canon." A/B: *Auto/Biography Studies* 9.2 (1994): 167–80.

Brooks, Cleanth, and Robert Penn Warren. *Understanding Poetry: An Anthology for College Students*. New York: Henry Holt, 1938.

Cain, Kathleen Shine, et al., eds. *The Mercury Reader*. Needham Heights MA: Pearson Custom Publishing, 2000.

Christensen, Charles. Personal interview. July 3, 1997.

Connors, Robert J. *Composition-Rhetoric: Backgrounds, Theory, and Pedagogy*. Pittsburgh: University of Pittsburgh Press, 1997.

Day, Henry. *Elements of the Art of Rhetoric*. Hudson: W. Skinner and Co., 1850.

Fulton, Maurice Garland. *Expository Writing*. Rev. ed. New York: Macmillan, 1912.

Golding, Alan C. *From Outlaw to Classic: Canons in American Poetry*. Madison: University of Wisconsin Press, 1995.

Hardison, O. B., Jr. "Binding Proteus: An Essay on the Essay." *Essays on the Essay: Redefining the Genre*. Ed. Alexander J. Butrym. Athens: University of Georgia Press, 1989. 11–28.

Harris, Wendell V. "Canonicity." PMLA 106.1 (1991): 110–21.

———. "Reflections on the Peculiar Status of the Personal Essay." *College English* 58.8 (1996): 934–53.

Lauter, Paul. *Canons and Contexts*. New York: Oxford University Press, 1991.

———. "Preface to the First Edition." *The Heath Anthology of American Literature*. Ed. Paul Lauter et al. 2 vols. 2nd ed. Lexington MA: D. C. Heath, 1994. 1: xxx–xl.

Lewis, Edwin H. *Specimens of the Forms of Discourse*. New York: Henry Holt, 1900.

McQuade, Donald M. "Composition and Literary Studies." *Redrawing the Boundaries: The Transformation of English and American Literary Studies*. Ed. Stephen Greenblatt and Giles Gunn. New York: MLA, 1992. 482–519.

North, Stephen M. *The Making of Knowledge in Composition: Portrait of an Emerging Field*. Upper Montclair NJ: Boynton, 1987.

Rasula, Jed. *The American Poetry Wax Museum: Reality Effects, 1940–1990*. Urbana IL: National Council of Teachers of English, 1996.

Sanders, Scott Russell. "The Singular First Person." *Essays on the Essay: Re-*

defining the Genre. Ed. Alexander J. Butrym. Athens: University of Georgia Press, 1989. 31–42.

Scholes, Robert. *Textual Power: Literary Theory and the Teaching of English.* New Haven: Yale University Press, 1985.

Smith, Barbara Herrnstein. *Contingencies of Value: Alternative Perspectives for Critical Theory.* Cambridge: Harvard University Press, 1988.

KAREN L. KILCUP

The Poetry and Prose of Recovery Work

Let our readers be assured that (as matters are managed among the four or five different cliques who control our whole literature in controlling the larger portion of our critical journals,) it requires no small amount of *courage*, to an author whose subsistence lies in his pen, to *hint*, even, that any thing good, in a literary way, can, by any possibility, exist out of the limits of a certain narrow territory. – Southern Literary Messenger, 1849

My title is intended not only to suggest the necessity of generic diversity in recovery work but also, of course, to underscore the efforts (the "prose") that underlie the pleasures of rooting around in rare book rooms and well-equipped research libraries (the "poetry"). Beyond gaining the satisfaction of ushering into print again such writers as Martha Wolfenstein and Onoto Watanna, I have been reminded that a number of nontrivial, nonintellectual realities help determine what can or cannot be accomplished in today's corporatized academy and its affiliated publishing culture. I will touch here upon the role of power and privilege of varying sorts in recovery work and in the anthologizing and criticism that complement it. With examples drawn principally from nineteenth-century American women's writing, because it is the field in which I have worked most, I will outline some of the central challenges in recovery work today. These challenges are aesthetic, political, and economic, and both internal and external to the subject field and to the profession; although I separate them for ease of discussion, they are inextricably interconnected. Some of the remarks that follow will be familiar to those who have completed anthologies, but I believe that the discussion as a whole will carry new insights for virtually everyone. Many of my observations have relevance for anthologizing in general, as well for the writing of white males, whose work has not enjoyed the recovery efforts expended elsewhere. At the heart of this discussion and the questions it raises resides my uncomfortable awareness of the degree to which economics drives the recovery process. As Duncan Wu has observed concerning the elements in anthologizing that scholars resist, those related to money are among the most common: "Scholars haven't traditionally needed to think about the commercial marketplace, and there remains the suspicion that it's improper for them to do so" (n.p.).

"Standards": The Politics of Aesthetics

Composing an anthology creates a miniature canon, no matter how resistant the editor is to the vexed notions of goodness and importance (see Kenneth Warren; Wu). By definition, what's in is important and good, and what's omitted is at least potentially questionable. Every responsible editor ponders long to formulate the best selection criteria. Traditionally, anthologies are compiled on three bases: excellence, representativeness (and/or comprehensiveness), and interest, often working in some combination.[1] These criteria were as important in the case of nineteenth-century texts, such as E. C. Stedman's *An American Anthology*, as they are for today's *Heath* and *Norton* anthologies of American literature. All three criteria frustrate precise definition. Excellence putatively refers to the Arnoldian aesthetic – the best that's been thought and said – and, as we know, the best tends to be self-perpetuating and conservative (in the negative sense). Ironically, although "excellence" has been deconstructed now for a number of years, literary scholars often still cling to this nebulous term in part because of its self-justificatory elements.[2] After all, if we aren't contributing to excellence, what are we doing? Advancing mediocrity? Making money? Reviews of Rufus W. Griswold's *The Female Poets of America* (1849) indicate that adjudicating excellence concerned our predecessors as much as it does us. The questions of who determines excellence and by what standards are still too often elided. This criterion, however, often polices the realm of the aesthetic in contradistinction from the political, a distinction I have explored elsewhere ("The Conversation").

"Representativeness" incurs other difficulties. Here there appears to be a more concrete, objective standard, but the difficulties of claiming representative status remain as tangled as those relating to excellence, especially in our multicultural era. In the creation of *Nineteenth-Century American Women Writers* I excluded more than four filing drawers of materials; the final volume in no way "represents" the concerns or aesthetics of thousands of texts that I eliminated in the early stages because of insufficient excellence. No anthology can make a serious claim to being characteristic until its editor has read virtually everything in the field, clearly an impossibility even in the nineteenth century, let alone in the twentieth. Here, too, political agendas can – and at this historical moment should – inform the selection process. For example, my anthology aimed to encompass authors diverse by region, ethnic group, and genre, among other categories, in an effort to convey the scope of the cultural conversation in which these writers engaged – to seek representativeness over a broad field, not necessarily always to represent individual writers by their best work. What (and whom) should we represent in our anthologies? What do we mean by such terms as *diversity* and *inclusiveness*? Too often, as I will explore in more detail later, class is elided as a principle of selection. Comprehensiveness – or breadth – is a related concept, implying perhaps a less refined selection process and a much larger scope – along the lines encompassed by Evart A. Duyckinck and George L. Duyckinck's 1856 *Cyclopaedia of American Literature*. Given the economic realities of publishing outlined below, today we can expect genuine comprehensiveness only in electronic formats.

"Interest" slips and slides as much as the two other selection criteria. As Nina Baym has indicated in her discussion of antebellum nineteenth-century novels, interest has been a consistent touchstone for evaluation in American literary history; the obvious question, again, is, interest to whom, and on what basis? I used this measure in combination with the criterion of diverse themes to help assemble my first anthology, aimed at a large group that includes students, scholars, and general readers. One extension of interest relates to the troublesome notion of popularity. Anthologies of popular genres such as humor and science fiction have ready markets; even putatively academic collections such as Nancy A. Walker and Zita Dresner's important *Redressing the Balance: American Women's Literary Humor from Colonial Times to the 1980s* (1988) and Mary Suzanne Schriber's *Telling Travels: Selected Writings by Nineteenth-Century American Women Abroad* (1995) have a much wider audience than collections of "serious" or canonical writing.[3] Perhaps those of us in the process of recovery work need to take Jane Tompkins's views about popular texts more seriously, to interrogate our assumptions about audience and pleasure (if a work is pleasurable and accessible, it can't be good), and to expand the audiences for our work. This strategy represents not simply a matter of appropriate politics – or better sales – but of breaching the artificial and self-interested boundary between the academy and the "real world," a boundary that has, for most of us in state universities and public colleges at least, already been breached by hostile forces interested only in such matters as "measurable student learning outcomes" and "efficiency."

A less frequently articulated selection criterion is "challenge." At first glance one might assume that I denote aesthetic excellence, but I intend rather to emphasize the ambition of the anthologist to invite or propel readers to interrogate existing standards, however murky or implicit such standards may be. For *Nineteenth-Century American Women Writers* I extended the principles of the groundbreaking *Heath*, which encompassed (for example) Sui Sin Far, a Chinese Canadian author who traveled and worked in the United States for a number of years, and I included other writers who were American in a flexible sense and who invited students to think in transnational terms.[4] Equally important, I wanted to include texts that were not, in the strictest sense, "literary," in both this collection and *Native American Women's Writing*. Hence, the former includes an obituary of Emily Dickinson by her sister-in-law, Susan Gilbert Dickinson, and cookbook writing by Catherine Owen, while the latter includes testimony to the U.S. Senate by Susette LaFlesche, as well as the coauthored report by Zitkala-Ša, *Oklahoma's Poor Rich Indians*, on the exploitation of the Western Indians. The important point here (as I've suggested with advice writing) is that putatively nonliterary texts exist on a continuum with literary texts, and understanding the aesthetics of the former can help illuminate the literariness of the latter ("'Essays of Invention'"). We should continue to expand the canon of great or good texts to include interesting ones that converse with more conventionally canonical forms.[5] This standard of challenge may seem to be incommensurate with my suggestion a moment ago that we consider expanding our audiences, but what challenges academic audiences might interest nonacademic readers.

With rigid conceptions of literary and nonliterary genres, restrictive notions of major and minor authors continue to diminish our conceptual scope and historical understanding. Our selection criteria often remain circumscribed by unconscious or unarticulated hierarchies of length and genre, as we see in the case of the brilliant sketch writer and poet Rose Terry Cooke, arguably one of the most important U.S. writers in the nineteenth century. In this case, as in many others, what we might call the "circularity of absence" governs her availability: a writer's continued omission from mainstream collections is virtually guaranteed by the publishers' resistance to critical work, even when, as in Cooke's case, a volume has been proposed by a distinguished scholar with cutting-edge books to her credit; simultaneously, the absence of a major book on a writer confirms her or his status as minor and legitimates exclusion from collections. Even when such irritating pressures are conscious, editors often cannot resist publishers' (or teachers') demands, as is apparent from the presence, disappearance, and subsequent reappearance of *The Scarlet Letter* in the Heath. The perpetuation of the "Star System" (see Shumway) for *writers* has powerful aesthetic as well as economic resonances, hampering development of the broader field because we spend our energies focused on a very small proportion of writers. I appreciate the fact that, politically, scholars in the field of nineteenth-century American women's writing (and other recovery fields) have to be careful about spreading ourselves too thinly and that too much breadth can also be counterproductive, dispersing limited energies.[6] Nevertheless, I wonder if, and how, *major* and *minor* continue to be useful terms for study. The Star System of writers, much more prevalent in the twentieth century than in the nineteenth, represents a form of cultural amnesia, with the advent of Modernism being the customary explanation (Clark; Golding); nineteenth-century anthologists like Griswold aimed at breadth rather than depth. We might usefully remember that most authors, even those we today consider major, wrote both "highbrow" and "lowbrow" work, to borrow Lawrence Levine's terms; we too rarely account for this fact in either our anthologies or our criticism. Sarah Orne Jewett represents just one example of an author whose popular work, such as her newspaper writing, has been virtually deleted from contemporary criticism and canonical significance (Johanningsmeier; Kilcup and Edwards).[7]

Martha Banta acknowledges the hospitality of anthologies to shorter works. For my collections of nineteenth-century American women's writing I determined that, aside from the fact that excerpts were generally problematic and that I would exclude them except in cases where a selection could stand alone, one principal consideration was the domination of the novel (and fiction more generally) and the elision of nontraditional and shorter genres in recent literary studies. On the other hand, representativeness trumped aesthetic concerns with form: if in a particular period I needed the perspective, say, of a Western writer, I chose that writer with the awareness that her excellence might be secondary to her interest. I also hoped to avoid cloning prior recovery work, merely reprinting now familiar texts that had achieved nearly canonical status, such as "The Yellow Wall-Paper" for Charlotte Perkins Gilman and "Old Woman Magoun" for Mary Wilkins Freeman. As Banta astutely underscores, "the anthology that works must be a sum of voices that are talking back and forth with one another to some purpose" (333). It is difficult for the anthologist to conceptualize this conversation if she is thinking about money – either the profit she will make or the commercial requirements of her publisher.

Economics: Publishers, Purchasers, Purveyors

My answer to the question of criteria was, in fact, partially informed by economic forces beyond my control: my publisher urged me to include at least a few familiar texts that would entice people to buy my first collection, although the final selections were mine – hence, "The Yellow Wall-Paper" was included, though in a newly discovered manuscript version. The power exerted by presses and publishers over the recovery process represents an important element in the economics of recovery work; as Wu notes, "commercial considerations will inevitably play their part in determining the contents of each different anthology; scholarly or pedagogical factors cannot be the sole determinants" (n.p.). Unlike Paula Bennett's visionary *Nineteenth-Century American Women Poets*, which was assembled from extensive primary research and took many additional years to find a publisher, too many anthologies represent little more than cut-and-paste compendia of now familiar works and writers; part of this phenomenon can be attributed to scholars who wish (or need) to profit, and part can be attributed to presses with the same desire.[8] Moreover, the sales price is determined by the press, often with significant pressure from the marketing department and equally often in departure from the contracted price.

If we were able to resist or evade the economic pressures of publishers, perhaps we could envision anthologizing in a comprehensive as well as individual sense, that is, to consider press series (or even the publishing landscape in individual areas) as another form of this activity. The ambitious Rutgers University Press American Women Writers Series has broken important new ground, but as the market indicates, their production quality – that is, costs – may be too high, for the press has not issued a new volume for a number of years. One of their success stories is Catharine Maria Sedgwick's *Hope Leslie*, which the press brought out in 1987. Since then this innovative 1827 novel on racial and gender politics has sold tens of thousands of copies at $15.00. According to on-line Books in Print, the book has been available beginning in 1972 from Irvington Press, but at a retail price of $29.50. In 1998 Penguin saw a good market opportunity and issued its edition for $13.95. On the one hand, researchers and teachers in the field can be grateful to have available two affordable editions framed by the fine scholarship of Mary Kelley (Rutgers edition) and Carolyn L. Karcher (Penguin). On the other hand, we might wish that the resources had been extended to encompass other, less profitable works so that our collective "anthology" of nineteenth-century American women's writing were expanded. This narrow focus on profitable authors may be exacerbated by the structure of – and political clout wielded by – single-author societies that, even if unwittingly, pit one writer against another; with only so many resources in the publishing world, those authors with institutional power and recognition dominate. Moreover, even for recovered writers, a single text (usually a novel or longer work) often dominates. Thus, in spite of the lack of a comprehensive collection of short stories – beyond the handful usually reprinted – by Sarah Orne Jewett, publishers are cashing in on her growing reputation, with reprints of *The Country of the Pointed Firs* included in volumes by David Godine ($20.00), New American Library ($3.95), Oxford ($8.95), Macmillan ($22.95), University Press of New England ($14.95), Library of America ($11.95), Viking Penguin ($8.95), Random House ($13.50), Norton ($9.95), and the ubiquitous Dover ($1.00), to cite only the most prominent.

Purchasers, the students, represent another node in the anthologizing matrix – the principal one, in fact. As Wu reminds us, "perhaps it is in the interests of publishers, who care only about profits, to discourage . . . enquiry" about the appropriate relationship of the student to the anthology (n.p.). Kenneth Warren asserts: "[We need] to continue reminding ourselves of the extent to which our students embody the conflicts we face in attempting to mediate between text and audience, between 'history' and people of the present. What we teach is inextricably linked to those whom we teach and our impressions of their deficiencies and needs; and our sense of what we ought to teach has changed, and will change, with our shifting student populations" (341). I agree wholeheartedly with Warren's perspective; but, beyond his observation, I want to explore, first, who are "our students" and (later in this discussion) who are "we"? Community colleges serve about 40 percent of the students in higher education in the United States; another large percentage attends regional state universities or small private colleges. Although many of the students at my home institution, a medium-sized doctoral-granting public university in the South, are middle class, a significant number come from families of the working poor; some are first-generation college students. "We," then, need to remember that when it comes to students' needs and priorities, *economic* diversity often matters at least as much as gender, ethnic, or racial diversity; "their deficiencies and needs" vary widely and include more than the lack of access to a particular literary text or understanding of a tradition.[9] Not too long ago one of my undergraduates came into my office to apologize that he had not done the reading because he had lost his job; there was no money left over for textbooks, but he hoped to have another job in a few days. Such situations require us (apart from individual action) to consider multiculturalism more fully and explicitly in class-based terms. How well can the academic literary anthology, a textbook, serve the vast majority of U.S. students, as well as their elite counterparts? How does it serve different populations differently? What roles do our students serve as audiences for anthologies – are they or should they be "guinea pigs" for the investigation of new canons, as Duncan Wu pointedly asks? Or, as he suggests, do they literally help pay for vacations in the Caribbean; and do we fill our anthologies with "what's good," or "what's good" for students, or "what's good" for the bottom line, our own or our publishers'?

Given the economic situation of most students, instructors in literary studies at the large majority of institutions in the United States are under heavy pressure to keep course-book costs low; students complain if they are required to buy a book and then only read a small portion. There is also a threshold price for books, and some students will not purchase a humanities textbook over fifteen dollars unless it's an anthology. Ironically, students' lack of time and money may help create a market for shorter works in anthologies; at my home institution, as at numerous others, many students have jobs, often full-time, and now more than ever they need access to inexpensive collections that provide a wide range of materials. This economic situation is exacerbated abroad, where the price of textbooks is sometimes 50 to 100 percent greater than in the United States. In addition to having sensitivity to cost, students are acutely attuned to locations of social and cultural power. Not only are "classic" novels perceived as "a good buy" – with paperbacks available from Dover, for example, for a dollar or two – but the privilege of novels over shorter genres, especially in the last twenty years, has significantly distorted the field of literary studies.[10] Collections of short fiction, especially by a single author, are difficult to sell, as witnessed by the disappearance of Judith Fetterley's important collection of sketches by Alice Cary in the Rutgers series. Aesthetically and politically powerful, Cary's writing nevertheless does not fit securely or tidily into canonical genre categories. When the profit-making enterprise of publishing – invading even the world of university presses – reinscribes the dominant scholarly model of major and minor authors and genres, our collective "anthology" of American women's writing is substantially diminished. This situation occurs in part because of the more limited student audience (usually upper-level undergraduate and graduate students) for many recovery collections.[11]

English departments are the purveyors of texts, including anthologies, and they are often at least as conservative as publishers. The "culture wars," "crisis in the humanities," and general retrenchment in English departments have often resulted in little self-examination. Instead, if a dean funds a line for a retiring colleague, there is a rush to replacement, because department heads are so concerned (often with good reason) that the line will disappear. Without attention to constructing goals for the future, we may foster outsiders' sense of our irrelevance as we cling to the institutionalized structures and writers of the past without fully articulated rationales for doing so. Such replacements often have other, equally inappropriate rationales. I know of one midsized department that recently decided to hire its fourth Renaissance specialist because "students want to take Shakespeare and we can't meet the demand." The consumer culture, not the future of the department or the profession, determines who will be hired. What this stagnancy and market-driven perspective mean for recovery work, especially for specialists in women's or minority writing, is obvious: if we replace retiring department members with people in the same fields or select colleagues based on the popularity of their subjects (usually Shakespeare and contemporary literature), much recovery work will remain undone.

Publishing (and Perishing)

In addition to these economic constraints constituted by the publisher, student, and department, recovery work is very time-consuming and expensive for the editor. For example, in the summer of 1995 alone I spent over twelve hundred dollars on photocopies related to my projects; travel costs to libraries were much higher. Working at the time at an "old" university in England, I was fortunate to have extensive institutional support and a teaching load of about 6.5 hours per week (with only twenty-three weeks of teaching over the year). For *Native American Women's Writing* I received institutional support in the form of numerous graduate student research assistants and hundreds of expensive interlibrary loan requests.[12] What does it mean to a field that only people with money (or significant institutional support, as I had) make the selections? In some cases the social class of the editor, as much as that of the consumer (student), affects what kind of work can be done. This reality suggests a relatively homogeneous perspective that potentially impoverishes scholarship, and it is connected at least indirectly to the Star System of scholars. Because this system influences what will count as literature and, of course, what will be included in anthologies, it becomes in some sense a stand-in for class, with academics at elite, well-funded institutions more frequently possessing access to the prestigious publishing outlets that effectively determine the canon.[13] In recent years, as anthologies have become standard fare for university and college survey courses and certain "star" scholars have capitalized, sometimes literally and cynically, upon their names to sell texts, repackaging the work of less famous editors has become more common. The obvious but necessary point here, to return to Warren's observation, is that "we" are not all the same.

From this angle it is possible to identify an important question neglected in the earlier discussion about selection standards: how might notions of excellence, representativeness, and interest – and hence selections – be circumscribed by the class of the anthologist? Such questions seem so transparent and familiar that we may forget to ask them. Some scholars may take for granted, for example, that individuals choose selections most amenable to their experience, whether in subject matter, genre, or form. Thus they might assume, with some justification, that a woman anthologist would decide to compile an anthology of women's writing or to emphasize women's literature in what publishers like to call a "mainstream" anthology. But how accurate is a similar assumption concerning the working-class anthologist who, with the education acquired in becoming an academic, can (and sometimes must) "pass" for middle-class? Supposing that we can even define "working-class" satisfactorily, is she more or less likely to include working-class voices in a collection, given that education? Today's anthologists have been trained by the descendents of the nineteenth and early twentieth centuries' academic elite, who tended to value some genres – principally, fiction, poetry, drama, and autobiography – over others. Advice writing, travel writing, children's writing, and the like were infrequently serious candidates for canonical inclusion, in part because they were not "excellent" (and "complex") and in part because they "interested" the wrong people (and hence, as Levine and Huyssen have detailed, couldn't have aesthetic merit). To a significant degree, although popular texts have engendered tremendous interest in recent years, they remain marginalized within the canon. I would argue that genre hierarchy offers one measure of class differentiation in anthologizing, and such a hierarchy may be fostered by the class structures of academe.

Although my understanding here may be based principally upon my knowledge of people who have engaged in recovery work, individuals at "major" research universities and/or those with the personal resources to undertake recovery work seem more likely to be predisposed to regard certain kinds of writing as "nonliterary" than those with different kinds of institutional and personal affiliations. This situation translates into an absence of recovery efforts, for example, on working-class writers; such collections as *The Lowell Offering: Writings by New England Mill Women (1840–1845)* and *The Factory Girls: A Collection of Writings on Life and Struggles in the New England Factories of the 1840s* were compiled by cultural historians, Benita Eisler and Philip Foner, rather than by literary scholars. While this different perspective brings a welcome diversity to the intellectual conversation, historians possess different values than scholars in literary studies. Even if a literary editor is aware of how her class situation influences her selections, however, acting on that knowledge is not necessarily straightforward. For one thing, the concept of the working class is at least as fluid in the nineteenth century as it is in the twentieth, where we see the emergence of a self-aware, explicitly proletariat literature. If a working-class editor, for a variety of reasons, might be reluctant to acknowledge her background, so too were authors.[14]

Recovering working-class writing often means more than reviewing the influential periodicals of the time; it might mean a commitment to archival research, an expensive and time-consuming effort. My recovery of the European travel diaries of the Boston domestic servant Lorenza Stevens Berbineau was supported by a Mellon Fellowship as well as by a series of substantial research grants from my home institution at the time, the University of Hull in England.[15] Even people who can "afford" to do the work, both financially and professionally, are often overburdened with other projects. Those entering the profession frequently cannot afford it financially, nor can they risk their professional futures by embarking on long-term studies of writers and works considered "marginal" ("it's only an anthology" is a refrain that echoes even at nonelite institutions among senior faculty judging the work of untenured faculty). Anthologizing work, in fact, can be so "innovative" that it is literally unrecognizable to some as a legitimate scholarly enterprise containing a rich intellectual critique; if it doesn't fit within, or reside at least at the edges of, some traditional field or theory, it may be denied as genuinely academic work, in spite of the current permeability of literary studies. In the most extreme case such work might never be published. That scholars are aware of this matter at some level is evident from the relative lack of critical work being done on nineteenth-century American women's writing, especially on poetry; despite the emergence of cultural studies and what we might expect to be the consequent diminishment of genre hierarchies, Judith Fetterley's 1994 lament concerning the significant gaps in the field remains largely accurate ("Commentary"). The disparity between workers within the profession, with starting assistant professors at many institutions teaching 4–4 loads, compounds the difficulties and contributes to what I would call canon calcification. Even if they have no intention of engaging in recovery work themselves but desire to teach recovered authors, those individuals with heavy teaching and service loads often do not have time to learn about new writers unless they make substantial professional – and sometimes personal – sacrifices.

Finally, such matters as permissions costs also influence who does the work and what is recovered. Anthologists complain endlessly about these costs, but colleagues who have not encountered the problem may be surprised at its significance. For example, I was forced to exclude from my first collection an early oral narrative by a Mexican American woman, Eulalia Perez, because the library that held the materials wanted two thousand dollars for roughly eight pages. To republish approximately seventeen pages of materials by Emily Dickinson cost about six hundred dollars. In this case the publisher covered the expenditure, although publishers sometimes limit their contributions severely. As I discovered when I applied to my home institution for permissions costs for another project, many – probably most – institutions have extremely limited funding for such purposes; more often these costs come out of the editor's profits – if, indeed, there are any.[16] If one is editing a recovery anthology, profits are often microscopic, whereas reprinting familiar authors can be very rewarding indeed. Dale M. Bauer's observation in another context is extremely useful here: "Who controls representation controls social power" (120).

(Identity) Politics

Recovery work and the accompanying criticism can often be profoundly influenced by identity politics. For example, in spite of Nelly McKay's recent call for a nonessentialist perspective on literary studies, white scholars are often discouraged or even excluded from recovery and criticism of nonwhite texts. Permissions-granting institutions and publishing houses may fail to appreciate careful work done by white scholars and to see the value of having minority texts appear in multicultural or pluralist anthologies. Because of the understandable concern about white scholars' appropriation of minority primary texts, libraries or historical societies may overcharge for permissions costs, preventing dissemination of important materials and unwittingly reducing the demand for additional minority work. Publishers may have anxieties about white editors' scholarship on minority authors or about readers' responses to it. Fortunately, the vision and energy of some minority scholars who support important white-edited recovery projects, as was true with Amy Doherty's collection of María Cristina Mena's writing, may counterbalance these forces. Another discouraging form of identity politics occurs when minority scholars, many of whom have no difficulty in acquiring excellent publishers for their collections, discover that their work on minority texts and writers is judged by their colleagues to be "unimportant" or "marginal" to the scholarly enterprise. I know of at least two cases in which bitter tenure battles arose because departments refused to take seriously the recovery work and scholarship of two women who were well-known in their respective fields.

The same dismissal of work occurs to "foreign" scholars working in American literature, who are, it is assumed, "behind" "the cutting edge," either because of the inaccessibility of materials or simply because they aren't American. Although such a perspective may strain credibility in the humanistic environment of the academy, I can confirm its accuracy from personal experience, having worked in England for several years, as well as from the experiences of friends and colleagues in Europe and elsewhere. The emergence of the Internet, with the availability of primary resources like the Making of America, has already started to level the playing field between scholars who work at well-funded, larger institutions and those who have traditionally lacked access, including foreign scholars.[17] Too often in the United States we fail to consider the complicated position of American literature abroad and of our colleagues who study and teach it. In the United Kingdom, for example, American literature is frequently regarded, when it is seen at all, as marginal and is sometimes taught in departments of commonwealth and postcolonial literature along with Australian, New Zealand, South African, and Caribbean literature. Our colleagues in the United Kingdom struggle against the added invisibility of American *women's* literature. Finally, these colleagues have a sense of urgency about the field – teaching and research – that comes when, as at Cambridge, one is asked to teach all of American literature in a short lecture series; or when, as frequently happens, even Americanist faculty members have to teach a broad range of subjects, including Shakespeare.

Another element of identity politics that works to police the borders of anthologizing (and literary studies more generally) is editors' understandable reluctance to include texts that are reprehensible or even questionable because of their racist, sexist, or classist perspectives. There are several such problematic texts included in *Nineteenth-Century American Women Writers: An Anthology*. "An Ex-Brigadier," by the Southern writer Sarah Barnwell Elliott, has as its protagonist a lively, racist Civil War veteran, con man par excellence, who has posed as a preacher; the narrator of Mary Mapes Dodge's "Miss Maloney on the Chinese Question" – one of Mark Twain's favorite stories – is a thieving Irish servant who depreciates a Chinese servant. Unquestionably offensive, both of these stories raise important questions about the authors' narrative stance. They also elicit for me, and I hope for other scholars, the tangled problem of how we should handle writers whose politics we find repugnant. This concern returns us to the question of representativeness that I raised earlier: how can an anthologist make any claim for this standard if she excludes offensive texts that accurately "represent" their historical moment? Moreover, some *aesthetically* excellent texts – including "An Ex-Brigadier" – incorporate such views. How should we handle the question, for example, of Charlotte Perkins Gilman's cultural eugenics? Rather than eradicating an ugly past, is it not better to expose it prominently for discussion?[18]

Another identity matter emerges in the creation and reception of anthologies. Few men undertake collections of women writers; few men take courses on women's writing. To be blunt, men often study and teach men; women, women, and too seldom do these paths converge (see Idol and Ponder). We need to foster an environment in which such crossover scholarship – not just by gender but also by race, class, and other social identities – is encouraged and recognized (see Wonham; Powell). We also need to couple a synthetic, pluralist approach with continued particularist efforts at articulating identity-based or minoritized traditions more fully. In addition, region limits our perspectives; in the field of nineteenth-century American women's writing there are still too few considerations of Southern and Western women other than a small group whose work has been recovered by such scholars as Judith Fetterley, Marjorie Pryse, and Melody Graulich.

Criticism and recovery work are two sides of the same scholarly project: anthologies – and rediscovered writers – cannot advance, or be taught, without becoming part of a critical conversation.[19] Here again identity matters. One obstacle to the advancement of both practical and theoretical criticism is the intense pressure on beginning scholars, some of our most innovative and challenging critics, to produce, to publish quickly. This pressure often leads to publications focusing on a single writer or small group of writers, most of whom must be canonical or neocanonical, or presses will reject their projects. That is, academic institutions themselves collude, however unwittingly, with publishers to ensure the maintenance of the status quo via its economic penalties: denial of tenure and promotion, the possible demise of a career. In concrete terms, while it is possible for a beginning scholar to master the major work of and criticism on Emily Dickinson, it can take many years – in spite of important work by David S. Reynolds on the subject – to understand her in the more complex context of her popular contemporaries such as Longfellow, Whittier, Larcom, and Elizabeth Barrett Browning, let alone within the vibrant poetic conversation encompassed by Frances Harper, Sarah Piatt, slave songs, patriotic songs, and the history with which this work is framed. The structures of the academy and the affiliated publishing world make the development of this breadth and sophistication extremely difficult, and they tend to reward hasty (and often inaccurate) generalizations – by established as well as beginning scholars – that advance neither recovery work nor criticism.

Future Directions

It is important to move beyond defining challenges. Many solutions are implicit in the analysis above: to conduct more primary research, negotiate with publishers, create more grounded theory, and initiate more self-interrogation. But as I hope I have emphasized, we have to refocus beyond understanding the aesthetics of recovery work to appreciating its politics and economics and to taking action based on this understanding. What are a few steps that we might take to respond to the realities of academic life as I have outlined them in relation to recovery work? First, we need to work in our own departments not only to urge colleagues to acknowledge the economic and political realities of the academy, particularly in the humanities, but also to engage them in actively formulating goals for the future. One of these goals might be to enable release time for scholarship and/or for teaching preparation in expanding fields with new writers. I must admit that I am least sanguine about this step, given the traditional inertia in many departments as well as the chronic lack of resources in some, but change in even a small number of departments, especially prominent ones that are often regarded as models for best practices, would have a large impact on students and faculty alike.

A few other steps can be undertaken with some confident expectation of success. First is the advancement of Internet libraries of materials. As I mentioned above, the availability of such materials is already deconstructing traditional hierarchies in international scholarship, although electronic access to materials will certainly not address all of the problems. Those of us doing recovery work can contribute to online resources that diffuse materials more widely than traditional print media, and we can point friends, colleagues, and students to useful sites. Another positive step we might take is working toward many more collaborations between those with a measure of power and economic security and those in more marginalized circumstances: between senior and junior people, tenured and part-time individuals, faculty and graduate students, U.S. and international scholars. Such collaborations would provide more access to the resources of the academy and the publishing world, at least partially buffer any potentially negative consequences of "controversial" or "marginal" work, and enhance scholarship with a much-enlarged intellectual conversation. Another fundamental step that we need to take is interpreting humanistic work for the general public. Although "community outreach" has become a buzzword for many university administrators in the corporate university culture, I know from many years of personal experience in the humanities councils in New England and North Carolina, as well as from community service programming in England, that interpreting for a broader audience what we do and how and why we do it can help create a foundation of support that we will need more and more as public funding for research in the humanities shrinks and continues to be awarded principally to those with elite institutional affiliations. As so many have argued so persuasively in discussions of the academic labor crisis of recent years, we have to look outside the academy for models of community action (Nelson).

A final (and in my mind crucial) intervention in the process of recovery scholarship is to involve our students. Although our colleagues represent an important audience for our collections, the work we have done is unlikely to last if it fails to have wide circulation. Undergraduate students at a wide range of institutions can, and should, be involved in the research process and the intellectual work of criticism and canonization. When I rediscovered Lorenza Stevens Berbineau's European travel diaries, I hesitated to share them with my students, concerned that the lack of punctuation and irregular spelling would alienate them from this domestic servant's text and would encourage them to dismiss it as insufficiently literary. Having assigned it now at three very different institutions, I have to acknowledge that I shortchanged them: students, unlike some of our peers, can be astonishingly open to unconventional texts and innovative perspectives, and they can help us to formulate our ideas more carefully and – if we are concerned with the economic diversity that is so often neglected in academe – more accurately.

Recovery work, one might say, should be its own reward. For me the most tangible rewards come in conversation with my students.

Reading Fanny Fern, Catharine Maria Sedgwick, and Frances Harper, among others, my students this past semester reiterated the astonishment I so often encounter: "We haven't solved any of the problems that this writer raises!"; "Nothing much has changed since 1826!"; "I had no idea these women were so political and so subversive!" They were, as always, furious: "How can a writer like Harper or Wolfenstein just *disappear?*"; "Why didn't anyone tell me about Lydia Maria Child before now?" And they were passionate: "Lazarus speaks directly to my situation as an immigrant"; "Wells-Barnett is a model for me." Students at every level appreciate not only knowing the writers but also learning about the economics and politics of canon formation; about such matters as the economics of publishing and the academic profession (permissions costs, for example, always shock them); and about the imbrication of these matters with intellectual freedom, access to ideas, and social critiques of American culture. Their energy, engagement, and insight are my best rewards. Perhaps, finally, I have provided readers with more "prose" and less "poetry" than they might have wished. But it's the prose that will continue to make the poetry possible.

Notes

The epigraph concerns Rufus Griswold's formative anthology, *The Female Poets of America*. The "cliques" to which this reviewer refers were the affluent, educated, powerful men in the Northeast who determined what counted as "good." By "recovery work" in the title I mean scholarship that emphasizes restoring the writing of unknown writers, or the unfamiliar writing of more canonical authors, to critical view.

   1. As Alan C. Golding explains in relation to poetry, early anthologists had a variety of aims, ranging from preserving culture and asserting a political agenda (in the late eighteenth century), to articulating the idea of a national literature and national identity (in the early to mid-nineteenth century), to providing inexpensive compilations that would help unify a diversifying United States. These goals overlapped at times, but each period had its own agenda, with inclusiveness being emphasized more (and sometimes apologetically) in the earlier period and excellence becoming a stronger value later. Nevertheless, merit was a theme in early assessments.

All evaluative and critical terms in my discussion, not just these three standards, should be understood by the reader as enclosed with quotation marks; I have supplied these marks where omitting them might have been confusing.

2. For discussions of "excellence," see, for example, Smith; Lauter, *Canons and Contexts*; and Sosnoski and Wiederhold. Morris provides a very helpful account of the history of literary value in his preface.

3. See also Janet Gray's collection of popular nineteenth-century American women poets.

4. It is important, as Robert K. Martin argues, not to colonialize the writers of American nations adjacent to the United States.

5. Of course, a number of anthologies, including the *Heath*, have already expanded the definition of the literary, but in my view they don't (and often can't, because of their publishers or because of space restrictions) go far enough.

6. Although my recovery work has concentrated on women writers, it also needs to be reiterated that many interesting nineteenth-century male writers need recovery and criticism. Clearly, not all writers deserve recovery, but we need a much larger conversation about the standards for such work and the economic forces surrounding it.

7. For example, Louis A. Renza's and Richard H. Brodhead's work on Jewett responds to these questions in very different ways.

8. "Profit" needs to be construed broadly, to include tenure, promotion, salary raises, internal and external grants, and status mobility.

9. Although I am sympathetic with Jay Fliegelman's list of desiderata for general American literature anthologies (which he establishes in response to the new [at that time, 1993] edition of the *Heath*), I wonder how or if his list would vary for students in different institutions and with different goals. I should clarify here that over the course of my career I have worked in institutions ranging from elite research universities to small colleges and regional state universities; hence, my observations about both students and institutions are informed by personal experience rather than speculation.

10. Ironically, these novels, as various sources in the last few years have emphasized, have to be short.

11. It may also occur because of the fractured structure of U.S. undergraduate education, where many students transfer from two-year to four-year schools, both often having different (and rarely coherent) requirements, either for the major or for general education.

12. Without this graduate student assistance, I could not have completed this project for many more years, and I was and am uncomfortable with the ways in which graduate student labor is relatively unrewarded. One of my responses has been to use the results of the recovery projects to help provide my graduate students with their own research opportunities, as well as to engage in joint publications. The situation of graduate students in the economics of the profession has fortunately enjoyed renewed discussion in recent years (Nelson), and there is hope for amelioriation of current exploitive conditions.

13. Prestigious institutions, while they demand originality and innovation, characteristically place boundaries on such originality and innovation, boundaries particularly salient in relation to recovery work. What "counts" for tenure and promotion at an elite institution, for example, will vary from what counts at many regional state universities and colleges: in elite institutions an anthology might be thought of as an interesting (and potentially profitable) sideline to the faculty member's "real" work of writing monographs – but if a faculty member "merely" compiled anthologies, what could be tolerated as a quirky side interest would become a failure of scholarship, even though compiling a truly innovative recovery anthology can demand more time and as much real critical thought as writing a monograph. As I note below, however, in the present job market state universities are increasingly able to apply the same standards for publication.

14. For example: Although, as Thomas Dublin, Benita Eisler, and Philip Foner remind us, many of the Lowell mill "girls" were from comfortable farming families and worked in the mills to earn money for a brother's or their own education, to obtain spending money for clothing, or for other reasons than subsistence, some were decidedly dependent on the income for their survival. Nevertheless, the pages of *The Lowell Offering* tended to include genteel selections as much as self-consciously or explicitly class-based texts. For many individuals membership in the middle class is something to aspire to and working-class antecedents are to be minimized or erased. With these understandings in mind, we can then ask, is Lucy Larcom a working-class author? Harriet Jacobs? What counts, or should count, in the category?

15. For a discussion of Berbineau and of the difficulties of understanding class in the nineteenth century, see my "Introduction: A Working-Class Woman's View of Europe."

16. It is worth observing that despite over ten thousand dollars in institutional grants, my two anthologies cost thousands more to complete. Two

colleagues paid three thousand dollars for a single story in their recovery anthology, an investment that took many years to recoup.

17. According to the Web site of the University of Michigan (with Cornell University, one of the recipients of a Mellon Foundation grant to complete the project), "The Making of America (MoA) is a digital library of primary sources in American social history from the antebellum period through reconstruction. The collection is particularly strong in the subject areas of education, psychology, American history, sociology, religion, and science and technology. The collection currently contains approximately 8,500 books and 50,000 journal articles with 19th century imprints." See http://www.hti.umich.edu/m/moagrp/ and http://cdl.library.cornell.edu/moa/.

18. The *Heath* has adopted this position, for example, with the inclusion of an excerpt from Caroline Lee Hentz's proslavery fiction. More of such problematic work needs to reappear in both pluralist and particularist collections.

19. Lauter has recently observed (Presentation) that to be successful, recovery work requires complementary teaching and criticism. I am abridging my discussion of criticism here substantially but would simply point out a few additional challenges that influence both critical and primary recovery work: the continuing absence of a comprehensive theoretical framework for the field (see Harris) and the inability to construct a "representative" or even meaningful theory because of an inadequate overview of primary materials; the need for more complex views of sentimentalism, including sentimentalism in male writers (see Bennett, *Poets in the Public Sphere* and "The Descent"; Camfield); the circularity of absence, described above, from the critical angle; the economic and professional penalties for recovery criticism; the gender segregation of critical discussions (see Buell and Reynolds for two exceptions); and the tendency to conceptualize in terms of periods, dates (see Warren and Dickie), and conventional genres. In relation to the last concern, a more specific illustration may be helpful: we need to account for the genre hybridity of much American writing, not just that written in the nineteenth century or by women (Kilcup, " 'Essays of Invention' "; Lauter et al.). Although I appreciate Kenneth Warren's concern that anthologies, "even revisionist ones, reinscribe a rather traditional relationship of Literature to audience," requiring "trained cultural priests [who] initiate willing novices into the mysteries of the process of reading and understanding the sacred texts" (341), I believe that a critical perspective that regards, say, Thoreau's *Walden* and Emerson's "Self-Reliance," as well as Fanny Fern's

newspaper columns, on a continuum with advice writing will go a long way to demystify the former, to dehierarchize the relationship between the professor/anthologist and the student/reader, and to make literary studies more immediate for students (see Banta).

Bibliography

Banta, Martha. "Why Use Anthologies? Or, One Small Candle Alight in a Naughty World." *American Literature* 65.2 (1993): 330–34.

Bauer, Dale M. "The Politics of Collaboration in *The Whole Family*." *Old Maids to Radical Spinsters: Unmarried Women in the Twentieth-Century Novel*. Ed. Laura L. Doan. Urbana: University of Illinois Press, 1991. 107–22.

Baym, Nina. *Novels, Readers, and Reviewers: Responses to Fiction in Antebellum America*. Ithaca: Cornell University Press, 1984.

Baym, Nina, et al., eds. *The Norton Anthology of American Literature*. 5th ed. New York: W. W. Norton, 1998.

Bennett, Paula. "'The Descent of the Angel': Interrogating Domestic Ideology in American Women's Poetry, 1858–1890." *American Literary History* 7.4 (1995): 591–610.

——, ed. *Nineteenth-Century American Women Poets: An Anthology*. Malden MA: Blackwell, 1998.

——. *Poets in the Public Sphere: The Emancipatory Project of American Women's Poetry, 1800–1900*. Princeton: Princeton University Press, 2003.

Brodhead, Richard H. *Cultures of Letters: Scenes of Reading and Writing in Nineteenth-Century America*. Chicago: University of Chicago Press, 1993.

Buell, Lawrence. *The Environmental Imagination: Thoreau, Nature Writing, and the Formation of American Culture*. Cambridge: Harvard University Press, 1996.

Camfield, Gregg. *Sentimental Twain: Samuel Clemens in the Maze of Moral Philosophy*. Philadelphia: University of Pennsylvania Press, 1994.

Clark, Suzanne. *Sentimental Modernism: Women Writers and the Revolution of the Word*. Bloomington: Indiana University Press, 1991.

Doherty, Amy. *The Collected Stories of María Cristina Mena*. Houston: Arte Público Press, 1997.

Dublin, Thomas. *Transforming Women's Work: New England Lives in the Industrial Revolution*. Ithaca: Cornell University Press, 1994.

Duyckinck, Evart A., and George L. Duyckinck, eds. *Cyclopaedia of American Literature*. New York: Baker and Godwin, 1856.

Eisler, Benita, ed. *The Lowell Offering: Writings by New England Mill Women (1840–1845)*. New York: W. W. Norton, 1998.

Rev. of *The Female Poets of America*. Ed. Rufus W. Griswold. *Southern Literary Messenger* (February 1849): 126.

Fetterley, Judith, ed. *Clovernook Sketches and Other Stories*. By Alice Cary. New Brunswick: Rutgers University Press, 1987.

———. "Commentary: Nineteenth-Century American Women Writers and the Politics of Recovery." *American Literary History* 6.3 (1994): 600–11.

Fetterley, Judith, and Marjorie Pryse, eds. *American Women Regionalists, 1850–1910*. New York: W. W. Norton, 1992.

Fliegelman, Jay. "Anthologizing the Situation of American Literature." *American Literature* 65.2 (1993): 334–38.

Foner, Philip, ed. *The Factory Girls: A Collection of Writings on Life and Struggles in the New England Factories of the 1840s*. Urbana: University of Illinois Press, 1977.

Golding, Alan C. *From Outlaw to Classic: Canons in American Poetry*. Madison: University of Wisconsin Press, 1995.

Graulich, Melody, ed. *Western Trails: A Collection of Short Stories*. By Mary Hunter Austin. Reno: University of Nevada Press, 1987.

Gray, Janet. *She Wields a Pen: American Women Poets of the Nineteenth Century*. Iowa City: University of Iowa Press, 1997.

Griswold, Rufus W., ed. *The Female Poets of America*. Philadelphia: Carey and Hart, 1849.

Harris, Susan K. *Nineteenth-Century American Women's Fiction: Interpretative Strategies*. New York: Cambridge University Press, 1990.

Huyssen, Andreas. *After the Great Divide: Modernism, Mass Culture, Postmodernism*. Bloomington: Indiana University Press, 1986.

Idol, John, and Melinda Ponder, eds. *Hawthorne and Women: Engendering and Expanding the Hawthorne Tradition*. Amherst: University of Massachusetts Press, 1999.

Johanningsmeier, Charles. "Sarah Orne Jewett and Mary E. Wilkins (Freeman): Two Shrewd Businesswomen in Search of New Markets." *New England Quarterly* 70 (March 1997): 57–82.

Karcher, Carolyn L., ed. *Hope Leslie*. By Catharine Maria Sedgwick. New York: Penguin Books, 1998.

Kelley, Mary, ed. *Hope Leslie*. By Catharine Maria Sedgwick. New Brunswick: Rutgers University Press, 1987.

Kilcup, Karen L. "Bigger Is Not Always Better: Teaching Medium-Length and

Shorter Works in Diverse Genres." *The Heath Anthology of American Literature Newsletter* 21 (2000): 3–6.

———. "The Conversation of 'The Whole Family': Gender, Politics, and Aesthetics in Literary Tradition." *Soft Canons: American Women Writers and Masculine Tradition.* Ed. Karen L. Kilcup. Iowa City: University of Iowa Press, 1999. 1–24.

———. "'Essays of Invention': Transformations of Advice in Nineteenth-Century American Women's Writing." *Nineteenth-Century American Women's Writers: A Critical Reader.* Ed. Karen L. Kilcup. Malden MA: Blackwell, 1998. 184–205.

———. "Introduction: A Working-Class Woman's View of Europe." *From Beacon Hill to the Crystal Palace: The 1850 Travel Diary of a Working-Class Woman.* Ed. Karen L. Kilcup. Iowa City: University of Iowa Press, 2002. 1–49.

Kilcup, Karen L., ed. *Native American Women's Writing, c. 1800–1924: An Anthology.* Malden MA: Blackwell, 2000.

———, ed. *Nineteenth-Century American Women Writers: An Anthology.* Cabridge MA: Blackwell, 1997.

———, ed. *Soft Canons: American Women Writers and Masculine Tradition.* Iowa City: University of Iowa Press, 1999.

Kilcup, Karen L., and Thomas S. Edwards, eds. *Jewett and Her Contemporaries: Reshaping the Canon.* Gainesville: University Press of Florida, 1999.

Lauter, Paul. *Canons and Contexts.* New York: Oxford University Press, 1991.

———. Presentation. "For What It's Worth: The Reappraisal of Antebellum Women's Writing: A Roundtable Discussion." Society for the Study of American Women Writers Conference. San Antonio TX. February 17, 2001.

Lauter, Paul, et al., eds. *The Heath Anthology of American Literature.* 3rd ed. Boston: Houghton Mifflin, 1998.

Levine, Lawrence. *Highbrow/Lowbrow: The Emergence of Cultural Hierarchy in America.* Cambridge: Harvard University Press, 1988.

Martin, Robert K. "North of the Border: Whose Postnationalism?" *American Literature* 65.2 (1993): 358–61.

McKay, Nelly. "Guest Column: Naming the Problem That Led to the Question 'Who Shall Teach African American Literature?': Or, Are We Ready to Disband the Wheatley Court?" PMLA 113.3 (1998): 359–69.

Morris, Timothy. *Becoming Canonical in American Poetry.* Urbana: University of Illinois Press, 1995.

Nelson, Cary, ed. *Will Teach for Food: Academic Labor in Crisis*. Minneapolis: University of Minnesota Press, 1997.

Powell, Timothy B., ed. *Beyond the Binary: Reconstructing Cultural Identity in a Multicultural Context*. New Brunswick: Rutgers University Press, 1999.

Renza, Louis A. *"A White Heron" and the Question of Minor Literature*. Madison: University of Wisconsin Press, 1984.

Reynolds, David S. *Beneath the American Renaissance: The Subversive Imagination in the Age of Emerson and Melville*. New York: Knopf, 1988.

Schriber, Mary Suzanne, ed. *Telling Travels: Selected Writings by Nineteenth-Century American Women Abroad*. DeKalb: Northern Illinois University Press, 1995.

Shumway, David R. "The Star System in Literary Studies." *PMLA* 112.1 (1997): 85–100.

Smith, Barbara Herrnstein. *Contingencies of Value: Alternative Perspectives for Critical Theory*. Cambridge: Harvard University Press, 1988.

Sosnoski, James, and Eve Wiederhold. "Querulous Inquiries." *symplokē* 7.1–2 (1999): 64–84.

Stedman, E. C., ed. *An American Anthology*. New York: Houghton, 1900.

Tompkins, Jane. *Sensational Designs: The Cultural Work of American Fiction, 1790–1860*. New York: Oxford University Press, 1985.

Walker, Nancy A., and Zita Dresner, eds. *Redressing the Balance: American Women's Literary Humor from Colonial Times to the 1980s*. Jackson: University Press of Mississippi, 1988.

Warren, Joyce W. *Fanny Fern: An Independent Woman*. New Brunswick: Rutgers University Press, 1992.

Warren, Joyce W., and Margaret Dickie, eds. *Challenging Boundaries: Gender and Periodization*. Athens: University of Georgia Press, 2000.

Warren, Kenneth. "The Problem of Anthologies; Or, Making the Dead Wince." *American Literature* 65.2 (1993): 338–42.

Wonham, Henry A. *Criticism and the Color Line: Desegregating American Literary Studies*. New Brunswick: Rutgers University Press, 1996.

Wu, Duncan. "Editing Student Anthologies: The Burning Question." *Romanticism on the Net* 7 (August 1997). Available at http://users.ox.ac.uk/~scat0385/dwu.html.

Zitkala-Ša [Gertrude Bonnin], et al. *Oklahoma's Poor Rich Indians*. Philadelphia: Office of the Indian Rights Association, 1924.

PART TWO

Innovations and Challenges

ROBERT L. MCLAUGHLIN

Anthologizing Contemporary Literature

In his essay for a volume called *Why I Write* David Foster Wallace extends a Don DeLillo metaphor comparing a book in progress to a "hideously damaged infant" who constantly demands the writer's attention and love. Wallace writes:

> And so you love the damaged infant and pity it and care for it; but also you hate it – *hate it* – because it's deformed, repellent, because something grotesque has happened to it in the parturition from head to page; hate it because its deformity is *your* deformity (since if you were a better fiction writer your infant would of course look like one of those babies in catalog ads for infant wear, perfect and pink and cerebro-spinally continent) and its every hideous incontinent breath is a devastating indictment of *you*, on all levels . . . and so you want it dead, even as you dote on it and wipe it and dandle it and sometimes even apply CPR when it seems like its own grotesqueness has blocked its breath and it might die altogether. (141)

Now I certainly don't mean to compare my experiences editing *Innovations: An Anthology of Modern and Contemporary Fiction* to Wallace's writing *Infinite Jest*, but I do think Wallace articulates wonderfully the conflicting feelings any writer (or editor) can have, feelings about the distance between conception and actualization, about the combination of self-critical awareness of the piece's flaws and the desire that others will love it, about the pride in one's accomplishment subverted by the knowledge of how much of the accomplishment was really out of one's control. Looking back over the course of events that led to the publication of *Innovations*, I can identify the ways that various considerations – aesthetic; cultural; pedagogical; and, unfortunately but inescapably, practical – worked together and/or at cross-purposes in influencing the anthology I ended up with.

The journey began in the summer of 1994 when I gave John O'Brien, the executive director of Dalkey Archive Press – a nonprofit literary publisher located on the campus of Illinois State University in Normal, Illinois – a proposal for "The Dalkey Archive Press Anthology of Contemporary American Literature." I intended to organize this much as I organize my undergraduate course in contemporary American literature. A substantial first section was to contain pieces illustrative of some of the fundamental characteristics of postmodernism: antireferentiality, self-reflexivity, intertextuality, indeterminacy, deconstruction of defining binary oppositions, conflation of subject and object, the death of the author, and so on. The second and third sections – at the time I saw a clear distinction between them, though I don't see it now – were to contain pieces illustrative of contemporary fiction's attempts to work within the theoretical implications of postmodernism to discover ways to talk about the world and to have some sort of social impact. John rejected my proposal for two reasons: first, while he wanted to publish an anthology, he didn't want to limit it to texts written in the United States after the Second World War; second, and more significantly, he disagreed with the argument of my proposed introductory material, that postmodern aesthetics is the product of specific sociohistorical events, trends, and ideas in the postwar world.

This latter point led to a counterproposal. John and then–editor in chief Steven Moore had for some time been wrestling with the problem of an anthology that would make a case for the historical primacy of the kind of formally and stylistically innovative fiction to which Dalkey Archive Press is dedicated. This anthology would argue and demonstrate that the confinement of prose fiction within the conventions of realism, as effected by F. R. Leavis, Ian Watt, and the editors of the New York Times Book Review, among others, greatly distorts literary history. In fact, the texts that account for what we call literary realism cover a fairly small historical period and are an aberration from the mainstream of literature. This mainstream, from The Arabian Nights to Empire of the Senseless, is of prose fiction playfully aware of its limitations in trying to represent an unrepresentable world; of the free play of language; of the text's place in an infinitely complex intertext; of the liberatory possibilities of exploding form; and, most important, of how all of these practices combine to re-create the human consciousness's experience of the world more successfully – if never completely successfully – than any simplistic attempt to hold a mirror up to nature. John compared literary realism to a small creek: to people who have never seen anything but that creek, it is a river. When they see a real river, the Mississippi, for example, they don't know what to make of it. (The *New York Times* would no doubt say, "It's not for everyone.") John's challenge to me was to produce an anthology that would open readers' eyes and let them see the Mississippi that is the innovative tradition of prose fiction. Through the many changes we made in the anthology over the next four years, the demonstration of this aesthetic principle remained its raison d'être.

I began developing a table of contents for this anthology, for which I had the working title "The (Other) Great Tradition." To help develop ideas (and to cultivate a potential audience of readers, many of whom would be in a position to adopt the anthology for classes), we ran a call for suggestions in Dalkey Archive Press's spring 1995 catalog. Assuming that most of the people who receive the catalog would be familiar with Dalkey Archive's aesthetic mission, I laid out the idea behind the anthology and asked for suggestions for texts that could be included and for the kinds of courses for which the text would be appropriate. I received around thirty responses, most of them enthusiastic about the project, some of them offering useful suggestions, most of them confirming possibilities we had developed within the office. There was one less than enthusiastic response, however, sent directly to my department chair, asking that I be given tenure immediately so as to spare the world my book. Well, we wanted to rattle cages.

By late spring 1995 I had established the following table of contents:

Apuleius, "The Story of Aristomenes," from *The Golden Ass*
Petronius, "Eumolpus," from *Satyricon*
Unknown, "The Story of King Shahrayar and Shahrazad, His Vizier's Daughter," from *The Arabian Nights*

Murasaki Shikibu, "A Picture Contest," from *The Tale of Genji*
Giovanni Boccaccio, from *The Decameron*
Rabelais, "The Birth and Early Upbringing of Gargantua," from *Gargantua and Pantagruel*
Margaret of Navarre, from *The Heptameron*
Miguel de Cervantes, "The First Sally," from *Don Quixote*
Margaret Cavendish, *Assaulted and Pursued Chastity*
Henry Fielding, book 5, chapter 1, from *Tom Jones*
Laurence Sterne, book 1, chapters 1–12, from *Tristram Shandy*
Denis Diderot, from *Jacques the Fatalist and His Master*
Thomas Carlyle, "Editorial Difficulties" and "Characteristics," from *Sartor Resartus*
Lewis Carroll, "Humpty Dumpty," from *Through the Looking-Glass and What Alice Found There*
Charlotte Perkins Gilman, "The Yellow Wall-Paper"
William Carlos Williams, from *The Great American Novel*
Gertrude Stein, *A Little Novel*
Djuna Barnes, "Prologue," "January," and "March," from *Ladies Almanack*
Felipe Alfau, "A Character," from *Locos: A Comedy of Gestures*
Stevie Smith, from *Novel on Yellow Paper*
James Joyce, from *Finnegans Wake*
Ralph Ellison, "Prologue," from *Invisible Man*
Jorge Luis Borges, "Pierre Menard, Author of the Quixote," from *Ficciones*
Flann O'Brien, chapters 13 and 18, from *The Dalkey Archive*
Donald Barthelme, "The Balloon," from *Sixty Stories*
John Barth, "Menelaiad," from *Lost in the Funhouse*
Nicholas Mosley, from *Impossible Object*
Gert Jonke, "The New Law," from *Geometric Regional Novel*
Joyce Carol Oates, "How I Contemplated the World from the Detroit House of Correction and Began My Life over Again," from *The Wheel of Love and Other Stories*
Gilbert Sorrentino, "Lady the Brach," from *Imaginative Qualities of Actual Things*
Ishmael Reed, from *Mumbo Jumbo*

Thomas Pynchon, "The Story of Byron the Bulb," from *Gravity's Rainbow*
B. S. Johnson, "Everyone Knows Somebody Who's Dead"
Grace Paley, "A Conversation with My Father," from *The Collected Stories*
Alf MacLochlainn, "Awake for Morning Looking through the Alice Glass," from *Out of Focus*
Angela Carter, "The Fall River Axe Murders," from *Saints and Strangers*
Salman Rushdie, "The Perforated Sheet," from *Midnight's Children*
Kathy Acker, "The First Part of Don Quixote: The Beginning of Night," from *Don Quixote*
Robert Coover, "You Must Remember This," from *A Night at the Movies*
John Edgar Wideman, "Surfiction," from *The Stories of John Edgar Wideman*
William Gaddis, "Szyrk v. Village of Tatamount et al., U.S. District Court, Southern District of Virginia No. 105–87," from *A Frolic of His Own*

Pretty ambitious, huh? In the process of putting this together I learned that my guiding aesthetic principle would necessarily be tempered, and frequently compromised, by other considerations. To complicate matters further, these considerations, each in itself valuable, frequently did not work together: from one point of view – for example, the aesthetic – a particular selection might seem fine; from another point of view – say, pedagogical – the same selection would offer problems.

Thus I found, as I tried to fine-tune the table of contents, virtues and curses – often in the same piece. For example, I had included a chapter from *Tom Jones*, one of the chapters opening each book of the novel, in which Fielding's narrator violates the suspension of disbelief and talks about his characters as characters and his book as a book; I wanted to make the point that Fielding, often cast into the mainstream of literary realism, was in fact self-consciously self-referential. This worked perfectly with the anthology's aesthetic goal, but it offered problems with pedagogy. Would this piece stand alone for a student reader – or, for that matter, any reader? Would the point I wanted to make by including this chapter be clear to anyone who had not already read all of *Tom Jones*?

And if one had already read *Tom Jones*, would one really need to have this chapter in the anthology? I had similar concerns about the selections from Diderot and Carlyle: they belonged in the anthology's aesthetic argument, but taken out of context, would they mean anything to a reader or have any use in the classroom? The problems arising from using selections taken from longer works would recur.

Similarly, thinking of possible classroom use, I included several pieces with intertextual connections. Thus instructors could make connections and point out important differences among Cervantes's *Don Quixote*, Borges's story, and Acker's *Don Quixote*. I wanted to include the same story as treated by Boccaccio and Margaret of Navarre; I was even thinking of bringing in *The Canterbury Tales* to show a third treatment. I thought instructors would have fun following the stylistic chaos of *Finnegans Wake* with O'Brien's presentation of a mysteriously surviving James Joyce who has abrogated experimental fiction. The problems with this strategy were twofold. Once again I wondered how successfully sections of longer texts taken out of the larger context of the whole work, especially the Acker and O'Brien, could be read or used in the classroom. Even more important, beyond demonstrating intertextuality, some of these pieces did little else to participate in the anthology's aesthetic; the Boccaccio and Margaret of Navarre read like rather conventional stories. And even in the cases of Acker and O'Brien there were better selections in others of their works that more aptly fit the aesthetic argument. I wondered to what extent the aesthetic argument was being compromised in order to offer the intertextuality, a useful pedagogical tool.

My most serious area of concern in these conflicting approaches to the selections was culture, especially cultural representation. I articulated these concerns on four levels. First, the anthology's argument was conceived in grand – perhaps grandiose – terms: to demonstrate a literary tradition spanning all recorded history and all the habitable continents. Clearly, the table of contents I proposed made only a few gestures to literature outside of Britain and the United States, and about half of it was made up of texts from the twentieth century. For the anthology's argument to mean anything, it would have to be much more inclusive than it was at this point. Second, the implications of separating the aesthetic from a text's sociohistorical moment came home here. How much was I distorting the texts by Murasaki and Rushdie, for example, by viewing them and asking the reader to view them through an admittedly Eurocentric aesthetic lens? In which other less obvious cases was I distorting texts by treating them aesthetically to the exclusion of their cultural contexts?

The third level on which I suffered a dilemma involved cultural representation. Like almost all the profession by now, I believe in the importance of showing students that there is a world of literature by authors other than heterosexual white men. In my proposed table of contents eleven of the forty-one pieces are by women, only three by blacks, only one by a Latin American, and none by other groups one might want to see represented. This, combined with the Eurocentric focus of the selections, made me fear that the anthology would be less multiculturally inclusive than I thought it ought to be. But simultaneously, I had to contend with another, contradictory fear: I had to admit that I had included some pieces *because* they offered cultural representation, even though it took quite a stretching of the aesthetic lens to see them working in the anthology's project. This is clearly true of the Paley story and the piece from the Smith novel, at least in its excerpted form. Cavendish's *Assaulted and Pursued Chastity* offers some interesting gender transgressions (at seemingly arbitrary points the narrator will switch from male to female pronouns and back again in referring to the novel's hero[ine]), but otherwise it is a conventional romance, and a very long one at that. I didn't want to purchase cultural inclusivity at the price of subverting the anthology's aesthetic claims.[1] This too would be a recurring challenge.

My fourth level of cultural discomfort came from the canonlike nature of the anthology's argument and contents. I recognized the valuable pedagogical work done, mostly in the 1970s and 1980s, critiquing the notion of the literary canon. I was concerned that even in offering an alternative to Leavis's great tradition, I was invoking an amorphous historico-aesthetic authority as the basis for the tradition (*tradition*, unfortunately, in T. S. Eliot's sense) the anthology sought to celebrate.

Indeed, this seemed to bring together many of the problems I've discussed above: although the subject of my anthology was innovation, I was building it with a very traditional – to be frank, outdated – theory of anthology making. In wrestling with problems of inclusion and exclusion and aesthetics and culture, I was also wrestling with Eliot's legacy and the recent theoretical response to it. I suspect that to one degree or another all anthology editors do.

On top of all of these considerations, at this point ugly practical concerns entered the picture. Although it was clear that for the anthology to fulfill its purpose I would need to add more pieces, the page count was already prohibitively high: I would also have to cut pieces. I also had to begin exploring which of these pieces were in the public domain and for which I would need to acquire permissions from the rights holders and how much permissions would cost. I had a limited budget for permissions fees. Over the next several months I met frequently with John O'Brien to talk about these problems as well as to tinker with the table of contents. During these meetings it became clear to both of us that the anthology was too ambitious and too unwieldy ever to work. I summed up my frustration one day when I told John that I couldn't imagine a course for which I would adopt the book. He thought for a minute and said neither could he. And that was the end of "The (Other) Great Tradition."

The next part of the story begins a few months after that, when John, still wanting to publish an anthology, suggested we try a more modest book: we would agree on ten pieces that we both liked; all ten would be examples of innovative prose fiction, but each, even if part of a longer text, would be readable on its own. I would write an introduction that would make the case for the tradition of literary innovation, and we would include a suggested list of further reading to make up for all the things we couldn't include in this volume. I added one condition: that we limit the pieces to fiction written by twentieth-century U.S. authors. Although this meant we would lose some great pieces (I especially regretted not being able to use a Borges story or Angela Carter's wonderful "The Fall River Axe Murders"), it seemed to me that the more we limited the parameters of the anthology, the less we would be guilty of leaving out. On a practical note this also gave us a clear marketing target: American literature courses. Thus was born *Innovations*.

This revised and simplified approach solved some, though not all, of my problems. After I had exchanged a number of memos with John, we settled on fifteen pieces instead of ten; for reasons I'll discuss below these were reduced to the following twelve:

Felipe Alfau, "A Character"
Djuna Barnes, "Ladies Almanack: July"
John Barth, "Menelaiad"
Donald Barthelme, "The Balloon"
Robert Coover, "You Must Remember This"
William Gaddis, "Szyrk v. Village of Tatamount et al., U.S. District Court, Southern District of Virginia No. 105-87"
Cris Mazza, "Is It Sexual Harassment Yet?" from *Is It Sexual Harassment Yet?*
Gilbert Sorrentino, "Lady the Brach"
Gertrude Stein, *A Little Novel*
David Foster Wallace, "Little Expressionless Animals," from *Girl with Curious Hair*
Curtis White, "Bonanza," from *Memories of My Father Watching TV*
John Edgar Wideman, "Surfiction"

Some of these pieces carry over from "The (Other) Great Tradition"; the new pieces here – the Mazza, Wallace, and White – came from my decision to eliminate pieces that were not autonomous and include more short stories. The resulting volume is thus, in my opinion, despite the many wonderful pieces that have been lost, more readable and more useful pedagogically. I've received complaints that the Barnes chapter – a highly stylized disquisition on rhetoric and sexual identity – does not make sense standing alone, but my experience in teaching *Ladies Almanack* makes me confident that it doesn't make sense any more easily in the context of the entire novel.

The change in focus from the entire history of world literature to formally and stylistically innovative pieces I like from a single country and century was in most ways liberating. I no longer had concerns about coverage: since the selections were no longer trying to demonstrate an argument, there were no holes to fill. I wasn't even claiming to be covering twentieth-century American innovative fiction comprehensively. Moreover, since the focus was now restricted to U.S. fiction of the last three-quarters of the twentieth century, I was no longer worried about applying an inappropriate interpretive lens to a text from another culture and thus misrepresenting it. I emphasized my decision to divorce the pieces from a version of literary and social history by arranging them in alphabetical order by the author's last name, not the chronological order I had used in "The (Other) Great Tradition."

The failure of these decisions, for me, is that as a scholar I believe the aesthetics of high Modernism and postmodernism are in many ways tied to the sociocultural atmosphere of the century. My selection criteria and organization scheme – if not actually denying this – certainly do not recognize it, and while my introduction gestures toward the social influences on and the social impact of innovative fiction, it foregrounds aesthetics qua aesthetics. Granting this failure, I maintain the value of the anthology as it stands in that it argues explicitly and, I hope, persuasively against the unexamined assumptions of many readers – especially students – that the tenets of realism define what literature is supposed to be. This in itself is socially valuable: theorists from Elaine Showalter to Catherine Belsey have indicted realist fiction for its role in transmitting and reproducing the ideological status quo; in this sense innovative fiction is both aesthetically and socially transgressive.[2] Considering all this, I shouldn't have been surprised to learn that *Innovations* is most frequently adopted for creative writing courses; instructors apparently want to show burgeoning fiction writers that forms and styles beyond realism are possible and are to be desired.

One problem that the change of focus in the anthology didn't solve was cultural representation. There are still fewer pieces by women and authors of color than I think an anthology like this ought to have. There are two reasons for this. First, a lesson I learned from the collapse of "The (Other) Great Tradition" is that it's a mistake to compromise one's selection principles to ensure complete representation.

The stakes were even higher with the smaller anthology – with so few pieces to offer I couldn't afford to make the book's purpose obscure. I considered many texts that either only tangentially connected with my aesthetic goal or couldn't quite stand alone. Rather than subvert the point of the anthology, I decided to swallow my disappointment and hope the critical reaction from readers wouldn't be too harsh. The second reason had to do with forces out of my control, as once again practical considerations intruded. Permission had to be obtained for every piece but one (*Ladies Almanack* is in the public domain), and while many of the publishers and agents I worked with were both helpful and sympathetic to a relatively small project from a nonprofit press, a few were not. I lost three pieces from *Innovations*, two by women and one by an African American, over rights issues. In one case, the most understandable, the author won't let the work be anthologized; the frustration here was from how long it took to find this out – the publisher, since it knows permission won't be granted, simply didn't answer my letters. In another case the publisher inexplicably demanded a payment more than twice as large as we paid for any other piece. It was beyond my budget, and the publisher rejected my pleas for mercy; thus I lost one of my favorite stories. In the last case the publisher – a medium-sized commercial publisher – never answered my letters or phone calls, not even after the author in question intervened with them. Had I been able to include these three pieces, I would have been happier with the cultural and gender mix of the anthology. Perhaps I'll be able to rectify the situation should we ever put out a second edition.

In contrast, an aspect of the anthology with which I continue to be pleased – and that was made possible with the transformation to the smaller book – is its streamlined pedagogical apparatus. As a teacher I generally prefer that students engage texts, even difficult texts, with as little mediation as possible. As I write in the anthology's introduction, I think confusion is an important – perhaps a vital – part of learning. It's through being willing to be confused and then working out that confusion that we reach new understanding and new knowledge. Thus when I teach I like my students to avoid material that will predigest the reading for them, and I wanted to avoid such material in *Innovations*.

Because of the broad historic argument of "The (Other) Great Tradition," its use of so many texts from unfamiliar times and places, and its use of so many excerpted pieces, I imagined (and had actually started writing) rather elaborate headnotes, which would outline the author's biography; provide relevant cultural information; and explain, where necessary, the selection's place in the larger text (I was especially looking forward to doing this last for the selection from *Gravity's Rainbow*). The new focus of *Innovations* meant that I needed only to supply some biographical information about each author, which I kept brief and removed to the back of the book so that it would interfere with the reading of the fiction as little as possible. My introduction was concerned with the big-picture argument for the tradition of innovative prose fiction and referred only briefly to the pieces to follow in the anthology. My goal was to supply an aesthetic context in which to read the fiction while preserving the challenge of the fiction's confusion, and I think I succeeded.

Another pedagogical feature of the anthology, "A Highly Eccentric List of 101 Books for Further Reading," caused more intellectual contention than any other aspect of the project. John O'Brien, I think, saw this as a chance to do what the original anthology was to have done – present a canon of the innovative-fiction tradition. I, still smarting from losing my battle with cultural-historical coverage the first time, wanted to treat it much less formally. As the title suggests, it ended up closer to my idea: it restricts itself to the second half of the twentieth century; but it does cover many countries, and if one wanted – for whatever reason – to propose a canon of postmodern fiction, this would be a good place to start.

If, as I argue above, learning comes from confusion, I learned a great deal while editing *Innovations*. I learned, on a practical level, how much more goes into the publication of such an anthology than I would have imagined. I learned how far a theoretical or aesthetic vision would take me before I had to compromise. And I learned some things about myself as a teacher and a scholar from the issues over which I was willing to compromise. In the end, four years after publication, there are aspects of *Innovations* that I still wish I could change, flaws of which, frankly, I'm ashamed. On the other hand, despite these flaws I find myself, in general, proud of the book. I had my wife take pictures of me holding it after we had discovered it in City Lights in San Francisco and the Fifth Avenue Barnes and Noble in New York (distribution coast to coast!). My heart irrationally sinks when I see that it's only the 586,703rd best-selling title on Amazon.com. Wallace's book/infant metaphor seems more and more apt.

In writing this essay I've had something of a change of heart about *Innovations*. Being so close to the project for so long, I had come to think of the book as a satisfactory substitute, but a substitute nevertheless, for the two more ambitious anthologies – the one on postmodern fiction, which never got off the ground, and "The (Other) Great Tradition." But with some distance now, and with the opportunity afforded by this essay to return to the process by which *Innovations* was built, I think the anthology I ended up with solves the problems associated with anthology making better than either of the other two could have. Writing this essay has also gotten me thinking about how a second edition might solve them even better. Perhaps the journey isn't over yet.

Notes

1. This, in my opinion, is the path taken by Norton's *Postmodern American Literature*; it's so concerned with cultural representation that *postmodern* becomes synonymous with *contemporary*, a serious distortion.

2. See, for example, Showalter's classic "Towards a Feminist Poetics" and Belsey's "Constructing the Subject: Deconstructing the Text."

Bibliography

Belsey, Catherine. "Constructing the Subject: Deconstructing the Text." *Feminist Criticism and Social Change: Sex, Class, and Race in Literature and Culture.* Ed. Judith Newton and Deborah Rosenfelt. London: Methuen, 1985. 45–64.

Geyh, Paula, Fred G. Leebron, and Andrew Levy. *Postmodern American Fiction: A Norton Anthology.* New York: W. W. Norton, 1998.

McLaughlin, Robert L. *Innovations: An Anthology of Modern and Contemporary Fiction*. Normal IL: Dalkey Archive Press, 1998.

Showalter, Elaine. "Towards a Feminist Poetics." *Women Writing about Women*. Ed. Mary Jacobus. London: Barnes and Noble, 1980. 25-36.

Wallace, David Foster. "The Nature of the Fun." *Why I Write: Thoughts on the Craft of Fiction*. Ed. Will Blythe. Boston: Little, Brown, 1998. 140-45.

CRIS MAZZA

Finding the Chic in Lit

In 1994 FC2, an independent publisher of alternative fiction, asked me if I would run and judge a book contest for women writers. This would mean receiving possibly hundreds of book manuscripts, screening them, selecting ten finalists, carefully reading all of those books, then selecting a winner (or finding an outside judge who would agree to do the job for little or no payment). FC2's lists had traditionally been male-dominated, so they wanted to discover new women writers who were working in nontraditional forms of fiction. This idealistic goal should've made me anxious to dig in and work for the greater good of womankind. But a book contest was *not* a task I was eager to undertake, for purely selfish reasons, especially with no assistance. So my argument was also idealistic: FC2 could unearth *more* women writers if it instead produced an anthology that could "discover" ten to twelve new authors. Creating the anthology could be considered the "screening" stage – we could then begin soliciting book-length manuscripts from these authors for FC2's regular editorial pool to consider. The director of FC2 agreed, and the project opened. Without any primary goal that the book would compete with a Norton anthology or be an antidote to similar mass-market projects, I barely gave a second thought to promotion or marketing or potential reviewers. "Talent search" really *was* the foremost goal, until the manuscripts started arriving. Then, distracted by hundreds of pages of a vaguely familiar taste or scent of similarity, a second unspoken goal emerged: could this book be different? But what did that mean? No familiar or marquee names? That wouldn't be a problem – it was FC2's trademark. The fiction inside standing as the marquee name? Was that possible? Perhaps fiction not only unique enough to let this anthology stand above the plethora of women's-writing anthologies already on the market but *also* different from the books by men through which FC2 had earned its reputation. Hadn't

I been taught that women's alternative fiction had not followed the exact paths of male trailblazers' formal innovation and self-reflexive metafiction? With the canon of literature being so prominently male, rebellious women writers really had no tradition to rebel against, so their revolt had to have a different tone than the now historic literary insurrection against the traditional canon. This is why – in answer to many male queries – we reserved this postfeminist book for women writers only. How could we showcase the ways women explore alternative forms of fiction without focusing on women doing it? We weren't expanding feminism by saying that now men were invited into the exploration of female expression experience.

"Why don't you do an anthology for men only?" male students asked me.

"You mean there haven't been any yet?" I answered. "How about most of the anthologies since the beginning of time?"

Nuts and Bolts

Our first point of difference came when I decided not to carry the whole responsibility myself (how utterly female of me) – so why not have a male coeditor for a women's anthology? There were no planning sessions; no discussions of our aesthetic, our agenda, our vision; no marketing blueprint; no publicity plans. Again how utterly female: I didn't even confer with the coeditor when I made the flier and set the reading fee at five dollars, ridiculously low in comparison to other projects being advertised at the same time. We only wanted to cover production costs – printing and binding – there was no need for a lump sum for an award winner. And no thought given to the possibility of paying the writers; naturally just being chosen would be reward enough. Shame on us for that. But it didn't keep the submissions away. Roughly four hundred of them were stuffed into my mailbox at the University of Illinois at Chicago.

In 1995 *Chick-Lit: Postfeminist Fiction* was released. Because FC2's initial goals were met – discovering writers and producing a successfully interesting book – *Chick-Lit 2* was quickly launched. After *Chick-Lit 2* was released in 1996, a review ran in the *Washington Post* that, besides trashing the book for not having enough good ol' plot, inaccurately represented the book as being not only full of lesbian sex but also supported by a grant from the NEA, "sure to give Jesse Helms a conniption fit." A family-values watchdog group, one that peruses newspapers looking for precisely this sort of information, brought the book – and the publisher – to the attention of a Congressional subcommittee. A Congressional attack on the NEA ensued, one that saw Jesse Helms waving another "scandalous" NEA-supported FC2 title aloft during a debate.

So with the spark being FC2's simple, and innocently ideal, goal of editing an anthology to discover new women writers, the inferno was the NEA gathering forces and successfully defending itself from the "Contract on America." The Republican forces in Congress have since then lightened their stance on abolishing funding for the arts – mostly on the strength of public outcry over the threatened elimination of NPR, but partially due to the strong support the NEA displayed in withstanding the 1996 Congressional attack.

One morning, five years later, I ran an Internet search, using only the term *Chick-Lit*. Surprisingly (or not), reviewers, authors, and publishing marketing departments alike are using *chick-lit* to define a wave of writing by young women, characterized most readily by the Bridget Jones books – the publishing industry's late 1990s version of the 1980s "Brat Pack," this time all girls. Do any of them give credit to the original *Chick-Lit* or the publisher and editors who first coined the term? Guess again. In fact, a British author of one of these airhead-girl books claimed that the "chick-lit" phenomenon was a British movement that the rest of the world was trying to imitate, similar to the British invasion of rock-and-roll.

I don't know if we helped start a wave – now called the second or third wave of feminism, depending on where you start counting – or if the wave was already building and we happened to put our boat into the water at the right time to ride it high (like Marines on D-Day) all the way to the beach. Most people who get credit for initiating a movement are actually just lucky enough to be doing the right thing at the right time and catch the motion just when it begins to accelerate. But this was a movement, a wave, a tide I honestly had no idea was there, let alone gaining momentum, at the same time I made my funny flier titled "What Is Postfeminist Fiction?" I thought I was being absurd and incongruous.

The evolution of the project – both explained in and exemplified by the introductions to the two books – shows that the endeavor was not an idea that resulted in a book, but actually almost the opposite. The whole experience was (is) a work in progress. What follows are the introductions to the two FC2 Chick-Lit anthologies – slightly revised for this format – which can give more insight into the germination and birth and evolution of ideas that editing these books created, for me and my coeditors and hopefully for readers as well.

Chick-Lit: *Postfeminist Fiction*, Edited by Cris Mazza and Jeffrey DeShell

When the call for manuscripts for (what was then titled) "On the Edge: New Women's Fiction" went out in June 1994, I asked for postfeminist writers working with alternative fiction. I just thought "postfeminist" was a funky word – possibly a controversial one if read *antifeminist* – so I didn't define it. I probably couldn't have if I wanted to. It was almost a joke, an icebreaker. I wanted to see what it would produce. I knew I was looking for something different, something that stretched the boundaries of what has been considered "women's writing," something that might simply be called "*writing*" without defining it by gender and yet at the same time might speak the diversity and depth that women writers *can* produce rather than what they're expected to produce.

I have discovered that outlining what was the different sort of fiction I was seeking was best accomplished by looking afterward at the pieces assembled between the covers. It was actually combining the four hundred manuscripts answering the original call for "postfeminist writing," with the perception of the editors selecting the eventual contents of the book, that produced an answer – at least our answer – to the question on the flier: *what is postfeminist fiction?*

Not antifeminist at all, but also not:

My body, myself
My lover left me and I am so sad
ALL MY PROBLEMS ARE CAUSED BY MEN
... BUT WATCH ME ROAR
Society has given me   an eating disorder
                   poor self-esteem
                   a victim's perpetual fear
... therefore I'm not responsible for my [stupid] actions.

Of our chosen twenty-two writers: I could tell these women were grinning (or sneering) as they wrote. Their fiction took an often irreverent slant on the very issues women *are* concerned about; their styles and forms were at times quirky, droll, jocular, frisky, ironic, but still their fictions carried weight and power. None were comedy, none written for laughs alone, the point not, in self-defense, to turn laughter *at* a woman's concerns into laughter *with* a woman. The trash of life can be funny, especially when, as writers, we're the ones in control. But irreverence is not mere dismissal nor a designation of insignificance. Maybe women are simply no longer afraid to honestly assess and define themselves without having to live up to standards imposed by either a persistent patriarchal world or the old feminist insistence that female characters achieve self-empowerment.

It was only after selecting the contents of *Chick-Lit* that I realized there *is* such a thing as postfeminist writing. It's writing that says women are independent and confident but not lacking their share of human weakness and not necessarily self-empowered; that they are dealing with whom they've made themselves into rather than blaming the rest of the world; that women can use and abuse other human beings as well as anyone; that women can be conflicted about what they want and therefore get nothing; that women can love until they hurt someone, turn their own hurt into love, refuse to love, or even ignore the notion of love completely as they confront the other 90 percent of life. Postfeminist writing says female characters don't have to be superhuman in order to be interesting. Just human.

Chick-Lit 2 (No Chick-Vics), Edited by Cris Mazza, Jeffrey DeShell, and Elisabeth Sheffield

NO VICTIMS, the antitheme

What is a *theme* anthology? Frankly, its theme is a marketing tool. Just saying, "This is a remarkable collection of stories," isn't always enough to sell a book, to either an individual reader or a prospective publisher. On the other hand, say, "Here's a book of great new stories *about* ——," and you've automatically got a hook . . . and, hopefully, a ready-made audience, created out of a preexisting camp. Love gone wrong, change of life, single parenthood, losing a baby, adoption, physical handicaps, attachments to pets, relationships with food or drugs or alcohol, abusive relationships, regional lifestyles, favorite childhood toys. Collections of stories have acquired the necessity of being about something, proving something, illustrating something, exploring something . . . one thing, a SUBJECT.

The theme possibilities could be limitless. However, perhaps with the growth of publicity-via-confessional on talk shows, tabloid news, and other media, a prevailing type of theme anthology is a victim theme, usually a victim-and-recovery theme: sharing the trauma but providing a glimmer of hope, an inspiration, a feel-good reason for grouping together stories about certain types of personal and/or intimate tragedies.

Since FC2 is a publisher of noncommercial fiction, it certainly wouldn't seem apt to do an anthology with a selling hook, especially a popular one, no matter how noble the editorial motivation for choosing the particular victimization as a motif. So an antitheme anthology seemed an obvious choice. However, a true antitheme anthology is not necessarily just one without any theme at all – that unsalable book of great stories – but could also be one that explores those fictions that don't seem to fit the favorite, marketable anthology themes. Thus **NO VICTIMS.** Actually, there's a more seriously contemplated reason for the theme **NO VICTIMS.**

In reading the four hundred submissions to *Chick-Lit* in 1994 we found that stories about women as victims are a popular trend for women writers. Is this trend *bad* or *wrong*? Not at all. Go ahead and continue to attempt to wake the world from its complacent slumber.

From the CHICK-LIT 2 *rejection letter:*

When I proposed the theme **NO VICTIMS** for the second *Chick-Lit* anthology, what I meant was: while we're looking for new or alternative voices in women's fiction, let's also look for story content without a trauma that comes from *outside* the character – unfortunate perpetrations like incest or sexual assault or the disease of addiction, caused not by an individual's choice or motive but by anything from neglectful parents to a patriarchal society to poverty to media to government to money and power all being in the hands of men (oh, I guess that's the same as patriarchal society) – things beyond the character's control that can then be blamed for the aftermath the victim is left to deal with. NO I DIDN'T MEAN "THEY" ASK TO BE RAPED/HARASSED/MOLESTED! Sexual assaults and harassments and injurious poor body images *do* exist and have waged a war on women (the American Medical Association says so too). But for this book I was interested in seeing what action(s) women (characters) can incite *on their own*, whether bad or good, hopeful or dead-end, progressive or destructive. We (the editors) hope that women aren't *only* what society has made them and that there is *some* individual identity to work with.

But . . . sample of the typical cover letter that we received:

Please consider my story for your "No Victims" anthology. Although the sixteen-year-old narrator is a victim of ——, she gains strength and breaks the cycle of abuse.

In victim-fiction a perfectly nice, promising person encounters **IT.** Incest, rape, mugging, sexual harassment, drug/alcohol addiction, sexual discrimination. The now-victim then begins to struggle with the **AFTERMATH.** Eating disorders, more addictions, self-mutilation, low self-esteem, dangerous passivity that allows further harassment or abuse. And that's the story's entire dramatic action.

This editor's defensive sidebar:

In my novel *Your Name Here:* ⎯⎯ a character has unconsensual sex as a partial result of "acting out" blindly – out of retaliation, resentment, and anger, out of wanting revenge for unrequited feelings. I intended for her to be a victim, not simply a victim of male society that rapes its women but of something more subtle (and more dangerous): a victim of whatever causes her to ignore the intellect she's been given, ignore the education she has, ignore the fact that she has a job she's good at, and be guided *only* by wanting a man to think of her as attractive, desirable, a potential sex partner. A goal more important than career or accomplishment. A goal that supersedes all other noble pursuits. And few women even realize they're doing it. No one forces women to do this. Perhaps that "evil" "society" encourages it, implants it, but if we're, by now, smart enough to recognize it, aren't we also smart enough to resist it? If not – THAT'S scary.

I suspect the troubled industry is subtly driving writers to use what has already proven to be moving material. If so, how about, just for this book if you want, instead of a fiction's drama beginning and developing because of something that happens – randomly, through fate or a fucked-up society – *to* someone, therefore creating an "inner conflict" that will then "develop," how about fiction by and about women where the movement or tension stems *primarily* from who a character is and what she wants? So OK, sometimes she'll still end up a victim, but the story itself isn't based on a thunderbolt from the blue targeting an innocent someone and determining the course of their future emotional duress or social difficulties or personal obstacles.

And yet you'll find some of the classic trappings of victimhood here – self-mutilation, S and M pornography, nonmutual sexual experiences – but there's a difference. These aren't stories about the traumas of, aftermath of, and recovering from victimhood. In fact, *certain writers don't seem to consider victimizing situations as victimizing, and the victims don't regard themselves as victims at all!*

Could this be a symptom of postfeminist writing?

From the original call-for-manuscripts for CHICK-LIT *in 1994:*

What Is Postfeminist Writing? If you have no answer or don't even know what the question means . . . *good*, perhaps *you're* a postfeminist writer. Just another absurd label, but it – like *all* labels – represents contemporary criticism's ongoing quest to locate, define, and thereby understand writers who, for reasons as individual as they are, haven't been embraced or appreciated.

When the first "On The Edge: New Women's Fiction Anthology" was released in October 1995, my icebreaker, aren't-I-funny-as-shit identification tag in the call for manuscripts had become the subtitle:

Chick-Lit: Postfeminist Fiction

All of a sudden I was *responsible* for something, expected to define and defend it, wear the plaque, lead the garrison. Trying to remain undaunted, I offered a complimentary copy to a senior faculty member in English and women's studies. "Postfeminist, huh? What's that? Hope you're not implying all the issues have been solved or are obsolete."

My abashed response:

No.

But then someone else said it better . . .

One generation of women wrote "Shit Happens." The next says, "Yeah, it still does, but I've stuck my fingers in it." *2 girls review*

Introduction by Cris Mazza for the *Chick-Lit Reading*, October 30, 1996, Guild Complex, Chicago

Before I get labeled godmother or umbrella or womb of any new movement, I'll have to reiterate the funky beginnings of this project.

FC2 wanted to publish more alternative fiction by women. A book contest only eventually showcases the work of one woman. A more efficient talent hunt would be an anthology.

First step: choosing a coeditor. I invited novelist Jeffrey DeShell. And at first I admit to the cowardice of using Jeffrey's first-name initial (J. DeShell) to hide his gender from the hoards of hungry-to-be-published women we expected to stampede our call for manuscripts. Instead this encouraged a few men to attempt to hide their gender on submissions by using the first-initial-only. Unfortunately, they didn't cross their name out sufficiently enough on their reading-fee checks, and their male names were clearly discernible.

Would a traditional call for manuscripts set the tone for a nontraditional anthology? All we knew was that we wanted "alternative" fiction by women. Alternative from what? We meant, of course, simply noncommercial or nontraditional narrative. (Can you be nontraditional without being noncommercial? Can narrative be noncommercial without being nontraditional?) Passing by a bulletin board on one of the floors of University Hall at UIC, I saw some kind of conference or symposium and noticed the word "postfeminist." Eye-catchy, funny, weird – I usurped the word (without dragging along whatever definition it already carried), stuck it on a flier, and waited to see what would stick to the flypaper. (Later, on another flier posted somewhere, I actually saw the word "postwomanist" and wondered if I should've used that one. And my friend Mark Amerika wondered if I'd like to do an anthology for male transsexuals and call it postmasculine fiction.)

Ha ha, it was a grand joke, and Jeffrey and I shared several evenings of intense discussion (i.e., irreverent chatter) about our project, along with Elisabeth Sheffield, whose story "Sugar Smacks" was the first selection for Chick-Lit. During these bull ... ahem, cow ... sessions Jeffrey suggested we call the book Clit-Lit. I agreed! He reconsidered. We compromised on Chick-Lit. To my surprise, when the book was published the cover said Chick-Lit: Postfeminist Fiction. Jeffrey's joke and mine had come together and now had a responsibility: to *mean* something.

Believe it or not, it *did* mean something. And to tell you the truth, I'm still learning what that meaning is.

Midway through our selection process for Chick-Lit, we discovered a pattern: the stories we chose were more often than not irreverent, sassy, in-your-face adventures of women characters with no hint of dealing with the oppression and liability of "growing up female in America" (Erica Jong – second-generation feminist). At that point, before Chick-Lit saw its first reviewer, I chose the theme for Chick-Lit 2: No Victims. This wasn't a different theme than Postfeminist Fiction; it was an *extension*. It was a phase in my growing understanding of just exactly what it was I was doing.

What did I mean? Simply put, no divorce, incest, rape, sexual harassment, general sexism, man-hating, mother-bashing, woe-is-me-I'm-a-victim-of-an-unfair-world fiction. (These things could be in a story without the story being *about* them.) You might still see traces of victims-of-an-unfair-world in Chick-Lit 2, but there is always a difference, an attitude, a quest not just to overcome victimhood but to probe completely different areas of experience: say, accidental auto theft, a profound and complex relationship with a horse, or how a couple can become a single organism – embodied in fiction by a pair of scissors.

Well, Chick-Lit 2 has now joined Chick-Lit in the real world. And suddenly, literary and arts publications are saying things like "The Perils of Postfeminism." A subtitle in the *New Yorker* (reviewing a new columnist in the *New York Times*) used the complete buzz-phrase: *Postfeminist Chick-Lit* (gee, I wonder where they got that funky terminology). Electronic literary and cultural sites on the Internet are featuring special issues like *ebr*'s "Writing (Post) Feminist" and a "news" site called the Postfeminist Playground. Graduate students are saying to me, "My book is feminist, but I'm afraid it's not *postfeminist*."

What?

And the reactions, the inevitable reactions, are the most mystifying development of all. Part of the introduction on the Postfeminist Playground said they were just wondering what comes after feminism has made its mark on our world. Respondents see only that the word *feminism* has been toyed with, has been altered and changed! They read *prefeminist* or *retrofeminist*. They see the word *postfeminist* and think they see

get ye back to the kitchen, wench.

Wait a minute. Can't you hear (or *read*)? What these postfeminist women are saying is that we're complicated organisms. We're smart and funny and talented and bold and mischievous and careless and selfish and rude and fun and dark and horny and nervous and creative and energetic and ambitious and sometimes mean and occasionally downright stupid. In other words, we're *more* than oppressed victims. We can *start* things instead of just react. We have so many significant things to say that have nothing to do with how

I wasn't allowed to have a paper route

or

MY BOSS TOUCHED MY BUTT

or

My man left me when I no longer looked twenty-one.

Here's the serious thing. On the whole, the media, the publishing industry, and culture in general only give women's experiences attention when they *are* victims' experiences: incest, abandonment, sexual assault, date rape, the glass ceiling, sexual harassment, the oppression of female stereotypes, breast cancer, drug abuse, alcoholism, brothers who get sent away to expensive universities while sister goes to junior college. Yeah, these things all happen. Yeah, let's continue to try to wipe them out. But no, let's not let the media insinuate *these* experiences are the only ones women have or can imagine!

Now I know what I meant with the No Victims theme. Now I know why I wanted to keep victims out of this precious little piece of literary territory. To give the rest of us some credit and attention too. In 1991 my second book, Is It Sexual Harassment Yet?, came out six months *before* the Clarence Thomas hearings – the title story's desired effect was to warp and confuse people's standard gut reactions to this murky territory of fucked-up gender relations. The *Wall Street Journal* was one of the places that gave it a feature review – calling it anarchistic and subversive – so a radio program called me to be a guest, asking me to deliver a copy of the book so the host could prepare. A week later I was politely informed my presence was no longer desired on the show because the book was fiction and I wasn't an *actual* victim of sexual harassment.

Well girls, here's the thing: our significance has become measured in how many times, and how hideously, we've been a victim. There have been studies to survey media attention given to women. The percentage of front-page newspaper stories that are about women: ——— (RIDICULOUSLY LOW PERCENTAGE NUMBER GOES HERE). Then the percentage of *those* stories that *are* about women but *only* because a woman was the victim of a crime: ——— (RIDICULOUSLY HIGH PERCENTAGE NUMBER GOES HERE). If the media and publishing industry only seek or will only give attention to women when they are victimized, if media only includes or highlights women's experiences as victims, then that becomes our only status. *It's starting to seem like our only importance to society is that our experiences as victims exemplify how fucked-up society is.* Period. The end. Even though part of that statement is basically true, I'd like to put forth: it's *not* our *only* importance to society.

As I see it, postfeminism is the logical *next* stage of feminism: time to look closely at ourselves; to admit our weaknesses as well as celebrate strengths; to *honestly* assess what we've *helped* make ourselves into, rather than only blaming the patriarchal world; to see how far we've come (or haven't come) since we've been aware of the feminist goals of the last three decades; and to explore *all* the other facets and types of experiences besides our oppression. Time to stop saying, "Give me a voice because I've been a victim," and instead say, "Listen to me, dammit, because I have something important and interesting and new to say!"

In some small way I helped allow forty women to say it.

Postscript, December 2000

One doesn't have to study a culture to be a product of it. Artists and writers shouldn't have to be students of the theory of an era before writing or creating material influenced by and emblematic of the era. The culture or movement or era is, in fact, defined by the literature and art that come organically out of its influence. So did I understand or appreciate what I was embarking upon? I didn't even understand the questions. When the editor of this volume – proving that good editors have some considered and carefully conceived agenda for what they want to accomplish *before* beginning to gather pieces and making a book – asked me, "Is postfeminist writing part of the third wave of women's studies/feminism? (Second wave being body politics.) What is the third wave of feminism, and what is/should be its relationship to women's writing?" my answer was basically, "Huh?"

Here's what I know: at a time when FC2 thought the NEA would never again risk including FC2 among the independent publishers who receive grant money, the director of FC2 – examining a sales report – muttered, "Thank god for *Chick-Lit*." A nationally known reviewer in a natural venue said not only, "Whatever happened to *plot*? Can't we read a *story* every once in a while?" but also, "Not many straight women here either" (it's the *either* I find astonishing, and transparent). To help explain what the reviewer understood after reading the book, another newspaper set up a chart showing "the evolution of a genre," with columns marked **prefeminism, feminism,** and **postfeminism** – when *white rice* appears under *prefeminism*, the other two columns have *brown rice*, then *sushi*. Eventually *Chick-Lit: Postfeminist Fiction* went into a second printing, as did, on its coattails, my own *Is It Sexual Harassment Yet?* And so far four of the *Chick-Lit* contributors have had books come out with FC2.

The significance of the *Chick-Lit* anthologies can be seen not only in the appropriation of the title, turning it into a literary buzzword, but in the way the books are used as texts in postmodern literature classes – sometimes representing the only postmodern writing by women in the course syllabi. Subtle significance can also be seen by doing the market research I should've at least contemplated before rushing headlong into the project: comparing these anthologies, their goals and agenda and intended readership, to other "similar" anthologies. *The Norton Anthology of Postmodern American Fiction* originally bought the rights to a story from *Chick-Lit: Postfeminist Fiction* but in the end didn't include the story in the volume, possibly to make room for more marquee names. But the reason given to FC2 was that the editors had decided their definition of postmodern fiction was stories that included or were about pop culture. Other anthologies of postmodern fiction have no living women writers included, or else assume all alternative women's writing is in the same vein as Kathy Acker, and certainly ignore the issue of two genders having different objects of and approaches to rebellion. In fact, the Chick-Lit anthologies had more to rebel against than we realized – not only (simply put) the way standard feminism wanted women to write and culture's designation that women are only significant in their victimhood but the notion that all writers would naturally rebel against the same traditions. And probably the editors not realizing all this was what allowed the books the abandon to accomplish what they did.

CARY NELSON

The Economic Challenges to Anthologies

One

It was in the spring of 1999 that I learned the British edition of my forthcoming *Anthology of Modern American Poetry* would have to be canceled. My publisher, Oxford University Press, had come to the conclusion they could never sell enough copies of the book to recoup the huge investment they were facing in reprint fees. They had hoped to make a profit on the project, not immediately, to be sure, but after a year or two. Now it looked as if the amounts they were being charged to reprint the poems we were including would throw the book permanently in the red. No small irony there, given the number of left-wing poets I had selected; politically and philosophically in the red, the book was now financially in the red as well. Capitalism was to get the final word in blocking the dissemination, at least on the continent and around the world, of some of America's fierce but forgotten political poets.

The publishing industry is a perfect example of the Marxist argument that base and superstructure are not only entangled and interdependent but also contingent and mutually determining. Yet many readers – Marxist and non-Marxist alike – assume a great deal more independence for the cultural realm than is warranted, especially where intellectual production is at stake. It is becoming increasingly clear that not only large expensive books like this one – an anthology with a total budget (including staff salaries) of over $200,000 – but also modest scholarly books with direct production costs of only $5,000 are dependent on specific markets and thus clear financial conditions of possibility. I want to review the intellectual and financial history of this book to give a detailed example of what I mean.

The largest single cost by far for an anthology reprinting previously published poems is permissions fees. Once I had established whether a poem was still in copyright, it was Oxford's job to track down the copyright holder and request the right to reprint the relevant work. Despite working very efficiently, it took my permissions editor six months to do the job. Sometimes it required several letters just to identify and track down the copyright holder. Then a significant number of publishers did not answer until multiple letters, faxes, and phone calls had been tried. In one case – Holt, Robert Frost's publisher – we received no reply despite five months of trying. So I asked Oxford to send an express mail letter saying we would reprint the poems (and give a fee of $50 per poem) unless we heard otherwise within forty-eight hours. That got a response.

This was merely one of a number of cases where we had to invent some unique way to handle an individual problem. Often Oxford and I had to play good cop/bad cop or the reverse. Only I, for example, could write a letter threatening to drop an author from the book unless a fee was lowered. It also fell to me to set recommended fee-reduction levels for the smaller presses and individual agents, since Oxford had more experience with the larger houses. When tensions rose with a given correspondent, we would routinely switch roles and start again.

Some publishers, like Random House, will set a fee per line of poetry that runs through their whole list of poets. Other publishers, like New Directions, have different fee structures for different authors and poems. Thus a short, famous, frequently reprinted poem may cost more to reprint than a longer little-known poem. We paid more to reprint a six-page excerpt from William Carlos Williams's "Asphodel, That Greeny Flower" (1955) than we did to reprint the entire twenty pages of his *The Descent of Winter* (1928). Farrar Straus charged more per line to reprint Randall Jarrell's universally anthologized "The Death of the Ball Turret Gunner" (1945) than for any other poem.

Despite the bad news about the consequences of high reprint fees for the British edition of *Anthology of Modern American Poetry*, the American edition was not threatened because the estimated market was much larger. But there too we steadily increased the permissions budget. It had started in five figures and was now in six. Tough bargaining by both Oxford and me was necessary to hold to even this substantially increased sum. We wrote the usual letters requesting reductions, letters every publisher's permissions department expects to receive, and most large publishers sent back the anticipated 15 to 20 percent cuts in their requested fees.

In some cases, however, when the requested fees were especially high, we had to be more aggressive. One literary agent, notorious for charging high fees and for refusing to reduce them, happened to be representing two poets we wanted to include. I wrote back with a simple offer: "Cut the fees by 50 percent or we will drop one of your writers, who will then get nothing; we'll let you know which one we're cutting when the book goes to press; it's up to you." Of course, I had to be willing to follow through with my threat, which indeed I was. As it happened, the agent agreed to cut the fees in half, and the poets both made it into the book.

Yet after six months of bargaining we were still over our increased budget. So I began to cut poems. The University of California Press was charging us $25 each for poems by Robert Creeley and Charles Olson. No need to cut there, and nothing to gain in doing so. So I cut an Elizabeth Bishop poem (Farrar Straus) and a James Merrill poem (Knopf), saving $1,000 or more for each poem. Three Robert Frost poems (Holt) hit the cutting-room floor at $500 each, as did two e. e. cummings poems (Norton/Liveright). Ditto with a Louise Erdrich poem (Holt). Another $500 saved. On the other hand, a prize-winning poet I very much admired, whom I shall not name, came in at $8.50 per poem; we obviously could use as many of his poems as space allowed.

Some publishers saw the Oxford anthology as a way to gain additional readers for their poets and thus as an indirect way of increasing sales of their books of poems. That is sound reasoning, especially in the current market, where the bookstore shelf life for volumes of individual poets' work can be very short. In many stores a volume of poetry that sells out in a few months is never reordered. Very few poets get to see a series of their books kept in stock, and many widely read and much-loved poets have no long-term bookstore presence whatsoever. A few major anthologies, however, do get reordered and restocked.

The Economic Challenges to Anthologies

They are one of the most dependable ways – and sometimes the only way – for poets to get new readers.

A major component of increasing reprint fees is short-term greed. Commercial publishers owned by conglomerates often refuse to look beyond the impulse to maximize this quarter's profits. So they charge what the market will bear. In the case of the British edition of my anthology, greed overwhelmed the book and killed it. That is an increasing danger for anthologies, one that puts the presence of poetry in the culture at substantial risk.

University presses often behave differently. I cited the University of California Press as an exception to the pattern of extortionate fee demands, and I could as well have mentioned a dozen other university presses. We were charged fair prices by such university presses as California, Illinois, Pittsburgh, and Wesleyan. At the moment the high rates charged by many commercial publishers – often twenty-five to fifty times what university presses charge – are balanced by the lower rates from campus presses. If universities upped their rates to commercial levels, the game would be over. Anthologies would die out overnight.

We also encountered notable and immensely welcome acts of generosity. Melvin Tolson's son gave us *Libretto for the Republic of Liberia* (1953) for free. In return we annotated the poem elaborately to make it fully available to readers for the first time. Yet our most memorable demand came from an individual poet, not a corporation. I had wanted to include several examples of the edgy punk poetry that emerged in the 1990s toward the end of the book. I succeeded with Sesshu Foster and Patricia Smith but failed with one other young poet.

I never talked with the poet himself; instead I talked and corresponded with his lawyer. The reprint fee requested for his poem – nearly $90 per line – came to more than ten times the highest rate we were paying anyone else. I explained that this was impossible, that we couldn't set such a destructively high standard for this book and others. The fee I offered instead, I was told, wouldn't even pay the poet's New York rent for a month. In response to my asking whether he was really so much better than Adrienne Rich or Michael Harper, the lawyer replied, "Yes. He's been on MTV; he's been on Broadway; they haven't." When I suggested that being included in the first comprehensive anthology of modern American poetry to be published might help the poet's career, the lawyer replied that he was doing just fine selling his small-press books by hand at performances. She then, however, volunteered that he might relent on the fee if Oxford gave him a contract (with a healthy advance) for his next book. I allowed as how I hadn't any authority over the way Oxford negotiates its book contracts. Then came the final madness. I was told that the poet might adopt a different attitude if I could help him secure a high-paying visiting professorship at the University of Illinois. I cut the poem from the book.

Not all the memorable exchanges, to be sure, were over money. It took a long time for Oxford to track down Joy Davidman's heirs so we could ask to reprint "For the Nazis" (1944). The rights, it turned out, were held by her two sons, products of her marriage with William Gresham, an American veteran of the Spanish Civil War, whom she left when she ran off with C. S. Lewis half a century ago. (You may recall that Debra Winger played her in the film *Shadowlands* [1994].) One son lives in the United States and granted reprint rights immediately. The other could only be reached through his Swiss lawyer. For whatever reason he refused us reprint rights. Again we had to devise an individual strategy, so I faxed a reply to the lawyer, saying I'd either reprint Davidman's anti-Nazi poem or explain in the anthology that the son was determined to suppress his mother's work, so the issue wasn't going to go away. It was their choice. A fax approving the reprint arrived shortly thereafter.

We were also flatly refused one reprint for financial reasons. Editors of American literature anthologies know that some publishers deny (or limit) reprint rights so they can offer more works by a given author in their own collections. Hemingway stories are a well-known example. In our case it was Hart Crane's *The Bridge* (1930). W. W. Norton, long a family-owned firm but now owned by its senior editors, would not let us reprint the poem sequence in its entirety, arguing that would undercut sales of Crane's *Collected Poems* (1966). Yet they already use all of *The Bridge* in the current edition of *The Norton Anthology of American Lit-*

erature (1998), an introductory text with proven sales much larger than anything we might hope for. So the real reason Norton refused, I conclude, is that they want to retain *The Bridge* for themselves. They publish the only competing anthology of modern American poetry, and its new edition can tout inclusion of *The Bridge* if they so choose.

Norton also charges high reprint fees for the poems they do allow others to reprint. Had they granted permission for all of *The Bridge*, they might well have charged $15,000 to reprint it, a sum we could not have paid in any case. Their high charges serve a dual purpose – maximizing immediate profits and burdening competitors with nearly disabling costs. Much the same set of impulses, I suspect, underlies their poetry publishing program as well.

Norton is very canny about bringing authors with growing reputations on board, not necessarily because sales of their individual volumes generate major profits but because control of the reprint rights for poetry is a great advantage in the potentially lucrative textbook market. Norton's individual volumes of poetry are often indifferently designed and printed. Rich's books, for example, deserve loving care in design and production, but they do not always receive it. The results are almost industrial in appearance.

Norton's control of modern and contemporary American poets – the poets from cummings to Rich for whom they own the rights and do not have to pay fees to other publishers – gives them about a $20,000 advantage in the permissions fees they have to pay to produce their own anthologies. That is part of what is virtually a monopoly publishing program for this imprint. A wide variety of anthologies from numerous publishers would be to readers' benefit, but reprint fees make that impossible. A large anthology can thus come only from a publisher with major resources. Direct costs of $200,000–$300,000 and more are to be expected. Except for Oxford and Cambridge, then, university presses cannot compete to produce such books. And no one can produce them for a general audience alone. Course adoptions are the only basis of long-term sales. There is likely to be no other market that can enable a publisher to recoup costs, let alone earn a profit.

A major anthology is as much a financial project as a cultural one.

Anyone who thinks this sort of book can flow unimpeded from intellectual reflection is simply unaware of the costs involved. Indeed, the Ellman and O'Clair *Norton Anthology of Modern American and British Poetry* has remained unchanged and unchallenged for so long because no one could afford the permissions fees they'd have to pay to challenge it. My own anthology became possible – just barely possible – because the seventy-five-year copyright limit under the old copyright law had begun to expire for a number of the texts of high Modernism. T. S. Eliot's *The Waste Land* (1922) used to cost $7,500 to reprint in an anthology. Now it's free. Ditto with Robert Frost's early poems. Despite the high rates charged for some contemporary poets, then, we were able to assemble a potentially viable package, though the book will be in the red for some time.

Poets would be better served by a more competitive, less financially prohibitive and monopolistic environment, but late capitalism is unlikely to grant them one. Would Crane support Norton's policies? Obviously he has no say in them. Nor are there a lot of Crane heirs out there benefiting from the market value of his poetry. What poets could do – if they wished to do so and thought about it – is negotiate with their publishers to limit the size of the reprint fees that could be charged at the time they sign their own book contracts. The young poet who wanted $90 per line may be unlikely to champion this proposal, but many poets would like to see their work more widely disseminated and read. As things stand now, the future of anthologies is very much in jeopardy. That, in turn, means American poetry will be less available and less widely read.

Two

Whatever intellectual and cultural decisions inform publishing projects, they are increasingly constrained by financial pressures and financial negotiations. Readers rarely think of such matters, but editors think of them all the time. My publisher (Oxford) was very tolerant of the growing cost of doing business with me. Nevertheless, they could hardly give me so much latitude that I would actually cause them to lose money on the project. My original contract called for me to produce a book of 950 pages in print. I had little confidence I could do the job properly and well at that length, but I had no hard proof at the outset and no firm page estimate of my own. So I signed the contract on a hope and prayer that all would work out. In fact, the complex mixture of poems, annotations, and headnotes – along with questions like whether to start each poet on a new page, what size type to use, and how many lines to place on each page – made estimating length very chancy. I did ask for (and receive) an agreement that Oxford would increase the number of lines per page in the printed book from the initial estimate of forty-eight to fifty-three to give me a little leeway with which to work.

I also checked journal and magazine publishing histories as carefully as possible to maximize the number of poems that would fall into the category of public domain. Many anthologists pay for permissions fees unnecessarily by using book (rather than magazine) publication dates. As a student of the old copyright law I also knew a few other obscure regulations of benefit to anthologists. If an author permitted first publication without a copyright notice – as a number of authors did during the Depression or when publishing in political magazines or issuing broadsides – then the poem was in the public domain from the outset. Similarly, even if a poem without copyright notice was published without the author's permission, the poem is in the public domain unless the author took legal action against the publisher. Langston Hughes considered taking legal action against the publisher of "Goodbye Christ" (1932), but his lawyer dissuaded him, so the poem is in the public domain.

Detailed knowledge of this sort saved us thousands of dollars in fees, no small matter when we were confronting high-priced publishers at every turn. Yet I also missed a few journal publications for poems, so we paid a few hundred dollars in fees that we could have avoided. We lost another $1,000 when publication was delayed to the year 2000; we had thus committed ourselves to paying for several poems that were actually in the public domain by the time the book appeared in January.

In the end financial pressures made a difference in how some poets were represented. When I had to cut a few poems from the book to bring me back within a budget already expanded more than once, I turned, as I said, to relatively expensive poems. Elizabeth Bishop's "Manuelzinho" (1965) was one of the poems I cut, not happily. It was there in part to show a major poet writing in what would now be a politically unacceptable way. The poem violates so many contemporary taboos that it is almost unthinkable from a late twentieth-century perspective. Yet it was, I felt, less critical to her career than the poems I did include. Sacrificing "Manuelzinho," however, made Bishop a bit more conventional, a result I still regret, though Farrar, Straus, and Giroux, her publishers, made the shorter Bishop selection inevitable because of their high reprint prices.

Only if price were no object could an editor include, say, as many Bishop or Merrill or Rich poems as he or she might choose. Early Frost poems, on the other hand, are in the public domain, and one may thus choose freely from them, though the question of balance with poets still under copyright necessitates some constraint. One could not very well routinely have huge selections from public-domain poets and tiny selections from expensive poets under copyright. My point is that, throughout a project like this, financial and intellectual or aesthetic questions are thoroughly entangled with one another.

Three

At times the entanglements are straightforward. Granting space to one poet uses up some of the available printing budget and thus must entail exclusions elsewhere in the corpus of modern poems. From the outset I was determined for the first time in any anthology to give adequate representation to long poems and poem sequences. Without them I do not feel either the cultural ambitions or the real achievements of modern American poetry can be recognized. But long poems and poem sequences take up more space, and they can be quite expensive to reprint. So printing a series of sequences in their entirety sent a kind of tidal wave through the poets who might otherwise have been included, significantly limiting the available space and thus sweeping aside a number of poets I had hoped to include in the book.

Poem sequences also have a nonrelational command over space. Printed in its entirety, Gertrude Stein's "Patriarchal Poetry" (1927) takes however many pages it takes. Ordinarily, anthology editors apparently ration space to approximate a hierarchy of importance. Eliot gets more space than Marianne Moore because he's more important. Edwin Rolfe cannot get as much space as Robert Lowell because he's less important. The page count cannot be impeccably administered in a canonical merit system, but one is to try one's best. I chose to set this strict accounting principle aside.

My aim was to make the experience of modern American poetry as I saw it available to readers in a single volume. The decision to include poem sequences in their entirety was enough on its own to dismantle any hierarchy of poets based on space allotments. A poet like Frost, who wrote mostly short poems, can be well-represented in relatively few pages. His twenty-three poems take up twenty-one pages, despite the inclusion of two longer narrative poems, "The Hill Wife" (1916) and "The Witch of Coös" (1922). These count as long poems for Frost, and, more important, they show his interest in presenting female characters in his narrative verse, but they are still much shorter than many other long poems in the book.

The poet with the most pages in the book, a total of sixty, is Tolson. I wanted to include his *Libretto for the Republic of Liberia*, a poem I consider as innovative as Eliot's *The Waste Land*. Not only that, moreover, but I wanted to provide it with full annotations for the first time, a task that Edward Brunner performed splendidly. Henry Louis Gates Jr. deserves credit for including *Libretto* in his *Norton Anthology of African American Literature* (1996) – "If this anthology," he writes, "does nothing more than recover the works of Melvin B. Tolson to a wider audience, that alone will justify its existence" (1328). Gates, however, does not add to Tolson's own annotations, which leave foreign-language passages untranslated and a great number of obscure historical references unidentified. Our notes to *Libretto* alone came to over one hundred pages of manuscript, a burden that Oxford took up without a word of protest. Eliot, by comparison, receives thirty-four pages in the anthology, not because he is half as important as Tolson but because I felt that was enough space to represent his major work. I include "The Love Song of J. Alfred Prufrock" (1915), "Gerontion" (1920), *The Waste Land*, "The Hollow Men" (1925), "Journey of the Magi" (1935), and "Burnt Norton" (1936). The decision to annotate *Libretto* fully would have been impossible had I been held hostage to a page-count hierarchy. The two-volume Library of America modern American poetry anthology uses only a small sample of *Libretto* because it links page count to cultural status. It is also, of course, an anthology edited by a committee. Reaching group consensus on a fully annotated *Libretto* might be difficult; a single editor with a committed and supportive publisher has as much freedom as finances permit.

Later in the book Muriel Rukeyser gets thirty-five pages because I include her long poem sequence "The Book of the Dead" (1938). It is the most important poem sequence by a progressive poet in the first half of the century and the single most ambitious poetic version of 1930s documentary style. Including it gives political and aesthetic counterbalance to Eliot and Ezra Pound. And it underlines the often forgotten fact that experimental Modernism was taken up by poets with diverse cultural aims and political beliefs.

In an essay-review ("Twentieth-Century American Poetry, Abbreviated") in the spring 2001 issue of *Parnassus* William Logan complains that "the Harlem Renaissance has received far more critical attention than its achievements deserve" (467), opines that Tolson's *Libretto* is "a ludicrous pastiche of modernist practice," and concludes that "it takes an editor without fear of God to favor Muriel Rukeyser over T. S. Eliot" (470–71). Rukeyser, he notes, receives thirty-five pages in my anthology, whereas Eliot receives but thirty-four. Although I would be willing to take credit for this gesture of lese majesty, the truth is I had no idea what the final page count would be. Perhaps Logan has no experience editing large, heavily annotated anthologies. Such books are still set from hard copy, typically photocopies of reliable editions of the poems and computer printouts of headnotes and annotations. With over five hundred different published sources with varying type sizes and line lengths and no way of knowing how the extensive notes would compress when typeset, it was impossible to calculate either the length

The Economic Challenges to Anthologies

of the published book or how many pages each poet would receive. As it happened, my two-thousand-page manuscript gave Rukeyser forty-two pages and Eliot sixty-one; Eliot ended up with one fewer page in the book because the elaborate notes to his poems took up less space. I suppose a properly respectful editor would go back and cut poems to preserve the expected hierarchy.

Presenting the story of modern American poetry fully, in my view, meant rejecting a strict pecking order for poets. At the same time I needed some notable generosity from poets' heirs and publishers to be able to include these long poems. Were Rukeyser and Tolson and Stein represented by Farrar Straus, Random House, or Norton, their long poems would not be in the book. I would not have been able to afford them. Instead Stein was represented by Yale University Press, which treated us very fairly and made it financially possible to reprint the whole of "Patriarchal Poetry," the most rigorously deconstructive poem of American Modernism and thus a poem in some ways decades ahead of its time philosophically. From Rukeyser's son and Tolson's son we also received generous treatment focused on helping their parents' legacies get wide distribution.

As a reader moves through this book, with numerous long poems and poem sequences – some of them unfamiliar – the legacy of twentieth-century American poetry begins to be reshaped. I have always been surprised, for example, that Rich's "Twenty-One Love Poems" (1976) is typically represented with excerpts rather than with the whole sequence; we print the sequence in its entirety, which gives a much more accurate portrait of the subtleties of Rich's thought and method. More unfamiliar still to readers of anthologies is Williams's *The Descent of Winter*, a dadaist and politically speculative mix of poetry and prose, perhaps Williams's single most experimental sequence and one that balances his exquisite short lyrics with a more complex form.

Perhaps most unfamiliar of all the poem sequences we print is Welton Smith's "Malcolm" (1968), one of the most interesting poems of the Black Arts movement but largely forgotten because Smith's literary career lasted only a few years. With no ongoing series of books appearing, we would typically only remember Smith if he continued to be anthologized. Smith did, as it happens, issue one pamphlet of poems in 1972, and "Malcolm" was included in the famous 1968 Larry Neal–Amiri Baraka anthology *Black Fire*. But his work, so far as I know, has not been reprinted since. I would not have thought about reprinting "Malcolm" but for Karen Ford's wonderful analysis of the poem in her 1997 book, *Gender and the Poetics of Excess: Moments of Brocade*.

Critics can revive a poet's reputation, but the only sure way to keep a poem alive is to anthologize it. Much more, I suspect, than people realize, anthologies shape our memory of poetic history. They help establish not only whether a poet will be remembered but also *how* a poet will be remembered. When a poet is represented in anthologies with one sort of poem but not another, to a large degree even specialists in the field will remember the poet by way of the poems regularly anthologized and not others. Those will after all be the poems faculty members reread and teach year after year. Those are the poems students will read. Those are the poems most available in bookstores. If the poet has no collected volume of poems, moreover, then buying a series of his or her individual books requires a certain dogged effort over time.

The power of anthologies to shape cultural memory was brought home to me most dramatically early in this process. As part of its marketing research Oxford sent out a questionnaire to modern poetry specialists. The questionnaire took the form of a detailed table of contents for a proposed anthology of modern American poetry. People could vote on whether or not to include each poem. There followed a supplemental list of additional poets with space to recommend whether or not to add them to the book. Finally, there was an opportunity for more extended commentary.

The Oxford editor who compiled the prospective table of contents, Tony English, later told me that he had made it as conventional as possible in order to get people stirred up and guarantee responses. Anyone who completed and returned the questionnaire received a $100 honorarium. As it happened, I was so annoyed by the table of contents that I threw the envelope aside, determined not to respond at all. I had no idea at the time that Oxford was contemplating inviting me to edit the book; if I had ignored the questionnaire they would probably have gone elsewhere. In the end I decided to write a response explaining how I would treat half a dozen of the poets included but suggesting that the contents needed a complete overhaul.

Once I had agreed to edit the book, Oxford tabulated the results of the questionnaire and sent me both the compiled statistics and the individual forms with the names of the respondents deleted. There were just over sixty complete questionnaires. Although I wasn't required to honor the results of the survey, Oxford did want me to think seriously about the financial consequences of dropping modern poets that people expected to be able to teach. Yet only a small number of poems received significant votes, and they were all poems I wanted to include in any case. So on that issue we had no conflict.

What was more interesting to me was how the existing anthologies had shaped peoples' attitudes. Only one respondent suggested adding Edna St. Vincent Millay's witty, rhetorically polished, and decidedly antiromantic sonnets to the book. These poems weren't on the list because they are not widely anthologized. No one seemed to notice the absence of her political poems. The only Millay in readers' minds was the ecstatically romantic Millay regularly anthologized. In the antiromantic category, among other poems, we reprint her entire "Sonnets from an Ungrafted Tree" (1923) and then end her section with three political poems, "Justice Denied in Massachusetts" (1927), "Say That We Saw Spain Die" (1938), and "I Forgot for a Moment" (1940). The effect, as with many of the selections, should be to change the way a poet is perceived and remembered.

Other absences from the Oxford survey were equally predictable. Sterling Brown was not on Oxford's list, and no one thought of mentioning him. Langston Hughes was represented as he usually is in anthologies, without his most searing poems about race, like "Christ in Alabama" (1931), and without his poems of the left, like "Come to the Waldorf-Astoria" (1931), both in our anthology. Only one respondent suggested, without being specific, that his section should be rethought. We give Hughes twenty-nine poems in twenty-four pages, deliberately placing him in the front rank of American poets. The lesser-known poets of the Harlem Renaissance remained unmentioned but are well-represented in the anthology.

There were nonetheless many good suggestions in the comments section of the questionnaire. One writer made a good case for how to present John Ashbery. Another argued for Adrian Louis, whom I much admire, and who is well-represented in the book. Often respondents were particularly knowledgeable about one or two authors, and they made detailed and interesting suggestions in those instances. So there was much of value in the results. Yet there was very little encouragement to make fundamental changes in how canonical poets should be treated. Most respondents saw little reason to alter the picture presented in existing anthologies, though it is also true that the list of respondents Oxford used emphasized established faculty who had been teaching modern poetry for some years. Few if any assistant professors were queried. This older group at least had cultural memories largely shaped by their textbooks.

Moore was thus substantially remembered as she is anthologized. A few people, I was pleased to see, did recommend including "Marriage" (1924). What we did instead was reprint her two most philosophically ambitious long poems, "Marriage" and "An Octopus" (1924). These poems also display her most complex use of quotations and the depth of cultural analysis she is capable of, without which her role in Modernism is severely slighted. I added two historically oriented poems, "Sojourn in the Whale" (1921) and "Spenser's Ireland" (1941), to complicate her image still further.

Moore is not the only canonical poet who receives revisionist treatment in the Oxford anthology. Except for Eliot, who is well-represented with the most extensively annotated version of his major poems in any anthology, every well-known poet receives a new treatment here. Crane's section includes a number of his early poems to give a better sense of how many different modern styles he integrated into *The Bridge*. Frost's section is focused on the darker poems that are slighted in many collections. Wallace Stevens has his early and late poems, the latter in particular little anthologized, given full representation. Pound's *Cantos* is not only given a generous selection but also chosen and annotated to make an argument about its structure that is absent from any other collection.

Less celebrated but still important poets are presented with work that will surprise many readers weaned on earlier anthologies. Carl Sandburg is here a diverse poet who writes not only about working-class lives but also about race and about the horrors of war. Amy Lowell takes up history and gender in her pages and writes some of the century's most beautifully rapturous poems. Vachel Lindsay is represented in part with two of his little-known late mystical poems about nature. Claude McKay's section gives him twelve poems, enough to show not only the variety of ways he addresses America's traumatic investment in race but also – for the first time in any collection – the 1940s poems that are just as strong as the better-known works of the 1920s.

For the first time in any comprehensive anthology we also give enough poems to reconstruct the historically important phenomenon of 1930s political poetry. Of the thousands of poems from the period we select those that are aesthetically and rhetorically most powerful. It has long been clear that no one aesthetic standard can account for the diversity of American Modernism, so we represent the several aesthetic traditions that shaped the period, including the best of its lyrical, experimental, and agitational poems. With the inclusion of scores of lesser-known poets, finally, the anthology reshapes the entire account of twentieth-century American poetry.

Bibliography

Gates, Henry Louis, Jr., and Nellie Y. McKay, eds. *The Norton Anthology of African American Literature.* New York: W. W. Norton, 1996.

Logan, William. "Twentieth-Century American Poetry, Abbreviated." *Parnassus* 25 (2001): 438–77.

ALAN D. SCHRIFT

Confessions of an Anthology Editor

Edit: verb, from Latin ēdit-us, past participle of ēděre, to put forth, from ē, out + dàre, to put, give – Oxford English Dictionary

Let me begin at the outset with a confession: I like to edit anthologies. I find it interesting, even exciting. I've edited quite a few: four have been published to date, and I'm presently working on a fifth – possibly a multivolume work (an issue to which I will return shortly). Each has been a different sort of collection. Some have been entirely my creation; others have been coedited with a colleague. Some have been entirely under my editorial control; others have been made to fit constraints imposed by a publisher concerned with "marketability" issues. Most have been motivated by what I'd call "pedagogical" concerns, although all have been informed by "intellectual" or "scholarly" concerns in a way that I hope problematizes the overly simplistic "pedagogy/scholarship" binary. In the following pages I'd like to recount my intentions with each of the anthologies I've edited, as well as some of the questions I'm wrestling with concerning my current, and biggest, anthology project. In so doing I hope to expose some of the functions that an anthology might serve and some of the factors that a good anthologizer must consider. I hope also to show what I might venture to call the attributes of "editorial intelligence," attributes that to some degree overlap but in other respects do and should differ from what might be called "authorial intelligence."

A Tale of Four Anthologies

My "first" anthology eventually emerged as two, and therein lies a tale. The story begins when I was in graduate school in the early 1980s, completing a dissertation in philosophy at Purdue University on Nietzsche and hermeneutics. Gayle L. Ormiston, a fellow graduate student, and I began talking about how the battle lines that had been drawn between recent French theory and the hermeneutic tradition missed the many affinities we saw between the two traditions. Our plan, and it seemed simple enough, was to compile a collection of readings to be titled "Hermeneutics and Postmodern Theories of Interpretation" that would do three things: chronicle the early hermeneutic tradition in German philosophy; survey the developments of that tradition in the middle years of the twentieth century; and collect what we regarded as recent interventions in that tradition that came from or were informed by contemporary French philosophy. Our goals were also simple enough: first, put together a collection of readings that chronicled the past two centuries in hermeneutic theory and that could serve as a basic text in a graduate or advanced undergraduate course in philosophical or literary hermeneutics; and second, intervene in the hermeneutic tradition by demonstrating that once one turned toward contemporary French philosophical theory, one did not need to leave this hermeneutic tradition behind.

Putting the table of contents together was easy, and fun. Nothing like this collection existed at the time, and setting the contents for the first two sections was straightforward: the first section, with the working title "Texts/Contexts: The Hermeneutic Legend," would include the first English translation of selections from Friedrich Ast's work, well-known but not easily accessible selections from Schleiermacher and Dilthey, and the relevant sections from Heidegger's *Being and Time*. The second part, "Fusions/Confusions: Dialogue, Ideology, Methodology," would focus on Hans-Georg Gadamer's work and the controversies that surrounded it, with selections – again some translated for the first time and others either hard to find or part of larger works – by Gadamer, Jürgen Habermas, Emilio Betti, and Paul Ricoeur. The last section, "Textuality and the Transformation of Reading," involved more challenging decisions about who and what to include, and we ended up with a selection of essays that included the first translation of Foucault's essay "Nietzsche, Freud, Marx"; a complete version of a Derrida essay on Heidegger and representation that had only appeared in part in a journal; a new translation of a short book by Jean-Luc Nancy on hermeneutics in Plato and Heidegger; newly translated essays by Werner Hamacher and Manfred Frank, which reconsidered Schleiermacher, and by Eric Blondel, on Nietzschean interpretation; and a reprint of an essay on psychoanalytic interpretation by Julia Kristeva. Very little, if anything, by Frank, Nancy, Hamacher, or Blondel had at that time been published in English, and we thought this last section would really make a mark on both the hermeneutic tradition and interpretation theory more generally.

But here is where the story takes an unfortunate turn. We did not have an easy time getting a publisher interested in committing to two relative novices, neither of whom had a book out yet. It took about six years before we finally were able to get a contract from the State University of New York Press, but they were unwilling to publish the book as a single volume, claiming it would be both too big and too expensive to produce. (In hindsight neither claim was true, as collections larger than ours were subsequently published by SUNY; at the time, however, we felt we were in no position to argue.) Instead, and contrary to the basic idea behind the project, they required us to split the German hermeneutic theory (what we had seen as parts 1 and 2) from the more radical French interpretation theory. The resulting volumes, *The Hermeneutic Tradition: From Ast to Ricoeur* and *Transforming the Hermeneutic Context: From Nietzsche to Nancy*, both appeared in 1990. Although it was nice to have two lines on my CV, I have to admit in retrospect that this was a very bad decision that really ran counter to the basic intellectual intention of the project, which was to show the continuing relevance of the hermeneutic tradition to the contemporary theoretical scene. I'm not sure whether SUNY Press imagined the two volumes being sold together, but they never really did sell as a pair. Instead *The Hermeneutic Tradition* has sold consistently for a decade and appears to be used fairly widely in a number of courses, while sales of *Transforming the Hermeneutic Context* have never been very good, and it has made little mark on the intellectual scene or the hermeneutic tradition, even though it includes several significant essays by major figures on the contemporary theory scene, essays that appear nowhere else in English.

Several years passed before I again considered putting an anthology together, and my second anthology project (and third anthology) – *The Logic of the Gift: Toward an Ethic of Generosity* – can be traced to a paper I wrote on gift and exchange in Nietzsche and Cixous.[1] In the process of researching this paper I found myself reading a wide range of fascinating material on gifts and gift-giving by anthropologists, literary theorists, and economists, as well as philosophers. The topic of the gift was at that time beginning to appear all over the critical map, in part a response to the appearance in English translation of Derrida's *Given Time* in 1992. The more I read on the topic, the more interested I became. And the more I read, the more I realized that there were a small number of texts that almost all discussions of the gift cited: in addition to Derrida's *Given Time*, there was near universal reference to Emerson's essay "Gifts"; Marcel Mauss's "Essai sur le don" and "Gift, Gift"; Georges Bataille's essay on expenditure; Émile Benveniste's "Gift and Exchange in the Indo-European Vocabulary"; and Claude Lévi-Strauss's *Introduction to the Work of Marcel Mauss*.

I decided to put together a collection of essays and excerpts that would bring together some or all of this material plus some of the other material that I personally found interesting and helpful in my own work on gift and exchange. My selections were guided by a couple of other factors, though. First and foremost there were pedagogical considerations: in 1995 I wanted to teach an advanced undergraduate seminar on gift and exchange in contemporary critical theory. I used this occasion as a testing ground for what might or might not work in a collection that could form the basis for such a course. Here, by "pedagogical considerations," I mean three things. First, what independent selections from a theorist are accessible and intelligible to bright undergraduate/graduate students in isolation from other works by that theorist? Second, what complete texts would I want to assign in addition to my anthology, such that selecting a section from this text to include in the anthology would not involve unnecessary duplication in my course? And third, what selections would work with and amplify one another?

When I isolate these three questions in this way, an interesting fact comes to the fore: for an anthology like this one the very same questions that I – as an editor – ask myself are the questions that I – as an instructor – would ask when first setting up a syllabus for a new course: What will be accessible and intelligible to the students? What texts will be ordered? What selections will work together? My answers to these questions were in some sense idiosyncratic, but in some sense not. To do the subject justice in a course I thought one should probably read all of Mauss's *The Gift* and all of Bataille's first volume of *The Accursed Share*, so omitting these entirely was a calculated gamble. I compromised on the Derrida, deciding that while many courses would also read *Given Time* in its entirety (as I myself do in my course), some would not, and so I decided to include that text's opening chapter. I did want to include the Mauss essay "Gift, Gift," which had never been translated into English, and rights to reprint Benveniste's and Emerson's essays were easy to acquire. It was fortunate that the rights to Lévi-Strauss's essay were owned by Routledge, my publisher, which meant I could reprint almost two-thirds of that short book in my own collection. My leanings were toward feminist and anthropological issues, and so I chose to include what some would regard as a disproportionately high number of selections addressing these issues, selections by Bourdieu, Cixous, Irigaray, Sahlins, and Strathern. I also oriented the volume toward the French theoretical discussions of the topics, again because that's my interest and that's the course I wanted to teach. I was forced, for editorial as well as some legal reasons, to omit any selections from Heidegger, Bataille, and Levinas, which are perhaps my only regrets, but I was able to invite some new contributions and was fortunate to have my invitations accepted by people (Gary Shapiro, Allan Stoekl, and Robert Bernasconi, respectively) who did address these theorists' works, as I did as well – in the cases of Heidegger and Bataille – in my editorial introduction.[2] I've since taught the course twice, and I think the collection does indeed hang together very well, a comment that I've heard from several others who have either read the anthology or used it in their teaching.

My most recent anthology, *Why Nietzsche Still? Reflections on Drama, Culture, and Politics*, has a different origin entirely, and in many respects it is a very different kind of collection from the previous ones. Unlike the others it is almost entirely comprised of previously unpublished essays, nor did I imagine this collection functioning as the basis for a class. And it owes its origin to a particular event, a session that I organized for the 1996 meeting of the International Association for Philosophy and Literature. For this session, which was titled "Nietzsche and the Dramas of Culture," I invited six scholars to address the topic. What emerged at the session was something quite remarkable: all of the papers fit together extremely well, with numerous overlapping themes and points of critical engagement and intersection. Immediately after the session I began talking to the presenters about a possible anthology on Nietzsche, drama, and culture, and we all agreed the papers would work together well in that context.

Over the following two years we revised our papers, and I used my contacts in the Nietzsche scholarly community to invite a number of other people whose work I respected to contribute something to a collection that now had broadened a bit. Since several of the initial papers also addressed political issues, it made sense to include this topic. Also, since several disciplines were represented in the initial panel and, more important, since I believe strongly that much interesting work on Nietzsche is being done outside philosophy departments, many of the people I invited were chosen precisely because they work outside the confines of an academic philosophy department. Two final themes, both somewhat polemical, were also addressed by the essays collected. First, I wanted to argue that contrary to comments coming from around the philosophical world, the intellectual energy animating the Nietzsche scholarly juggernaut of the past three decades had not completely disappeared. And this was connected to the second theme, namely, that although the enthusiasm surrounding the "French Nietzsche" might have passed (especially in France), there was exciting, innovative, and serious Nietzsche scholarship going on throughout the English-speaking scholarly community. That this volume could bring together a collection of excellent essays by scholars from the United States, Canada, England, Wales, and Australia, scholars working in departments of comparative literature, English,

German, philosophy, political science, political theory, rhetoric, and women's studies, would testify to the continuing and widespread interest in Nietzsche's thought.

Observations

When I think back on these projects, a couple of general themes emerge. First and foremost is intellectual coherence: for an anthology to work the pieces must hang together; they must build on each other and, if not articulate a thesis, at least give voice to several related theses. In this respect putting an anthology together is not unlike authoring a book. This is what I referred to earlier as the overlap between "editorial" and "authorial" intelligence. But second, and here unlike authoring a book, editing an anthology requires careful consideration of the anticipated audience. In the end this consideration may be indistinguishable from the publisher's concern for a market. But here I want to introduce a (hopefully not entirely self-serving) distinction between anthologies that have some fundamental intellectual merit and anthologies that serve to cater to an already existing market. In the latter category I would place the dozens of anthologies that serve large introductory courses at large universities. These anthologies make a lot of money for their editors and their publishers. I have no doubt that the next edition of some trade publisher's "Introductory Readings in Philosophy" or "Contemporary Moral Problems" text will sell more copies, at a higher price, in six months than my four anthologies will sell in their lifetimes. While I don't want to claim that these introductory anthologies are devoid of intellectual value, I think they serve needs – both intellectual and financial – that are fundamentally different from the needs that my anthologies seek to serve. Of course, this is not to say that an intellectually significant anthology need make no money. I don't know the exact figures, but I would guess that Walter Kaufmann's edition of *The Portable Nietzsche* has, since first published in 1954, sold an awful lot of copies, even as it has for many years served to introduce quite admirably a large number of readers to Nietzsche's works.

So what then do I mean by anticipating an audience in an intellectually meritorious way? In the grandest of senses I suppose this means something akin to creating a tradition, whether it be the abridged tradition of hermeneutic theory, as my first anthology sought to bring together, or the sorts of traditions that the anthologizers who put together the Norton anthologies of this or that seek to create. But it can also mean something much smaller than tradition creation; it can introduce a new field to an audience that should be interested but doesn't yet know enough about the particular field to be interested. This was, I think, the genius – the "editorial intelligence" – behind one of the most significant "theory" anthologies I know, David B. Allison's *The New Nietzsche: Contemporary Styles of Interpretation*. By bringing to the American audience, for the first time, English translations of the new French Nietzsche scholarship by Derrida, Deleuze, Kofman, Granier, Klossowski, Blondel, Blanchot, and so on, Allison's collection intervened in and transformed definitively Nietzsche scholarship in America. It would be in some cases fifteen years before some of the major works from which these selections were excerpted would appear in English translation, but in those years a lot of people came to know Allison's "new Nietzsche." It is, I think, too easy to say after the fact that of course an anthology with Derrida, Deleuze, Kofman, Klossowski, Blanchot, and so on, was a sure thing. For if we go back to 1977 we find nothing of Blanchot's nonfiction or of Klossowski or Kofman in English; only Deleuze's Proust book had been translated at that time, and it would be five more years before Deleuze's Nietzsche book would appear and seventeen years before a publisher would decide that the English-speaking world was ready for *Difference and Repetition*. This to me is the primary sign of a truly successful scholarly anthology: it fills an intellectual void that even some of the practitioners of that scholarship don't yet realize exists.

Creating a Canon, or Telling a Story

This brings me to my current project, one that involves several of the issues already addressed, as well as a few others. I am working on a reader that seeks to be sufficiently large and broad to satisfy virtually any instructor interested in teaching a course that surveys the twentieth century in French philosophy. I imagine writing a brief introduction sketching the historical evolution of French theory throughout the century, and I will also include brief (one- to two-page) introductions to each of the authors included (concentrating on biographical details and a broad overview of their importance, rather than a summary of what the reading selections present), adding a bibliography of important works published and perhaps including important secondary source materials. As should be clear from my previous anthologies, I do not believe in aggressive excerpting and so will work to include the most important and most representative complete selections (either complete essays or complete book chapters). The selections themselves will be organized into five sections, which I list below, along with the names of some of the figures whose work I am considering including:

1. *Early Years*: selections from Alain, Bergson, Brunschvicg, Mounier, Teilhard de Chardin, Wahl, Weil
2. *Existentialism and Phenomenology*: selections from de Beauvoir, Camus, Dufrenne, Levinas, Marcel, Merleau-Ponty, Ricoeur, Sartre, Tran Duc Thao
3. *From Existentialism to Structuralism*: selections from Aron, Bachelard, Bataille, Blanchot, Breton, Canguilhem, Castoriadis, Césaire, Fanon, Klossowski, Kojève, Lefort, Lefebvre, Memmi
4. *Structuralism*: selections from Althusser, Barthes, Hyppolite, Lacan, Lévi-Strauss, Saussure
5. *Poststructuralism*: selections from Badiou, Balibar, Baudrillard, Bourdieu, Bouveresse, de Certeau, Cixous, Debord, Deleuze, Derrida, Descombes, Foucault, Granger, Guattari, Hadot, Irigaray, Jankélévich, Kofman, Kristeva, Lacoue-Labarthe, Le Doeuff, Lyotard, Marion, Nancy, Rosset, Serres, Wittig

This list gives a sense of the scope of the project and should also give a sense of the scope of the problems. Part of what I'm wrestling with is how to decide what "should" be in the collection (in terms of establishing the narrative I wish the collection to support) vs. weighing issues of classroom vs. library utility, "affordability," "readability," and audience (scholars vs. students). There is also the more general and global question of whether, having been given the option, I would like to produce this collection as a two-volume work. Before addressing what sorts of factors I am considering as I think about each of these issues, let me say a little more about what has motivated me to consider this project in the first place, for this bears directly on how I will proceed.

As a historian of philosophy who has focused increasingly on recent French philosophy, I have come to be distressed by the lack of attention among English-language students and scholars to the historical unfolding of philosophy in France in the twentieth century. This lack of attention is most apparent in the cases of post-1960 "poststructuralist" French thinkers, and it manifests itself in a number of ways. First, there is the general sense that many of these thinkers respond to some extent to their structuralist predecessors but are inspired more directly by German philosophers: Husserl, Heidegger, Nietzsche, and Hegel, in particular; by chronicling the entire century and recalling some of the lively philosophical debates in its first six decades, I hope to correct the conjoined misconceptions that "French philosophy" began with structuralism and that it functions in large part in response to the German master thinkers. A second, related point concerns a "cult of genius" that has surrounded many of the leading French philosophers of the twentieth century, a cult that some of these thinkers have themselves cultivated, with the result that the interlocutors with whom they were engaged and the teachers from whom they learned are often completely eclipsed from view. The fault is not always with the French, however, as their eager English-speaking audience is all too happy to ignore the hints that they themselves sometimes give. So, to take a well-documented example, in Foucault's inaugural address upon taking his position at the Collège de France he credited Dumézil, Canguilhem, and Hyppolite for the roles they played in his intellectual evolution. Yet how many scholars who have published on Foucault would have to confess to not having read a word by any of these three? There have been throughout the century a number of great "teachers" whose influence on French philosophy has been enormous – teachers like Alain, Kojève, Bachelard, Canguilhem, Hyppolite, Jankélévich, and Wahl – and by bringing some of their published "lessons" to the fore I think a better sense of the evolution of French thought can be garnered.

A third and final point is also worth mentioning. The enormous popularity of the major figures in contemporary French philosophy – Derrida, Foucault, Deleuze, Lyotard, Kristeva, Irigaray, Lacan, and so on – has not only led to many very influential figures from earlier in the century being largely if not totally forgotten but has also eclipsed the significant work of a range of other contemporary philosophers. These two eclipses have different causes and reflect different phenomena. The latter – those important figures in France who have not yet been or are only just being "discovered" by an English-speaking audience – include figures like Jacques Bouveresse, Clément Rosset, and Alain Badiou, who for differing reasons have just never caught on sufficiently to justify the expense of translating and publishing their work.[3] But it is the former – the "forgetting" of earlier influential figures – that is, I think, more intellectually interesting, as it has a great deal to do with the abrupt and rather odd dismissal of all things existentialist that followed the rise of structuralism. To be sure, much of this had to do with a typically Oedipal French intellectual gesture, namely, the exiling of Jean-Paul Sartre from theoretical relevance. One could certainly argue that no intellectual force exercised so dominant an influence on French thought this century as did Sartre, which makes his disappearance all the more suspect. But not only has Sartre been overlooked. In addition, almost everything that had any connection with him – and this was quite a lot – has also been ignored for quite a while. I mean here not only Sartre's major "existential" interlocutors Merleau-Ponty and de Beauvoir but also the religious critics to whom he was responding like the Personalist Mounier or the Catholic Marcel, and the various Marxist controversies that he was a party to during the 1940s and 1950s. And then there was his influence on and support for the challenges to colonialism raised by, among others, Fanon, Césaire, and Memmi.[4] Things are changing recently for the better in this regard, and there is, to be sure, now some renewed interest in the work of Merleau-Ponty, de Beauvoir, and the so-called black existentialists; there is even renewed interest in circles other than undergraduate existentialism classes – where his popularity has never waned – in Sartre. But there are still important figures and developments, particularly in the first decades of the twentieth century, and in the years between the Second World War and the rise of structuralism, that should be recalled if the story of the French twentieth century is to be told philosophically. And that is what my current project seeks to do.

But how am I going to do this? For, as should be clear, my intention is not to write a monograph narrating the century but to create an anthology that, with a little editorial guidance, will facilitate the telling of one version of the century's self-narration. And here come the problems I alluded to earlier: What is my anticipated audience for this anthology? And which selections will best communicate the historical narration I want the selections to tell? The anthology intends to be comprehensive, but what exactly does that mean: a single essay by each important figure or multiple essays reflecting the differing positions of some of the major figures? Part of the problem here is finitude, textual finitude: a volume can only be so large. And that means making difficult decisions like choosing between an all but forgotten piece by Marcel that addresses the Catholic objection to Sartre or including a late Derridean essay like "Khōra" to supplement his earlier, better-known, and more influential essays.

As I think about these questions, I continue to return to the basic question of audience (or "market," as my publisher keeps reminding me). And what this really means is: do I want to construct this volume to function well in a course (or several courses), or do I want it to be the sort of collection that scholars, libraries, and only serious students will likely consult? The answer to this question will lead to different answers to the previous questions. For example, the question of accessibility or readability becomes less pressing when the volume is not being targeted to a certain pedagogical setting. To take a concrete example, one that I am confident of but that I think will also be controversial: I have been teaching an upper-level twentieth-century continental philosophy course to bright undergraduates for over a decade at Grinnell. On the basis of my experience with this class in the early years I came to the conclusion that Derrida's most famous essay, "Différance," is to a large extent unreadable by undergraduates. Derrida is in general hard enough, which I think explains why, if my experience is at all typical, Foucault is far more popular with undergraduate students than Derrida. But there are particular problems with "Différance," problems one doesn't face trying to teach, say, "Structure, Sign, and Play in the Discourse of the Human Sciences" or "Signature Event Context." The reason is simple, I think: "Structure, Sign, and Play" and "Signature Event Context" are self-contained essays; Derrida tells you enough about Lévi-Strauss in the former and Austin and Saussure in the latter to allow you to see how his deconstructions, and deconstruction in general, work. To appreciate what is going on in "Différance," on the other hand, requires knowing Nietzsche, Freud, Heidegger, Levinas, Saussure, and Hegel, and a little knowledge of French grammar and syntax doesn't hurt either. The average, even well-above-average undergraduate just won't know this stuff, and while "Différance" may in the end be the more significant essay, it is not obvious that it belongs in an anthology designed with primarily pedagogical concerns in mind.

But should pedagogical concerns be the primary concerns? That's, I suppose, what I'm really wrestling with as I decide what "should" be in the collection. And here is where the question of one vs. two volumes becomes critical. For it is not clear that a two-volume work will sell as a classroom collection: it will be too big in terms of pages – fourteen hundred pages of French philosophy is much more than any semester course could handle – and probably too expensive, especially if, as is likely the case, instructors will also want to assign some complete texts of their particular favorites. But it's not clear that a single volume can make anything like the intellectual statement that I hope this anthology will make. For realistically, a successful (both pedagogically and financially) single-volume work could, I think, be easily constructed, but it would include at best perhaps a little Bergson; the usual Sartre, Merleau-Ponty, and de Beauvoir; some Saussure, Lacan, and Althusser; and the predictable two or three essays by Derrida, Foucault,

Deleuze, Lyotard, Kristeva, and Irigaray. But this is probably already larger than a single volume could support if in fact complete essays and representative essays from the figures listed were to be included.

Which is why, as I begin the process of making the entry selections, I'm leaning toward a two-volume work. And I'm also leaning toward making my editorial interludes do more of the work, so that not everyone will be represented with a textual selection (*tant pis pour* Brunschvicg, Dufrenne, Aron, and probably quite a few others) and some of the less well-known writers of the less well-known periods (vitalism vs. neo-Kantianism, early phenomenology, the orthodox Marxist response to Sartre) will be quickly described and paraphrased rather than represented and read. Even with two volumes, in other words, the totalizing dream of constructing a canon is unrealizable. But in the end, at the close of the twentieth century in French philosophy, if anything is clear it is that the project of totalizing canon creation is not only impossible but undesirable. We can only tell stories of what now seems important to recall, to bring together, to allow to speak for a little while longer. And the story I want to tell will have some surprises. It will recall existentialism in a way that tries to show de Beauvoir and Merleau-Ponty as equal players with Sartre in the unfolding of those decades. It will present the anticolonialist "black existentialists" as a major development in the French century. It will present some nonphilosophers – not just Saussure and Lacan but also Bataille, Lévi-Strauss, Bourdieu, Cixous – as major philosophical voices. It will, to my regret, not include all the important essays from the "big names" that I and others want to teach, but it will do so in order to make room for some of the teachers who nurtured these individuals – Kojève, Bachelard, Canguilhem, Jankélévich, Hyppolite – and for some of the other, less popular but important thinkers with whom these "big names" studied, conversed, reviewed, and responded.

I hope the story this anthology tells will be a good one, which is to say, an honest story, informative and insightful, sometimes predictable and other times surprising. Not the whole story, by any means, but a story worth telling.

Concluding Un-Market-Friendly Postscript

Since I originally wrote this essay several years ago, the status of my anthology of twentieth-century French philosophy has changed significantly, and while the considerations I address in the preceding remarks remain, in my view, crucial for producing an intellectually valid anthology, a postscript is in order. After deliberating carefully for over a year, I decided against a two-volume work, not wanting to repeat the mistake of my first anthology/ies by dividing up a collection whose raison d'être was precisely to bring together selections that were not normally conjoined. And I did in fact create a table of contents for a collection that would do justice to the rich and diverse history of philosophy in France in the twentieth century. As I began to contact publishers to request the rights to reprint the selections I had chosen, I ran into what became insurmountable problems. As I allude to above, the differences in what publishers charge for reprinting selections vary considerably, and while I had more than a few publishers willing to grant me permission to reprint selections without charge or with only a nominal charge, other publishers were not so generous. The situation was compounded by the fact that my publisher (Blackwell) operates both in the United States and in the United Kingdom, which often made it necessary to request permissions to reprint a selection from two English-language publishers (one owning the U.S. rights, the other owning the UK/Commonwealth rights), effectively doubling the number of permissions required. This was frequently the case with the older, and more expensive, selections from the existentialist writers (Sartre, Camus, de Beauvoir), whose copyrights were likely determined before "world rights" became the norm.[5] The end result of these requests was a total for permissions that approached forty thousand dollars, almost four times what my publisher thought was the maximum amount for the volume to be producible. I've tried to pare down the selections to a size that will make the anthology feasible to produce, but this has resulted in a volume that will not do what I had hoped, namely, both represent those selections that everyone would expect to find in an anthology of twentieth-century French philosophy and also include selections from thinkers who should be represented in such a collection but for various reasons usually are not. I am still negotiating with my publisher, trying to get them to think about a "hybrid text," something like a small monograph or reference work with selected readings appended that are drawn almost exclusively from the writings of those philosophers normally overlooked in the bigger, classroom-oriented anthologies. But publishers seem uncomfortable with a volume that is neither a monograph, textbook, nor anthology, and I'm not at this point certain that this "hybrid text" will be approved. So, to bring this postscript to a close, while I have begun putting together yet another anthology of new essays, with the working title "Modernity and the Problem of Evil," for Indiana University Press, it is not clear to me right now whether my work on twentieth-century French philosophy will appear as my own monograph or as a text with selected readings, and if the latter, whether it should still be considered an anthology at all.

Notes

1. This essay was originally written for and published in another anthology: "On the Gynecology of Morals: Nietzsche and Cixous on the Logic of the Gift," in *Nietzsche and the Feminine*, edited by Peter J. Burgard. The final, revised version of this essay appears as chapter 4 of my *Nietzsche's French Legacy: A Genealogy of Poststructuralism*.

2. It is perhaps worth noting here that in the case of anthologies that reprint already published works, questions of copyright permissions and costs often play a large role in determining what can and will be included in a collection. This is no doubt why some anthologies reprint older, and in some cases far inferior, translations of the selections they reprint. It is also, I suspect, a reason why some collections fail to include what would seem to be obvious selections. The cost differential is in some cases quite large: some journals will literally give their essays away, while some trade presses I have dealt with have charged thirty dollars a page, and this has been in the context of a scholarly anthology that will have a limited audience at best. There are problems other than cost, however, and although I have not yet had to omit a selection I wanted because the permission to reprint it cost too much, I was forced to exclude Bataille's essay "The Notion of Expendi-

ture" from my gift anthology because the University of Minnesota Press has a rule that prohibits their granting permission for selections that account for more than 10 percent of the total pagination of the resulting anthology.

3. That there has been to my knowledge no critical discussion or even acknowledgment that Bouveresse, an "analytic" philosopher and Wittgenstein scholar, now holds the Chair in Philosophy at the Collège de France that was previously associated with the history of philosophy and was held by Gilson, Guéroult, Hyppolite, and Foucault, is not unrelated to some of the problems that this particular anthology project seeks to address.

Badiou's situation has changed significantly in the past few years, as four of his books and an anthology of his writings have appeared in English translation since 1999, with at least two other of his works soon to appear. After teaching for thirty years at the University of Paris VIII–Vincennes, Badiou was appointed Professor of Philosophy at the École Normale Supérieure in 1999.

4. It should be noted that Sartre himself could be charged with obliterating the philosophical world out of which he and his colleagues emerged. After all, how much does Sartre acknowledge the debates – Bergson and the vitalists vs. Brunschvicg and the neo-Kantians – that provided the backdrop against which his entire philosophical education took place, or the religious existential humanisms like those of Mounier or Teilhard de Chardin to which his own atheistic existentialism was a response? It is perhaps ironic that when, for example, Derrida almost completely ignores Sartre and cites Husserl and Heidegger as his early inspiration, he repeats the very same gesture Sartre performed a half-century earlier.

5. This gave new meaning for me to the idea of the "materiality of the text." In fact, to take one specific example, I am now persuaded to the idea that one of the reasons why the philosophical writings of Albert Camus are almost never included in collections of French philosophy, and are increasingly rare in any anthologies other than those devoted exclusively to existentialism, is that they are prohibitively expensive and difficult to justify when other equally important writings can be reprinted at one-quarter the cost.

Bibliography

Allison, David B., ed. *The New Nietzsche: Contemporary Styles of Interpretation.* New York: Dell, 1977.

Bataille, Georges. *Consumption*. Vol. 1 of *The Accursed Share: An Essay on General Economy*. Trans. Robert Hurley. New York: Zone Books, 1988.

———. "The Notion of Expenditure." *Visions of Excess: Selected Writings, 1927–39*. Ed. Allan Stoekl. Trans. Allan Stoekl, with Carl R. Lovitt and Donald M. Leslie Jr. Minneapolis: University of Minnesota Press, 1985. 116–29.

Benveniste, Émile. "Gift and Exchange in the Indo-European Vocabulary." *Problems in General Linguistics*. Trans. Mary Elizabeth Meek. Coral Gables FL: University of Miami Press, 1971. 271–80.

Burgard, Peter J., ed. *Nietzsche and the Feminine*. Charlottesville: University of Virginia Press, 1994.

Deleuze, Gilles. *Difference and Repetition*. Trans. Paul Patton. New York: Columbia University Press, 1994.

———. *Nietzsche and Philosophy*. Trans. Hugh Tomlinson. New York: Columbia University Press, 1983.

———. *Proust and Signs*. Trans. Richard Howard. New York: G. Braziller, 1972.

Derrida, Jacques. "Différance." *Margins of Philosophy*. Trans. Alan Bass. Chicago: University of Chicago Press, 1982. 1–28.

———. *Given Time. 1. Counterfeit Money*. Trans. Peggy Kamuf, Chicago: University of Chicago Press, 1993.

———. "Khōra." Trans. Ian McLeod. *On the Name*. Ed. Thomas Dutoit. Stanford: Stanford University Press, 1995. 89–127.

———. "Signature Event Context." *Margins of Philosophy*. Trans. Alan Bass. Chicago: University of Chicago Press, 1982. 307–30.

———. "Structure, Sign, and Play in the Discourse of the Human Sciences." *Writing and Difference*. Trans. Alan Bass. Chicago: University of Chicago Press, 1978. 278–93.

Emerson, Ralph Waldo. "Gifts." *Essays and Lectures*. New York: Literary Classics, 1983. 535–58.

Lévi-Strauss, Claude. *Introduction to the Work of Marcel Mauss*. 1950. Trans. Felicity Baker. London: Routledge and Kegan Paul, 1987.

Mauss, Marcel. "Essai sur le don: Forme et raison de l'échange dans les sociétés archaïques." *Année sociologique* 2.1 (1923–24): 30–186. Rpt. in *Sociologie et anthropologie*. Paris: Presses Universitaires de France, 1950. 143–279.

———. *The Gift: The Form and Reason for Exchange in Archaic Societies*. Trans. W. D. Halls. Foreword by Mary Douglas. London: Routledge, 1990.

———. "Gift, Gift." *Mélanges offerts à Charles Andler par ses amis et ses élèves*.

Strasbourg: Istra, 1924. 243–47. Rpt. in *Oeuvres*. Ed. Victor Karady. Paris: Editions de Minuit, 1975. 3: 46–51.

Nietzsche, Friedrich. *The Viking Portable Nietzsche*. Trans. and ed. Walter Kaufmann. New York: Viking, 1954.

Schrift, Alan D., ed. *The Logic of the Gift: Toward an Ethic of Generosity*. New York: Routledge, 1997.

———. *Nietzsche's French Legacy: A Genealogy of Poststructuralism*. New York: Routledge, 1995.

———. "On the Gynecology of Morals: Nietzsche and Cixous on the Logic of the Gift." *Nietzsche and the Feminine*. Ed. Peter J. Burgard. Charlottesville: University of Virginia Press, 1994. 210–29.

———, ed. *Why Nietzsche Still? Reflections on Drama, Culture, and Politics*. Berkeley: University of California Press, 2000.

Schrift, Alan D., and Gayle L. Ormiston, eds. *The Hermeneutic Tradition: From Ast to Ricoeur*. Albany: State University of New York Press, 1990.

———, eds. *Transforming the Hermeneutic Context: From Nietzsche to Nancy*. Albany: State University of New York Press, 1990.

PART THREE

Attitudes and Responses

JEFFREY J. WILLIAMS

Anthology Disdain

What do we usually think of anthologies, in particular literature and theory anthologies?[1] As scholarly work they are usually deemed inferior entities. As pedagogical tools they seem a necessary evil. Simply as books they are disposable, worth only as much as the used market will carry, literally worthless after they are superseded by a new edition. Accordingly, in formal evaluations of our work – yearly reports, salary documents, and so on – they are not credited in the same blue-chip category as scholarly books or articles, and often not even credited as research, but consigned to the prestige-deprived category of teaching or the default category of service. In critical responses they are taken to task for their reductiveness. Like Cliffs Notes they are found wanting insofar as their headnotes and other introductory apparatus represent received opinion and simplify complicated views and their arrangements delimit their respective fields in various ways.[2] In general conversation they are usually mentioned with a long-suffering nod or dismissed with disdain.

But if we think so poorly of anthologies, why do so many of us still use them? And if we use them, why do we feel compelled to speak ill of them? To put this another way, although anthologies might represent received opinion, what are the stakes of our more sophisticated received opinion that anthologies are inferior intellectual enterprises?

While there are no doubt better and worse anthologies, there is a strange dissonance between our commonplace attitude toward them and their actual use and value. I do not mean to be an apologist for anthologies nor to brush their limitations aside (in fact I've examined some of their formal constraints in a previous article, "Packaging Theory"), but here I would like to focus on the ambivalence they induce. That ambivalence, I believe, reveals as much about how we fashion ourselves as academic professionals as it does about their objective qualities. It taps into a realm of what I have called "academic affect," which encodes a hierarchy of values and in a significant way makes us the professional subjects we are, constituting or "performing" our social position. Elsewhere I have looked at a number of other signposts of our professional life, such as "the life of the mind," tenure, and name recognition. Tenure, for instance, refers in our official discourse to the objective job protection of due process (it is not a guarantee of a job but a protection against unfair firing). But tenure in our actual working lives and practices far more often connotes the affective relations within departments, among faculty, and one's own feeling toward one's job – and perhaps one's life.

The ambivalence toward anthologies taps into another strata of academic feeling. I look at anthologies because they are one of the most common objects of our professional life, indeed that permeate our everyday experience, and because they register the tension of our positions between the commercial and the academic, teaching and research, the middle class and the elite, the common and the sophisticated, and paraphrase and complexity. We typically define our positions according to the latter terms, in turn suppressing the former; part of my argument is that this enacts a misrecognition that operates to assure our positions as professionals but that finally is not only inaccurate but has debilitating consequences.

First, the commercial and the academic. One element of our ambivalence toward anthologies, I believe, rests on their being a concrete reminder of the commercial in the academic sphere, which we hold as separate in our professional imaginary.

Anthologies, it often seems, are ubiquitous in literature departments, bowing the shelves in our sections of the campus bookstore, weighing down the backpacks of our students, and splayed open on the rows of desks in our large survey courses. They are a quintessential physical object of our academic environment, distinctive to the university (beyond the generic white-collar appointments of filing cabinets and computer stations) and to our discipline (other disciplines typically use introductory textbooks). But though they collect texts of presumably high cultural value, they themselves have little cultural value;

they fall into the realm of practical use, rather than the realm of aesthetic uselessness (recalling Kant's definition of the aesthetic, of purposiveness without purpose) and are obviously commercial products, manifest in their cash buyback value at the end of term, when students stand on long lines to sell them. More generally, they signal the market relation of the university, one that students experience directly, functioning as a controlled market, paying not only for books but for tuition, fees, housing, food, and so on. Students are often all too conscious of this cash nexus, of pay in exchange for accreditation, when they complain of how expensive anthologies are or tell us that they (or their parents) pay our salaries. It is also a market relation that we participate in whenever we assign an anthology – indeed, as publishers know very well when they shower us with flyers and catalogs, periodic visits, and free examination or desk copies.

Our ambivalence or disdain projects a distance from this basic market relation. It draws on the general opposition, familiar in the "ivory tower" cliché, of the university and business and of the monastic and the worldly. More specifically, it enacts what I would call a defensive professionalism, staving off threats to our distinctive position. The tension between the market and the academic is a familiar crux of professionalism, whereby professions draw legitimation by claiming a disinterested remove from the commercial (see Larson; Robbins). Doctors, for instance, claim to work for the good of humankind, rather than for venal motives like fees. Most of our rationales for professing literature – to preserve culture (the conservative justification), to promote critical thinking (the more progressive rationale), to contribute to the discipline (the intraprofessional rationale), or to expand human knowledge (the extraprofessional rationale) – operate at this level, casting a space outside the market and our motives as ideal rather than material. Our ambivalence toward anthologies derives from their less than ideal significance and expresses our disinterest.

The problem with ambivalence or disdain, however, is that it fosters a denial rather than a recognition of the market relation of the academy and proffers a self-assuring judgment of taste (such concerns are beneath us) that disables an effectual response. The stakes of this misrecognition were especially clear in the Yale graduate student strike of 1995–96, when the faculty rejected the unionization effort. They did so because they held that the university was a space apart, outside the normal operation of market enterprises (hence becoming a patronage system), so unions were not appropriate. While one might supportably claim a separate status to justify the freedom to pursue certain kinds of intellectual work, this professionalist denial fosters a misrecognition of our role as labor and thereby debilitates any effectual political response in negotiating our terms of labor, other than appealing to the beneficence of patronage.

Similarly, our imaginary remove from the market allows us to sidestep or deny the market relation that students experience. That is, anthology disdain might be not just an assertion of our special status but an avoidance of the discomfiting recognition, especially for those of us with the liberal or progressive hope of equal opportunity for education, of the conscription of students as a captive market, visibly of books we assign, less visibly as an indentured class (given the massive growth of student loans; see Lipsky and Abrams). One conclusion is that we should disdain not anthologies but this conscription of students. Another is that we should advocate and initiate programs for free books, co-ops rather than franchise campus stores, and nonprofit publishing of academic texts, rather than simply seeing anthologies in and of themselves as degraded goods.

Second, teaching and research. Another – and perhaps the foremost – element of our ambivalence toward anthologies turns on their standing in for teaching, from which we project a distance in our current professional self-definition as researchers.

Anthologies, in their seeming omnipresence, not only invoke the market but serve as persistent reminders of the classroom and the hours we spend there, as well as preparing, grading, holding office hours, and so on. Because extant modes of professional distinction value discourses and practices conducted under the auspices of research, we often begrudge or resent that time and work, which seem precisely to impede research. One can see this especially in the normal usage of *work* (see Levine 7). By it we do not mean the courses that we teach Tuesday–Thursday, not to mention the six committees we are on or the hour when we go over a paper with an earnest student, but our individual research – in the humanities, the article or book we are preparing for publication. (If asked what you are working on, at a conference or in the mythic tableau of a cocktail party, what do you answer?) This is not out of perversity or self-delusion, but because we define "work" on the model of the techno-industrial research university and its structure of rewards, which places foremost value on research that presumably lends prestige to the institution. In this sense anthology disdain turns not on the questionable merit of anthologies but precisely on their pedagogical value. This disdain extends to other pedagogical instruments, like primers, surveys, and syllabi.

Though research is a fully naturalized expectation for us, it is a relatively recent development, based on the protocols of the Cold War research university (see Lewontin). By 1970, as Christopher Jencks and David Reisman report in *The Academic Revolution*, professors saw their foremost task as research rather than teaching. As a point of comparison, in the previous era a prominent part of the program of the New Critics was not only their critical writing but their series of text-anthologies, such as *Understanding Poetry* (1938), *Understanding Fiction* (1943), and *Understanding Drama* (1946), compiled by Cleanth Brooks, Robert Penn Warren, and other leading figures. There is no contemporary parallel – for instance, *Misunderstanding Poetry* or cognates, edited by Paul de Man and J. Hillis Miller.

In one sense the distance from teaching is a misrecognition, insofar as most faculty, according to MLA statistics, publish relatively little and research universities constitute only 15 percent of higher education.[3] In a different sense it reflects a contradiction inherent in the research university, which claims a special role in generating new, specialized knowledges through research while at the same time invoking teaching as its primary public justification, especially at state colleges and universities, whose mission statements and formal measures still claim teaching, not research, as our primary task. This mirrors a contradiction of professionalism, claiming both a specialized autonomy and a larger public use. The peculiarity of some of our affects toward teaching – whether complaisance, lackluster dutifulness, or resentment – is that it is our primary public justification.

One obvious conclusion is that we should change not only our attitudes toward teaching but our reward structure, so that teaching is not secondary to or a trickle-down from research but as highly valued. However, what has happened instead through the 1990s is a more entrenched division between research and teaching, resulting in what George Levine calls "the two nations" of English, the higher literature faculty and the lower writing faculty. This has also happened in the division of labor between full-time literature faculty who teach upper-level courses and flexible faculty who teach literature surveys and other anthology-based courses. This recognizes the contradiction of the research university but if anything intensifies the subordination if not abjection of teaching.

Third, class. Alongside the professionalist hierarchy of teaching and research, another dimension of ambivalence to anthologies turns on their emblematizing the social hierarchy of class – the tenuous class position of the people and places that tend to use them, from which we distance ourselves to assure our elite standing.

Anthologies are pervasive reminders not only of teaching but specifically of all the lower-level "service" courses we teach and the students who take them – usually poorly prepared, one often hears. In a pointed look at the *Norton Anthology of Women's Literature*, "Is There Class in This Text?," Lillian Robinson describes this predicament quite bluntly: "Within the profession, complaints about the anthologies themselves are not always distinguishable from complaints about the kind of course for which they are assigned and even about the students to whom such courses are addressed" (61). In other words, our response stems not from their objective merit but from their social significance. Anthologies signal the class status both of students and of the universities where they, and we, are located, as Robinson further observes: "The less 'gentlemanly' the institution, in terms of intellectual tradition and student origins, the more likely it is to rely on Norton anthologies in the apposite courses – that is, they are used extensively by students who are the first generation of their families to attend college" (61). Anthology disdain, in this form, expresses a class disdain.

It is not that professors come from the upper class; in fact, it is far more likely that they come from the middle class or perhaps from the working class, and in any case professors assume an amorphous class position, somewhere in the middle (probably with low-middle income) but affecting high cultural standing. The tenuousness of our standing represents a quintessential professional-managerial class quandary, one that Barbara Ehrenreich examines in *Fear of Falling*, in which she deciphers its fraught "inner life." The professional middle class, Ehrenreich argues, attains its position through educational credentials rather than inheritance, which engenders a constitutive class anxiety because its toehold is insecure, dependent on the vicissitudes of the symbolic worth of a sheepskin rather than the anchor of wealth. The extended and repeatedly reinforced procedure of tenure, instead of a short-term probationary period that a civil service worker might experience who effectively gains tenure, makes precisely the anxiety of falling a structural part of our employment. Disdain or contempt for anthologies plays out a class anxiety, projecting an elite status to counter the rude reminder of the less-than-elite standing of many of the schools where we work and the students we teach.

One conclusion is that we should not only value teaching as a humanistic good but, particularly for those of us who claim liberal or progressive politics, see it as a mode of redistribution of resources, one that helps to remedy class inequality. However, the intensification of the job market has only exacerbated our class anxiety, as hiring seems all the more uncertain if not fortuitous. It has also led to a greater disparity between the status of the institution where one has been trained and where one teaches, those with elite credentials landing berths at schools several steps down in the hierarchy, which we tend to feel as a class insult, generating more rather than less disdain.

Fourth, the common and the sophisticated. As a corollary to the issue of class, anthology disdain expresses the valuation of sophistication over common knowledge, one that assures our cultural distinction.

Anthologies are decidedly middle-brow products, ones that, as Robinson puts it, are "a non-elite packaging of elite content" (60). Our professional hierarchy – and a large part of our training – privileges difficult, elite, specialized discourses over nonelite, colloquial discourses. As Pierre Bourdieu and Jean-Claude Passeron argue in *Reproduction in Education, Society, and Culture*, there's a considerable stake in creating an elite language, or what they call the "magisterial discourse" of the "university idiom" (109, 108). Studying efficiency in teaching, they find, somewhat disturbingly, that most pedagogical communication fails, is inaccessible to students, and intentionally works to generate misunderstanding.[4] This functions to assure professional distinction; as they remark, the professor "may have abandoned his ermine and his gown, he may even choose to descend from his dais and mingle with the crowd, but he cannot abdicate his ultimate protection, the professorial use of professorial language" (110). (This bit of satire neatly points out that simply by wearing jeans to class or putting desks in a circle, we do not necessarily abandon our position of authority or distinction.) It also functions to separate students by class (which they show, in typical Bourdieuan fashion, in myriad statistical charts), insofar as students from higher classes are more likely to understand these elite languages, as well as to select some students interested in pursuing the game of education.

This suggests, somewhat perversely, that the problem with anthologies is precisely their accessibility and role in making discourses understandable. One would have thought that a worthy aim, but they then give up the distinction that we affect. Bourdieu relentlessly points out that we establish class standing or "distinction" through cultural capital, which we accrue through the demonstration of taste, valuing the rarefied and sophisticated over the common and pedestrian. Disparagements of anthologies, in this regard, work as an assertion of our sophistication. They turn, again, not on objective merit but on cultural capital. Disdain is an expression of taste, and to put my argument in a nutshell, our response to anthologies relies primarily on judgments of taste rather than logical or cognitive judgments.

Bourdieu's analysis also suggests that a significant part of what we teach is the codes of cultural distinction, encouraging and rewarding their reproduction in our best students. Thus education is a form of redistribution, but it is a skewed one, to those who demonstrate sophisticated taste. One might wish to redress the inequitability of redistribution, but this foregrounds a fundamental dilemma: redistribution depends on the established place of cultural capital, which we can then rechannnel; if democratized it then dissipates the distinctive value of that capital.

Fifth, paraphrase and complexity. A further inflection of our ambivalence toward anthologies rests on their modal form, which is reductive and paraphrastic, in contrast to the complexity of literature and theory. (This point I will spend a bit of time on because, while related to the question of sophistication, it addresses the general theoretical issue of anthologies' objective form.)

Anthologies by definition are reductive. They filter a vast and complicated web of original material into a composite unit and, in making their texts accessible through editing and introductory material like headnotes, operate as paraphrase or synopsis. In contemporary theory paraphrase has been a nodal point, taken up by Cleanth Brooks in "The Heresy of Paraphrase," the culminating chapter of his New Critical classic *The Well-Wrought Urn*, and in surprisingly similar terms by Paul de Man in his foreword to Carol Jacobs's *Dissimulating Harmony*, a précis of deconstructive protocols and caveats for criticism. They both find fault with paraphrase because it extracts propositional rudiments from and substitutes them for literary or theoretical language. For Brooks it yields only "statements" about a poem, "a rack on which the stuff of the poem is hung" (199), eliding the distinctive language of paradox and irony that for him constitutes poetry. Brooks's particular target is the scientific impulse in criticism, and he goes to lengths to distinguish legitimate literary criticism from the propositional form of scientific or philosophical discourse. In de Man's case paraphrase projects the illusion of coherence, "the sequential coherence we associate with a demonstration or with a particularly compelling narrative" (222), which in turn serves to "blur, confound, and hide discontinuities and disruptions in the homogeneity of its own discourse" (220). Like Brooks, de Man rejects paraphrase because it reduces literary or theoretical language to the level of a scientific proposition, which blanches the distinctiveness of that original language. Unlike Brooks, who attributes to good poetry an "achieved harmony" and organic unity, de Man insists on the discontinuities and disruptions in meaning. For him true reading or legitimate literary criticism is attuned to the failure of unity, which paraphrase glosses over. This parallels de Man's objection to translation, which purports an equivalent meaning but, as he argues in his last essay, "Conclusions," always fails its task. Anthologies in this light are always and necessarily failed insofar as they represent paraphrases or vernacular translations of literary or theoretical texts.

Though this line of argument has a certain cogency, it finally relies on a contradiction. It measures the validity of paraphrase based on an idealist conception of knowledge, tacitly assuming that there is an originary core of meaning, embodied in the literary or theoretical text, that paraphrase or translation by definition falls short of or fails. Like imitation for Plato, paraphrase is a degraded representation of the true text. In this light the bias against anthologies participates in the by now familiar metaphysics of presence, devaluing them as secondary and derivative; if, taking the insights of deconstructive or antifoundational critics (like de Man himself) to heart, one instead assumes that there is no primary core or absolute ground, then all knowledge is always secondary and derivative – that is, a form of paraphrase, translation, or rewriting. This is not to say that all forms of rewriting are equal but that one cannot dismiss or invalidate paraphrase, or by extension anthologies, as illegitimate or worthless.

Still, this does not account for the difference between paraphrase and primary texts. That difference, I believe, is best framed in terms of genre and stages of learning. The argument against paraphrase assumes the frame of epistemology and the certainty of knowledge, rather than that of hermeneutics and the processes of interpretation and of pedagogy and the lived practices of how one learns. This is a wrong turn, which leads to the dead end of the failure of paraphrase. If one works instead from the assumption that meaning is constructed, never complete but always in process, and derived from practices rather than from a metaphysical essence, then paraphrase might be seen not as delivering a false knowledge but as playing a constitutive role in interpretation – the "rack" or preliminary steps upon which you build interpretation or that interpretation complicates. In pragmatist terms what matters is what proves useful in building a viable picture rather than what proves true to some higher conception of knowledge. Applied to anthologies, though their paraphrastic traits – received opinion, predictable packaging, and limited selections – fail to a certain degree in representing the full complexity of literature or theory, the more salient issue is their use and place in pedagogy and in helping students build an interpretive repertoire. Against received opinion about paraphrastic genres, Gerald Graff points out that "it is easy to disdain these cribs, but marketing pressures have actually forced their producers to think through the problems facing the average literature student more realistically than have many department curricular planners. Cliffs Notes supply students with the generalized things to say about literary works that the literature program takes for granted they will somehow get on their own" (41).

How after all does our object of study, our course matter, get passed on? How do students actually come to an understanding of what they read or hear, especially if they're reading or hearing it for the first time? How did we start reading and learning the vast lineage of literature or difficult discourse of theory? I would submit primarily through paraphrase, through what Richard Rorty calls redescription, through summary and translation. Paraphrase is in fact a primary mode of teaching, especially in undergraduate classes. In this light anthologies do not represent a failed knowledge but a different genre that accords with a particular stage of learning, or more broadly the manipulation of conventions and genres at hand to construct a scheme for understanding.

One familiar genre that anthologies present in their headnotes is biographical narrative. Another, in their normatively linear arrangement, is historical narrative (usually literary history or history of ideas). Biography has been discredited under the New Critical rubric of "authorial intention," a prohibition continued through poststructuralist criticism, despite proclamations of intertextuality, in the general rejection of humanism. However, though one cannot ascertain a necessary cause or definitive intention of a text from biography, I would argue that biography works rhetorically rather than logically. That is, it is a useful fiction and does productive pedagogical work in providing a "narrative correlative" for ideas. Similarly, though historical narratives might be convenient fictions or paraphrase, they productively construct a framework or scheme for learning. Part of the problem in talking about such pedagogical modes is that they are rhetorical and affective and thus difficult to measure or prove, but I would argue that pedagogy works most indelibly through narrative in three ways: in giving a coherence to what often must seem a bewildering array of facts, whose "compellingness," as de Man puts it, draws students to learn the topics at hand; in providing mnemonic keys and a mnemonic thread to hold ideas in mind; and in projecting models for emulation, which, as Aristotle points out in the under-read second book of the *Rhetoric*, is a primary mode of learning. These affective dimensions – compellingness, memorability, emulation – are usually set outside the realm of critical discussion because they are intangible and not logically demonstrable, but they are central to pedagogy, if not to thinking.[5] Such narratives are what students look to not only in learning a set of views but in fashioning their own intellectual personae.

To give an example drawn from my experience as one of the editors preparing *The Norton Anthology of Theory and Criticism*: in writing the headnote for Henry Louis Gates Jr. I discovered that he had initially attended Potomac State Community College, near where he grew up in West Virginia, but, encouraged by an English instructor, he transferred to Yale. (In his memoir, *Colored People*, he testifies to being a product of affirmative action.) This is no doubt a contingent fact, but a striking one that makes Gates's story more compelling and memorable and that suggests a model of emulation, one that has obvious relevance to students at the state universities where I've taught. While at Yale Gates worked on the gubernatorial campaign of John D. Rockefeller IV (D–West Virginia), writing his senior thesis on the campaign, and traveled for a year on fellowship in Africa. Both of these biographical facts likewise carry some compelling interest, and they also provide some explanation for his generally assimilationist rather than radical position, bridging Yale theory and African tradition and propounding an African American canon but working inside dominant institutional structures. They are accidental circumstances of his life but provide a correlative for the problematic that he works through in his essay in the anthology on the assimilationist Alexander Crummell.

Translation or paraphrase provides a correlative through which students can not only ascertain but affectively engage the texts they have in front of them. According to neuroscientists like Antonio Damasio, ideas do not arise from a separate faculty of "pure reason" but are thoroughly tied to affect and emotion. We need a better way to talk about the affective dimensions of pedagogy, because they are a crucial part of teaching, and we teach not only texts and ideas but affects. We also need a better way to talk about and understand how affects or feelings play a formative role in constructing us as professionals, both for good and ill, because change does not arise from ideas alone.

Notes

1. I concentrate on literature and theory anthologies because I know them best but more consequentially because they structure the basic curriculum in English. This obviously leaves out the vast plethora of composition anthologies, which perform a different role in the curriculum and have different principles of organization. They call for fuller examination, but for now I would say that their inferior status bespeaks a similar relation to teaching and to students.

2. Critics have argued that their synoptic character is not innocent but has negative conceptual and political consequences: they promote a detached rather than dialogical model of literary or critical discourse; they decontextualize their selections apart from larger cultural or social history; and they foster the ideology of liberal individualism, or worse, of dominant, white, Eurocentric culture. (For instance, see my colleague Laurie Finke's essay in this collection.) The impetus of 1990s anthologies, notably the *Heath* as well as newer editions of the *Nortons*, tends toward dispelling the dead white male charge, adding women, people of color, and alternative texts, although it's an open question whether this is finally disruptive or assimilative. The new Longman anthologies attempt to present literature more contextually, and a number of recent theory anthologies try to present theory in terms of critical debates and applied readings.

One nagging question, beyond reconfiguring the contents of anthologies, concerns the structural relation of university teaching. Evan Watkins argues that, "just by virtue of being taught in English, *any* text – 'radical' or 'conservative' or whatever – is already caught up in the social constructions of class, of race, and of gender. . . . For as part of the *social organization* of work in English, these texts occur in the midst of the social circulation of people" (26). I do not think that this negates the value of canon reform, but it does remind us that it should not stop there.

3. As Walter Metzger observes in general, "While all or nearly all academics teach, only a quarter of them account for what may deservedly be called research, and only a tenth of them account for nine-tenths of all scientific and scholarly publications" (163).

4. See also the complementary study, *Academic Discourse*, which focuses on "linguistic misunderstanding."

5. The neuroscientist Antonio Damasio has argued powerfully that emotion is not separate from reason but thoroughly tied to it; in a sense thinking stems from emotion. Damasio distinguishes between affect as a primary physical response and emotion as its cognitive result; I use *affect* here because of its currency in recent theory and because its colloquial sense encapsulates something of visible behavior.

Bibliography

Bourdieu, Pierre, and Jean-Claude Passeron. *Reproduction in Education, Society, and Culture*. 2nd ed. Trans. Richard Nice. Thousand Oaks CA: Sage, 1990.

Bourdieu, Pierre, Jean-Claude Passeron, and Monique de Saint Michel. *Academic Discourse: Linguistic Misunderstanding and Professorial Power*. Trans. Richard Teese. Stanford: Stanford University Press, 1994.

Brooks, Cleanth. "The Heresy of Paraphrase." *The Well-Wrought Urn: Studies in the Structure of Poetry*. 1947. San Diego: Harcourt Brace Jovanovich, 1974. 192–214.

Damasio, Antonio. *Descartes' Error: Emotion, Reason, and the Human Brain*. New York: Putnam, 1994.

de Man, Paul. "'Conclusions': On Walter Benjamin's 'The Task of the Translator.'" *The Resistance to Theory*. Minneapolis: University of Minnesota Press, 1986. 73–105.

———. Foreword. *The Dissimulating Harmony*. By Carol Jacobs. 1978. Critical Writings, 1953–1978. Minneapolis: University of Minnesota Press, 1989. 218–23.

Ehrenreich, Barbara. *Fear of Falling: The Inner Life of the Middle Class.* New York: Pantheon, 1989.

Graff, Gerald. "Taking Cover in Coverage." *Profession* 86 (1986): 41–45.

Jencks, Christopher, and David Reisman. *The Academic Revolution.* New York: Doubleday, 1968.

Larson, Magali Sarfatti. *The Rise of Professionalism: A Sociological Analysis.* Berkeley: University of California Press, 1977.

Levine, George. "The Two Nations." *Pedagogy* 3.3 (2001): 7–19.

Lewontin, R. C. "The Cold War and the Transformation of the Academy." *The Cold War and the University: Toward an Intellectual History of the Cold War Years.* By Noam Chomsky et al. New York: New Press, 1997. 1–34.

Lipsky, David, and Alexander Abrams. "Indentured Students." *Late Bloomers: Coming of Age in Today's America: The Right Place at the Wrong Time.* New York: Times Books, 1994. 107–26.

Metzger, Walter. "The Academic Profession in the United States." *The Academic Profession.* Ed. Burton Clark. Berkeley: University of California Press, 1987. 123–208.

Robbins, Bruce. *Secular Vocations: Intellectuals, Professionalism, Culture.* New York: Verso, 1993.

Robinson, Lillian. "Is There Class in This Text? On *The Norton Anthology of Literature By Women.*" *In the Canon's Mouth: Dispatches from the Culture Wars.* Bloomington: Indiana University Press, 1997. 49–66.

Watkins, Evan. *Work Time: English Departments and the Circulation of Cultural Value.* Stanford: Stanford University Press, 1989.

Williams, Jeffrey J. "The Life of the Mind and the Academic Situation." *The Institution of Literature.* Ed. Jeffrey J. Williams. Albany: State University of New York Press, 2002. 203–25.

———. "Name Recognition." *minnesota review* 52–54 (2001): 185–208.

———. "The Other Politics of Tenure." *College Literature* 26.3 (1999): 226–42.

———. "Packaging Theory." *College English* 56.3 (1994): 280–99.

NANCY CIRILLO

Anthologizing the Caribbean, or, Squaring Beaches, Bananas, and Nobel Laureates

"Anti-Muslim Writer Wins Nobel." So Chicago's largest newspaper announced V. S. Naipaul's receipt of the Nobel Prize for Literature on October 11, 2001. In the aftermath of September 11 such a headline accomplished a few tasks with a minimum of effort. Mostly it justified the award of the prize to a possibly otherwise obscure and therefore perhaps undeserving writer by declaring that the writer's political loyalties were at least beyond reproach. At the same time it defined "literature" as if not entirely then profoundly political, in two senses: first, in the ideological and activist sense, in that it must inevitably take sides; and second, more pragmatically, in that writers (however obscure) on the correct side will be awarded big prizes.

The handling by a major American newspaper of the receipt of the Nobel by Naipaul illuminates (among other things) many of the complexities of anthologizing the Caribbean in the United States. The underlying assumption of the headline that the readership would not accept the idea of a Caribbean laureate without some justification, despite the fact that it was the second in a decade, reveals a fundamental problem: can the North American metropole take the Caribbean margin "seriously"? The dismissal of Naipaul's work as "anti-Muslim" and the implication that that is what got him the prize reveal a reading of a readership admittedly during a time of crisis, when marketing loyalty and power would sell newspapers; Naipaul was, however, easier to dismiss given his unlikely national origins.

Marketing Nobels, at any rate, to a particular public can throw in bold relief how that public is thought to perceive the culture from which the writer comes. Nine years earlier the American press appeared somewhat startled that Derek Walcott, from the Caribbean, had won the prize, there having been again some question of whether the Caribbean had a literature, not to mention literatures. What the press tended to provide for both Walcott and Naipaul was not information but justification, heavy with the implication that they had won Nobels despite their Caribbean origins. Whether the Nobel conferred a kind of legitimacy to the Caribbean was simply putting the question about metropole and margin in different words. We Americans who teach Caribbean literature in the United States sink to this level on occasions of claiming the Nobel in "justifying" what we do in both academic and nonacademic settings. My experience with two Immigration and Naturalization Service officers four years ago on my return from Kingston, Jamaica, where I had examined a book collection, might sum up the latter; incredulous and suspicious at my explanation that I had spent three days in Kingston looking at books, they responded with acid sarcasm: "Caribbean books?" On the other hand, it is often difficult in the American academy to insist upon the particularization of the Caribbean, either as a region or as discrete cultures and nations within the region, while it is subsumed for reasons both pragmatic and ideological under the general rubric of the postcolonial or, even more frequently, under African American or Latin American studies. Consequently, to argue for both Walcott and Naipaul as part of the Caribbean, as part of a century-long tradition of thought and art, and not to see the Caribbean as dignified by their presence, or the laureates as either necessarily anomalous or spontaneous, is problematic in the United States, although less so in Canada and Britain.

Proximity has much to do with this problematic perception of the marginal Caribbean in the metropolitan United States. If geography is destiny, then it was rarely beneficent in the Caribbean. Proximity to the United States created a neocolonialism that thrived on the residual British colonial structures at the same time that it invented forms of political and economic exploitation more adaptive to American interests. Proximity to the United States made it difficult if not impossible to exoticise the region, and consequently it has been represented neither as having a heart of darkness nor as the jewel in anybody's crown. It has not even been able to bask in some reflected glory, as an island paradise, like Bali and the Pacific Islands do for the metropolitan mind in the reflected glory of Asia. Proximity has shaped the marketing of the Caribbean in the United States as a cheap, quick fix to the anxieties of mainland metropolitan life and has helped to commodify the region as the discount paradise. Proximity has probably accounted for much of the indifference to the written part of Caribbean culture, the sense that it is so close we must already know all there is to know about it, and what we know about it precludes literacy, much less art or thought.

This proximity has much to do with the almost tropistic need to justify the written word from the Caribbean, since proximity had everything to do with the neocolonial practices, especially since the turn of the twentieth century. These forms of economic domination – especially the maintenance of single-crop economies and particularly the spectacular rise of the largely American-controlled tourist industry after the Second World War – would produce seemingly unending cycles of poverty, emigration, and instability, all of which proximity renders visible. Marketing these particular economies on the mainland through the all-too-familiar images of beaches and bananas and sun-drenched idylls reinforces and rereads the more than three-hundred-year-old colonialist perceptions of the region as a now convenient, not-too-expensive not-quite-Eden. When political instability and the endless whisper of drug-related crime threatened to staunch the flow of tourists early in the 1990s, the hotel industry responded by putting in place on virtually all the islands the all-inclusive, which is a walled hotel complex, a mutant born of the mating of Disney World with the gated community. Guests can engage in interchange with the citizens of these areas by ordering drinks or fresh towels.[1] The all-inclusive as an architectural signifier is worth an essay all on its own about, at the very least, race and class, North and South.

One way, then, to describe this particular kind of marginalization of the region is to borrow a term from the historians of the Caribbean in their varying but rather consistent description of British policy from the beginning of the nineteenth century – *indifference* – and to use it as a means of representing American attitudes and policy.² Although this indifference has had its own genesis in the United States from, again, proximity, it mirrors and reshapes that older form of indifference of the colonial legacy, of conventions and laws that account for the contemporary "fragmented nationalism" and impenetrable poverty of the Anglophone Caribbean.³

Britain's historic practice of indifference was realized as forms of economic and political negligence; a studied lack of policy; or what the Guyanese intellectual Walter Rodney has called in another, not dissimilar context underdevelopment. This indifference, as the historians variously develop it, describes Britain's handling of the region following the failure of Caribbean sugar and cotton in the world markets by the early nineteenth century and the loss of the American colonies. Imperial attention turned eastward, especially to India: more strategic, wealthier, appropriately exotic, and appropriately hierarchical.⁴ The Caribbean languished. Dealing with the region as a backwater effectively created a backwater. The continuing maintenance of single-crop economies, as punishing to the society as to the soil, through the replacement of slave labor with indentured labor in the mid–nineteenth century, maintained as well a level of subsistence living for the majority of the population that still pertains. The introduction of indentured labor largely from South and East Asia into an area heavily populated by newly freed – but thoroughly unaccommodated – black slaves created tense, often inflammatory relationships that, again, still pertain. In 1938, a year that could well win a world prize for indifference, the Moyne Report to the British Parliament on the state of the colonies listed the barrackyards housing South Asians in Trinidad as exhibiting the worst conditions in the Empire. This was not by design, legislative or otherwise, but a consequence of a century of forgetfulness, of, really, indifference.

Certainly, the discovery of oil a couple of decades earlier in Trinidad and the increasing labor strife did much to jog the collective official memory and possibly even conscience, which resulted in Lord Moyne's mission. If Trinidad, which would eventually supply over 60 percent of the Empire's oil, had suddenly become more interesting, it had also become more dangerous. The increasing labor strife in the oilfields of Trinidad and in shipping and allied industries in Jamaica during the 1930s brought the cauldron of political and cultural energies to the boil. Nationalism and the push for independence manifested themselves as much in the labor struggles as in the appearance of poetry magazines. If marginalization meant indifference in the metropolitan worlds, it had not finally bred passivity in the islands. That activism that Frantz Fanon describes as intrinsic to the expression of a developing national culture had already manifested itself in his native Caribbean.[5] There was, however, no place for these energies to go except into the streets. The institution of the oppressive crown colony structure in almost all the British Caribbean following the Morant Bay uprising in Jamaica in 1865 politically crippled the populations – all of them, white, black, of color – with its travesty of self-governance for the century following.[6]

As a consequence of this history, the Caribbean, as Caribbeans will often say, is a place to be from. At the same time the Caribbean is itself a place of exiles, African, South Asian, East Asian, European, there being almost no indigenous population left except in Guyana and a small preserve in Dominica. The Caribbean, then, as "home" is often ambiguously treated, both passionately loved and profoundly repudiated. The majority of English-speaking Caribbean writers live somewhere else at the same time that they write, almost always, about the Caribbean or about being Caribbean somewhere else. Many, like such visible writers as George Lamming, Kamau Brathwaite, and Walcott, go home for part of the time but mostly live and work in places like London, New York, Boston, or Toronto. Paule Marshall, born in Brooklyn of Barbadian parents, sets almost all her novels in the Caribbean, although she identifies herself as diasporic. She nonetheless appears on at least one list, from the University of the West Indies at Cave Hill, Barbados, as Barbadian.[7] Caryl Philips, born on St. Kitts and taken to England at the age of five, identifies himself almost entirely with the black British movement and only occasionally writes of the Caribbean, although he took over as general editor of Faber and Faber's brief and abortive venture in publishing Caribbean books in 1997.[8]

The point of the foregoing is to ask, since historic circumstances have driven whole populations out of the region, especially its most talented, who is Caribbean? Even the Nobels complicate the answer: while Walcott's acceptance speech, entitled "The Antilles," was a lavish encomium to his native region, Naipaul, in his statement to the press acknowledging the prize, mentioned his adopted homeland, Britain, and his ancestral homeland, India, but gave not a nod to Trinidad or the Caribbean, an omission that did not surprise many of his readers, actually. The two Nobels dramatize from their own perspectives in their responses to the prize the same issues of cultural identity taken up in the marketplace by Chicago's largest newspaper, including, for each, a certain level of justification for this identity. For Walcott the encomium was both polemical and didactic, attaching himself and his work profoundly to the Caribbean. For Naipaul – and this was not a formal acceptance speech but a press release – his work was most explicable through his attachment to one modern power and to an ancient tradition but not to the place in which he spent almost the first two decades of his life.

Are both Nobels Caribbean? If we are preparing an anthology on the Caribbean, may Naipaul opt out? And by the same token may Paule Marshall opt in, so to speak? Is Naipaul, after a half-century of residence in Britain, more at home in an anthology of contemporary British literature? Marshall in an American or African American anthology? Caryl Philips, discussing such questions of identity a few years ago, quoted Michael Ondaatje as saying he didn't care if he was identified as Canadian, Sri Lankan, or diasporic, as long as he got published.[9]

Ondaatje's pungent remarks about identity are relevant here in imagining who qualifies as Caribbean, particularly if we apply them to the group at hand by particularizing the Caribbean diaspora in its historic moment. The major immigration from the region began in 1949, primarily to Britain and Canada, producing in the last half of the twentieth century more than two-thirds of what we might think of as the corpus of English-language Caribbean writing. Although a majority of this group was born in the region, increasingly among the younger group there are individuals who, like Philips, emigrated to the metropolitan centers as small children with families; as the twenty-first century begins there will be new generations born in these metropolitan centers. The term *transnational* is perfectly serviceable for the discussion at hand, particularly in that, among other things, it includes the idea of dual or even multiple identities. The poet Kwame Dawes is an excellent example of this: born in Ghana, the son of the Jamaican novelist Neville Dawes, he returned to Jamaica at the age of eleven and remained there for over a decade before emigrating to the United States, where he has lived and worked for almost twenty years. The center of his work is almost exclusively Caribbean. There are at least three different kinds of anthologies in which Dawes's work would be perfectly at home.

The transnational Caribbeans, like so many other populations, are in more than one sense holders of two or more passports, none of which gets revoked on possession of another. Using this as a model for our purposes here, there is no reason that the Caribbean writer cannot claim a place in two or more anthologies: Naipaul, for instance, in a Caribbean anthology; in one of contemporary British writing; certainly in one of world literature (however that is defined); or in an anthology of South Asian writers of the diaspora.

The question is not so much, what is an authentic Caribbean, as what is an authentic Caribbean anthology at this moment? For anthologies are marked by their temporality and, like those time capsules placed in the cornerstones of local public libraries, freeze a culture at a particular moment. Although there still ain't no black in the Union Jack, no respectable anthology of contemporary British literature would omit black British, and even while Aboriginal suits for full rights of citizenship are still being heard in the Australian courts, Aboriginal writing appears in recent anthologies of Australian literature of various kinds despite the unwillingness of the indigenous Australians to adopt either "Australian" or "Aboriginal" as a form of national identification.[10]

That the anthology comes into being during the heyday of the nation-state is a truism, and that the "founding" anthologies were in one sense or another essentially a kind of nation building as well as a process of canon formation is equally a truism. The dramatic transformations of these traditional anthologies are already in hand for some time, growing even weightier as they grow more inclusive in their battle for the university marketplace. Whether these testify to a new kind of nation building, or to the creation of a new kind of civic, social space that ceases to be national, or to a transnational dynamic so rapid that the idea of the anthology will only be able to survive in the future as some interactive hypertext, is mercifully nothing I can take up here except in the context of the Caribbean.

An inclusive, general anthology of the English-speaking Caribbean at this moment, prepared for the American, probably mostly academic, marketplace, would be a time capsule of largely twentieth-century writers, all of whom identified closely with Caribbean themes and aesthetics. Caribbean themes and aesthetics enlarge the issue of readership beyond the metropole-margin polarity at the same time that they are functionally, organically, a part of it. What Caribbeans write about and how they write about it are both responsive to and independent of their historic, forcible engagement with the metropolitan world. Caribbeans almost always, one way or another, write about history, mostly lost; politics and power; race; poverty; the crumbling vestiges of colonialism; and the glaring signs of neocolonialism. They write about these issues most often in varying linguistic ranges and registers, usually in the same work and frequently shaped by decentered, seemingly fragmented structures.

The readership of such an anthology is likely a student one, but students would not necessarily be particularly different in how they think initially about the Caribbean from that readership of the newspaper discussed earlier. Despite this description, students are inevitably enthusiastic after reading Caribbean writers, although they usually preface their remarks with "I had no idea . . . ," or "I never realized . . . ," acknowledging the general attitude of mainland to region, which forecloses any expectation of print culture. And if they are enthusiastic, and they are, they comprehend the issues with difficulty at first, but then with growing interest, some even abandoning an earlier, openly professed position that history is boring and politics uninteresting. These latter comments are not only anecdotal, the fruits of over a decade of "teaching the Caribbean," but have surely been a focus for generalized professional attention: for example, at the Caribbean Literary Studies conference in November of 2000, a plenary session was devoted to the teaching of Caribbean culture in the United States. The drift of the discussion, and certainly an underlying focus of the panel, was how to address and displace the attitudes and lack of knowledge of mainland, mainstream students. The discussion touched inevitably as well on the sensitive questions of the historic American presence in the region and was protracted, various, and at variance. Anthologizer, take note.

Those rich and complex themes and forms that define Caribbean literature and much of its discourse are rendered even more complex by almost a century of diaspora, although it is mainly a postwar, Cold War phenomenon. The Caribbean immigrants of the 1950s and 1960s were both participants in and witnesses to the dismantling of one empire and the simultaneous creation of new ones. They were of the region, both urban and rural, largely unemployed, with the exception of the few Island Scholars, one from each island annually, subsidized by the British government. They were of color, sometimes South Asian but predominately black, and in the first wave of writers almost exclusively male. Official citizenship was not a problem at the time they emigrated to Britain or Canada; they all carried British passports. Citizenship in every other sense was often catastrophic, culminating in the Notting Hill riots of 1968. The encounter with the metropolitan world of the postwar, disintegrating Empire is represented through finally multiple and shifting identities: Naipaul's mimic man, Lamming's emigrants, Samuel Selvon's Londoners.

Those many students who respond enthusiastically do so initially to fiction and poetry, often because they already know "something" about Caribbean music. That this fiction and poetry – and the music as well – were shaped by the historical and political comes as a revelation: the historical and political as lived experience, under the spell of which history and politics cease to be boring and uninteresting respectively. The Caribbean presence in the United States and the dazzling growth of the music industry, with its infinite cosmopolitan appetite responding to an ever-expanding audience through rapidly adapting technology, have come to create their own sensibilities in the generation to whom this music has become available. In this respect the center/margin polarity is beginning to erode culturally, at least in a specialized sense, in the production and consumption of music, if not hegemonically, that is, politically and economically. However, the availability of calypso and reggae and the occasional Caribbean cuisine not only does not stimulate much expectation of an equally vibrant, elaborated print culture but can work against it; hence the "I had no idea" responses of my students and the plenary sessions at Caribbean conferences that deal with this.

The anthologizer planning an anthology of the Caribbean for the likely American university market, aware of but undaunted by all the foregoing, would have some fundamental questions to answer about the historic U.S. metropole–Caribbean margin positioning, even while taking into account the growing familiarity with island music. Perhaps the first question would be, should two centuries of American involvement in the region be discussed, and is that possible to do without sermonizing or soft-pedaling? If anthologizers deal with the American presence, more significant as neocolonialism, then they must discuss imperialism and colonialism, both historically and theoretically; they must, that is, make intelligible that nearly impenetrable web of European alliances and misalliances that gave the Caribbean its unfortunate sobriquet, the Cockpit of Europe. American anthologizers must confront somehow the issue of a literature and body of discourse that are not separable from historical and political forces that shaped them. To repeat at this point that this is an unfamiliar idea to an American readership is simply to be redundant.

Formal or literary questions concerning what genres to include are not isolated from these issues either. Narrative, for instance, to explore only one genre here, holds a crucial position in the literature of the region, not – and this has been much discussed critically and theoretically by Caribbean writers – as a bourgeois form but as a recuperative and regenerative form in its capacity to reimagine and re-create lost histories, especially African and Asian, an imagined more than an imaginary past, as it can represent through rich and varied language the energy and liminality of the present.[11] Consequently the novel is a major form of Caribbean literature, in all the local languages (nation languages) as well as in the four colonial languages. The omission of all but short narratives is an omission that is, of course, a given with any anthology, but since the novel is a primary form in the Caribbean, should it be acknowledged in some way, through lists of recommended reading or the reproduction of sections of certain novels?

Although this discussion has completely focused on the Anglophone Caribbean, the echoing unasked question – and one the anthologizer would need to consider – is, would it be possible to establish the essential cosmopolitanism of the entire Caribbean basin? But is this doable or even desirable? Even in the same colonial grouping, islands historically had little to do with each other, for reasons of both distance and colonial policy; yet the sense of the region as a region, of regionality, if that is a word, has been growing in the latter half of the twentieth century and into the twenty-first. Even the abortive attempt at federation in the Anglophone Caribbean in 1963 attests to that, but the impulse is even clearer in the cross-cultural interchanges: regardless of language group, everybody knew about, or read in translation, that founding generation, Marcus Mosiah Garvey and Césaire and Fanon, José Martí and C. L. R. James, just to start the list. Since an anthology is as much about time as it is about place, it would seem unnatural to leave this out. Including a section with selections from some of these intellectuals and activists would not only render a more accurate picture of the cosmopolitanism of the region but would restore these influential thinkers to their rightful place as central to the debates of the latter half of the twentieth century.

Anthologies are about time in another sense, not only being aware of themselves as historic artifacts but having a place in the history of that artifact. Among the many reasons anthologizers might spend time looking over their shoulders, looking at what came before is primary. Needless to say, aspiring contemporary American anthologizers of the Caribbean have little to look at except the select (very select) pieces of Caribbean literature that have been included in those bloated tomes of that ever-increasing flood of "world" literature. But that is contemporary. The not-very-lengthy history of Caribbean anthologizing in the United States, however, deserves a mention here.

What appears to be the earliest, or certainly one of the earliest, exemplars of a Caribbean anthology published by an American press for an American readership was produced as a paperback for Pocket Books in 1974 and was likely not intended for the university marketplace, being relatively unencumbered with what is known in the business as "editorial apparatus." There had been some publication of Caribbean writing in the United States for the twenty-year period preceding this, but it had been sporadic and was mostly the product of simultaneous publication in the United States and Britain or Canada by a British press. Such a joint publishing venture produced an earlier anthology – and this does appear to be a first – but clearly for a trade readership, as its title would suggest: *From the Green Antilles: Writings of the Caribbean*. More a sampler than an anthology, *From the Green Antilles*, edited by Barbara Howes, is a sort of aerial view of writing from the four colonial languages through short stories, essays, and poetry. Given its year of publication, 1966, it is likely the publisher, MacMillan, was testing the marketplace at the height of the American civil rights movement to expand the consumership of Caribbean – that is, largely black – literature, already growing in Britain.

The Pocket Books anthology, eight years later, shows marks of awareness of changing relations in the society and the consequent changes in consumer patterns. Even as an artifact, or perhaps especially as an artifact, through its title and cover design, it produces an image, richly unstable, of the relations between mainland and region. This image would be the predictable idiom for the production of Caribbean books for almost the next twenty-five years. The title, *Caribbean Rhythms: The Emerging English Literature of the West Indies*, occupies the top half of the cover, and the remainder bears a color photograph of unidentified but likely Trinidadian steel drummers, palm trees rampant. Particularizing the Caribbean to those of us in Caribbean studies typically means working locale by locale and generalizing, or theorizing, only very cautiously. The Caribbean is particularized in another way, however, for the metropolitan markets by metropolitan presses, and that is iconographically, on its book covers: bright colors; flora abundant and exuberant; black people, preferably dancing. The book itself becomes, thus announced, an unexpected artifact.

This particular cover, for example, can be read in at least two ways that appear contradictory but bear the relationship of something like the reversible reaction in chemistry (is it a gas or a liquid?) or an iconic rendering of the chiasmus, in which each element of the cover subverts the other in organic relationship. In one reading, for example, the title, *Caribbean Rhythms*, in bright red, picks up the possibility that if a reader knows anything about the region it would likely be music, and this is reinforced by the photograph of the drummers. The interplay between the title and the photograph as the first presentation, the cover, of a book of Caribbean writing can be seen as a form of reassurance to the purchaser, almost exclusively metropolitan or presumed to be, that the Caribbean can still be defined by its nonliterary culture, that there has been no noticeable shift in power. The subtitle, *The Emerging English Literature of the West Indies*, would confirm that: whatever this is, it is at least "English," but merely "emerging." "Emerging" is, of course, a redolent term. It assumes the "from." The title and the photograph control the idea of that place from which this writing emerges, and this could be as close to a heart of darkness as the Caribbean would ever come. However dark, benighted, wordless that place is from which this writing is emerging, it is emerging as English, which in its turn gives rise to at least a couple of readings. The first is that these people (playing their drums) are really praiseworthy, worth saving. The other reading is that English somehow won in some contest in which drums and palm trees figured prominently; it has emerged. The word "rhythms" also underscores the power of English literature to "emerge" as it stimulates an image of the primal and of blackness. This word powerfully evokes as well the worst of racial stereotyping in the United States, and this is emphasized by the accompanying photograph. Read in this way the cover reinforces every metropolitan preconception of race and the primitive as it reinforces an unassailable sense of dominance.

There is, of course, the opposite reading, the one that subverts. In this reading the particularization of the Caribbean represented by the cover is associated with the natural and the vital, and the steel drums and palm trees become metonyms for an energetic culture and an exuberant landscape. English literature in this reading does not emerge from some passive primal soup but comes actively out of the vitality represented by the cover. It is something willed. In 1974 even the word "rhythms" could be read differently: in the light of the Negritude doctrine of Aimé Césaire and Léopold Sédar Senghor and its effect on the American black power movement, where the African is seen as intrinsically vital and energetic and possessed of a creative imagination superior to the desiccated linearity of the metropolitan mind. In this reading the emergence of English literature is not so much the more passive process of hybridization but the more creative one of syncretism. In the more recent criticism and theory from the Caribbean, in the work of such writers as Derek Walcott and Wilson Harris who ultimately repudiated Negritude, powerful ideas of syncretism, of re-creation out of the chaos of colonialism, of the "shards" of empire, shape writers' work.[12] For over twenty-five years Caribbean books – whether published in Britain (mostly), in the United States (occasionally), or by the fragile publishing industry in the Caribbean – were immediately identifiable by such covers. What is distinctly possible is that the very instability of these images has made this iconography a marketable truism.

As something of a founding anthology, and indeed certainly an early although not founding publication of Caribbean writing in the United States, *Caribbean Rhythms* represents certain approaches to the marketing of the print culture of the Caribbean in its text as well. James T. Livingston, the editor, opens his introduction by quoting James Weldon Johnson, providing, not quite twenty years into the civil rights movement, a familiar name, a presumption that readers of this anthology would naturally be readers of African American literature. As a market strategy in 1974 this was by no means wrongheaded, nor would it be even now. As a means of providing insight into Caribbean cultures and Caribbean history, it can be misleading for many reasons, but primarily because the black populations are majority, not minority, in the Caribbean and because for three centuries the region was under European domination. Livingston seems aware of this and moves immediately on to the Caribbean itself, providing some generalized background on colonialism in the region and acknowledging that American images of the region are "the frivolous product of tourism" (2). His introduction is a masterful attempt to place this "emerging" literature in its historic and political setting for the American reader, but it is only fourteen pages, itself a comment on editorial assessments of the depth of interest the general readership of a trade book might have.

The selection of texts and their organization are rational in the context Livingston identifies: the introduction of the "literature" of a region of which the assumed reader only has "frivolous" images. Writers are identified by nation, and selections are prefaced with brief critical biographies. The contents are divided into sections by genre, another reassurance of the familiar, of organizing principles well-established.

Since 1974 Caribbean studies in the United States has grown slowly but steadily, partly nourished by the energies of African American studies and Latin American studies, then in the late 1980s by postcolonial studies. Likely primed by these developments, ten or more years ago there was a small flurry of reprint publishing of such writers as C. L. R. James, following his death and attesting to his political rehabilitation in the United States twenty-five years later and postmortem. This was mainly the work of university presses buying reprint rights from largely British publishers, but since university presses are attuned to academic markets, however small the flurry, it acknowledged a stirring of interest in the culture of the English-speaking Caribbean in institutions that could guarantee group adoptions, although in this case not, of course, mass adoptions.

Public interest spiked when Walcott won the Nobel in 1992, although largely in Walcott himself, which suggests that Nobels are interesting but not necessarily where they come from. Although this is anecdotal, bookstores display both Walcott and now Naipaul as Nobels, not as writers from the Caribbean.

Publishers typically publish only if there is a market, and this truism is especially true for the more expensive, complex, and time-consuming project of an anthology. By the mid-1990s certain Anglophone Caribbean literature was available in single paperbacks, either reprints of canonical writers, like the Jamaicans Roger Mais and V. S. Reid, or contemporary writers, like the Belizean Zee Edgell or the Jamaican Michelle Cliff. The translations of, again, certain select contemporary Francophone writers like Maryse Condé (Guadeloupe) or Patrick Chamoiseau (Martinique) receive the kind of critical attention – the *New York Times Book Review* and the *New York Review of Books* – to which publishers are very alert. Translations from the Spanish, especially from Cuba and the Dominican Republic, are receiving more critical attention aimed at the general public.

The first generation of Caribbean writers, those who arrived in Britain starting in 1949, were indeed founding fathers, and if they had been preempted by the redoubtable Jamaican poet Una Marson, who emigrated to Britain for a brief period in the 1930s, it was their generation that was known as the "boom." By the 1980s the majority of Caribbean writers available in print were female, a phenomenon that has received a good deal of attention. Predictably, an anthology of Caribbean women writers appeared in 1990, Daryl Cumber Dance's *Out of the Kumbla*. Other specialized anthologies like *New Writing from the Caribbean* (MacMillan/Caribbean) and *The Caribbean Writer* (University of the Virgin Islands) are hardy annuals that also appeared in the early 1990s but are not readily available in the continental United States.

If the American markets, both general and academic, did not appear to be especially ripe in the 1990s for a wide-ranging anthology of Caribbean literature, certainly Britain and Canada were, with their numerous and well-established Caribbean populations and the growing and expressive presence of Caribbean intellectuals especially in the British universities. Consequently, the first and the only anthology to date of the Anglophone Caribbean that attempts a wide-ranging selection over the entire twentieth century is British and is published by Routledge, a firm that comes close to specializing in postcolonial literature, theory, and criticism. Entitled *Reader in Caribbean Literature*, it was published simultaneously in London and New York in 1996. The anthology is clearly for academic use exclusively, judging from the critical essays written by the two British academics, Alison Donnell and Sarah Lawson Welsh, who edited it. Like the critical essays in most anthologies these are addressed to some general academic reader, a divisible category between teacher and student, somewhere between the specialist and the uninitiated. But the simultaneous publication renders the categories even more divisible by geography and culture; that is, like all anthologies this one is about place, but in a somewhat more complicated sense. The Anglophone Caribbean, once colonial and now Commonwealth, is geographically distant and culturally present in Britain, while in the United States the Caribbean is geographically close enough for intense economic and political engagement yet far less culturally present on the mainland. In the case of this anthology the idea of place, the representation of the literature of one place to readers in another, is then further complicated by what the editors can or cannot assume about the readership, or, what would be truer here, readerships, about how they think, critically, theoretically, politically, and historically.

The general introduction announces exactly on page 1 the purpose of the anthology: "to generate more readers of Caribbean literature and readers of more Caribbean literature." A political statement of purpose, its multiple subtexts would include an address to the almost two centuries of indifference from the colonial power as it addresses its primary readership in that one-time colonial power itself. As a theoretical statement it argues for the erosion of the center/margin polarities and for the repositioning of Caribbean literature/theory in postcolonial discourse. As a historical statement it redresses a cultural imbalance in attempting to return materials unavailable or ignored for over half a century to at least academic and possibly even public attention. The statement of purpose is meaningful to both sets of readers on opposite sides of the Atlantic, in that Caribbean literature has been conspicuous by its absence; how this might be explained in each metropolitan locale would look very different.

The political statement of purpose above, in its directness, its unselfconscious moral sense, the presence of a voice, is more common in British critical and historical texts and sets a tone for the entire twenty-seven-page introduction with its forthrightness and lucidity. American students, especially graduate, are not unaware of this, and some find this distinctive voice "opinionated." This distinctiveness of tone and approach between British and American critical writing is as clear a marker of cultural differences in readership as any. Certainly another, one that addresses methodology, constitutes a section in the introduction and is entitled "Locating Theory." Locating theory takes about a page. Although there is nothing that directly identifies any school of thought, culture, nation, or readership in this section, the usual suspects are likely in the American academy, where theory has a far stronger hold: "Although 'theory-speak' can disguise its own value-laden assumptions within a cumbersome costume of elaborate language games, it can also work to unmask areas of intellectual activity in which covert . . . cultural biases masquerade as clarity and universal truth" (Donnell and Welsh 9).

Although few would argue that point even on this side of the Atlantic, the judiciousness employed by Donnell and Welsh suggests a stronger awareness of the twinned birth in New York and London of this volume in this brief discussion of theory than elsewhere. Their general caution about the use of theory, however, reinforces a point they make elsewhere, one every student of the Caribbean must make, that Caribbean theory is intrinsic to the subject and that, in respect to the rise of poststructuralist theory in the metropolitan world, it is often prior and typically influential; also, at the intersections of European and postcolonial theory, "the Caribbean . . . has been the crucible of the most extensive and challenging post-colonial theory" (Ashcroft, Griffiths, and Tiffin 144). In their effort to "generate" more readers of the Caribbean they do much to set the record straight in positioning Caribbean literature and theory and in adjusting the ways by which the metropolitan universities see this positioning, which leads them to a final caution at the end of this section: "In the 1990's fetishization of theory, it is also our aim to alert readers to the problems of constantly proliferating critical discourse without an accompanying attentiveness to literary texts" (Donnell and Welsh 10).

The anthology is also markedly British in the transparency with which it treats Caribbean and British colonial history, both factually and conceptually. For example, the statement that the Caribbean aesthetic embodied "a desire to decolonize and indigenize ... a geography and a people who had been dominated by British Victorians" (Donnell and Welsh 4) would mean a great deal more to a British student than to an American. Even American students who have "done" a survey that includes Victorian literature or a course in Victorian literature would not respond to the allusion easily and instantaneously. The introduction is full of statements like this that are perfectly meaningful to any reader who knows at the very least British colonial history. American teachers end up teaching the essays as well as the literature and would do well to require a history of the Caribbean as a companion volume.

For American readers uninitiated in Caribbean (or British colonial) history the organization of the volume into historical sections covering decades, with brief prefatory essays, offers some relief. Although this runs the danger of artificiality and arbitrariness, it at any rate shows progression and relationship in this still-unfamiliar literature. It also provides a connective tissue around the gaps and holes any anthology suffers. The necessary exclusion of the novel does not necessarily mean the exclusion of the novelist, and many are represented here by either short fiction or essays. Their selection is as justifiable as any, and to argue that they should have included V. S. Reid rather than Roger Mais is simply frivolous. On the other hand, the exclusion of Derek Walcott and V. S. Naipaul is announced up-front and justified on the grounds of the expense of reprint and the accessibility of their work. Fair enough.

The Routledge *Reader in Caribbean Literature* is thoughtfully done. As it is the only volume of its type available at the moment, there is even more reason to be grateful for the intelligence and lucidity with which it has been put together. For the American market Routledge might consider a special preface in the next edition. Or some other publisher might consider an anthology exclusively for the American market.

What might that look like? From the foregoing the answer is clear: first, a much more extensive historical section, one that focuses not only on Caribbean history and British colonialism but also on two centuries of the American presence. Second, because of the proximity of the region, its cosmopolitanism is much more apparent, even if it is not thought of in quite that way. The Spanish-speaking Caribbean has a visible presence on the mainland, for example, and the Dutch-speaking islands attract a considerable amount of tourism. The French Caribbean is probably best known through the painful history of Haiti (and the vexed American presence there) and the Haitian communities in the United States, although Martinique and Guadeloupe attract their share of tourism. Including some work from these non-English-speaking areas would render a far clearer picture of the region, one that would synthesize a sense of the place an American reader might already have from various experiences. Even more important, this would ensure the inclusion of seminal thinkers and artists like Césaire and Fanon, Martí and Nicholás Guillén.

These are the names, along with others like C. L. R. James, Kamau Brathwaite, and George Lamming, whose work appeared immediately following the end of the Second World War and took the game beyond the boundary and declared the very rules by which it existed to be fraudulent, bankrupt, and hypocritical: "Europe is morally, spiritually indefensible" (Césaire 32). The cosmopolitanism of the Caribbean took on new meanings as these writers emigrated: back to, of course, the old – or the new – colonial powers, where there was enough wealth to publish books for a readership; to London, Paris, Toronto, and New York. Much of what they wrote became foundational in the debates of the latter half of the twentieth century. A Caribbean anthology for Americans might provide a certain sophistication to the national perspective by addressing a cosmopolitanism that exists outside the consumerist models.

It is not only the cosmopolitanism of the Caribbean but the historic experience of the region that places it so often in the central debates on world poverty, health, education, political stability, race, the environment; the list is long. For example, if this essay appears uncoupled from the now-growing field of postcolonial studies for its lack of specific reference to methodology, concept, or theory, it is not, of course, nor can it be. To repeat the earlier point, to read the Caribbean historically – to read, that is, those texts of the 1950s especially – is to read certain of the earliest articulations of what would subsequently earn the name "postcolonial," as reading Caribbean texts in general provides the corrective for turning postcolonial theory indiscriminately and hegemonically against the dense, complex weave of island and diasporic texts: "the . . . emphasis on literary critical theory is as hegemonic as the world which it attacks" (Christian 459).

Further, in almost every way we might intend this, the Caribbean is an invention of colonialism, or, what is far truer, the protean forms produced by colonialism in all its stages and the responses, reinventions, and re-creations of the populations upon whom these were visited. As the only region of the world entirely populated for three centuries by exiles, voluntary and involuntary, in the service of the colonial powers and for whom, therefore, the indigenous was always somewhere else, the Caribbean can be best understood in these terms of this essential historic condition.

Perhaps because of the exceptionalist nature of Caribbean texts, or perhaps because of the institutional nature of postcolonial programs in the United States, or perhaps because the Caribbean, or at least the Spanish-speaking Caribbean, was taught in Latin American or Americas programs, the Caribbean does not show up as frequently in most postcolonial programs in the American academy as South Asia and Africa do. Certainly, one reason for this is that these two areas weigh more and have done so for the past two hundred years, in the strategic and economic balances of the metropolitan world. Also, the early creation (by the 1840s) in South Asia of a British-educated indigenous class to help administer the rapidly expanding Raj helped as well to create a few decades later an increasingly independent tradition of intellectualism on the subcontinent. The dominance of South Asian postcolonial theorists today is a posterity of this. Theorizing South Asia and Africa on economic, strategic, or cultural grounds, on relations between the colonizer and the colonized, on the significance of the indigenous, on ruling elites, on versions of the past – the list is very long – yields little that pertains to the Caribbean.

Yet the very exceptionalism of this region, where institutions are almost entirely the invention of colonialism and cultural response was almost entirely an effort to exorcise it and synthesize a new consciousness, would however argue that the study of the cultures of the Caribbean can produce, as it already has, penetrating insights into the nature of colonialism and its aftermath. This would be one compelling argument for teaching Caribbean studies as part of postcolonial programs. Teaching Caribbean studies as part of postcolonial studies also engages more profoundly the European origins of Caribbean colonialism and would provide a fair counterbalance to the appearance of Caribbean subjects in gender studies, as a consequence of the wave of major Caribbean women writers of the past two decades, and in African American studies, where interest in the relationship between the mainland and the region is widening to include issues of the diaspora, itself, of course, a subject quintessential to the study of colonialism. Finally, since for three hundred years the region experienced cycles of intense exploitation and complete neglect of its environment, a subject ubiquitous in Caribbean writing of all kinds, there is an increasing interest in environmental or ecocriticism.[13]

But again, there is no way to detach these disciplinary approaches to the Caribbean from the fact of its colonial invention and the historic struggle against it. That postcolonial studies is a vexed and contentious arena – that its practitioners cannot agree on what constitutes it, how to spell it, or whether the "post" properly begins with the appearance of the first bootheel in the sand or when the Union Jack was run down the mast and a brand-new flag run up – is a mantra often recited. That there is no simple answer, nor should there be, is yet another truism. Particularizing a region, reading its texts, historicizing it, may at least lead to clearer questions and, to repeat an earlier point, vitiate the excessive generalizing, the intellectual bullying, that can proceed from the exclusive reliance on the theoretical.

This is a function anthologies perform well, if spottily and selectively, as an introduction. The anthology for an American readership outlined earlier could particularize the region in a way meaningful to Americans. Such an anthology might do very well in the American market. It might also – to move this discussion from the commercial, the who sells what to whom – offer an antidote in some small way for American indifference to the region. In any of the many and sometimes conflicting ways Naipaul's oft-quoted remark, that the Caribbean is the third world's third world, might be taken, there is no disagreement that it sharply illumines the fierce economic, social, and political conditions that describe the region. Proximity has rendered the United States both an agent and a witness of this. Such an anthology might speak of these things.

Notes

1. Nobody said it better on this subject than Jamaica Kincaid in her polemical work on her native Antigua, *A Small Place*, the text of which provides the screenplay for the recent (2001) Jamaican documentary *Life and Debt*, on the predations of the World Bank.

2. See the work of Gordon Lewis, Eric Williams, Philip Sherlock and Hazel Bennett, Jan Rogozinski, and Franklin W. Knight.

3. See Franklin W. Knight, *The Caribbean: The Genesis of a Fragmented Nation*. Elie Wiesel, in his dedication speech for the Holocaust Museum, referred to indifference as "the worst of crimes."

4. Among the best discussions of this particular phase of the Empire is David Cannadine's *Ornamentalism*.

5. See Fanon's *The Wretched of the Earth*.

6. See especially the epilogue to Eric Williams's *History of Trinidad and Tobago*.

7. This information is from their acquisitions librarian.

8. He has written of the Caribbean in three novels: *A State of Independence*, *Higher Ground*, and *Cambridge*.

9. Philips made these remarks at the Dusable Museum, February 1997.

10. Paul Gilroy made the remark about the Union Jack and later used it as the title of a book: *"There Ain't No Black in the Union Jack": The Politics of Race and Nation*.

11. Certainly a seminal work on Caribbean narrative is George Lamming's *The Pleasures of Exile*.

12. The notion of the "shards" of empire is from Walcott's Nobel acceptance speech, published as *The Antilles: Fragments of Epic Memory*.

Syncretism is a consistent theme sounded in Wilson Harris's work, for one example, as a "principle of justification" that "set up an alteration in textures of imagination" (3).

13. A call for submissions to a volume entitled *Caribbean Literature and the Environment: Between Nature and Culture*, from Elizabeth DeLoughrey (English)

and Renee Gosson (French), at Cornell University, in July 2002, suggests the immediacy of this topic.

Bibliography

Ashcroft, Bill, Gareth Griffiths, and Helen Tiffin. *The Empire Writes Back*. London: Routledge, 2000.

Cannadine, David. *Ornamentalism*. London: Allen Lane, 2002.

Césaire, Aimé. *Discourse on Colonialism*. Trans. Joan Pinkham. New York: Monthly Review Press, 2000.

Christian, Barbara. "The Race for Theory." *Cultural Critique* 6 (1987): 51–63. Rpt. in *The Post-Colonial Studies Reader*. Ed. Bill Ashcroft, Gareth Griffiths, and Helen Tiffin. London: Routledge, 1995. 237–41.

Dance, Daryl Cumber. *Out of the Kumbla*. Trenton NJ: African World Press, 1990.

Donnell, Alison, and Sarah Lawson Welsh. *Reader in Caribbean Literature*. London and New York: Routledge, 1996.

Fanon, Frantz. *The Wretched of the Earth*. New York: Grove Press, 1965.

Gilroy, Paul. *"There Ain't No Black in the Union Jack": The Politics of Race and Nation*. London: Hutchinson, 1987.

Harris, Wilson. The Whole Armour and The Secret Ladder. London: Faber and Faber, 1962.

Howes, Barbara, ed. *From the Green Antilles: Writings of the Caribbean*. New York: Macmillan, 1966.

Kincaid, Jamaica. *A Small Place*. New York: Plume/Penguin Books, 1988.

Knight, Franklin W. *The Caribbean: The Genesis of Fragmented Nationalism*. London: Oxford University Press, 1990.

Lamming, George. *The Pleasures of Exile*. New York: Allison and Busby, 1984.

Lewis, Gordon K. *The Growth of the Modern West Indies*. New York: Monthly Review Press, 1968.

Livingston, James T., ed. *Caribbean Rhythms: The Emerging English Literature of the West Indies*. New York: Pocket Books, 1974.

Philips, Caryl. *Cambridge*. London: Bloomsbury, 1991.

———. *Higher Ground*. London: Viking, 1989.

———. *A State of Independence*. London: Faber and Faber, 1986.

Rodney, Walter. *How Europe Underdeveloped Africa*. London: Bogle-L'Ouverture, 1968.

Rogozinski, Jan. *A Brief History of the Caribbean*. New York: Meridian, 1992.

Sherlock, Philip, and Hazel Bennett. *The Story of the Jamaican People*. Kingston: Ian Randle Publications, 1998.

Walcott, Derek. *The Antilles: Fragments of Epic Memory*. New York: Farrar, Straus and Giroux, 1993.

Williams, Eric. *History of Trinidad and Tobago*. New York: Praeger, 1964.

ANGELINE O'NEILL

Distinguishing the Map from the Territory

Before the name: what was the place like before it was named? – Paul Carter, "Spatial History"

In recent years the instability of notions of text and textuality has impacted significantly the academy, the publishing industry, the reading public, and relations among them. Indigenous writers, orators, academics, and editors have been empowered by this, and an increasing number of anthologies of Indigenous literature have appeared, the content and very existence of which make strong political and social statements. The relationship between this phenomenon and the politics of literature and theory inside and outside the academy requires close scrutiny. Indigenous literature and orature directly challenge academic assumptions of "good literature" as evidenced in the Western literary canon, highlighting the restrictions of this canon that have supported and been supported by the academy, often to the detriment of the establishment of an Indigenous voice. The transformation of an oral into a written tradition is a case in point, prompting us to ask what Indigenous literature is and does. How is it anthologized, and to what effect? What are the problems inherent in the selection/editing/publishing process? Cross-cultural issues demand consideration, and in this context the process of anthologizing is simultaneously a movement toward others and a study of that movement, particularly where it involves collaboration between Indigenous and non-Indigenous editors. Recent anthologies, such as *Reinventing the Enemy's Language: Contemporary Native Women's Writings of North America*, edited by Joy Harjo and Gloria Bird, exemplify power relations in Foucault's sense, not as static situations but as processes or dynamic systems resulting from the interplay of multiple sites of power. Other examples to be discussed here include Daniel David Moses and Terry Goldie's *Anthology of Canadian Native Literature in English* and an Australian collection, *Those Who Remain Will Always Remember: An Anthology of Aboriginal Writing*, edited by Anne Brewster, Rosemary van den Berg, and myself. Each of these anthologies provides a space for dialogue between those who work in the literal and/or metaphorical "territory" of the Fourth World, such as Native North American and Aboriginal Australian writers and orators, and those who try to map it, including non-Indigenous editors and academics.

Perhaps the best place to begin any consideration of such a complex area as that of anthologizing is with a brief look at the changing notion of "literature." Andre Lefevere proposes that "a literature . . . can be described as a system, embedded in the environment of a civilization/culture/society, call it what you will" (465). He proceeds to say that "the system is not primarily demarcated by a language, or an ethnic group, or a nation, but by a poetics, a collection of devices available for use by writers at a certain moment in time" (465). This latter statement would be disputed by many Indigenous writers and orators as an ethnocentric generalization that seeks to separate the indistinguishable strands of literature: language, ethnicity, and poetics. Well-known American Indian writer Leslie Marmon Silko, for example, poses the pertinent question, "What changes would Pueblo writers make to English as a language for literature?" and asks her reader "to set aside a number of basic approaches that you have been using and probably will continue to use, and, instead, to approach language from the Pueblo perspective, one that *embraces the whole of creation and the whole of history and time*" (49, italics mine). According to the Pueblo, "expression resembles something like a spider's web – with many little threads radiating from the center"; each word-thread has its own story. Language, then, *is* story (Silko 49–50), and the story is the people, who will absorb and transform whatever linguistic materials are available in order to perpetuate the web – in this case the English language, the language of the colonizer.

Although Silko contests Lefevere's dissection of "literature," she seems to be in agreement with Lefevere when he describes the emergence of "a kind of hybrid poetics" resulting from the interaction between two systems: a historically dominated system (for the purposes of this essay, Native North America and Aboriginal Australia) and a historically dominant system such as the English one. In the early stages the latter, according to Lefevere, constrains the production of literature within the dominated system. The resulting "refraction" of the dominated system has, until recently, been the material of Indigenous anthologies in the domain of educational institutions. Such collections, whether consciously or not, were united in their assumption of "the white man's civilising mission and of his superiority," and this consensus was maintained by "undifferentiated patronage" (466–67). In these conditions unique elements of the dominated system either vanish or go underground, until a readership develops that acknowledges and accepts the hybrid poetics (Lefevere 469). I would add that it is at the moment of such acknowledgment that many recent anthologies have come into being, coupled with the academy's realization that a literary canon must of necessity be flexible and dynamic. Collections of Indigenous "writings" in English are finding an increasing non-Indigenous and Indigenous readership and a number of publishing houses willing to support them (for economic as well as ideological reasons). They are proving useful tools for cultural and linguistic empowerment. In the words of Native American writer Kateri Damm: "We can fight words with words. Then, with the weakening of colonial attitudes we can move together towards greater cultural, artistic and creative forms of expression that reflect the changing faces of who we are. . . . We will look with two sets of eyes and hear with two sets of ears and we will speak from the place where we stand with full confidence in the power of our voices. Indigenous literatures will resist the boundaries and boxes. . . . More importantly, we will open the borders to each other" (24).

In recent years the revisiting of the Western literary canon has seen the opening up of notions of text and textuality, which amounts to a reconsideration of the acts of writing and reading, and speaking and listening. This has obvious implications for the process of anthologizing, as "any reflection on the dualism work/text oscillates between two extreme poles: one where the work and its author are practically identical and the other where the text is a set of signs coded by multiple keys" (Chevrel 61). If a text is a set of signs bearing meaning, then the hegemony of the historically dominant system may be called into question, and the way is opened for new and different uses of language and modes of interpretation. What Chevrel labels "paraliterature" – "all the texts which are not canonised by institutions or those which institutions have trouble accepting" (47) – is foregrounded. Much Indigenous writing falls into this category.[1]

Ironically and with some justification, literary theory – a tool often used to question the process of canonization – is frequently coupled with canonization as a way of changing or remaking Indigenous stories, the reworked or reinterpreted versions of which are then anthologized by the literary establishment to the detriment of both. Lefevere warns of this when he recommends that literary scholars must now show a deep awareness of noncanonized and "refracted" texts. Happily, he says, "the hybrid poetics has produced its hybrid patronage: the canonization of works and writers that is now going on" (470).[2] He warns that while "systematisation" on this basis may be valuable, we run the risk of giving it "some kind of ontological status" and confusing the map with the territory. This danger can be avoided by means of "continuous feedback between those . . . who work in the territory itself, and those of us who try to make maps" (470). Anthologies can provide this sort of feedback.

In her essay "Native Literature: Seeking a Critical Center" Native American poet and academic Kimberly Blaeser, of the Ojibway, discusses the theorizing of American Indian literature and calls for "a critical voice and method which moves from the culturally-centered text outward toward the frontier of 'border' studies, rather than an external critical voice and method which seeks to penetrate, appropriate, colonise or conquer the cultural center" (53). In her discussion she focuses on the difficulties arising from the transformation of Native languages into English, and oral into written forms. Blaeser is critical of attempts to resolve these difficulties using Western literary theory, according to which the worth of the literature is essentially validated by its demonstrated adherence to a particular literary mode, dynamic, or style (55–56). Although admitting that some scholars in Native studies have not applied the theories in this colonizing fashion, she vigorously maintains that the authority granted to the mainstream critical center marginalizes Native texts. She takes as her prime example the oral tradition, elements of which "have been dismissed as primitive, rediscovered and translated into 'literary' forms, used as models for contemporary literary and cultural movements, altered and incorporated into mainstream works of literature, and almost theorised into their predicted 'vanishment'" (54). In other words, Blaeser, like Lefevere, seems to be calling for a revision of the relationship of Indigenous writers and orators with literary critics and academics. However, she sees an emerging group of Indigenous, bicultural "word warriors" addressing this issue through "literary self-consciousness and intertextuality, the multiple connections with oral tradition and the theorising within the literary works themselves" (61), thus focusing on past race relations and opening Native American texts on their own terms to a broader contemporary readership.

The issue of the relationship between past and present looms large in Joy Harjo and Gloria Bird's *Reinventing the Enemy's Language: Contemporary Native Women's Writings of North America*. In fact, the two are inseparable, so much so that the introduction assumes the form of a dialogue between the editors, behind which is heard the constant buzz and hum of their women ancestors' voices in dialogue with their unborn daughters and granddaughters. We are told that "*Reinventing the Enemy's Language* was conceived during a lively discussion of native women meeting around a kitchen table. Many revolutions, ideas, songs and stories have been born around the table of our talk made from grief, joy, sorrow, and happiness. We learn the world and test it through interaction and dialogue with each other, beginning as we actively listen through the membrane of the womb wall to the drama of our families' lives. . . . The kitchen table is everpresent in its place at the center of being. . . . . We welcome you here" (19). From the opening words to the final poem, suitably entitled "Perhaps the World Ends Here," the anthology cheerfully answers contributor Kimberly Blaeser's fears that literary theory and analysis will kidnap Native American writing and announces the triumphant emergence of an empowering discourse. The anthology exhibits a strong suspicion of the written word, and the editors explain that historically the written word in English was a weapon of destruction for their peoples and their strong oral traditions. For this reason the prose and poetry in *Reinventing* is framed by "oral" pieces, and each contributor "speaks" a brief, personal commentary on her piece, herself, and why she writes, establishing a link between herself and her ancestors. Family and particularly children, as the modern heirs to these living traditions, figure prominently: "We wished the collection to be as solid as a kitchen table and imagined creating that kind of space within the pages of a book, a place where we could speak across the world intimately to each other" (21). Building on this solid foundation, the editors sought to politicize as well as transform literary expression, providing as they did so a forum for self-expression for eighty-seven women writers from various tribes and backgrounds, representing fifty tribal nations. Not surprisingly, the anthology became a book as much about the process of writing and speaking as about survival and being Native/Indian and female. *Reinventing* is fundamentally concerned with power relations in Foucault's sense. In this case power emanates from myths and stories and from the women who have communicated them and will continue to do so. Power also resides in the written (and published) word in English, which, as the title suggests, will be "reinvented" as a result of the interplay between these sites of power.

Harjo and Bird solicited work from a diverse group of Native American women "to speak . . . to become empowered rather than victimized by destruction" and to return to the traditional "power of language to heal, to regenerate, and to create" (21). So too, in their introductory dialogue in *An Anthology of Canadian Native Literature in English*, Daniel David Moses and Terry Goldie establish the text as a space for the interplay of different sites of power. Like Harjo and Bird, Moses comments on his people's need for self-expression and "the variety that results, the different ways this English language is being nuanced and danced about on these pages" (xxix). Goldie, a non-Indigenous editor, establishes his role in this interplay when he says that one of his aims in the anthology was to "do a little bit to get the Native voice heard" rather than to comment on it (xix), and Moses agrees that it is a space where Native writers can tell their own stories and the dominant community must "just . . . sit back and watch" (xxvi). Similarly, *Those Who Remain Will Always Remember* is a collaborative effort that developed from enthusiastic discussions, motivated by a desire to see Western Australian Aboriginal people better represented nationally.

In an effort to achieve these goals and in recognition of the inherent limitations of the written word in English, each of the anthologies is only loosely structured. *Native Literature* is arranged chronologically, with the first and second sections devoted to traditional songs and traditional orature, while the pieces in *Reinventing* and *Those Who Remain* are very loosely grouped according to the contributors' predominating concerns. Joy Harjo and Gloria Bird proceed from a section entitled "The Beginning of the World" to "Within the Enemy: Challenge," followed by "Transformation: Voices of the Invisible" and finally "Dreamwalkers: The Returning." At the suggestion of the publisher, *Those Who Remain* has no visible divisions at all, allowing each piece to flow into the next. All of the collections may be said to blur genres, containing a mixture of songs, stories, poems, orature, memoirs and commentaries, letters, and pieces that simply cannot be categorized in any of these ways. Not surprisingly, many of the writers disregard the expectations of standard English. Nor is it surprising that the anthologies focus on similar issues: cultural regeneration, family and gender, race relations past and present, social problems such as domestic violence, alcohol and drug abuse, all of which convey a steely determination to survive.

These concerns show the writers' resolution to empower themselves and to correct the sort of representation by a dominant society so often found in early anthologies of Indigenous literature, which are clearly "owned" by their non-Indigenous editors. While they were compiled with the best of intentions, the fact remains that many provide a greater insight into the editors' and publishers' vision of Indigenous peoples than that of the contributors themselves. In this respect they are representations of the Indigene, who is reduced to the status of "a semiotic pawn on a chess board under the control of the white signmaker" (Goldie 10). However, it is all the more insidious as it occurs in the guise of the Indigene's self-representation. The selection of pieces and the strictness of editing to conform to standard English and the expectations of a white readership establish the white self as Subject and the Indigenous Other as object. Interestingly, in doing so such anthologies may be seen as repressive forerunners of later collections borne of what Goldie describes as the process of "indigenization": the dominant society's need to become "native," to partake in "the impossible necessity of becoming indigenous" (13). Having said this, it is important to note another recent tendency in mainstream representations of Indigenous peoples. Gareth Griffiths notes an inclination to "[overwrite] the actual complexity of difference" (237), resulting in a discourse as oppressive and self-reflexive as those that have preceded it. An awareness of these tendencies highlights the importance of collaboration between Indigenous and non-Indigenous editors. In the anthologies here discussed both Harjo and Bird, the editors of *Reinventing*, are Native American women whose work also appears in the volume. However, the other anthologies are collaborative efforts: Daniel David Moses, a writer of poetry and drama, is of the Delaware people (*Native Literature*), and Rosemary van den Berg, writer and academic, is Nyoongar (*Those Who Remain*), while Goldie, Brewster, and O'Neill are non-Indigenous academics.

This connection with the academy is of particular interest, as it represents a changing attitude inside and outside traditionally conservative educational institutions to Indigenous peoples – a growing number of whom are university-educated. Nevertheless, Greg Young-Ing, Native writer and manager of Theytus Books, is critical of white academics and the body of work produced by them in relation to Indigenous peoples. He describes it as tending "to reduce the emotionally, historically and culturally-charged issues to dry information-laden legalise [sic] and/or academic jargon. Furthermore, by creating a recognized school of experts who are a relatively 'low risk' to publishers, and by saturating the market with a wave of books *about* Aboriginal peoples, this wave of academic writing has the effect of ultimately blocking-out the Aboriginal Voice" (182). This raises the issue of the selection, production, and publication of Indigenous anthologies. That the academy is gradually acknowledging this literature's significance amounts to the modest beginnings of a philosophical change. Different ideals of literature coexist, and literature produced on the basis of these differences is published and read by different groups of readers. Each of the anthologies discussed here exemplifies this process, which is closely connected to the question of identity.

Australian anthropologist Jeremy Beckett acknowledges and unwittingly exemplifies the tension that exists between what Aboriginal people say about themselves and what others say about them, and the way notions of Aboriginality and non-Aboriginality are constructed. He suggests that "ethnicity" results from the linkage of three elements: "an 'original' culture, located in the more or less remote past; a living 'folk' which is the repository of this culture, *perhaps in an impure form;* and a 'modern' population who are its heirs" (212, italics mine). While these three elements are the complex core of each of the anthologies discussed here, Beckett's emphasis on "purity" requires further comment, as it is disputed by most contributors. Joy Harjo explains its inappropriateness when she raises the issue of tribal self-identification: "For this anthology we did not require previous publication, but the contributors were asked specifically that they be 'tribally identified' – that is, that they be culturally part of a particular tribal nation. We wanted the anthology to be made of the voices of those who have directly experienced being Indian in their everyday lives. It seemed such an obvious request, but it was not to be this easy. It was to become a very charged issue" (26).

Judgments of cultural "impurity" are, then, best left to the discretion of the peoples concerned. Yet such judgments are frequently made. In Canada, for example, many "non-status Indians" were created "through massive adoption and baby stealing that took place in the earlier years of this century" (Harjo and Bird 27). Shamefully, this policy was adopted in Australia to similar effect.[3] As editors of *Those Who*

Remain we faced the same issue as Harjo and Bird: what is cultural "impurity" when culture itself is dynamic? We looked for guidance to tribal elders, several of whom were themselves urban-dwelling. It seems, then, that the issue of individual and tribal/group identity is the site of a power struggle in Indigenous and non-Indigenous communities alike.

Along with the question of contributors come the questions of which pieces to include in an anthology and how to approach the editing process. Evidently, traditional Anglo-European standards of what constitutes "good literature" must be discarded. Editor and contributor Gloria Bird elaborates on the problems faced by all editors, whether Indigenous or not, in the compilation of anthologies:

> This process of editing has brought many issues into focus: audience/readership; questioning my own integrity or right to say what writing is acceptable; questioning by whose standards I was reading; and acknowledging my own biases in making those decisions. In reading the manuscript submissions, I had to learn to read differently, or to unlearn the critical aspect of reading that I have been taught in creative writing workshops and in university literary courses. Basically, I had to confront my own internalized views on what constituted literature and recognize the learned preference of written over oral literatures in academia. I had to acknowledge the oral nature of the submissions and value the literal testimony of the women's voices that came through their writing. (28)

Terry Goldie expresses his own discomfort with the necessary process of selection when he says that "rightly or wrongly, we are capturing things at a point when there is more than enough material to justify the project but at a point where no one has sifted through that material" (Moses and Goldie xx). This is history in the making, and the impact of each piece must be carefully evaluated, bearing in mind that the standards established by the academy are valueless in this context. As Moses comments, "the decisions are definitely political, especially with a literature that is emerging even as we speak" (xx).

It is generally acknowledged that "the modern nation state is the major locus of power in the contemporary world" and that all power relations within it are "ultimately circumscribed by this dominant stage of power" (Ariss 131). This is the greatest problem faced by Fourth World peoples in their attempts to construct their own discourses. In the case of Aboriginal Australia and Native North America power relations are dominated by the white colonial state, which controls not only information and expertise but also the means for its propagation. In Australia government-funded agencies provide the only means of entry for Aboriginal people, returning us once again to Foucault's notion of power relations as a site of confrontation. Robert Ariss pursues the issue of the role and place of Aboriginal literature as a discursive field in the context of power relations between the Aboriginal community and the dominant Euro-Australian community, and his argument further illuminates the context in which Indigenous anthologies come into being. Consider the following poem by Robert Bropho, taken from *Those Who Remain:*

> atsic
> all these gifts
> the white man gives us
> like atsic
> > they're
> > like
> > time
> > bombs[4]

In recent times ATSIC (the Aboriginal and Torres Strait Islander Commission) has been heavily criticized by both the Aboriginal and non-Aboriginal communities for, among other things, irresponsible handling of finances. Robert Bropho is a well-known activist and writer, and leader of the Swan Valley Nyoongar community. In "atsic," on behalf of his people, he publicly criticizes what he sees as yet another federally funded government initiative that, ultimately, has done his people more harm than good. Bropho regularly writes to Western Australian newspapers, and his letters are occasionally published. In doing so, however, he is forced to conform to the standard means of expression in a forum run by and for the dominant community. In *Those Who Remain*, as in his autobiography *Fringedweller* (1980), he takes a mainstream forum and uses it as a means of self-empowerment, confronting reader expectations. *Fringedweller* was for this reason well-received by influential Aboriginal poet Oodgeroo Noonuccal.[5] She describes it as an "unedited narrative" characterized by a "monotony and lack of system" that communicate "a culture of poverty" in which are heard "the voices of people calling to the . . . government to lift them out of their misery and degradation" (qtd. in Ariss 139). In "atsic" Bropho elaborates on these concerns. So too he challenges the mainstream genre of anthologizing in English by submitting a piece that breaks with the conventions of standard English and is not easily categorized. "Success Hill Sacred Spring Ceremony," which is also in *Those Who Remain*, functions similarly. It is based on a speech given by Bropho in commemoration of generations of his people, the River People, and their relationship with their land.[6] In both instances he advocates an Aboriginality of "concrete otherness," a black discourse that seeks "to demystify, to expose the hypocrisy and unreality of government policy, and to reassert a more realistic ideology of self-determination" (Ariss 133). He, like many other writers included in *Those Who Remain*, is directly challenging colonialist history and seeking to re-present it as Aboriginal history, a history of the oppressed. As noted above and developed earlier in relation to *Reinventing the Enemy's Language*, a significant part of this process is the "fixation into writing" (Ariss 139) of an oral tradition, which itself becomes a political statement. It highlights "the problem of interpretation arising when two cultures attempt to redefine the channels through which each communicates to the other, one seeking to actualise its uniqueness in stressing its insurmountable cultural differences, while simultaneously adapting the discursive practices of the culture it is seeking to distance itself from" (Ariss 133).

The anthologies under consideration here are examples of the present state of the production and publication of Indigenous literature and the need to control the "strange technology we're dealing with, this writing our words down on paper" (Moses and Goldie xxv). Fremantle Arts Centre Press, publisher of *Those Who Remain*, is a small yet successful publishing house in Western Australia that has produced a significant number of texts by Aboriginal writers. Also of note in Western Australia is Magaballa Books – a small publishing house located in the northwestern town of Broome that only publishes Aboriginal writers. In this respect it is akin to Theytus Books, run by and for Native North Americans and situated in Penticton, British Columbia, and Pemmican Publications in Winnipeg, both established in 1980 in response to the paucity of mainstream publishers willing to promote Indigenous literature. It is noteworthy, however, that *Native Literature* and *Reinventing* are both published by well-respected, mainstream publishers – Oxford University Press and W. W. Norton – which suggests the increasing acknowledgment of the role and value of Indigenous writing by a general as well as a specialized readership. Accordingly, it is important that the contributors "own" their anthology. The fact that each text has a substantial introduction describing its aims and the process of its creation is an important statement by the editors and publishers on the need for their transparency, as is the fact that notes on contributors are supplied, along with a very brief note on the editors themselves.

According to Joy Harjo, *Reinventing* "gradually became a book about the process of writing and speaking" (26). I would add that each of these anthologies is also about reading and listening, particularly in the cross-cultural context. Cross-cultural interpretation has the potential to be an enormously enriching process, although it is also by necessity problematic, raising as it does the fundamental question of how one culture communicates to another. If "all codes depend upon an agreement amongst their users and upon a shared cultural background" and "codes and culture interrelate dynamically," as John Fiske says, then the challenge for readers and editors with a different cultural background from that of the writers is obvious.[7] Armand Ruffo, of the Ojibway, suggests that for the outsider seeking to come to terms with Native people and their literature, it "is a question . . . of involvement and commitment, so that the culture and literature itself becomes more than a mere museum piece, dusty pages, something lifeless" (174).

The anthologizing of Indigenous literature and orature thus has tremendous social, political, and philosophical implications. This can be seen in the compilation, production, and consumption of such anthologies as *Reinventing the Enemy's Language*, *An Anthology of Canadian Native Literature in English*, and *Those Who Remain Will Always Remember*, which exemplify and promote recent changes in the literary establishment and in the way it relates to the demands of an increasingly powerful Fourth World and its changing readership. Indigenous literature and orature directly challenge academic assumptions of "good literature" as evidenced in the Western literary canon. They highlight the restrictions of this canon and call into question notions of text and textuality traditionally adopted by the academy to the detriment of the establishment of an Indigenous voice. The transformation of an oral into a written tradition is a pertinent example of this. Consequently, issues of identity and authenticity are foregrounded for Indigenous and non-Indigenous communities alike. What is Indigenous literature? How does a non-Indigenous reader fathom the complexities of cross-cultural interpretation? The process of anthologizing stimulates debate, particularly when it involves collaboration between Indigenous and non-Indigenous editors, positioned both inside and outside the walls of tertiary institutions. The demand that literary theory not be used by academics as a tool of further colonization and the belief that literature is a means of empowerment reflect changing race relations, as well as the role that possession of the written word in English plays in them. Recent anthologies of Indigenous writing are self-conscious examples of power relations, as they center on the contributors' determination to empower themselves and to challenge representation by the dominant society. The task of editing such anthologies – to let the collection speak for itself and not inadvertently to frame or shape it or interfere with the contributors' self-representation – is challenging. It mirrors the changes occurring in the present social and political climate and requires an appreciation of the complexities of cross-cultural communication. This is seen in the editors' and readers' need to question their right to determine standards. In many respects the process of anthologizing Indigenous literature and orature requires a reconsideration of "literature" and of the acts of writing and reading, speaking and listening. In other words, it becomes a matter of establishing a dialogue and creating a space for the working out of power relations.

Notes

1. At this point it should be noted that "Native" is the preferred term by Indigenes of Canada, while those of what is now the United States prefer "Indian." "Aboriginal" is the all-encompassing (colonial) term used to describe Australia's Indigenes.

2. It is debatable whether an "Indigenous canon" is under construction. If so, we must ask, by whom is it being constructed, and for whom? Such a canon could easily recolonize the literatures that have only just been freed from the influence of the Western canon.

3. Officially formulated in the infamous Western Australian "1905 Act," the painful consequences are well-documented in Stuart Rintoul's anthology *The Wailing*.

4. See *Those Who Remain* (130). ATSIC, the Aboriginal and Torres Strait Islander Commission, was established and funded by the federal government and is staffed and managed by Indigenous Australians.

5. Oodgeroo, of the Noonuccal people of Stradbroke Island, was formerly known as Kath Walker. Her poetry is most concerned with universal love, rights, and dignity and with love and peace for Australia.

6. At the time of the writing of this essay, Bropho and his people, the Swan Valley Nyoongar Community, are engaged in a dispute with the Western Australian government over the land described in "Success Hill Sacred Spring Ceremony," on which the government seeks to build a jail.

7. John Fiske is quoted in Ruffo's "Inside Looking Out" (163).

Bibliography

Ariss, Robert. "Writing Black: The Construction of an Aboriginal Discourse." *Past and Present: The Construction of Aboriginality*. Ed. Jeremy Beckett. Canberra: Aboriginal Studies Press, 1994. 131–46.

Beckett, Jeremy. "The Past in the Present; The Present in the Past: Constructing a National Aboriginality." *Past and Present: The Construction of Aborigi-*

nality. Ed. Jeremy Beckett. Canberra: Aboriginal Studies Press, 1994. 191–217.

Blaeser, Kimberly. "Native Literature: Seeking a Critical Center." *Looking at the Words of Our People*. Ed. Jeannette Armstrong. Penticton: Theytus, 1993. 51–62.

Brewster, Anne, Angeline O'Neill, and Rosemary van den Berg, eds. *Those Who Remain Will Always Remember*. Fremantle: Fremantle Arts Centre Press, 2000.

Bropho, Robert. "atsic." *Those Who Remain Will Always Remember*. Ed. Anne Brewster, Angeline O'Neill, and Rosemary van den Berg. Fremantle: Fremantle Arts Centre Press, 2000. 130.

———. *Fringedweller*. Sydney: Alternative Publishing Cooperative, 1980.

Chevrel, Yves. *Comparative Literature Today: Methods and Perspectives*. Trans. Farida Elizabeth Dahab. Kirksville MO: Thomas Jefferson University Press, 1995.

Damm, Kateri. "Says Who: Colonialism, Identity, and Defining Indigenous Literature." *Looking at the Words of Our People*. Ed. Jeannette Armstrong. Penticton: Theytus, 1993. 93–114.

Goldie, Terry. *Fear and Temptation: The Image of the Indigene in Canadian, Australian, and New Zealand Literatures*. Montreal: McGill-Queen's University Press, 1993.

Griffiths, Gareth. "The Myth of Authenticity." *The Post-Colonial Studies Reader*. Ed. Bill Ashcroft, Gareth Griffiths, and Helen Tiffin. London: Routledge, 1995. 237–41.

Harjo, Joy, and Gloria Bird, eds. *Reinventing the Enemy's Language: Contemporary Native Women's Writings of North America*. New York: W. W. Norton, 1998.

Lefevere, Andre. "Interface: Some Thoughts on the Historiography of African Literature Written in English." *The Post-Colonial Studies Reader*. Ed. Bill Ashcroft, Gareth Griffiths, and Helen Tiffin. London: Routledge, 1995. 465–70.

Moses, Daniel David, and Terry Goldie, eds. *An Anthology of Canadian Native Literature in English*. Toronto: Oxford University Press, 1998.

Rintoul, Stuart, ed. *The Wailing: A National Black Oral History*. Port Melbourne: William Heinemann Australia, 1993.

Ruffo, Armand Garnet. "Inside Looking Out: Reading *Tracks* from a Native Perspective." *Looking at the Words of Our People*. Ed. Jeannette Armstrong. Penticton: Theytus, 1993. 161–76.

Silko, Leslie Marmon. "Language and Literature from a Pueblo Indian Perspective." *Yellow Woman and a Beauty of the Spirit: Essays on Native American Life Today.* New York: Touchstone, 1997. 48–59.

Young-Ing, Greg. "Aboriginal Peoples' Estrangement: Marginalization in the Publishing Industry." *Looking at the Words of Our People.* Ed. Jeannette Armstrong. Penticton: Theytus, 1993. 177–87.

RICHARD S. PRESSMAN

Is There a Future for the *Heath Anthology* in the Neoliberal State?

One

For many people the *Heath Anthology* represents a valuable effort to help us achieve a more truly democratic literature through greater inclusiveness. Its success is attested to by the fact that it remains in the arena of critical debate, that all other anthologies have moved in the same direction, and that it is now in its third edition. This is all to the good, as I and many, many others believe. But the gains that can be made through such a progressive anthology in our time are, I also believe, severely limited. As has been widely observed, an anthology, rather than being a mere collection, is a statement of canonical authority, albeit in a given moment of history. However, in a postmodern age, in which we have become so accustomed to imagining the *anti*authoritarian, it's difficult to imagine on what basis an authority could be developed to unite a society not only so multicultural but so fluid in its multicultural identities.

A little history: If I ask my students when the major leagues were integrated, they will tell me, inevitably, the late 1940s, with Jackie Robinson. Not so. They were integrated shortly after the Civil War – then, with Jim Crow, steadily unintegrated. While that integration was never deep, because of the majors' low level of development and the relatively few black athletes available out of slave conditions, it nevertheless existed ("African-Americans in Baseball").

I find a pattern that's similar in the development of American literary anthologies, a pattern culminating in the *Heath Anthology* of 1990. It's true that blacks hardly appear at all until the immediate post–Second World War period, and then only in terms of folk material, in only one or two anthologies. But all the way back to the nineteenth century women appeared, and in numbers larger than many of us saw in our undergraduate anthologies. Yet in 1889 an extraordinary ten-volume anthology (hardly intended for classroom use!), titled *A Library of American Literature* (Stedman and Hutchinson), was coedited by a man *and* a woman – though in the twentieth century a woman would not be an anthology editor until 1985, nearly a hundred years later. The earliest years covered in the 1889 anthology had a proportion of twenty men to each woman, but even early on, then, women *were* represented. The latest years, the post–Civil War period, saw that proportion increase extraordinarily to nearly 30 percent. So the proportion of representation may be rather near the proportionate rate of publication. And most of the women authors rediscovered and republished in the last generation appeared back *then*. Even a few Jews, writing before Abraham Cahan in the 1890s, appeared.

In the time of the modern two-volume teaching anthology, beginning in the post–Second World War period, we see various experiments attempted, including giving an international perspective, through the use of foreigners (mainly British) to comment on American life and through the translation of reports of the early French and Spanish explorers, on the grounds that they provided the *roots* for the American identity, one we *now* call multicultural. Albeit in small numbers, blacks and women were represented and were not relegated to the category of regional or local-color writers, a common deprecatory device.

But in the 1950s, most assuredly under the pressures of McCarthyism and the Cold War, these concessions to the nondominant disappeared, in the name of offering the reader literature only of "high literary merit" – offerings determined, of course, by white Anglo-Saxon males. This concept, which would remain the major criterion pronounced by nearly every anthology until the first *Heath* in 1990, had the effect of eliminating nearly every minority voice that had had at least some hearing before. The editors argued that more attention needed to be paid to the so-called major writers – none of whom was a woman (except, in most cases, Emily Dickinson) or a black or a Native American. Such other groups, while well-represented in the socioeconomy, did *not* exist in the anthology.

The most philosophically idealist of these anthologies, perhaps, *American Poetry and Prose* (1957), editor Norman Foerster prefaced thusly: "Especially I have tried to achieve a more steadily prevailing 'literary tone.' I have sought a higher average of artistic excellence in the selections, have increased the previously large representations of major authors, and have adapted the book to a more philosophical and aesthetic analysis and evaluation" (v). In the entire two volumes only nine women appear and only a handful of white folk songs. No blacks. There is no questioning of what constitutes "excellence" and what determines "major"; determinants are allegedly aesthetic, not sociohistorical. And it is not without significance that this most reactionary text was edited by one man, for the pattern had been not only that editors would be male but that they would decide in small groups.

In the late 1960s this pattern began to reverse, perhaps under the accrued mood of the civil rights movement, the new feminism, and the reformatory pressures of the Vietnam War. These same white Anglo-Saxon male editors began to notice, or notice again, some of the subaltern groups – those best represented in the economy and with the strongest voices in the political arena: women and blacks. Little by little, women were restored to the canon, and blacks – albeit at first just males – began to appear, not merely as singers of folk songs but as writers with individuated voices. In 1967 the predecessor to the famous Norton Anthology of American Literature, called *The American Tradition in Literature* (Bradley, Beatty, and Long), published a postwar high of thirteen white women and one black man. The first edition of what became the standard, the *Norton Anthology*, issued in 1979 (Gottesman et al.), a scant eleven years before the first *Heath*, in volume 2 (from 1865 forward) published twenty-two white women, eight black men, and one black woman.

Editors began to add criteria of a more social nature. The first edition of the *Norton*, for example, added "many new authors and selections . . . because they are of high literary merit *and* because their presence is needed in order to make sense of the literary history of our age" (Gottesman et al. xxiii). It seems to me that the essence of the first clause ("high literary merit") is a concession to the idealist, masculinist, authoritarian past, while the second ("make sense of literary history") signals the process of undermining that standard.[1] It implies that to understand the Romantic age, for example, we can't just read the traditional canonical figures, but we must also read their *context*, which implies that works in the context may well have been underrated. The authoritarian standard is further undermined by the editors' statement that "this principle of copiousness in selection is designed to allow teachers to set up their own reading lists" (xxiv) – perhaps the first recognition that teachers wish to make choices more than be told what is proper to teach, which act of choosing undermines masculinist authority.

In the mid- and late 1980s anthologies were increasingly accepting the more open ideas from the past and going beyond to admit still more groups. The second *Norton*, for example, in 1985, added to its editorial board of six men its first woman, Nina Baym. That anthology included twenty-three white women, nine black men, and five black women. But *The Harper American Literature* (first edition 1987) among its seven editors had three women and revived the work of early explorers, as well as included a number of Indian narratives. And, while omitting the explorers and all folk material, the Macmillan *Anthology of American Literature*'s fourth edition (1989) included thirty-two white women, eight black men, five black women, and perhaps the first Mexican American, Tomás Rivera. By the time the first *Heath* emerged the following year, the principles on which the *Heath* was based had not only been used in the past but, over the previous twenty years, had been slowly reviving.

Two

So the *Heath* was not startlingly new. Nevertheless, *The Heath Anthology of American Literature* represented an enormous pluralistic advance. General editor Paul Lauter formed the largest-yet editorial board, at fourteen members: "In its initial composition the board had equal numbers of men and women, minority and white participants; members came from every part of the country, taught in virtually every kind of institution, and specialized in most of the periods and varieties of American literature" (xxxv).

A call went out to the profession at large asking for suggestions, with more than 500 authors recommended (xxxv). Then the editors worked inductively. The result was the inclusion of over 300 authors, versus the next highest, the *Harper*, with about 225 (Johnson 129).

One of the techniques used to make all the anthologies increasingly inclusive was to extend the number of pages.[2] Whereas texts in the postwar period had about two thousand pages, those of the late 1980s had about five thousand. The first *Heath* grew to fifty-five hundred pages, now including the explorers; Indian folk material; and, for the first time, formal Native American writing. For the first time, too, an array of minorities were given space: not only many more blacks, especially women, but also Asians and Hispanics. Along with large numbers of Native Americans, volume 1 alone, which covered the period up to the Civil War, would have thirty-three women, four black men, and five black women – more than any other anthology had given us in *two* volumes. To accommodate still more people, the second edition (1994) reached sixty-one hundred pages, and the latest (1998) – despite removing the full texts of *The Scarlet Letter* and *Huckleberry Finn*, now offered in a separate, optional paperback – increased by nearly one hundred pages.

In part through its size, the *Heath* has become the standard toward which all anthologies are pulled, for the others steadily incorporate more of what the *Heath* does. Of course, the *Heath* has been part of the culture-wars controversy, attacked mainly from the right, but even from the center, for allegedly failing to uphold aesthetic standards. Upon its release in 1990 it was greeted variously with celebration, puzzlement, concern, and dismay. Some reactions, as in the culture wars in general, were vituperative, but most were thoughtful, attempting to be fair-minded, and in the process pointed out some genuine weaknesses that have been addressed in subsequent editions.[3]

However, the essence of the dispute was, predictably, as Lillian S. Robinson put it in a review of the first edition, "Is the diet really enriched by the additions, or have Lauter and his co-editors cut out essential nutrients, only to replace them with junk food?" (22).[4] In reducing the proportion of and emphasis on traditional canonical figures – even though such authors remained with proportionately the largest amounts of space – the *Heath* led some critics to be concerned about a loss of aesthetic standards and a presumably long-established tradition. Those concerned or opposed tended to see the newly introduced material as aesthetically inferior to what it replaced, which led to accusations that the anthology's purpose was not literary but political.

Arguments then ensued about whether it was possible to separate the two. Mark Edmundson, for example, said that "the editors seem to want things both ways: they want the anthology to have the prestige and respectability associated with a unified literary tradition, but also the moral rectitude that comes from refusing to 'privilege' ... one sort of writing over others" (1133). Seeing the anthology as outright political, as opposed to aesthetic, he argued that in effect it is not an acceptable teaching device: "They [the editors] would declare unequivocally that the task of teaching students to read and write and speak better was, given contemporary social exigencies, far too narrow, and that professors of English should strive to convey progressive political values directly" (1133). That is, the aesthetic is one concept, the political quite another, and the twain cannot meet. Richard Ruland, in a lengthy review/commentary, agreed that the twain cannot meet, that what the *Heath* "has undertaken is the marriage of two distinct theories of art that have rarely cohabited comfortably" (343). Like Fliegelman, Ruland saw that many choices were being made for political reasons – though Fliegelman wanted a better balance of the political choices, whereas Ruland, like Edmundson, expressed a concern about allegedly choosing politics *over* aesthetics.[5]

Lauter, however, saw the "marriage" quite differently. In a response to Ruland he stated that "the notion, insisted on largely by conservatives, that one must chose between *pluribus* [i.e., innovation] and *unum* [i.e., tradition] has the political effect – as it always has had – of marginalizing what is different for the sake of stressing the unity any group with power in a commonwealth finds necessary to maintain its authority" ("On the Implications" 331). To a great extent the two sides talk past each other. Lauter insists that there is no necessary split between his critics' aesthetics and politics, seeing the criticism itself as evidence that their aesthetics are politically motivated. The critics insist that there *is* such a split and that the *Heath* editors do not realize they are using the wrong standard for selecting a canon, a contemporary, temporary, political one.

In attempting to make the anthology more inclusive, the *Heath* matches developments in American society. One might see the *Heath* as a kind of literary affirmative action, creating more equal opportunity in a society traditionally racist and sexist.[6] In this the *Heath* seems genuinely to advance democracy by giving the subaltern much more of a voice.

Three

But for all its progressive intent the *Heath* can also be seen as a function of neoliberalism and hence in its way also conservative. While minority advancements are due in large part to painful political struggles, they are also due to the changing needs of capital. In this the *Heath* seems typically liberal, even idealist, for it all but ignores class – whereas capital, which poses as classless, is generally conscious of its class needs. A major impetus to the integration of the workplace is, after all, its need of personnel. If capital can gain its ends by promoting racism, as it has traditionally, it will; but if in order to so gain it must come to rely on these same victims of historical racism, it will be to some degree antiracist. On the one hand, capital wishes to divide, creating groups deemed exploitable. On the other, it wishes to at least create the *impression* of unity, proving that it is the answer to democratic fulfillment. As the nation becomes more "multicolorful," while demands for equality increase, racism – at least at the higher levels – becomes an albatross.

So in this sense the *Heath* becomes implicated in the neoliberal pseudodemocratic agenda, as with all those minority faces doing TV news – faces that represent a decided advance but whose presence also creates the illusion of a society far more egalitarian than it really is. In line with such corporate dominance, anthologies, beginning with the *Norton*, have come to be referred to by their publishers, rather than their titles or chief editors (Johnson 114) – what I call "corporate graffiti," by which corporations put their names on everything in society they can. The *Heath* is not, after all, referred to as the "people's anthology."[7]

In its defense the *Heath* could perhaps be seen as taking part in John Beverley's concept of a new United Front, as developed in his recent work *Subalternity and Representation* (or what Ernesto Laclau and Chantal Mouffe call a "coalition of new social movements"), one based on a vast coalition of self-identified subaltern groups.[8] "The unity of the people rests," says Beverley, "precisely on a recognition and tolerance of difference and incommensurability" (90). The very act of reifying multicultural identities within the text, be they social or literary, for the supposed purpose of giving them voice to advance democracy, points back to the capitalist-exploitative origins of those identities: "it is the instrumental reason of the state, not to speak of corporate merchandising and advertising strategies, to separate populations into classifiable identity groups. [Hence] mainstream multiculturalism is the 'cultural analogue of the liberal welfare state'" (144).[9] As such, in a version of identity politics the exploitation remains. Beverley may be right about the social text. But for reasons of class I have my doubts about the literary.

My doubts flow from the fact that the anthology is a function of the university. And a university education – despite its increasing necessity and the increasing percentage of the population pursuing it – remains a means to upward mobility. Generally, ethnic consciousness has been seen more as a function of subalternity. But in the very process of ethnic university students' learning about their own origins, they become *less* subaltern, as they learn the language of the academic establishment: while the anthology teaches them about where they come from, it also teaches them who they are becoming. They are no longer subaltern because now they *can* speak for themselves. One reason that college anthologies, including the *Heath*, have never paid much attention to class is that class is more threatening to capital than is ethnicity. As a best-selling textbook, then, as a part of the literary establishment, the *Heath* has less reason than ever to pose a problem to class patriarchy. Hence, as Ernesto Laclau says, "the very condition of emancipation – its radical break from power – is what makes emancipation impossible because it becomes indistinguishable from power" (*Emancipation(s)* 101).

Similarly, even as the anthologies have become fluid in content, so, as I see it, does multicultural identity. As time passes people's identities become increasingly multiple; individuals themselves become multicultural and multicolorful. On my campus, St. Mary's University of Texas, which is 65 percent Hispanic, 95 percent of these Mexican American, hardly an eye bats when a Hispanic and an Anglo pair off. Etienne Balibar says that "the real obstacle to the mixing of populations is [not ethnicity but] class" (103). The union of the Hispanic and the Anglo is generally accepted because both will be college graduates. But as university-trained individuals, the minorities then steadily lose their subaltern class identities, even as the group identity as a whole loses its force. If that identity can be renewed, it can come only from below, from the working class – the class one strives to escape by *going* to college. That can be dealt with only by a recognition that college graduates, to a great extent, nevertheless *remain* working-class – and that recognition, despite recent white-collar strikes, seems a long way off (though in that lies some hope). In acknowledging that the *Heath* did not deal with class well, Lauter observes that "the various conceptual frameworks which we [professors of American literature] use to talk about class are not very well developed" (Hill 179). Nevertheless, he recognizes that "the proletarianization of work within the university has in fact taken place. And you have large numbers of workers, both intellectual workers and manual workers, in colleges and universities, who are by any definition working class" (Hill 180).[10]

Then, too, there is the problem of recognizing who all the subaltern groups *are*. As the years pass we discover more categories of human beings demanding to be heard. A generation ago few imagined homosexuals as a group, let alone imagined a homosexual literature. Other categories of potential socioliterary identity – all fluid – are Haitian Americans, the elderly, the young, AIDS victims, victims of ecological brutalization, farmers who are losing their way of life, and subdivisions of presently recognized groups.[11] Much is being said, for example, about important differences *between* Hispanic groups. The more voices that are admitted into the dialogue, the more still other voices cry out for recognition. Under these circumstances it seems a horrendous task to organize an anthology or even a meaningful social change, let alone a revolution. While more groups are created, or emerge, or assert themselves, providing more voices for a United Front voice of the people, these same voices are subsumed into the homogenized mass of a pseudo-middle class. Ethnicity as an indicator of class, then, remains too unstable. Some time ago Werner Sollors cited the question posed by William Boelhower, in his *Through a Glass Darkly: Ethnic Semiosis in American Literature* (1984): "Who can predict when the ethnic difference will surface and why?" (277). He then argued that today "ethnicity is being recognized as a dynamic phenomenon" (278).

Hence, as the anthology democratizes itself, the content exceeds the form. The voices in the text become a carnival mocking what little editorial authority remains. So the ever-expanding anthology bursts its bounds.[12] As Glen M. Johnson puts it, "The anthologies of American literature have opened up the canon by stuffing themselves fuller. . . . This is either a step toward anarchy or pluralism made manifest" (126). Where then does it go? Perhaps it dies, with the understanding that the people cannot unite but must remain as separate, ever-changing voices. Perhaps we become inundated with infinite choices of anthologies infinitely refined, such as one on Jewish poets of New Mexico.[13]

Or perhaps the future is in the seemingly infinite capacity of technology. Anthologies will be available on-line, with students printing out professors' choices. But then from where would the guidance, the canonical authority, come for the professors to *make* those choices? For every day each of us becomes expert on less and less of the vast array of areas available. Perhaps there would be available an array of experts from whom one could choose in order to help one choose, ad infinitum.

I end as I began: in a postmodern age, in which we have become so accustomed to imagining the antiauthoritarian, it's difficult to imagine on what basis an authority, in particular a canonical authority, could develop a coherent enough society, one not only so multicultural but so fluid in its multicultural identity. It's difficult to imagine a form to fit such a content. For me the *Heath* represents a valuable, indeed a valiant effort to help us achieve a truly democratic literature. But it also may prognosticate the end of a national literature, and the impossibility of coalition, as it tumbles over the *Heath*-cliff.

Notes

1. This was observed, perhaps first, by Glen M. Johnson in his far-reaching study "The Teaching Anthology and the Canon of American Literature: Some Notes on Theory in Practice."

2. This was perhaps first noted by Johnson (125).

3. Jay Fliegelman, for example, suggested that including the literature of Revolutionary patriotism, but not the literature against which it was reacting, that of Toryism, and including the literature of abolition, but not that of proslavery writers, "not only embarrassingly reproduces a cultural history of winners, but cheats the student of confronting the discourses of paternalism and patriarchalism against which so many American texts are written" (335).

4. Despite placing the negative in the second, stronger position, Robinson's inclination was strongly toward the first, the positive.

5. Such conservative ideas privilege what is and has been over whatever challenges that, seeing the latter as ephemeral if not outright evil. But it has often been argued that conservatives tend to see whatever has been extant as the normal and hence the good, even though whatever has been the norm once replaced another norm that in its time was itself considered the norm. In a 1982 MELUS dialogue Judith Fetterley and Joan Schultz noted that a 1900 anthology, *A Literary History of America*, which included no women at all, featured as the nation's premier authors Oliver Wendell Holmes, Henry Wadsworth Longfellow, and James Russell Lowell – whereas current heroes Nathaniel Hawthorne, Henry David Thoreau, and Herman Melville did not appear at all. These latter acceded to the prime position through a previous struggle mounted by critics such as Harry Levin, Richard Chase, and Charles Fiedelson in the 1950s and 1960s. Significantly, all argued for these authors on the basis of formalist criteria. See Fetterley and Schultz.

6. Lauter himself sees the *Heath* as a product of the civil rights movement (Hill 170).

7. It is true that the third edition of the *Heath* (1998) was published by Houghton Mifflin. But it would have been foolish for the new house to change a name, albeit not their own, that is so well-established.

8. See, for example, *Hegemony and Socialist Strategy*.

9. Beverley cites Fraser (87). A similar complaint is made by some critics of the *Heath* who argue from the conservative assumption that ethnic identity divides people, in what should be a society that is color-blind, such that ethnic division is attributed not to capital but to those who call attention to ethnic division already extant.

10. For a full analysis of the condition of university labor, see Cary Nelson's *Manifesto of a Tenured Radical*.

11. Paul A. Smith himself, D. C. Heath's editor for the *Heath Anthology of American Literature*, admitted as much when he acknowledged "minority constituencies" other than the ones the anthology focuses on – women, African Americans, Mexican Americans, Native Americans, and Asian Americans – in this case facetiously listing "teenagers, the elderly, 'rednecks,' evangelicals, Canadians, etc." (Ruland 358).

12. Sollors, in 1986, recognized the problem in noticing that calls for more democratic anthologies assumed a concept, like the frontier, of endless space (255).

13. See Joan Logghe and Miriam Sagan's *Another Desert: Jewish Poetry of New Mexico*.

Bibliography

"African-Americans in Baseball." Exhibit. Afro-American Historic Museum. Philadelphia PA. Summer 1985.

Balibar, Etienne. "The Nation Form: History and Ideology." *Race, Nation, Class: Ambiguous Identities*. By Etienne Balibar and Emanuel Wallerstein. New York: Verso, 1991. 86–106.

Baym, Nina, et al., eds. *The Norton Anthology of American Literature*. 2nd ed. New York: W. W. Norton, 1985.

Beverley, John. *Subalternity and Representation: Arguments in Cultural Theory*. Durham: Duke University Press, 1999.

Bradley, Sculley, Richmond Croom Beatty, and E. Hudson Long, eds. *The American Tradition in Literature*. New York: W. W. Norton, 1967.

Edmunson, Mark. Rev. of *The Heath Anthology of American Literature*. *Times Literary Supplement* 4586 (October 19, 1990): 1133.

Fetterley, Judith, and Joan Schultz. "A MELUS Dialogue: The Status of Women Authors in American Literature Anthologies." *MELUS* 9.3 (1982): 3–17.

Fliegelman, Jay. "Anthologizing the Situation of American Literature." *American Literature* 65.2 (1993): 334–38.

Foerster, Norman. *American Poetry and Prose.* Boston: Houghton Mifflin, 1957.

Fraser, Nancy. "From Redistribution to Recognition? Dilemmas of Justice in a 'Post-Socialist' Age." *New Left Review* 212 (1995): 68–93.

Gottesman, Ronald, et al., eds. *The Norton Anthology of American Literature.* 2 vols. New York: W. W. Norton, 1979.

Hill, Mike. "Editing the Anthology: An Interview with Paul Lauter." *minnesota review* 48–49 (1998): 169–81.

Johnson, Glen M. "The Teaching Anthology and the Canon of American Literature: Some Notes on Theory in Practice." *The Hospitable Canon: Essays on Literary Play, Scholarly Choice, and Popular Pressures.* Ed. Virgil Nemoianu and Robert Royal. Erdenheim PA: John Benjamins, 1991. 111–35.

Laclau, Ernesto. *Emancipation(s).* London: Verso, 1996.

Laclau, Ernesto, and Chantal Mouffe. *Hegemony and Socialist Strategy.* London: Verso, 1985.

Lauter, Paul. "On the Implications of the *Heath Anthology*: Response to Ruland." *American Literary History* 4.2 (1992): 329–36.

———. "Preface to the First Edition." *The Heath Anthology of American Literature.* Ed. Paul Lauter, et al. 2 vols. 2nd ed. Lexington MA: D. C. Heath, 1994. xxx–xl.

Logghe, Joan, and Miriam Sagan, eds. *Another Desert: Jewish Poetry of New Mexico.* Santa Fe: Sherman Asher, 1998.

McMichael, George, gen. ed. *Anthology of American Literature.* 2 vols. 4th ed. New York: Macmillan, 1989.

McQuade, Donald, et al., eds. *The Harper American Literature.* 2 vols. New York: Harper, 1987.

Nelson, Cary. *Manifesto of a Tenured Radical.* New York: New York University Press, 1997.

Robinson, Lillian S. "I, Too, Am America – I." *The Nation* (July 2, 1990): 22–24.

Ruland, Richard. "Art and a Better America." *American Literary History* 3.2 (1991): 337–59.

Sollors, Werner. "A Critique of Pure Pluralism." *Reconstructing American Literary History.* Ed. Sacvan Bercovitz. Cambridge: Harvard University Press, 1986. 250–79.

Stedman, Edmund Clarence, and Ellen Mackay Hutchinson, eds. *A Library of American Literature from the Earliest Settlement to the Present Time.* New York: Webster, 1889–90.

PART FOUR

Theory, Pedagogy, and Practice

GERALD GRAFF AND JEFFREY R. DI LEO

Anthologies, Literary Theory, and the Teaching of Literature

JEFFREY R. DI LEO: You've thought a great deal about the institutionalization and professionalization of literary studies in America. What role have anthologies played in the institutionalization and professionalization of literary studies?

GERALD GRAFF: The roles and effects are obviously multiple and overdetermined, but let me start, being the curmudgeon I am, with one of the worst pedagogical results of literature anthologies: legitimating the primacy of literary texts and their supposed transparency and obscuring the importance of criticism and interpretation (not even to mention theory) for the literature classroom.

DI LEO: Why does foregrounding the significance of criticism and interpretation make you a curmudgeon? I would say just the opposite. I don't think that teachers have really thought enough about how to incorporate theory into the teaching of literary texts. The result is either a misappropriation of theory and criticism in their classroom or an avoidance of theory and criticism in the classroom. The worst instance of the former is what I call the "cookie-cutter approach" to theory, which works something like this: Apply literary theory "A" to literary text "B." Result: a valid interpretation of literary text "B" (and a successful use of literary theory "A"). With this strategy students think that criticism and theory are some kind of game wherein points are scored for the production of valid interpretations. Textbooks like many of the volumes in the Bedford series Case Studies in Contemporary Criticism that have primary texts along with selections like "What Is Deconstruction?" and "What Is Feminism?" promote this type of trivial use of theory, albeit I think unwittingly. In other cases theory and criticism are entirely avoided in the classroom either because they are perceived by the teacher as beyond the ken of the students or because the teacher wants to promote the illusion that literary studies just involves a close reading of the primary literary text at hand.

GRAFF: I agree. Students and teachers who pick up an anthology get the illusion that studying literature is a matter of closely reading a bunch of primary texts and letting those texts in themselves somehow tell them what to *say* about the texts in class and in student writing. This obscures, conceals, and mystifies the fact that what we say about a literary text, though certainly *accountable* to the text itself – and this is important in ways I hope we can pursue – is generated not by the text but by the critical questions we ask about it. These questions come from the secondary conversation of readers and critics rather than from the text itself.

DI LEO: I like this as a general way of approaching the teaching of literature but worry about placing the onus of criticism on the asking of the right critical questions. For me questions can both lead us to find new aspects of the text at hand as well as delimit our discovery of the text. I'd put the emphasis on the "conversation" part of your comment, rather than the "critical question" part. We should encourage our students to enter a conversation about a text. Specifically, the members of this conversation are the people who have written and commented on this text. The student can gain entry into this conversation only by acknowledging the scholarship of its members. His or her questions should concern the terms of the discussion, its assumptions and its conclusions. The arbiter in the conversation should be the literary text in question. In this context the approach to literary texts is one of entering a discourse community or discussion of the text. Students should recognize that the questions they ask about the text are determined by the terms, assumptions, and conclusions of the discourse community concerning the text. These questions are "critical questions" because they are meaningful within a particular critical context, not because they are questions in an anthology or what are perceived to be perennial questions.

GRAFF: Anthologies tend to efface the mediating intervention of criticism in literary study by reducing criticism to its dullest common denominator – informational headnotes and footnotes, arbitrary questions for study, and so on – thereby propping up the illusion that responding vividly to a literary work is fundamentally a stripped-down encounter of the student up close to the text, with the critical conversation about the text factored out or even seen as an unwelcome form of professional interference.

DI LEO: I never thought about this before, but I think that you are right. A strong case can also be made that headnotes and footnotes short-circuit entry into a critical discourse community. One way that they can do this is by leading the student to believe that these headnotes and footnotes are sufficient conditions of entering this community. If I read the headnote, then I have the necessary background information to enter into a critical dialogue with the text. Perhaps even more dangerously though, they can lead the student to believe that this is all that is worthwhile to say about the text. Students have little understanding of the process of editing a textbook and tend to believe that if it is in the textbook, then it is all that they need to know to read a particular text. There is a myth then about the sufficiency of editorial apparatus that cuts against the inclination to either supplement the editorial apparatus with more secondary materials or note that there are other important things to say about this text.

GRAFF: Anthologies thereby help produce the transparency illusion that I'm talking about – that what teachers and students try to do in their classroom responses to literature is produce how the primary literary works would speak for themselves if they could speak criticism.

DI LEO: It's funny that you should mention the transparency illusion because my experience seems to confirm what you say. During the course of my introductory course on theory and criticism, I generally have the students compare Jean-Paul Sartre's "What Is Literature?" and Roland Barthes's *Writing Degree Zero* – not because I have to but because it allows me to discuss the relative transparency and opacity of literature. I tell the students that transparency is the belief that literature is like a window to the world, whereas opacity makes literature out to be more like a wall that we cannot see through. Most agree with Sartre that literature *should* be like a window, and consequently they tend to both read it this way and value literature that they believe is more "transparent." Literature should reveal what it has to say. If not, it is in some way lacking. Reading otherwise is relatively unfamiliar to them. I think that this is more than anything else a consequence of the way that they have been trained to read and write about literature, because with only marginal effort I can help them to begin reading differently.

GRAFF: The explicative papers most commonly assigned presumably represent what John Milton's "Lycidas" or John Keats's *Odes* or Toni Morrison's *Beloved* would say if they could speak in critical talk – which is why students aren't expected in such papers to bring any critical conversation (it's assumed they are better off not knowing about such conversations or aren't ready for them yet) to bear on the text and thereby to pose a problem about the text. Am I making any sense here?

DI LEO: You are making a lot of sense here and are perhaps speaking to at least one tacit belief shared by many practitioners of literary studies today that most would be rather embarrassed to acknowledge: namely, that the most widely used anthologies today are grounded in fundamental ways on New Critical ideologies of the text or, more generally, in the tradition of explication of the text.

GRAFF: Yes, especially the assumption that the best way to initiate inexperienced readers into literary study is through an ideally preconceptionless close reading of the text itself, with as little mediation by supposedly "external" factors as possible. This assumption is preposterous, but it remains foundational to literary pedagogy even for many otherwise cutting-edge professors.

DI LEO: Well, then they really aren't cutting-edge, are they? It seems to me that their pedagogy has more in common with New Criticism than new frontiers in criticism.

GRAFF: This thinking is New Critical, yes, but it predates New Criticism and is found in anti–New Critics like Allan Bloom – that is, the view that texts in themselves tell us what to say about them, so who needs criticism, theory, and so on, and historical context can be covered in anthology headnotes and footnotes.

DI LEO: I agree that this approach to texts predates New Criticism and that there are positions coeval with New Criticism, like Bloom's, that support similar strategies. However, Bloom and others were not major forces in the shaping of the contemporary literary studies pedagogy. The traditions of both New Criticism and explication of the text (à la Eric Auerbach) first and foremost asserted the primacy of the text. Literary studies begins (and in some sense ends) with the selection of the "right" set of texts according to these traditions. If one has the right text before one, then "criticism" and "interpretation" are simply a matter of paying close attention to what this text "says." If the text has the "right stuff" (New Critics would look for things like irony, tension, and paradox, whereas the more advanced contemporary critic would look for things like race, class, gender, and sexuality), then a successful interpretation of the text necessarily follows from its close reading.

GRAFF: Exactly, though again I think New Criticism should not take the rap for a view that is older and more pervasive than any one school. If the text has the "right stuff," as you say, it will in itself induce an appropriate critical response in the student brain, and if it doesn't it's the student's fault for not reading carefully enough. That's why it's so important in this view to read texts that have the right stuff, ones that have passed the test of time, and so on, though, as I say, canon revisionists hold versions of this view too.

DI LEO: Yes, but their power in the formation of the English department curriculum, pedagogy, and canon was not close to that of the New Critics. I would maintain that even though progressive contemporary critics of the text are concerned with implicating the text with cultural and political concerns, their pedagogical strategy of focusing on the close reading of the right choice of primary texts does not move far beyond ideologies of the text that they would view as reactionary.

GRAFF: In many cases, yes.

DI LEO: Isn't it true that informational headnotes and footnotes direct the students (and teachers) toward what the text is "supposed" to be saying to them and study questions make sure that students do not drift far from this text as the locus of their critical attention? In other words, doesn't the editorial apparatus support this reactionary view of texts and textuality?

GRAFF: Generally yes, though I think the headnotes and footnotes are not seen as directing students toward what the text is supposed to be saying to them so much as they are seen as the preliminary background information students need in order to make sense of the text *and therefore*, at the next stage, be able to emit in their critical response what the text wants them to say about it.

DI LEO: Anthologies continue to legitimate and reinforce the primacy of literary texts even if the domain of what is a (literary) text has shifted and the range of things that texts (should) "say" has changed. The "new" progressive cultural studies canon of texts is anthologized as though it speaks to the student in much the same way as the "old" reactionary great books canon did, with the proviso that what it "says" is different. This, of course, is the message that is legitimated by anthologies that update their selection of texts while failing to alter their presentation of these materials.

GRAFF: Yes again.

DI LEO: So I tend to agree with what you say but have two related sets of questions for you. First, what is the alternative to anthologies that, as you say, "obscure, conceal, and mystify the fact that what we say about a literary text . . . is generated not by the text but by the critical questions we ask about it"?

GRAFF: Anthologies and casebooks that provide students with critical conversations about literary texts that the students can enter and see the point of entering. These are very hard to produce, since most academic criticism and even Sunday book-reviewing are not addressed to students but presuppose an initiated audience.

DI LEO: The Bedford volumes that I mentioned earlier don't seem to give the student a good reason to enter the conversation or even a good point of entry. For example, Ross Murfin's edition of Conrad's *Heart of Darkness* (1996) for Bedford anthologizes five "perspectives" on the text: reader-response criticism, feminist and gender criticism, deconstructionism, New Historicism, and cultural criticism. Using this "cookie-cutter approach" to theory in fact even seems to turn students off to theory and criticism. For them it just amounts to a clever response to a text, and the point of making it is remote aside from the grade that one might gain. Part of the weakness of editions like Murfin's is not that they use theory but that they give very little indication of why anyone would believe that this theory is important or significant, or from whence it came.

GRAFF: The Bedford "critical controversy" texts of Mark Twain's *Adventures of Huckleberry Finn* (1995) and William Shakespeare's *The Tempest* (2000) that Jim Phelan and I coedited are an attempt to produce such texts, which provide students with critical conversations that they can enter along with the texts. My sense is that we've succeeded only unevenly at this goal, but we're still working on it.

DI LEO: I think that the strengths of these two textbooks are quite obvious. I have used the *Huckleberry Finn* volume and can tell you that students feel as though they have entered a critical conversation on *Huckleberry Finn* and that they are thereby licensed to interpret or at least ask critical questions. However, what are the weaknesses that you see in these two textbooks?

GRAFF: I think they tend to be too difficult for students who don't already command the vocabulary and conventions needed for entering critical discussions and debates, especially ones who are uneasy about debates and arguments of any kind.

DI LEO: I tend to agree with you concerning the difficulty, but I also think that they provide a good opportunity for the students to learn the vocabulary and conventions through critical practice. Too often the vocabulary of critical theory is presented in isolation from critical practice. The recent glut of "dictionaries" of modern literary and cultural criticism only further validates this practice and encourages it. If one side errs on the side of the primacy of the text, the other errs on the side of the primacy of the theory – or at least the theoretical vocabulary. One of the ways in which students, as observers of critical practice, can gain entry into critical controversies is simply by asking questions about the vocabulary of the piece. What does the author mean by "hegemony"? What is "patriarchy"? This allows students, unwittingly, to enter the debate through their demand for clarity and understanding. From their growing understanding of the meaning of the terms, and their conventional use in critical practice, the students can then build up to more complex questions concerning the foundations of critical theory, including its key assumptions. Good anthologies will present critical readings that allow this kind of entry by the student into the conversation. Another key here is the willingness of the instructor to entertain the same bemusement as the student with the vocabulary and conventions of the critical practice. There must be a willingness on the part of both the instructor and the student to actively engage the critical practice with the end of understanding not only its general position on the text at hand but also the meaning of its vocabulary and the nature and assumptions of its mode of argumentation.

GRAFF: The first time I assigned the Huck text, in a midlevel undergraduate course at the University of Chicago, I felt that for some of the students several of the critical essays were too long and complicated. Some also expressed the view that Twain had written the book to entertain, so it was therefore perverse to pick it apart and quibble over it in a solemn academic way. They invoked Twain's opening warning that readers who find a moral in the story will be banished.

DI LEO: I agree with you about the length of the critical essays. For various reasons I think it is important for today's student that the selections be as brief as possible. Of course, this is no excuse for including trivial or shallow commentaries, but it is a mandate to select critical articles that conform to the temperament and reading capacities of today's students. Nothing is worse than selecting a good article for your students only to have them come to class saying that it was too long and complicated and therefore they gave up on it. I always think that it is better to err on the side of a shorter piece with a tighter argument, rather than a longer piece with a more profound but also looser argument. Providing students with successful engagements with critical theory encourages them to take on more complicated and longer pieces later in the course. Textbooks that are organized according to such principles are more useful in the classroom and address some of the objections to critical theory at their source.

GRAFF: As it happens, Phelan and I "empowered" such objections in our introduction to students when we noted that Twain might seem to agree with some disaffected literature students that literature is to be read for fun and not for the "hidden meanings" you can get out of it. Some of my students found that so convincing a position that I had to spend considerable time in class making a case for finding serious issues like racism in the book, as well as for debating how they are handled. I ended up feeling that for students who aren't already insiders to lit-crit discourse, something more basic is needed, a text that would present criticism, critical debate, and their justifications with fewer assumptions taken for granted.

DI LEO: But can't this be done by closely studying the criticism? In other words, perhaps it is the case that the criticism presumes things that do not hold in the primary text. If this is so, then shouldn't we be obligated to pursue this with the students even if it risks derailing a "contemporary controversy" like racism or the homoeroticism of *Huckleberry Finn*? This opens the door for more serious general questions as to how and why we validate readings of the Twain classic. Should we respect them just because they are anthologized? Or do they need to "prove" themselves irrespective of their position in the contemporary critical landscape? Sometimes the naiveté of students with regard to these questions can turn the teacher into the student: what we take to be the topoi of critical practice regarding texts like *Huckleberry Finn* become empty and unsubstantiated academic talk. It also brings us to even more important questions: Why do we read? What is it to read with understanding? What is the role of the critical community in answering these questions? Entering a discussion of contemporary debates on *Huckleberry Finn* need not be an exercise in validation of the debate. However, it also need not be an opportunity for the students to exercise their penchant for emotive and subjective responses to the text. In any event, isn't it the case that anthologies are still being published with headnotes and arbitrary questions because teachers use them and even demand them?

GRAFF: Yes, but then it's also the case that many of the same teachers have cut back on their expectations for what most students will be able to do – that is, it's generally not assumed that more than a minority of A students will really enter the critical conversation about literature, and it's okay if the rest get turned on by some books and respond vividly. If they can't produce a literate version of critical discourse, then, well, that's only to be expected.

DI LEO: But entering the critical conversation is not the same as producing a literate version of it. Students can read a bunch of articles on *Huckleberry Finn* and ask some questions that they never would have asked without reading them, but at the same time almost all of them would be hard-pressed to produce a version of the conversation.

GRAFF: Right, which is what I was trying to get at above – if it's a "literate version" of the conversation that we want from students, and I don't think we're doing them justice if we settle for less, then it's a problem if the gap between the critical debate and the level at which students appropriate and respond to it remains large. I think that simplifying the debate helps to close that gap and eventually helps students become more sophisticated down the road.

DI LEO: My other question from above is, why do you think that there is still such a strong at least tacit belief among teachers of literature today in the primacy of the text? Why is this still the case despite the belief by many of these same teachers that we are in the age of cultural and critical studies, with its concomitant devotion to the gendering, socialization, racialization, and sexualizing of the literary text?

GRAFF: In a way I'm a believer in "the primacy of the text," in the sense that my reading of any text – your questions here, say – has to be guided by or accountable to the text I'm reading. But I don't confuse this kind of primacy – accountability to the text – with sufficiency.

I think there's a lot of confusion about this issue, which we don't after all discuss very much, plus a lot of residual Platonism, plus the fact that if we committed ourselves to teaching criticism – that is, to seeing that that's what "teaching literature" entails, teaching students how to speak and write criticism – we'd have to do some work to figure out how to clarify the culture of criticism for students, and of course we're already overworked.

DI LEO: Well, if New Critics are not entirely to blame, then neither are the Platonists! What do you mean by "accountability to the text," and how is it disassociable from the idea of the "primacy of the text"? It seems to me that the former assumes the latter.

GRAFF: I'm glad you ask – a key question. By "accountability to the text" I mean the responsibility we have as readers to read the text on its own terms or to put ourselves in the author's shoes; by the "primacy of the text" (perhaps not the most precise phrase) I mean the fallacy that the text tells us what to say about it. These notions are often confused, so that if you deny, as I do, that a text tells us what to say about it you may be accused of (or praised for) denying that we can or should read a text on its own terms. Traditionalists make this mistake from the right, accusing you of relativism if you argue that texts don't tell us what to say about them; theory people make this mistake from the left, accusing you of retrograde objectivism if you argue that readers can or should read texts on their own terms.

DI LEO: Let me see if I understand you correctly: asserting accountability to the text means that we are obligated to interpret the text with an eye toward the cultural, biographical, and societal forces inscribed in the text though not necessarily openly revealed by the text, whereas asserting the primacy of the text means that we are obligated to interpret the text with the knowledge that everything that we can know about the text will be told to the active reader by the text. The difference is that the former does not tell you how you should read the text, whereas the latter does. Both positions focus on the text as the center of critical understanding of the text, but one emphasizes the text as the be-all and end-all of criticism (the primacy view), telling us what method to use to interpret it as well as its meaning, whereas the accountability view says that while a text says what it means, it cannot tell us how to determine what it says (what method to use to interpret it). Have I got it right?

GRAFF: Let me give a primitive example: someone who read a restaurant menu as an epic poem would be refusing accountability to the text, that is, misreading it. One could even say that the menu says to its readers, "Read me as a menu, not as a poem." But it doesn't follow that the menu tells anyone how to describe it in a given situation, which depends on the context and involves selection from the infinite number of possible things that can be said about any object. If my audience already knows the text is a menu, or if the question I'm asked is "What color is that text?" it would make no sense for me to answer – "It's a menu." The point has relevance to the selection of what to pick out to notice and talk about when we teach and study literature. Teachers who think texts tell us what to say about them have trouble seeing why their students fail to see what they see in those texts: here the text is signaling the students what to say about it and the student is mute or confused or says the wrong things, so the problem presumably is in the student. In fact, having a sense of what to say about a text, what aspects or problems to pick out, requires familiarity with the critical conversation about the text. When we expect students to make statements about literature without reading criticism (the anthology effect), we're asking students to enter a critical conversation that's withheld from them or to produce criticism without reading any.

DI LEO: But isn't it also true that according to the accountability view of texts, it is very well the case that some "contemporary critical debates" concerning them are inconsistent with reading the text on its own terms? That while issues of gender might be at the forefront of our critical attention, and have generated a lot of critical controversy, still they might not have crossed Twain's mind? It seems to me that this is one of the implications of your position.

GRAFF: Yes, quite so. In saying that we have to read the text on its terms I didn't mean to suggest that we can't or shouldn't also read it on our terms or in the light of contexts and issues that weren't of concern to the author at all. In fact, this doubleness structures reading: when we read a text we're concerned with its or its author's questions (I'm eliding that distinction for the moment) and with our questions, which stem from our own interests and biases or from problems that have arisen since the text was written (how does the glorification of war in the *Iliad* look in the wake of twentieth-century carnage?). In saying that texts don't tell us what to say about them, I was trying to say that the text in itself doesn't tell us which of the author's questions we should talk about, much less which of our own questions.

DI LEO: But even though a critical controversy may be a hot one today, it is also possible that this controversy is not accountable to the text. Maybe this is what your students were getting at when they doubted a "controversy" about race and racism in *Huckleberry Finn*?

GRAFF: This in fact is exactly what they thought: since racism is more of a hot issue for us today than it was for Twain (doubtful, but let's concede them that premise), we're misreading his text if we read it as being centrally about racial issues. Their skepticism was even more pronounced toward our section on gender issues: since feminist issues are of interest to us now more than they were to Twain, we're misreading his text if we ask how it deals with gender. I tried to convince them that one is not necessarily misreading a text – failing to be accountable to it – when one raises questions about it that weren't on its or its author's radar screen: there may have been no feminism in Shakespeare's day, but there were men and women and socially defined gender roles that his plays reflect, problematize, or whatever. So it's possible to be "accountable" to a text while going beyond its horizon of intentions and assumptions.

DI LEO: You know, this doubleness that structures reading that you are talking about sounds a lot like the hermeneutics of Hans-Georg Gadamer. Reading, for Gadamer, involves this interplay and dialogue between the past and the present. Reading a text like Twain's *Huckleberry Finn* prompts us to ask questions about our own interests and biases. We, in turn, bring these questions and biases to bear on the text of *Huckleberry Finn*. Understanding this text involves our ability to reconstruct the question to which it was an answer. For Gadamer – and it sounds like for you as well – understanding is productive, and meaning is never exhausted by the author's intentions. This view is consonant both with your position on accountability to the text as well as with your rejection of the primacy of the text. On this Gadamerian model it would make sense to anthologize readings of *Huckleberry Finn* that were firmly identifiable with our own interests and concerns and to use them to dialogue with Twain's text. The understanding here would be that we are not trying to understand in any absolute sense what Twain meant in *Huckleberry Finn* but rather are trying to understand what Twain meant in *Huckleberry Finn* relative to our own interests and biases. Better anthologies will contain materials that allow for us to do this, whereas worse anthologies will present Twain's book as though the absolute meaning of it were possible or as though it could speak for itself. What do you think? How much of a Gadamerian are you at heart?

GRAFF: Not much of one, I'm afraid. My impression is that Gadamer's notion of horizon-fusion fogs over rather than usefully problematizes the distinctions between past and present and subject and object. My own view is that it's constitutive of making sense of reading that we assume the distinctions between past and present and subject and object. It's constitutive of making sense of reading that we assume the possibility of distinguishing between what Twain meant (though I'd say that's a matter of probable inference, not of absolute certainty) and how we view that meaning in the light of our own interests and biases. That is, it seems to me that we need to be able to distinguish between the author's and his or her culture's questions and our own questions in order to bring these things together fruitfully. In other words, a degree of objectification, of the otherness of the author, has to be assumed. I don't think Gadamer and other Heideggerians allow this objectification – the past for them is always already inseparable from the present; that is, there's no getting at what Twain inferably meant as a subject independent of us. I think this confuses an already vastly confused issue that we evade rather than confront in teaching (mea culpa too), leaving students grasping at clichés like "We can't know the author's intention," "Literature's always ambiguous," and so on. But maybe I've misread Gadamer and Heidegger on this point. I've always found their writings murky.

DI LEO: Well, it is probably best not to get into a debate at this point as to what Gadamer did or did not mean in *Truth and Method* or the relative "murkiness" of Gadamer and Heidegger on this subject, but it would be interesting to hear who you consider your predecessors to be in terms of pedagogical method. Or should I say "anthological method"? If not Gadamer, whose work has most strongly influenced your own take on the shape and directions anthologies should assume to be most effective in the classroom? What did you take from their work? Do you view your own position to be more novel than derivative? Or more derivative than novel?

GRAFF: Tough questions. I sided with E. D. Hirsch against Gadamer/Heidegger back in the fun old days when the current fault lines were opening up around questions of the objectivity and/or historicity (and subsequently the politicality) of interpretation. Hirsch unfortunately has since then compromised himself with his questionable arguments about cultural literacy and education, and in retrospect I think there were problems with his theories of interpretation, but I still agree with him that to think of reading in a coherent way there needs to be some kind of distinction between what Hirsch calls "meaning" and "significance" (or what the author can be inferred to have intended) and how the reader recontextualizes that intention in the light of his or her or a different period's interests, which may involve reading against the grain. This argument amounts to a reassertion (a sophisticated one, I hope) of the old subject-object distinction that I gather Gadamer and Heidegger would dissolve into historicity or Being or what have you. The whole argument is fascinating and remains unresolved.

DI LEO: But Hirsch as well was not immune to the "fogging of the issue" that you ascribe to Gadamer and Heidegger. His distinction between "meaning" and "significance" heavily draws on Husserl's notion of an "intentional object." Meaning for Hirsch is not reducible to the psychological acts of Twain, nor is it independent of the mental processes of the author of *Huckleberry Finn*. Hirsch's "meaning" is some type of ideal object that can be expressed in a number of different ways and still "mean" the same thing. For me this is just as foggy a notion as the horizon-fusion thesis of Gadamer. However, regardless of the relative fuzziness of these ideas, why keep the allegiance to the "meaning" side of Hirsch's equation? Why not regard language and literature as purely social matters? Or leave them on the side of "significance" if "meaning" is destined to be a perennially fuzzy object/topic?

GRAFF: It's always good to find another fan of the Hirsch/Gadamer debate, a diminishing breed, I suspect. I have always found Hirsch's Husserlian take on meaning as an "intentional object" a bit hard to grasp, but I don't have a problem with meaning being in principle self-identical even when expressed in different ways. Hirsch has an essay on synonymity in *The Aims of Interpretation* (1976) that seems to me a good defense of this idea – a no-no for New Critics and Gadamerians, to be sure – of the separability of meaning from how it's expressed. I would like to think, though, that this Hirschean argument about synonymity is not incompatible with Derrida's concept of "iterability," or repetition with a difference, in "Signature Event Context." (This essay is found in *Limited Inc.* [1988], which I edited. Derrida's response to me in an interview [see 142–53] makes me think this convergence may not be as improbable as it sounds.) That is, for a meaning to be a meaning it has both to be itself (self-identical, in Hirsch's sense) and to differ from itself.

DI LEO: I'm familiar with Hirsch's essay, which also appeared in the first volume of *Critical Inquiry*. Hirsch's argument in "Stylistics and Synonymity" concludes that style depends on there being alternative ways of saying the same thing as well as a notion of synonymity. I think that a number of people have provided very good arguments against Hirsch's notion of synonymity. The main thrust of these arguments is to free the theory of style from the constraints of synonymity and from misleading oppositions like style and subject, form and content, what and how, and intrinsic and extrinsic. I tend to believe that Hirsch's notion of synonimity is too strict, as are the views of those such as Nelson Goodman who reject the notion of synonymity *in toto*. I would suggest that we take up a weaker sense of synonymity. Instead of "strict identity" and "sameness," our notion of synonymity should be weakened to account for the fact that while no two terms have exactly the same meaning, some terms are closer to the meaning of others, so that a choice between the two terms in a discourse situation would provide subtle shifts in meaning. This notion of synonymity would be closer to what I think Derrida finds agreeable – if anything – in Hirsch's notion. It captures the "sameness with a difference" that you spoke of regarding Derrida's concept of iterability. So I can see a link between Hirsch (albeit modified) and Derrida (albeit loosely conceived).

GRAFF: I like the idea of "weakening" Hirschean self-identity to make it compatible with the Derridean idea that "self-identity" itself is always already constituted by difference. That's in fact what I was trying to say myself. For an example of what we're talking about, look at what I just did: I said the *same* thing as you said – we need to weaken Hirsch's notion of self-identity – by *changing it*, putting it in other words, summarizing it, paraphrasing it. If I'd simply replicated your words, quoted you without restatement, what I would have produced would be not the same meaning but no meaning: summaries reproduce the same meanings by changing them, putting them into other words, but words that, in order to qualify as a summary, have to be recognizable *as* synonymous with the original. This seems to me a vindication of Hirsch's argument that some notion of self-identity must be presupposed to make sense of communication, but amended by Derrida's argument that self-identity is always constituted by difference, iteration, spin, or what have you.

DI LEO: So what does all this have to do with literature anthologies?

GRAFF: Well, when I said at the outset that anthologies tend to assume that great texts tell students and others what to say about them (i.e., they isolate the texts from the critical discourse that students are asked to produce about the texts), this was another way of saying that conventional anthologies rest on an inert notion of self-identity in which the student is somehow to reproduce the sameness of the text without the intervention of criticism, much less theory. Phelan and my "critical controversies" editions assume that the self-identity of *Huckleberry Finn* and *The Tempest* can be replicated only in interpretive controversies.

DI LEO: So great books are only great from within the context of interpretive controversies? If these books cannot contribute to the critical conversations of our day, then should they be overlooked? This is a recipe for a continuously shifting canon determined by a set of contingent conditions: conditions that are more times than not politically determined. How do you feel about resting literary studies and the contents of anthologies on politics?

GRAFF: It doesn't follow for me that books are great only if they contribute to critical conversations and should be overlooked if they don't. If *Moby Dick* is a great novel, as I think it is, it was as great when it was overlooked and ignored by the critical conversation as it was and has been since its revival after the First World War. There's a sense in which a book is what it is independent of what readers and critics see in it – the flower in the forest can still be beautiful even if never seen by a human eye. Here's where I want to preserve some notion of the objectivity of the text independent of its contextualization. The best theorist I know on this question, by the way, is John Reichert in *Making Sense of Literature* (1977), an unfortunately overlooked *Moby Dick* of literary theory. Reichert argues cogently that there's a sense in which, if we agree that a text says or does something, then presumably it always said and did it and doesn't stop saying and doing it from one historical period to the next. The same would follow for whether it's good or not, although (a big although) Reichert acknowledges that there's also an important sense in which goodness and badness are purpose- and context-relative – nothing is just good in itself but has to be good *for* some purpose. Whatever makes a text good or bad, then, is an objective property of the text, but the standards by which we judge it as good or bad change historically and culturally. I'm afraid I'm running over this too quickly, but Reichert lays it out well in chapter 4 (especially 121–28).

DI LEO: Well, I think that we should probably stop here before your comments on Reichert draw us into a long discussion on the metaphysics of literary value and related matters.

GRAFF: I agree.

Bibliography

Conrad, Joseph. *Heart of Darkness*. Ed. Ross C. Murfin. 2nd ed. Case Studies in Contemporary Criticism. New York: Bedford/St. Martin's, 1996.

Derrida, Jacques. "Signature Event Context." *Limited Inc*. Ed. Gerald Graff. Evanston IL: Northwestern University Press, 1988. 1–23.

Hirsch, E. D. "Stylistics and Synonymity." *Critical Inquiry* 1.3 (1975): 559–79. Rpt. in *The Aims of Interpretation*. Chicago: University of Chicago Press, 1976. 50–73.

Reichert, John. *Making Sense of Literature*. Chicago: University of Chicago Press, 1977.

Shakespeare, William. *The Tempest*. Ed. Gerald Graff and James Phelan. Case Studies in Critical Controversy. New York: Bedford/St. Martin's, 2000.

Twain, Mark. *Adventures of Huckleberry Finn*. Ed. Gerald Graff and James Phelan. Case Studies in Critical Controversy. New York: Bedford/St. Martin's, 1995.

TERRY CAESAR

Anthologies, Literature, and Theory in Japan

For the past two years I have been teaching American literature in Japan. No one I know uses an anthology, not in my department, not anywhere else. Fearing my experience might be too restricted, I asked an American friend who has taught in Japan nearly twenty years. He told me a story about how, some years ago, at one of Japan's best private universities, everyone teaching American literature seminars (more or less equivalent to third- and fourth-year upper-division courses in the United States) was expected to use an anthology. Which one? He said he had forgotten – "some monstrous two-volume thing. I must have it buried somewhere."

At that time he was only interested in teaching the Beats, principally Gary Snyder and Kenneth Rexroth. So he went to the Japanese head of his section and asked, very slowly, if the anthology was compulsory. The man replied, even more slowly, "Come [pause] back [pause] in [long pause] half-hour." Half an hour later the section head handed my friend a piece of paper, upon which was written the following: "Yes, you must use the anthology." My friend told me two more things: he didn't use the anthology (but carried a volume to class "in case anybody was watching"), and the head of the section was a Dreiserian.

He didn't have to clarify why the chair declined to speak to him. Japanese professors of English will often go to absurd lengths to avoid speaking English to their native-English-speaking colleagues. They simply are not accustomed to speaking English; most studiously avoid doing so to their students in the classroom and lack any reason to do so outside the classroom. Why should they speak English? Regional or national conferences are almost exclusively in Japanese. It is fairly easy to avoid foreign colleagues, if there are any. No wonder the editor of a guide to teaching English in Japan – in which grammar and translation prevail in the system, driven in turn by unremitting examinations until university – characterizes the result as "inarticulate literacy" (Wordell 4).[1]

I didn't have to ask why my friend decided to add an identification of his section head in terms of a Major Figure. To this day most Japanese professors of English so comprehend themselves. Hence, for example, as I write, the second year of a course on Jane Austen continues to be taught by a colleague in my own graduate program, whose head is a Shakespearean. Last year I was introduced by another of my colleagues, whose specialty is Fitzgerald, to his friend, whose specialty is James. And so on. Curtis Kelly and Nobuhiro Adachi emphasize how, "in Japan, to an even greater degree than in the West, scholarship is regarded as expertise in a narrowly defined subject. . . . The more classical and specialized the area of research, the greater the prestige . . . 'not just anyone can comprehend Wordsworth or Shakespeare'" (161).[2]

Must such legitimating emphasis on Major Figures result in a de-emphasis on the use of anthologies? At first this might not necessarily seem to be the case. Although some anthologies strive to break new ground, most are content to enshrine hallowed ground. Why else use them to teach? The policy of the American literature section head in my friend's former department suggests, however, quite another purpose: to have a uniform course offering, period; the logic is administrative, not curricular. Part of my thesis in the following discussion will be that teaching English or American literature in another country illuminates instrumental reasons such as this one with startling clarity. In most countries, I believe, anthologies are chosen for such narrowly and purely practical reasons as to confound a theoretically wary American professor about what an "anthology" is in the first place.

The rest of my thesis will be perhaps even more disturbingly simple: the use of anthologies in countries such as Japan has little to do with theory. Of course, their use – anywhere – can be theorized. What use can't? But the process need not necessarily be conducted according to the precepts of current theorizing about anthologies in the United States, which is as nation-specific as Japanese practice, although Japanese practice, so unlike the American, neither proposes nor needs to be so self-conscious. The burden of an anthology is different in a foreign country, where the teaching of literature is far more inseparable from the teaching of language and where consideration of another country's literary canon has less to do with intervening in the issues responsible for its very constitution than with providing for students some fundamental cultural literacy, if only in the form of names and dates.

This literacy continues the logic of English-language acquisition itself, whose prestige in a foreign country is more or less wholly convertible into what John Guillory has termed – following Pierre Bourdieu – cultural capital. The study of literature in English does not change this logic and, if anything, only enhances the chances for an individual to convert her or his knowledge of the English language into real economic value. In any case, the politics of acquisition itself remains the same. In a very real sense the teaching of literature in English in Japan resembles the teaching of Latin literature in the provinces under the Roman imperium. "The primary fact about the teaching of Latin literature," Guillory explains, "was . . . not that it conveyed Roman cultural values but that it was the vehicle for the teaching of the Latin language. This goal was important enough to overwhelm any objection that might have been raised to particular Latin works whose contents may not have been wholly compatible with the norms of the imperium. As carriers first and foremost of *linguistic capital*, these works could then become the vector of ideological motifs not necessarily expressed within the works themselves" (61).

Or, one could add, they could not.³ In any case, first things first: in the study of a foreign literature in a foreign country imperial norms and even ideological motifs come last. The imperial center understands this. Unless a correct, careful study of the language comes first in the provinces, nothing else of cultural value (from anyone's point of view) will follow. Therefore it is vital that the provinces adhere to the hegemony of the center, granting the space of the native – native speakers, native sources – final authority in all things. With respect to English, the rest of the world is in the position of provinces to the two major English-speaking nations, England and the United States. Japan is typical of a country that has no vested interest in challenging this state of affairs. Japanese schoolchildren endure six years of English instruction before college. Knowledge of English is widely accepted as a route to professional success of all kinds, from serving tea down the hall to writing faxes around the world.

And yet the cultural capital of the language is the paradoxical reason why its literature is such a dispensable commodity in Japan and why anthologies of literature in English are so empty of theoretical provocation. Of course, the institutional scene of study matters. No less than the United States, Japan has its elite institutions, where students know English very well and where literature can be read in a more theoretically rigorous setting than is common. Institutional hierarchy represents one of a number of distinctions that I will set aside here. However, a particularly important one will have to be conceded by the end: the distinction between foreign and native professors. My conviction is that no Japanese professor would be prompted to write the following discussion, much less feel the need to work through the issues in the way that an American would. Why not? Not necessarily because he or she is not aware of these issues. Some Japanese professors are. Instead because the circumstances – national, professional, ideological – in which everybody teaches in Japan make these issues superfluous, except for those who feel otherwise because they have been shaped by quite different theoretical mandates, as inseparable from the literature, to them, as their own construction as national beings.

One

What is an anthology? Perhaps in many cases a bastard child of generic and commercial interests, at once something more and nothing more than the commodity form of a "textbook." Insofar as literature in English is concerned, I will use the term *anthology* to refer to many different kinds of texts, from special editions of small books consisting of a selection of stories by individual authors to large volumes consisting of a collection of poems, stories, excerpts from novels, and plays over the course of several centuries. The small book, unlike the large, often has very little editorial apparatus. Far more interesting, however, if we consider the case of English taught abroad, is the fact that a local edition of a small, single-author anthology can be so overdetermined by the language native to the country as to be lodged indeterminately between that language and English.

I have before me, for example, the following book: *Yellow Trains and Other Stories*, by Penelope Lively. It is only published in Japan. Four stories are included. A page-and-a-half note, in Japanese, precedes the stories, providing an outline of Lively's career and reputation. Notes in Japanese face every English page (there are 102 in all), translating into Japanese various unfamiliar words, idiomatic usages, or local allusions. A few more pages appear at the end of each story, consisting of questions – in English – on "narrative" (fill in the blank), vocabulary (match synonyms), and basic comprehension of the plot. These last are more open-ended in nature and could be ultimately taken to be interpretive, although in context their basic thrust is as factual as questions such as whether the student knows the correct meaning of the word *complacent* or if the main character of "Yellow Trains" eats all her pizza by the end of the story.

That this book is an anthology – that is, a selection from some larger body of work – is not open to question. What it is an anthology *of*, on the other hand, is. Ostensibly, *Yellow Trains* is intended to be used in literature courses. However, the book is so carefully packaged as a foreign-language text as to disable the difference between literature and language. Of course, teaching literature abroad arguably confounds this difference at every turn. Students for whom English is not a native language are not equivalent to native English speakers because their basic competency cannot be taken for granted, especially with respect to the core definitions of the most common (to natives) words. Consequently, there is a constitutive moment teaching nonnatives when the putatively aesthetic or hermeneutic realm of the English text – considered as literature – suffers a fall into the realm of the literal, considered only as language.

Of course, people who do not try to teach literature in English, as literature, to nonnative speakers must be forgiven for wondering if this fall is not ultimately the very condition of any teaching, anywhere, in any classroom. In other words, even if one chooses to believe in some dubious notion of the self-evidently "literary," it always remains language, whose referential meaning alone is never stable and is instead fraught with contradictions, ambiguities, and provocations.[4] Let me give an example. The other day I chanced to ask one of my students whether she thought the geisha in the film *Teahouse of the August Moon* was a prostitute. "Prosecute?" she replied confusedly. I realized that my question had been too sudden. But my point is merely that some instabilities are more profitable to pursue than others and, furthermore, that some are so "unstable" as to be completely null. A slender anthology such as *Yellow Trains* exists for good reason, especially for students who have always studied English as an exotic variant of Japanese, much less those who have only had at most a basic language class from a native speaker.

Are anthologies such as the Lively one mandated to hasten the fall into the literal or to prevent it? In some respects, of course, it is hard to say. Much depends upon the teacher; much depends upon the students. Some even depends upon the publisher – and so I note that another anthology from the same publisher's list, *Contemporary American Women Writers*, not only has the same basic format (although the translations into Japanese are all at the back rather than on facing pages) but also lacks any rationale for why these stories by these particular authors (Ann Beattie, Bobbie Ann Mason, Ursula Le Guin, Alice Adams) have been selected. Is this anthology conceived of as a sop to Japanese professors about a fashionable foreign category or as a special treat for language students? To me this book – more than the Lively – in its way challenges a limit-notion of what an anthology is in the first place. Surely there is a difference between a random assemblage and a reasoned selection?

Contemporary American Women Writers seems to me precisely the sort of book that would not be published in the United States because it appears to possess no theoretical pretension, not to say inner logic. It is as if the use to which the text can be put is the reason for its existence in the first place. This use is a matter of pedagogical occasion, which is not foreclosed by the publisher or the editors (or rather, language annotators) in any particular way. The book exists because it does not have any theory, not because it does. If someone wanted to disagree that, on the contrary, the very title is the product of a substantial and ongoing theoretical history, I would only reply that this history falls away in another country. Of course, it can be mentioned. Indeed, it must be. But theorizing can easily overcome the specific anthology in question, which begs to be allowed to offer nothing more of itself than its utility for language instruction. No matter that this utility in turn effectively defeats the potential for the text to be used for the purpose of literary instruction – whether critical history, theoretical orientation, or anything else. How can the latter study be realized if the former accomplishment cannot be taken for granted?

Last semester I taught the first semester of a two-year seminar, beginning in the junior year. Such seminars are common in Japanese universities, where students are only free in their last two years to take – nay, choose! – more intensive, specialized courses. Mindful both of the novelty this seminar would be to the students and of the difficulty of their reading more extensively in English, perhaps for the first time, I inclined to that most fateful authorial choice of English professors abroad: Hemingway. Challenges to the canon be damned, I resigned myself; at least my students could be expected to have heard of Hemingway (arguably the most famous American author throughout the world) and therefore to be pleased accordingly. Moreover – feminism forgive me, at least for the moment – we would vigorously contest Hemingway's representation of women as the semester wore on, I vowed. Meanwhile, my most crucial consideration was much simpler: Hemingway is easy to read. That is, his words are monosyllabic. At least students would not feel the need (I hoped) to roll over every English word into its Japanese equivalent.

Therefore I ruled out a third anthology by Yumi Press, *Hemingway's Youth in Michigan*, despite, for once, the presence of some principle of selection to the five stories. Although I wanted more stories, the real reason for my decision was that this anthology contains a whopping thirty-six pages of annotations in Japanese. Granted, some of this material begins – in Japanese – by setting each story in some critical or historical framework, and, better yet, occasional translation of individual words, phrases, or sentences refers to previous critical commentary. Nonetheless, there was entirely too much looming authority of Japanese everywhere. What I proposed to do was to try to expunge entirely at least any outward encouragement for the fearsome fall of the literal in our reading by substituting another anthology, *The Snows of Kilimanjaro and Other Stories*, published in London rather than Tokyo and containing absolutely no Japanese.

The seminar was hard going anyway. The students could make little sense of some theoretical material on feminism about which I had them do reports. Better, say, if I merely tried to demonstrate the "reading position" presumed by certain passages than if I used such terminology. Best of all, alas, if I just gave them the literal meaning of these passages, word-by-word – in effect becoming the lost annotator for the Japan-specific anthology of stories that I had decided not to use; Japanese students scribble Japanese characters next to English words with such definitional zest as to make a foreign teacher wish that we could just scrap the foreign language entirely and go straight for the kanji every time. Japanese anthologies of writing in English may not be the correct ones for Japan because they inscribe the moment of the fall into the literal. Yet this moment will not be avoided by choosing a text that has no Japanese.

And, of course, not all literalities are semantic in nature. One day we paused during our consideration of "The Doctor and the Doctor's Wife." It was one of those times when I felt we were being too plodding. I wanted the students to appreciate Hemingway's artistry, especially with respect to the very American subject of violence. We did not discuss precisely what the doctor means when he says to the Indian trying to pick a fight with him, "I'll knock your eye teeth down your throat." I took for granted that the students knew what these words meant. But could they understand the subtle menace conveyed by the Indian's reply? "Oh, no you won't, Doc." How many other things could he say! A curse might appear more violent. American culture, unlike Japanese, is saturated with verbal violence. I asked the best student in the class what *else* the Indian could reply, just to check that all were at least sensitive to the issue here. With her exquisite tentativeness, Kyoko replied that he could have said the following: "Excuse me."⁵

Not even possible annotations in *The Harper Anthology of American Literature* are going to help the foreign instructor at this moment. More to the theoretical point, the issues that animate *The Heath Anthology of American Literature* take place far above the cultural comprehension of students who assume that social life consists of blunting aggressions and expressing verbal concessions at every turn.⁶ At times their understanding of American literature is as alien to its social construction or its fundamental meaning as that of the perhaps apocryphal African students who couldn't understand why Hamlet was so upset, because in their country an uncle marries his dead brother's wife as a matter of course. Consequently, the first thing to say about the relationship between theory and anthologies from the perspective of a foreign country like Japan is that, whatever the relationship is (particularly as construed back home), it does not matter at all in the classroom.

Two

Eighteen years ago I taught for a year at a provincial university in China. At a sort of book center near campus there were some English books available. I still have a two-page list, crudely typed. Titles and authors include *The Elements of Style*, by "W. Struck"; *The Scarlet Letter*, by "Howthorne"; *Collected Short Poems*, by "Ezra Pond"; and *Shakespearean Tragedy*, by "A. C. Beadly." No anthologies of English or American literature are listed. As I recall, the university library did not possess any either. But the English department did! The anthology was the department's own, typed on special thick brown paper, word-by-word, on an old typewriter, by one of the department secretaries. The department ran off dittos of each page and stapled them all together. I eventually lost the copy of the anthology I was once given in order to teach the second semester of the one-year sequence on the English literature survey.

We began with the Romantics. Of course, Blake's "London" was included. I tried to lecture about it with requisite ideological fervor.

Along with "To a Skylark," a poem of Shelley's that I'd never heard of, "Song to the Men of England" was also included. I could not lecture about this slight revolutionary ditty with the same ideological fervor. It was a relief to get to Keats. I spent two whole enthusiastic periods on "The Eve of St. Agnes." But I never felt that the students were emotionally connecting with the poem. Why not? All so much bourgeois aestheticism? Nobody was saying, and since there were a hundred students, I couldn't really ask. The moment I remember best took place toward the end, after we had marched as far as Tennyson's "Ulysses." I must have spent fifteen minutes explaining – no, propounding on – the meaning of the line "I am become a name." After the lecture was over a student rushed up to me. I had not seen anybody so excited all semester. He had one question: "What is the meaning of the line, 'I am become a name'?"

What to make of this experience today? Of course my student of Tennyson was so giddy with his fall into the literal that it had become an ascent. But what do the larger conditions of textual production in this instance tell us about some more comprehensive relation between theory and anthologies? That even when the conditions are so restricted as to be virtually private, a theory-driven anthology such as the one with which I was presented will always collapse under canonical pressures? Perhaps. "The Eve of St. Agnes" should not have been included. Come to that, Keats himself probably should have been banished. But then – it could be objected – why have a survey course of English literature in the first place in a Chinese university? If the purpose is to politicize literature, the thing can be both more efficiently and more thoroughly done by reading Chinese. If, on the other hand, the purpose is to learn English, then it ultimately does not matter what is read in a survey course.

Eighteen years ago, I think, my survey course was a special instance of what I take to be Guillory's incontestable claim: that "the fetishized mass cultural form of the list, as an instance of the social imaginary, determines the form of the critique of the canon in the university, the fixation on the syllabus as an exclusive list" (36). The list might not be "fetishized" in the same way or for the same reason in China as in

England or the United States. Undoubtedly, the canon is not critiqued there in the same way, if at all. (The department could have reread English literature and compiled a completely different list; instead its list was almost identical with one available in any native provincial department.) Nonetheless, what we had in my anthology is a radical example of not only how arbitrary a syllabus can be but finally how pointless for canonical questions, as perceived back home. What mattered to this Chinese university – not to say the People's Republic – was that there be a survey course in English literature, rather than what exact selections were chosen to comprise this literature. Moreover, what was important about these selections was not – in Guillory's words – how "an imaginary cultural unity" projected "out of a curriculum of artifact-based knowledge" is "never actually coincident with the culture of the native state" (38). This coincidence is only important to natives. What was important instead to the Chinese was how the selections could be read as putatively amounting to a national core. Such a reading is, I believe, crucial for the student's acquisition of symbolic as well as linguistic capital.[7] For this sole purpose any syllabus – in effect – will do as well as any other, even though some will of course be better, that is, nearer to the imperial source, than others.

I have before me the course offerings in English – complete with descriptions (in Japanese) and required texts – of a large university in Tokyo. There are courses in everything from Old and Middle English, through Shakespeare and nineteenth-century American women, to female Gothic literature and postmodernism. Even more offerings are available in English conversation and linguistics. A number of reading courses are covered by anthologies, including an Everyman *English Short Stories 1900 to the Present*, and *The Penguin Book of American Short Stories*. Of course, there are a number of survey courses, addressing both the whole of English and American literature and selected periods. Texts include the Prentice-Hall *Concise Anthology of American Literature* and, most often, the latest edition of *The Norton Anthology of English Literature*. Regarding all these texts recalls for me an old dream: to consider canon formation as it abides not in the United States or England but in the rest of the world. But then I remember that I had this dream before I awoke – somewhere between teaching in China and in Egypt three years later – to a harsher reality: the rest of the world quite contentedly teaches the same canon that is so disputed back home.

Or, to put it another way, the rest of the world receives the results of native disputes, most venerably textualized in the form of anthologies. If specific countries are rich enough, unlike China, to produce their own anthologies of English or American literature, they instead simply import them entire, as produced in their countries of origin. It may not always be cheaper to do this rather than to generate anthologies of their own. However, it does enable the country in question to continue the basic cultural equation through which literature in English is studied in the first place. A foreign country is subordinate not only to the authority of native literature but to the theoretical conditions by which the writing continues to be textualized and studied in the classroom, as well as to the social and cultural traditions in which the words continue to be written.

Any one foreign country that takes upon itself the business of teaching literature in English no more presumes to intervene upon the theoretical conditions of its teaching than it presumes to alter the traditions of its writing. Back home it matters terribly which poems by major authors ought to be included in the latest anthology, not to mention which authors get to be accorded "major" status, according to what criteria. Abroad, though, these controversies do not matter much at all, for the simple reason that the literature itself, whatever the selections, is already foreign enough. Is an author gay? How important are considerations of social class? Is race always a decisive factor, either in the construction of canonical authors or in their reception? Such matters may or may not prove profitable to pursue. But it will not be profitable to pursue them at the cost of securing some minimal ground either of language competency or of cultural comprehension.

You simply cannot raise the subject of a gay author in an English text without at least being mindful of how anything to do with homosexuality may have been – as in Japan – effectively effaced, on the basis of social and moral codes operating in a wholly different society and, of course, in another language. Just so, it will be a much less relevant task to raise the issue of race in a society such as Japan's, before students who have hardly ever seen an African American and who lack the faintest idea of how acute and insistent racial concerns abide in a multiracial society such as the United States. Gerald Graff's injunction to "teach the conflicts" is well-known. Not only, though, does it presuppose the very core of literacy (cultural as well as linguistic) that is always already in dispute in the foreign-language classroom.[8] Teaching the conflicts also assumes a nation-specific identity. A methodology that is laudable for Americans (as on the whole I think Graff's is) may be self-indulgent or superfluous for Japanese.

In the searching discussion that introduces his anthology *The Random House Book of Twentieth-Century French Poetry* Paul Auster quotes a friend and former British cultural attaché on the intelligence that every anthology has two types of readers: "the critics, who judge the book by what is *not* included in it, and the general readers, who read the book for what it actually contains" (73). American students, I think, are today either in the position of Auster's critics or are situated by their teachers to be in this position (whether their teachers make it explicit for them or not). One reason why I have not used anthologies in Japan is because I am disabled from uttering what I used to on the first day of class in the United States: we must be vigilant about discovering the principles by which the selections in our anthologies were made, and we must never forget that we could be reading a quite different syllabus.[9] Such words would serve no purpose here, for my Japanese students are situated instead in the position of Auster's general readers.

Reviewing the two new anthologies of the Library of Congress series American Poetry: The Twentieth Century, Brad Leithauser at one point makes the following qualification: "These volumes call for eventual revision. It seems safe to say that had they been assembled ten years ago they would look quite different. Ten years hence, they will demand a new shape" (73). This is so, I believe, as a general condition of anthology making, as it is widely understood in the United States today (and not only as a special condition either of contemporary literature or of poetry in general).[10] Leithauser is expressing a truism – for Americans. Anthologies need to be made new, just like computer programs, automobiles, and fast-food menus. "Making it new" is not merely a motto by Ezra Pound and not only an imperative for literary study in the United States. It is an ideological condition of American life, into which a special volume like this one on the relationship between theory and anthologies fits very nicely, thank you.

For better or worse, however, "making it new" does not describe an ideological condition of Japanese life and certainly not an imperative of literary study in Japan about writing in English. On this basis alone such study here has no power to intervene in native debates about theoretical horizons of teaching literature. However, in addition, it suits Japanese academic purposes just as well to concede all authority for innovation to native countries as it has traditionally served Japanese business purposes to allow for innovation elsewhere than Japan.[11] Let foreign professors thrash out the sociopolitical criteria whereby, for example, South Asian writing is deemed part of English literature or Hispanic writing part of American literature. Whatever makes its way into present or future Penguins or Nortons will suffice for Japanese purposes – supplemented, of course, by locally produced textbooks and handbooks. What does not suffice in these native anthologies simply will not be taught. Failure to eliminate or ignore an individual writer will not occasion the scandal (real or theoretically imagined) that it well might in England or the United States. In any case – the reasoning concludes – these countries are so absorbed in the circumstances of their own study that whatever happens in Japan, or anywhere else, will not interest them.[12]

So if we compare the theoretical situation with respect to anthologies in Japan to that in the United States, we face a rather wondrous irony: the very widely anthologized values that so vex the study of literature back home are precisely the ones presumed to be studied so unproblematically abroad. Take a recent critique – which appeared in *College English*, no less – of *The Norton Anthology of World Masterpieces*. Waïl S. Hassan charges that the newest edition "more subtly than ever reproduce[s] the canon's ideological underpinnings" (39). He concludes that, alas, he is "forced" to use the *Norton* anyway, "for lack of a viable alternative," and therefore is challenged anew to correct "the Eurocentric image of the world which the Norton Anthology suggests to the students who so much as read its table of contents" (46). From a number of comments that could be made, I would emphasize two. First, only once, at the end, does some register of a purely practical consideration appear. I have already noted the moment of the practical as crucial in teaching abroad, where an anthology seems usually to be chosen for no better reason than to dispense with the troublesome matter of appropriateness. Hassan, however, dismisses the consideration as if it possessed no theoretical interest.

But it does – in the United States. Why does Hassan go with the Norton, despite its reprehensible ideological profile? Not only for practical reasons. Surely, in addition, because this anthology delivers the cultural capital of the course more efficiently and directly than any other; indeed, the Norton is by now arguably more canonical than any of the authors or texts to be found inside it. How to teach the impossible subject of world literature and not be intimidated by the Norton's reputation? One may as well dispute the very cultural fact of Europe itself, which in a sense Hassan wants to do, albeit not so wholly that he has to worry about what cultural fact to substitute for it or, worse, what reasons he might provide for a substitute, given the curricular assumptions of the syllabus, the departmental program, or – ultimately – American society itself. In Japan, on the other hand, Hassan would not have to worry about any of this. World literature would not exist as a course. And if it did, it would exist in order to provide the Eurocentric view of the Norton – just as the normative, timeless British or the American "view" is provided now by its respective Norton or suitable counterparts.

Of what exactly does this view consist? To a degree the components are aesthetic. John Fiske speaks of the difference between the aesthetic and the popular by which the artwork is self-contained: "It is completed, finished, and contains within itself all that is necessary to appreciate it: the work of art awaits only the cultured sensibility that has the key to unlock its intricate secrets" (105). The study of literature in English is designed to foster the development of this sensibility, by means of which cultural capital can be purchased (not to say certified).

At the least – and here the matter becomes more broadly cultural – a whole *imagination* of the world is made available to the foreign student who studies another nation's literature, particularly at a time when even the culture of the United States is what Arjun Appadurai characterizes as "only one node of a complex transnational construction of imaginary landscapes" (4). The individual who would learn to negotiate among these landscapes is one who first studies them within the confines of their national constitution.[13]

This last point is crucial, although not one that Appadurai makes himself. His classic article concludes, on the contrary, by speaking of culture in the following way: "What I would like to propose is that we begin to think of the configuration of cultural forms in today's world as fundamentally fractal, that is, as possessing no Euclidean boundaries, structures, or regularities" (20). In other words, culture is not, whatever else, purely national. (Appadurai terms it instead "polythetically overlapping.") However, nothing could be further from the Japanese classroom, whether or not an anthology of English or American literature is on the syllabus. In such a classroom the national organization of knowledge – however complex and varied – remains the determinant of last resort. The important thing about American literature, for example, is that it is *American*. Contra Fiske, perhaps finally it is not absolutely crucial that (or rather, how) the literature be seen as literature. Yet it must be seen as venerably American. Unless the national boundaries of a literature hold firm, its peculiar networks of affiliation, its thematic configurations, its whole history as a national project might be thrown into doubt.[14] In consequence, literary study could not be so readily invested in the form of cultural capital.

The burden of a theoretically alert American literature classroom in the United States today may be to abet this doubt. The burden of this classroom in Japan – whether or not theoretically alert – is certainly to forestall it, at least at the level where an anthology is used. The reason can be given simply: teaching literature in English in a foreign country such as Japan ultimately accomplishes none of the cultural or social work that animates the study of this same literature back home. British or American critiques to the contrary, the same old canon suits Japan just fine. In a recent critique Stuart Hall confronts "a blank and uncomprehending Englishness" with "the basic building blocks of the new global universe," including African, Indian, and Caribbean elements (12). But a Japanese student will first want to learn about this "Englishness," whose study already is, from his or her perspective, a route into the very global universe that Hall only sees being effaced by the same thing! The venerable imagination of a national heritage may in fact be precisely what recommends it to foreign study, despite the fact that such stability, from a native point of view, is exactly what opens it up to the contestation that emerges from actual, lived social and political experience.

A foreign country, of course, possesses none of this experience.[15] Consequently, it is no more readable in another nation's literature than, say, the nuances from abroad of the oversized, "too-big look" of contemporary fashion, whose emancipatory "message" for Japanese women has, as Donald Richie explains, "no social relevance. It is a message without a context" (105). The foreign study of literature in English, I believe, is similarly decontexted, *if* what is most theoretically provocative about such study in its native countries today is proposed as most necessary. At most the literature will be – as Richie explains about the too-big look – "taken over unexamined" (106). The appropriation may not matter much when it comes to clothes. (Fashions change; "messages" from elsewhere converge or overlap; culture here is not exclusively school culture.) Usage becomes rather garishly ironic when it comes to the study of a national literature, especially when the very occasion for its study at home is elsewhere an examination that cannot take place.

Or else, perhaps, abroad it just appears idle to undertake such a study driven by the latest in sophisticated domestic theorizing. Carolyn Porter concludes a lengthy reconsideration of the American national heritage thus: "A field reconstellated by an historicized politics of location should open out onto the Pacific as well as the Atlantic and should address the pre-colonial cultures of Aztec and Algonquin as well as the post-colonial careers of Quebec and Haiti" (521). What purpose is served by this expansion in Japan? To dislodge Eurocentrism? But what if the rationale of a pedagogic occasion is to establish Eurocentrism in the first place? To promote multicultural discursivity? What if an agenda impeccably "diverse" in American terms can become confusing and diffuse in Japanese terms? Of course, in the end it may not matter very much anyway. A course is just one course. It exists to provide a grade. To this inescapable instrumental end one can just as easily put Aztecs as Puritans on the second-year midterm – anywhere; Japanese students certainly could not be expected to care much. And one can lecture to fourth-year students on Chinese immigration just as profitably as on African slavery; most students throughout the world would not likely be aware of the American cultural politics that can make the very choice politically (if not theoretically) reprehensible.

Three

I own a brand-new anthology, *Asian-American Literature*, edited by Shirley Geok-lin Lim. The subject is hot. The time is ripe – for American students, who need to be instructed about the latest phase of (and the newest academic field within) the debates concerning multiculturalism. During a visit to the United States this past summer I emboldened myself to call up the publisher and order an examination copy of the book, sent to my institutional address. What did I have in mind? Not using the anthology as a required textbook. Perhaps nothing more than reading it myself, as a means of either remembering when I participated in a curriculum in which such a book made sense or imagining such a curriculum in my present position, in which the book makes no sense. Maybe I just wanted to see if the publisher would honor my request. To my delight, it did. To my surprise, a copy of the anthology had arrived by the time I had returned to Japan.

Now what? Next semester I have two classes in American literature. If this anthology is too strenuous or just plain lengthy for the undergraduate seminar, what about the graduate one? I've been thinking of postmodernism. But such a subject has two immediate problems. First, it is theoretical. Theory is difficult for my students to read. Second, a course on postmodernism slights the most venerable – not to say typical – sort of graduate course, which would be on a single author. In Japan – in such contrast to the United States – the surest route to respectability, probity, and all other manner of canonical as well as professional virtues is through an Author, even and especially at the graduate level. Perhaps – it could be reasoned – I would simply be disdaining the culture out of which my students emerge, and back into which they must return, if I proposed a course on postmodernism, as opposed to, say, a course on Thomas Pynchon. Pynchon – too difficult, too contemporary – would be bad enough. But not as bad as postmodernism, or less bad in a more conventional, acceptable way.

Lately, though, I have been thinking about Asian American literature. As part of my absorption in Japan I had become interested in this subject anyway – writing reviews of some studies as well as teaching novels by Joy Kogawa and Kyoko Mori in earlier courses in American culture and literature. *Asian-American Literature* now enables me to further think of the subject as a fully academic one and not merely a chance interest or a haphazard curiosity. Anthologies do this. They dignify – not to say create – a field, according it a degree of range that might not have been suspected or a measure of depth that could not have been easily realized. Suddenly an assortment of texts together acquires weight, heft, authority. What about competing fields? The nice thing about choosing an anthology on Asian American literature in a foreign country is that one doesn't have to fret about not choosing instead an anthology on African American literature or Native American literature. In Japan literature in English does not compete with itself in this way. There are no compelling reasons why it should. Subjects – nay, whole departments – come about for entirely different, thoroughly social reasons. Insofar as I can tell, for example, the man who teaches Jane Austen in my own department does so because he used to teach in our director's former department. Even if some specialties are to be preferred over others – better Austen than Pynchon – it really would make no difference what his specialty is.

So, I could well reason, it finally does not matter what I choose to teach in the graduate course. Why not Asian American literature then? Ironically – to me – for the very reason that it now becomes – in some hapless Japanese sense – possible: that is, the volume *Asian-American Literature*. An anthology makes the subject seem more serious than I wish it would be – now a field, complete with its very own anthology! Granted, Guillory is correct: "In no classroom is the 'canon' itself the object of study." He continues thus: "The distinction between the canonical and the noncanonical can be seen not as the form in which judgements are actually made about individual works, but as an effect of the syllabus as an institutional instrument, the fact that works not included on a given syllabus appear to have no status at all" (30). This last point, I believe, is especially exacerbated in a foreign country, when the status of the works not included is the least of their problems. In fact, these works will have no existence. No other courses will "cover" them. The absence of the "coverage" model is perhaps the most decisive difference between the constitution of English departments in England and the United States and in Japan. Hence, the canon will consist of only what is taught – and only what is taught will constitute the canon.

The anthology before me could not be more different from the one I was given eighteen years ago in China, especially with respect to the current text's theoretical provenance. No matter that the issues of *Asian-American Literature* are hedged at every turn. We read in the preface, for example, that the volume offers "a broad sampler of works whose critical reception has already marked them as belonging to an Asian-American canon or which represent emergent voices, communities and concerns" (xv). How to tell the difference? Similarly, if what we have is "a rich diversity that parallels the heterogeneity of Asian-American communities" (xvi), then what about the subsequent claims of the introduction that the anthology "seeks to suggest a collective set of new American identities now emerging as Asian American" (xxii)? How much does "a transnational construction of American identity" change things? Could there be identities somehow "American" *before* they become "Asian American"? (The introduction strives to position itself in terms of earlier anthologies, on this very point.) Finally, one could ask, is Asian American literature a coherent object for academic study or merely a theoretical fiction? Alas, the editor does not offer enough additional materials for the student to read the book as the one rather than the other.

The foreign student, I think, will care about this distinction (if at all) in a different way than the American student. Guillory speaks of "a principle of specious unity" as being "implicit in the construction of any syllabus" (34). The foreign student can be assumed to be concerned about the unity, while the American student can be assumed to be concerned about its specious nature. Abroad, the lost cultural totality of which any one syllabus is merely a specious expression cannot be presumed to function if the literature is foreign. Back home, on the other hand, this same totality easily becomes all that functions. It is the first condition of any syllabus, conceived of (according to Guillory's argument) as the displaced condition of canonicity, which is in turn the stand-in for the fragmented nature of culture itself. A foreign student can be forgiven for failing to appreciate that on a syllabus the cultural totality of another country is already lost.[16] Why? Because there is no wider urgency for finding it, much less any concrete social reality in which either the loss or the recovery of the cultural tradition of another nation is in any way as important as comparable questions about one's own.

I do not know if I will use *Asian-American Literature* next semester. If the students will not worry about lost totalities, I will. But then, I have to admit, I am an American. If I am not responsible in some way for this totality, then why was I hired in the first place? Do any of my colleagues care if I choose a book that has my students reading selections from India or the Philippines rather than Texas or Alabama? Probably not; my command of the totality will be unquestioned. Will the students care? Most likely they will be concerned once again first and foremost with making some literal sense of whatever they have to read. Meanwhile, what about postmodernism – which is in part another way, now formidably theorized, to displace the matter of totalities, particularly on the national level? The more I flip through the pages of the anthology before me, the more I begin to suspect that it might enable me to imagine two courses for the price of one. According to one reading, it could be argued that Asian Americans are already postmodern and maybe always already were. I linger, for example, over the selection from Abraham Verghese, who was born in Ethiopia.

Let me not care what an Ethiopian is doing in an anthology of American literature that consists entirely of writing by Asians. At least the selections are indisputably in English. The language, as language, has of course nothing necessarily to do with theory, unless it can be demonstrated that each English utterance is embedded at once in a national and transnational economy. Consider a moment in the Verghese pages when the author, a doctor who had his medical training in India, meets an Indian physician at a cafeteria while being interviewed for a residency position in Los Angeles. By her features he imagines the woman is from Bombay or Delhi. She turns out to be from Birmingham, England. She explains that her family fled from Uganda. She has never been to India. Then there is the following exchange: "When I told her I was born in Ethiopia, she tried her Swahili on me and I my Amharic on her. Neither of us got very far with that and so we retreated to English" (499). If this moment may not illuminate postmodernism so well, it certainly illuminates the foreign teaching of literature in English. Such teaching takes place during a time when much of the rest of the world must retreat to English in order to communicate with each other.

National boundaries can be reconstructed in order to contain these people. And so, among other things, there abides on the university curriculum in Japan something called "American literature," in which the national totality comprehends all – maybe even Ethiopians. However, my feeling is that the actual study of any national literature will always feature, well, a retreat, especially when conducted abroad. To what? To the language in which it was written, considered in terms not of its ideological freight or cultural determinants but just of the simplest and most basic communicative needs between people. Since neither the freight nor the determinants can be either taken for granted or theorized away, especially when people are native to other languages, it might be better to try to confront the needs directly. How do people from other countries *ever* understand each other? Granted, anthologies do not make it any more possible to answer this question than other kinds of texts. At best, though, they do offer more occasions for the needs to be exhibited. I suspect that *Asian-American Literature* offers more than most.

This may not be reason enough for a Japanese professor to put it on the syllabus. It is not even reason enough for me. But the anthology just might suffice anyway – not only because I am inescapably an American, although this is part of the reason: just because I cannot teach the significance of conflicts does not mean I can any more ignore them than I can ignore the background of either myself or my students, who have been socialized to learn the importance of – of all things! – consensus. Moreover, the modest notion of English as a retreat may enable a more crucial practical result. It can forestall a further retreat – into Japanese. English is the language that my students and I must use in order to communicate. A Japanese professor would neither be so fearful nor, I believe, so anxious as I am, lest the very language of the literature in question be lost. And not lost just to Japanese, but to "Japanese" as the name of some untheorizable prior pedagogical condition in which what ceases to matter is not only the contents of the syllabus or its national construction but the language in which the text is written in the first place.

Notes

1. Compare McVeigh: "The Japanese education system has appropriated English for its own purposes, and transformed the language of the Other into a sort of impractical non-language" (74). See also the articles by Nozaki; and Kelly and Adachi, both in the Wadden collection. It might be added that the sheer amount of complaint – oral as well as written, in Japanese as well as English – concerning the astounding and predictable difficulty of teaching English in Japan enjoys the dubious status within Japan of being virtually a discourse of its own, quite apart from its pedagogical occasion, enshrined in the monthly magazine *The Language Teacher*, published by the Japanese Association for Language Teaching. For a typical mainstream example of this complaint see Clark.

2. Of course, such is the case with professionals anywhere, who strive to distinguish themselves from laypersons through specialized knowledge as well as specialized discourse about it. Japan, however, is in this respect a typically Asian country, I believe, informed by special Confucian traditions

of its own that put the educated man in a more elevated – not to say mandarin – position with respect to uneducated people than is more common in the West. See Reid for a recent popular account of this tradition, although his emphasis is more on the broad-based opportunity at point of entry than the elite status at the pinnacle of success. More generally, on the composition of academic departments in Japan, see Ivan Hall, who emphasizes that – apart from scholarly record and "promise" – permanent appointments are made "at the better universities" not so much on consideration of field as "on some previous connection with the hiring institution or its incumbent staff" (94).

3. I set aside here the question of literary language in linguistic capital, about which Guillory (63–71) may be recommended. As he notes, literary language may change more slowly than extraliterary language, or heteroglossia (in Bakhtin's definition), but this is not the fruitful theoretical provocation in the foreign classroom that it is in the native one, for the simple reason that canonical literature – ever the guarantor of both high and low linguistic usage – enjoys abroad little of the living, spoken contrast with either licensed or unlicensed grammatical abuses that it enjoys at home. This difference, in turn, "can be made to take the charge of many other differences constitutive of social struggles" (Guillory 70). In a foreign country, on the contrary, the difference is open to no such charge – which is one reason why any language is foreign to another in the first place. About the general question of the global hegemony of English, see Phillipson, whose concern, however, is what he terms "linguicism," and not the place of literature within this ideology, which in turn purchases some of its power by disconnecting "culture" from a purely instrumental view of language as a "tool" (287).

4. See, for example, de Man, most preeminently or scandalously, depending upon one's theoretical predilections. Compare Burgess's desire for an anthology of modern English literature in Malay translation. He had to abandon it: "Only when the thunder began to speak in Sanskrit would *Tanah Tandus* [*The Waste Land*] make sense to the East but we did not get as far as that. *The Waste Land* revealed itself, while the cats were chewing raw snake, as a very ingrown piece of literature which had nothing to say to a culture which had no word for spring and did not understand the myth of the grail" (404).

5. To be fair to the student, the Yumi volume, *Hemingway's Youth*, although it does not translate Dick's reply, does give an editorial opinion – citing an

American critic! – about the doctor's previous words to the effect that he is not being the gentleman that he should be (67).

6. For another and less happy example of a foreign reading overcoming any other response to an English text, see Mark Salzman's account of teaching Shirley Jackson's "The Lottery," in *Iron and Silk*. Salzman does not say whether he taught this chestnut from an anthology. Of course, such responses have a quite different status when the "text" in question is from popular culture – and therefore Fiske celebrates, for example, Australian Aboriginals "reading" Rambo as racially subordinate (104). For more on how the discrimination proper to popular culture clarifies the quite different discrimination proper to literature – at least as presumed in the culture-fraught "highbrow" foreign classroom – see below.

7. Guillory distinguishes in his introduction between linguistic capital – or "socially credentialed and therefore valued speech" – and symbolic capital, defined thus: "a kind of knowledge-capital whose possession can be displayed upon request and which thereby entitles its possessor to the cultural and material rewards of the well-educated person" (ix). That these "rewards" will be different in a country such as China from one such as Japan will not, I must trust, vitiate my modest point. For an individual to make such a display, some minimal knowledge of a nation *as* a nation is important (and some knowledge of that nation's literature is probably in this regard decisive).

8. Of course – once more – the problems of the foreign-language classroom overlap with those of the native classroom. Bialostosky is one of a number of critics who note how Graff's classroom lacks gradation: "Graff tells us to teach the conflicts, but he does not tell us which ones to teach first-year undergraduates and which to reserve for senior seminars" (399).

9. See Caesar, "Pieties and Theories."

10. Maria Damon is undoubtedly correct in the following statement: "Poetry, as any quick survey of literary nationalism will reveal, is far more easily pressed into the service of national identity formation than other forms of writing and seems to carry a symbolic weight in the national Imaginary that makes such civic service important" (468).

11. This particular point has by now become a commonplace in foreign commentary about Japan, capable of more expansive strictures such as the following by Smith, reminding Americans of the folly of assuming that, like them, Japanese are "somehow caught in a permanent state of aspiration": "Japan, as the world's premier learning culture, can absorb anything and still

go on being Japan. Nothing the Japanese import – not chopsticks, not constitutional law – remains quite the same once they adopt it. A millennium before the Americans arrived, the Japanese were awash in Chinese culture and civilization. But they never became Japanese" (309).

12. American studies – not so burdened by a formalistic concern about the constitution of the status of the "literary" text and instead mandated to address questions of national identity that English departments can safely either assume answered or ignore – is another matter. Its call to "integrate the work of scholars outside the U.S," as the last outgoing president of the American Studies Association put it (welcoming work that locates the United States in a global context), has been virtually a disciplinary imperative for some years now (Kelley 9). See, for example, Desmond and Dominguez, who argue for "not just an internationalization of views, a way of giving voice to foreign scholars who rarely get read or heard by U.S. humanities specialists, but for the activation of institutional and intellectual grounds for the generation of a new kind of scholarship about the United States" (484). Mary Kelley herself mentions the recent establishment of the International American Studies Association.

13. This individual is someone who would be known as *kokusaijin* (international person) in Japan, whose ideological construction in terms of *kokusai ishiki* (international consciousness) or *kokusai rikai kyoiku* (education in international understanding) is a crucial, if by now somewhat clichéd, component of Japanese education. For more on the system see Smith.

14. For an example of such doubt see Parker.

15. That is, not as expressed in English. The question of how writing in English can become for the provinces – to recall Guillory – "the vector of ideological motifs not necessarily expressed in the works themselves" is a separate one, whose consideration would require another discussion entirely than the one I am attempting here.

16. Again, I pass over the question of whether or not this is also the case in the classroom back home. To cite Gillory: "The function imposed upon schools of acculturating students in 'our' culture often . . . requires that texts be read 'out of context,' as signs of cultural continuity, or cultural unity. We need not deny that the text tradition can sustain intertextual dialogue over centuries and millennia, however, in order to insist that what is revealed by the historical context of this dialogue is cultural discontinuity and heterogeneity" (43).

Bibliography

Appadurai, Arjun. "Disjuncture and Difference in the Global Cultural Economy." *Public Culture* 2.2 (1990): 1–23.

Auster, Paul. Preface. *The Random House Book of Twentieth-Century French Poetry*. 1981. Rpt. in *The Art of Hunger: Essays, Prefaces, and Interviews and The Red Notebook, Expanded Edition*. New York: Penguin Books, 1997. 199–237.

Bialostosky, Don. "Is Gerald Graff Machiavellian?" *Style* 33.3 (1999): 391–405.

Burgess, Anthony. *Little Wilson and Big God*. London: Heinemann, 1987.

Caesar, Terry. "Pieties and Theories: The Heath in the Survey, the Survey in the Discipline." *Arizona Quarterly* 51 (Winter 1995): 109–40.

Clark, Gregory. "Overcoming Japan's English Allergy." *Japan Quarterly* (April–June 1998): 46–53.

Contemporary Women Writers. 3rd ed. Tokyo: Yumi Press, 1995.

Damon, Maria. "From Outlaw to Classic: Canons in American Poetry." *Contemporary Literature* 39.3 (1998): 468–75.

de Man, Paul. *Allegories of Reading*. New Haven: Yale University Press, 1986.

Desmond, Jane, and Virginia Dominguez. "Resituating American Studies in a Critical Internationalism." *American Quarterly* 48.3 (1996): 475–90.

Fiske, John. "Popular Discrimination." *Modernity and Mass Culture*. Ed. James Naremore and Patrick Brantlinger. Bloomington: Indiana University Press, 1991. 103–16.

Graff, Gerald. *Beyond the Culture Wars: How Teaching the Conflicts Can Revitalize American Education*. New York: W. W. Norton, 1993.

Guillory, John. *Cultural Capital: The Problem of Literary Canon Formation*. Chicago: University of Chicago Press, 1993.

Hall, Ivan. *Cartels of the Mind: Japan's Intellectual Closed Shop*. New York: W. W. Norton, 1998.

Hall, Stuart. "Whose Heritage? Un-settling 'The Heritage,' Re-imagining the Post-Nation." *Third Text* 49 (Winter 1999–2000): 3–13.

Hassan, Waïl S. "World Literature in the Age of Globalization: Reflections on an Anthology." *College English* 63.1 (2000): 38–47.

Hemingway, Ernest. *Hemingway's Youth in Michigan*. 3rd ed. Tokyo: Yumi Press, 1995.

———. *The Snows of Kilimanjaro and Other Stories*. London: Arrow Books, 1994.

Kelley, Mary. "'Taking Stands': American Studies at Century's End. Presidential Address to the American Studies Association, October 29, 1999." *American Quarterly* 52.1 (1999): 1–22.

Kelly, Curtis, and Nobuhiro Adachi. "The Chrysanthemum Maze: Your Japanese Colleagues." *A Handbook for Teaching English at Japanese Colleges and Universities.* Ed. Paul Wadden. New York: Oxford University Press, 1993. 156–71.

Leithauser, Brad. "No Laughing Matter." *New York Review of Books* 47 (September 21, 2000): 70–74.

Lim, Shirley Geok-lin, ed. *Asian-American Literature: An Anthology.* Lincolnwood IL: NTC Publishing Group, 2000.

Lively, Penelope. *Yellow Trains and Other Stories.* Tokyo: Yumi Press, 1995.

McVeigh, Brian. *Life in a Japanese Women's College.* London: Nissan Institute/Routledge, 1997.

Nozaki, Kyoko Norma. "The Japanese Student and the Foreign Teacher." *A Handbook for Teaching English at Japanese Colleges and Universities.* Ed. Paul Wadden. New York: Oxford University Press, 1993. 27–34.

Parker, Hershel. "The Price of Diversity: An Ambivalent Minority Report on the American Literary Canon." *College Literature* 18.3 (1991): 15–29.

Phillipson, Robert. *Linguistic Imperialism.* Hong Kong: Oxford University Press, 1992.

Porter, Carolyn. "What We Know That We Don't Know: Remapping American Literary Study." *American Literary History* 6.3 (1994): 467–526.

Reid, T. R. *Confucius Lives Next Door.* New York: Random House, 1999.

Richie, Donald. *A Lateral Review: Essays on Culture and Style in Contemporary Japan.* Berkeley: Stone Bridge Press, 1992.

Salzman, Mark. *Iron and Silk.* New York: Random House, 1986.

Smith, Patrick. *Japan: A Reinterpretation.* New York: Vintage, 1998.

Wordell, Charles. "Diverse Perspectives on English Teaching in Japan." *A Guide to Teaching English in Japan.* Ed. Charles Wordell. Tokyo: The Japan Times, 1985. 3–19.

SIMON MORGAN WORTHAM

Anthologizing Derrida

One

The texts of Jacques Derrida are gathered or collected together in an almost bewildering variety of ways. Essays, selected passages, fragments, and excerpts drawn from Derrida's enormous and rapidly growing corpus are included in numerous anthologies (too numerous to mention) alongside the work of many other critics, writers, and thinkers. These sorts of anthologies often aim to introduce students, as well as other interested parties, to apparently "representative" slices of writing that might be taken, by synecdoche or example, to illustrate, convey, or describe the key concerns of particular thinkers – and frequently, by extension, the intellectual and historical traditions and trajectories underlying the vast field of so-called literary or critical theory in which they play their part. Such collections obviously locate and present Derrida differently each time of asking: Derrida the poststructuralist; Derrida the literary theorist (although rarely Derrida the serious philosopher); Derrida as a figure associated with the (re)thinking of Marxism, psychoanalysis, feminism, New Historicism, or postmodernism (although too rarely Derrida the [re]thinker of phenomenology, from Hegel to Husserl and to Heidegger); and so on and so forth, et cetera, et cetera.[1] Bearing in mind the near global circulation of "Derrida," mediated nevertheless by very specific local, national, and transnational circuits, relays, nodes, contexts, and institutions of production, dissemination, archiving, and reading, it is obviously the case that the different and diverse impressions given of "Derrida" or of "deconstruction" by dint of the plural possibilities of such framing or scaffolding depend in part on the reception and translation (in the very broadest sense) of his work at a particular time or in a particular place. Anthologies devoted to the work of Jacques Derrida alone are also available, of course, and seek to combine or recombine different parts or elements of Derrida's writing (both essays and interviews), especially for the relatively inexperienced reader. Additionally, a host of textbooks or guides abound, which gather – or, if you like, anthologize – a whole range of different readings, emphases, or approaches potentialized by Derrida or by deconstruction. Rather like the published proceedings of certain conferences devoted to questions and issues raised by *deconstruction* or by Derrida's work, these sometimes include a contribution by Derrida himself. And, of course, Derrida's own published texts – many of his so-called books – often compile or gather together a body of essays, lectures, or writings that can hardly be read or understood as amounting to consecutive, sequentially ordered stages or developments contributing to an entirely unified thesis or argument taking shape in general. Lastly, there is also that handful of books that physically juxtapose Derrida's writing with the text of another writer, sometimes in two columns or bands, so as to stage an encounter of sorts between them.

In other words, then, the reception – indeed, often the production or publication – of Derrida's work is profoundly shaped by anthologization in a variety of guises. One might even suggest that "Derrida" is anthologized to a wider extent and in a greater number of ways than almost any other contemporary thinker in the theoretical field, which would suggest that Derrida's work supplies a most fruitful context in which to put the question of anthologization itself.

For some, however, anthologizing Derrida may give cause for concern. In the face of an increasingly immense Derrida industry, if one can call it that, are we encouraged to gobble up only the more digestible snippets, often forgetting to restore key quotes, passages, or indeed entire essays to their original context of writing or publication? Do we now tend to neglect the lengthier expositions that take place in Derrida's "classic" texts, the books published in 1967, for example, whereby sustained, patient, and rigorous attention to certain philosophical or intellectual problems on Derrida's part might more clearly identify him as a serious philosopher "in" or "of" the Western tradition? Via the work of anthologization, does Derrida's relationship to other thinkers and to various traditions of thought become far too malleable, with the frequent result that Derrida is presented rather abstractly, vaguely, and sloppily as some sort of "postmodernist," rather than as a particular thinker emerging out of a more clearly determined or locatable intellectual milieu? If such is the case, one might even say that the often-claimed pliability or iterability of "Derrida" or of "deconstruction" de jure, supposedly facilitating a limitless number of juxtapositions or contextualizations, de facto tends to promote, via the work of anthologization, anthologies that indeed proscribe, limit, and even exclude certain ways in which Derrida might appropriately be positioned, situated, and read.

Alongside the question of whether anthologies covering the texts of a variety of critics and thinkers generally tend to misrepresent or distort the tenor and specificity of Derrida's work itself, not least in their function as pedagogic tools for students, there are also problems and issues that attend the business of compiling anthologies devoted to Derrida's work alone. Let us look at just one recent case. In the introduction to *The Derrida Reader*, published in 1998, Julian Wolfreys suggests that, while his anthology tentatively but usefully "bring[s] together a number of key issues, or what might be called abiding interests or concerns, in Derrida's writing" (6), nevertheless the deconstructive texts of Jacques Derrida, as singular critical engagements or textual performances, paying heed on each occasion to very singular issues of translation or idiom, simply do not yield or evince "the parameters, the rules, the protocols, of a systematised methodology which could be said to operate in the same manner each and every time" (4). Thus the pieces Wolfreys decides to collect together cannot, "through a process of reading, assimilation and homogenisation, become reified as typical or representative of a particular approach" (6). Wolfreys therefore questions any programmatic reading or "combinatory logic" (1) that might be applied to or extrapolated from any compilation of "Derrida," whereby each or any selected "part" might in some sense be taken to figure the whole as exemplary instance or illustrative example. Wolfreys insists that in his selection (or in any other for that matter) "there is not the possibility of joining the dots and getting a complete picture, for there is no complete picture to be had, and anyway, the dots can always be joined in different ways" (5).

Anthologizing Derrida

This introduction by Wolfreys to *The Derrida Reader* raises an interesting question, going beyond his own handling of the problem of anthologizing Derrida. Is it the case that the almost limitless pliability and therefore appliability that is frequently claimed or assumed on behalf of Derrida's texts by those not so closely affiliated with deconstruction – which often enables more "generalist" anthologizers to consider all sorts of permutations and combinations in the field of theoretical writing – should now be seen as being reserved and reinscribed within an *internal* economy of circulation, reading, and iteration "*in*" Derrida, perhaps by those very same supporters and defenders of his work who at the same time often question or even repudiate such absolute malleability once Derrida is exposed to the *external* marketplace of more generalist anthologization? I do not think this necessarily follows from Wolfreys's reflections on anthologization. (For one thing, application and iteration may not mean the same thing, certainly as far as deconstruction is concerned.) Rather, it would seem that the (de)limiting effects that arise de facto as the product of the *institution of* anthologization imposed on (but also to some extent emerging out of) the de jure malleability or iterability of "Derrida" or "deconstruction" occur not just in the vicinity of the more generalist anthology; equally, they impose themselves on the possibilities thrown up by collecting Derrida's writings alone. For here, lurking behind the perhaps rather anxious tone Wolfreys adopts in discussing the matter, is the sense that any anthologization of Derrida's work – whether it stands alongside the writings of other authors or next to other bits of "Derrida" – will yet inevitably propose or suggest a "combinatory logic," however stealthily or implicitly, notwithstanding the best intentions of the anthologizing editor. Indeed, one can also look to the other side of the coin where this problem is concerned. If Wolfreys is at all persuasive in claiming that what is found in Derrida's work "cannot be reduced to a restricted economy of interpretive functionality which operates with a predictable consistency," so that key terms, motifs, philosophical issues, and moves deployed across different (selected) essays "do not remain constant . . . do not retain constant meaning-value in the general economy of Derrida's text" (11), then the division or borderline that some might presume to exist between the internal or "restricted" economy of "Derrida" and the external or "general" economy of "Theory" cannot confidently be inscribed or re-marked. For to set off or set aside "Derrida" as rather more fluid, iterable, or even "undecidable" when juxtaposed with his own work, and yet more demanding of a "correct" grounding or locatedness when gathered together with other writers or texts, would be to isolate, partition, delimit "Derrida" in a way that would obviously tend to suggest a certain sort of distinctive operation, an exclusive or interior effect that, as it were, "stops" at the edge of Derrida's text in general, precisely so as to limit or restrict the freer or more undecidable kind of "play" or iterability that is otherwise imagined to characterize his deconstructive procedures and performances. Given that the distinction between Derrida "in him- or itself" and Derrida "with others" therefore begins to collapse or become untenable almost as soon as it is made, howsoever it is made (remembering that many if not most of Derrida's texts remain infinitely attentive to a constitutive relation with a number of interlocutors), it may be difficult to consider these two forms of anthology separately and in isolation from one another. Indeed, the differences between them, while undoubtedly important, may be seen as being gathered up (although certainly not effaced) in a more viral sort of problematic that concerns the extent to which the anthologized "part" can – or should – be taken as typical, representative, or delimitable in terms of a larger "whole," whether this "whole" goes under the different names of "Derrida," "Deconstruction," or "Theory."

How might Derrida or deconstruction help us to think the relationship of the "part" to the "whole" as a, if not the, constitutive problematic of anthologization?[2] Let us turn to a very, very singular text of Derrida's, *Glas*. *Glas* is one of the more difficult, bewildering, and unplaceable "bits" of Derrida's writing, proving itself not easily assimilable to those general accounts or presentations that attempt to typify or explain "Derrida" more broadly. And yet, as something other or something more than just another "part" of the "whole" (so far as these sorts of accounts are concerned) of "Derrida," something more or something other than just another "object" in the "series," *Glas* gathers up, propagates, grafts onto the body (of the texts of Jacques Derrida) precisely this problematic of anthologization that is constitutive not just of the reception but indeed, and inseparably, of the very *production* (in the way that Wolfreys describes it) of Derrida's work itself. It would be irresponsible at this point not to acknowledge that the relevance of *Glas* to questions of anthologization has been noticed and remarked upon before. In her preface to *A Derrida Reader: Between the Blinds*, appearing in 1991, Peggy Kamuf worries about cutting out excerpts by Derrida from texts whose length, patient exposition, and "complex patterns of *renvois*" might otherwise seem entirely necessary, achieving over many pages crucial effects of "intricacy, balance, and counterplay" (x). However, Kamuf nevertheless states:

> I garnered a certain courage to excerpt so ruthlessly from Derrida's own repeated insistence on the partialness of any text, a partialness that is not recuperable in some eventual whole or totality. Moreover, the notions of cutting, grafting, piecing together – extracting – are everywhere in evidence in Derrida's texts, both as themes and as practices, until they are virtually coextensive with the text he is always interrogating and performing. Indeed, the masterful *Glas* may be read as a long reflection on cutting, which is always culpable, put into practice. This is one reason I have placed a series of brief passages from that work into the spaces between the sections. (xi)

Appropriately, the following quote from *Glas* begins this "series": "Let us space. The art of this text is the air it causes to circulate between its screens. The chainings are invisible, everything seems improvised or juxtaposed. This text induces by agglutinating rather than by demonstrating, by coupling and uncoupling, gluing and ungluing rather than exhibiting the continuous, and analogical, instructive, suffocating necessity of a discursive rhetoric" (75).

However, in her subsequent introduction to *A Derrida Reader* Kamuf more or less sets aside the question (which bears a multiple syntactical weight or force) of anthologizing Derrida that is imposed or demanded by *Glas*, in favor of presenting us with a quite dazzling polylogical discussion devoted to the topic of, among other things, the difficulties and issues surrounding the term *Reader* itself. As Wolfreys recognizes in the introduction to his own anthology *The Derrida Reader*, this "consideration" is sufficiently "exhaustive" that, instead of seeking to summarize its various trajectories and concerns, one could do no better than simply refer the "reader" (ha ha) to it. But – to draw a little on the language of film – given that such a cut from *Glas* allows Kamuf to take a shot at this question or problem of the "Reader," before then "spacing" or cutting up each excerpted "bit," each little scene from Derrida, by quotation from *Glas* itself, it does seem worth returning again to this "long reflection on cutting."

When thinking of anthologizing Derrida, let us re-turn therefore to *Glas*.

Two

An anthology is, literally, quite literally, a flower-gathering.

Although, most obviously, the standing of the "literal" is immediately complexified in the vicinity of the flower as, in *Glas*, "'the poetic object par excellence,'" or as the very "figure of figures" so far as rhetoric is concerned (14).

Derrida, in *Glas*, quite understands the root of *anthology* in the gathering of flowers.

Glas, which gathers together Hegel, Genet, Sartre, so many, so many others . . . *Glas*, with its two great columns, its two (tree)stumps of writing, standing rigidly upright like pillars, like towers, or like tombstones, risking perhaps a fall into the deadening (castrating) monumentalization of the work. But two columns that are also wound about or wound around – two columns that indeed grow up from the ground – by what is planted and propagated in *Glas*, so as to compose the text "in liana and ivy" (18). "Liana and ivy": namely, that which weaves, braids, binds, grafts, overlaps, and sews together the parts of the text that would otherwise appear to stand apart, banded, erect. Genet, for example, "has made himself into a flower. While tolling the *glas* (knell), he has put into the ground, with very great pomp, but also as a flower, his proper name, the names and nouns of common law, language, truth, sense, literature, rhetoric, and, if possible, the remain(s)" (12).

Which puts the question: what happens to the proper name, and all the effects of the proper name, in anthologization? (Derrida's name, among others, for instance.) And also a further question: what of the remains? What survives, lives on, remains, in anthologization, where flowers grow up and are gathered from the (burial) ground of the proper name, the (apparently) finished corpus (the corpse)? Liana and ivy weave, braid, fold, bind together, graft all these issues and questions, one on to the other(s).

In gathering flowers *Glas* (already) anthologizes.

So that the style of *Glas*, at its summit, has everything to do with "the erectile stem – the style – of the flower," which, when opening up, nonetheless sees "the petals part" (21–22). The part of the flower (a point of de-part-ure?) will therefore necessarily concern us in any attempt to think through Derrida's relation to the anthological. The part of the flower, in *Glas*, carries a multiple and pluralizing syntactical charge, gathering (and parting) itself in the vicinity of flowers. The parting of the petals, or of the leaves (of a given text), in anthologization or anthological textual production, sets off a number of problems and issues here. As does the question of the graft, without which anthologies cannot propagate themselves. Or the matter, perhaps, of cutting the stem, castrating the part as a part, a-part. Or, indeed, the problem of the flower as a part, a figure or example, of the whole of rhetoric or poetics (philosophy or literature is also necessarily implicated here), which, as "'the poetic object par excellence,'" as the very "figure of figures," the flower nevertheless partitions, sets apart, distinguishes, determines, delimits in general.

Indeed, questions of the cut and of the graft immediately become highly complicated in the vicinity of this very same problem. It is a problem that means that the flower cannot simply be thought to be cut and gathered in anthologization, as exemplary part of a larger whole, but that the flower also precisely sets apart that whole as a-part. If, as Derrida therefore notes, the flower comes to "dominate all the fields to which it nonetheless belongs," then, in a sense, at the very same time it stops "belonging to the series of bodies or objects of which it forms a part" (14). By effectively setting apart that which would set it apart as exemplary figure or instance, the flower becomes something more or something other than just another example of the whole (of rhetoric or poetics), so that in a certain way it therefore exceeds, overwhelms, interrupts, threatens to break the very same (daisy) chain to which it is strung. The flower, in anthologization, thus becomes, as Derrida puts it, "(de)part(ed)" (15). No longer just a bit of a larger whole, but the very part that actually allots or partitions a generality, thereby effectively deconstructing its normative workings, the flower holds or harbors in itself "the force of a transcendental excrescence" (15). This "transcendental excrescence" suggests an odd outgrowth or projection, an "extra" part that both enlarges a figure (the flower), making it larger than the whole (of itself), larger than the rhetoric or poetics it comes to distinguish or define, and also distorts, ruptures, and interrupts the entire economy and very idea of a whole, or of a generality of which it nevertheless remains an (excrescent) part. Obviously, one can detect here the logic of supplementarity inscribing itself at the very origin of what is supplemented. The anthologized part becomes an outgrowth and supplement that in a nevertheless entirely *originary* way both constitutes and deconstitutes, constructs and deconstructs the whole, the body (of texts, for example; of Derrida's texts, for example).

The flower, the anthologized part that is gathered, is nonetheless "(de)part(ed)" by force of this "transcendental excrescence" that sets it apart from the "series of bodies or objects of which it forms a part." The anthologized part is therefore *singular*. The singular is not to be understood here in terms of that which is just uniquely individual. Rather, the anthologized part is *singular* in the sense that it is what insistently *remains*, in perpetual de-construction if you like, after the problematic of "transcendental excrescence" that we've just described has come full circle. The anthologized part might then be understood as an aftereffect (but also occurring from the outset) of this problematic. It is in this sense also that the anthologized part is, to recall Derrida's term, "(de)part(ed)." It is (de)part(ed), in a ghostly sense, as what nevertheless *remains* after the part and the whole are subjected to "the force of a transcendental excrescence" that accompanies anthologization, or the gathering of flowers. The ghostly remains that might be taken to characterize the anthologized, "(de)part(ed)" part are therefore always already "at work in the structure of the flower" – the structure of the anthological – as a "practical deconstruction of the transcendental effect" (15).

All of which is to say that, in terms of deconstruction, anthologization may not necessarily be a bad thing, so far as Derrida is concerned. Or rather, perhaps: all texts in deconstruction are also in some sense already in anthologization. For Jacques Derrida, that is, all texts.

Although, of course, to gather flowers is not only to weave, braid, bind, and graft (copy and cut this phrase again, as with so many others!) but still, irreducibly and inseparably, to cut, to cut the head, to decapitate. As in Genet's *Our Lady of the Flowers*, of which Derrida says, in *Glas*: "To be decapitated is to appear – banded, erect: like the 'head swathed' (Weidmann, the nun, the aviator, the mummy, the nursling) and like the phallus, the erectile stem – the style – of a flower" (21). To gather or anthologize a part of Derrida, then, is to decapitate, but decapitate so as to *appear*, appearing in print, leaving an imprint on anthologized leaves, like the appearance of a ghost. We have seen how Derrida suggests that Genet "has made himself into a flower. While tolling the *glas* (knell), he has put into the ground, with very great pomp, but also as a flower, his proper name" (12). Equally, to anthologize Derrida is to decapitate the head and in a sense to bury the proper name, admittedly risking a monumentalization of it once rigor mortis sets in, rendering stiff and rigid the cuttable part. But as the death knell sounds, to anthologize Derrida may also be to witness or release a ghost-effect, a ghostly survival, living on or remaining, in the vicinity of the (de)part(ed). Look again at another bit of *Glas*: "In little continuous jerks, the sequences are enjoined, induced, glide in silence. No category outside the text should allow defining the form or bearing (*allure*) of these passages, of these trances of writing. They are always only sections of flowers, from paragraph to paragraph, so much so that anthological excerpts inflict only the violence necessary to attach importance (*faire cas*) to the remain(s). Take into account the overlap-effects (*effets de recoupe*), and you will see that the tissue ceaselessly re-forms itself around the incision (*entaille*)" (25).

The (de)part(ed) part, the decapitated head, is perhaps the very figure of figures, the figure par excellence, of a "transcendental excrescence," the (cuttable) head being a more or less elevated outgrowth of the body (of texts) of which it is not just a part but that (via the effects of the proper name as a head or heading) it sets apart, partitions, divides, or distinguishes, as that of which it is nonetheless a part. Once again, this would be the problematic that surrounds and engulfs the relationship of the proper name, the cuttable head, to the body of texts of, for example, Jacques Derrida. The (proper) name (the head) lives on in anthologization (as a process that is, in any case, *originary* in Derrida's text); but, again, it remains as a singular remnant (a ghostly imprint) of the problematic of "transcendental excrescence," which puts in persistent and perpetual deconstruction the "transcendental effect," along with the normative relationship of part to whole. Excrescence, outgrowth, the effects of supplementarity, are what remain after cutting the cuttable head (although they remain in an *originary* relation to decapitation and to the [de]part[ed]), so that "anthological excerpts inflict only the violence necessary to attach importance (*faire cas*) to the remain(s) . . . you will see that the tissue ceaselessly re-forms itself around the incision (*entaille*)."

The re-forming of tissue around the incision, ceaselessly, afterward and from the outset, thus provides a useful description of anthologizing Derrida.

Three

To recap, from *Glas*. The flower, which is gathered in anthologization and in which is gathered the very question of the anthological, therefore comes to "dominate all the fields to which it nonetheless belongs" so that, in a sense, at the very same time it stops "belonging to the series of bodies or objects of which it forms a part" (14). Thus the gathered flower, rather like Derrida or deconstruction itself, is both always and never a-part, always both somewhat lonely or alone and at the same time never isolated, an "excrescence," an outgrown part.[3] This means that one can never either simply take or leave the flower that is gathered in anthologization and in which is gathered the very question of the anthological. One can neither ever simply set it aside or apart nor ever unremittingly include, absorb, embrace, welcome it wholly.

How might these reflections on the anthological relate to the pedagogical? How might the question of anthologizing Derrida relate to that of teaching deconstruction?

At the beginning of "Otobiographies," itself a text originally presented as a lecture at the University of Montreal in 1979 and followed by roundtable discussions in which participated a select assembly of distinguished colleagues, Derrida has this to say:

> I would like to spare you the tedium, the waste of time, and the subservience that always accompany the classic pedagogical procedures of forging links, referring back to prior premises or arguments, justifying one's own trajectory, method, system, and more or less skillful transitions, reestablishing continuity, and so on. These are but some of the imperatives of classical pedagogy with which, to be sure, one can never break once and for all. Yet, if you were to submit to them rigorously, they would very soon reduce you to silence, tautology, and tiresome repetition. (3–4)

For Derrida it is neither that the academic conventions of a more or less orthodox pedagogy can simply be ignored, surpassed, or abandoned nor that they permit themselves to be unquestioningly defended and thereby unproblematically reproduced. Rather, any teaching necessarily partaking of pedagogical tradition that tries nonetheless to remain wholeheartedly devoted to an unsupplemented reinscription or conservation of the method or the system that allows and enables it to set out will inevitably dwindle into circularly self-justifying practices that actually inhibit and eventually preclude everything to do with the *event* of (a) teaching, of teaching as a singularly performative activity and, of necessity, as a finally incalculable form of address to an *other*. One can therefore neither simply take nor leave "classic pedagogical procedures," and in fact one must to some extent both take (partake of) and leave them at one and the same time in order for teaching to take place at all. (Here the apparently flippant and irresponsible tone of

Derrida's remarks above would seem, on closer inspection, to convey a more strongly responsible standpoint on quite difficult and complex issues.) In the face of this complication of otherwise easily polarizable positions on the issue of pedagogical tradition, Derrida therefore proposes a "compromise" to his audience, having to do with a deconstructive procedure that presents its practitioner as engaged in some sort of settling of accounts on a number of problems, rather than aspiring to the teaching of "truth" as such. Derrida anticipates that, for some, such an approach will seem too "aphoristic or inadmissible," while others will accept it as "law," and yet others will "judge [it] to be not quite aphoristic enough." While it would be easy enough to translate such categorizations into very familiar groupings, perspectives, or positions regarding Derridean deconstruction in general, what is perhaps more interesting here is that, on the basis of just this "compromise," whereby deconstruction presents itself as neither just entirely inside nor outside "classical pedagogy," Derrida begins to question or, one might even say, *recalculate* the possibilities of academic freedom in the very process of what would seem to be an appeal to it.

Derrida insists that, since he does not wish to "transform myself into a diaphanous mouthpiece of eternal pedagogy" (4), a fountain of self-proclaimed truth, untrammeled authority, and self-sustaining mastery (Derrida himself already having indicated the inevitable atrophying of any such teaching, although also its unavoidable persistence to some extent), his "compromise" or procedure is therefore one that would seem to somewhat liberate his audience or the "students" of his teaching, so that "whoever no longer wishes to follow may do so." "As everyone knows, by the terms of *academic freedom* – I repeat: a-ca-dem-ic free-dom – you can take it or leave it," he says (4). Here Derrida not only alerts our attention to the somewhat contradictory elements inscribed within our usual evocations of pedagogical tradition, which stress both teacherly authority and freedom of inquiry. More than this, a certain ironic tone becomes evident, underlying what seems to be a quite deliberately repeated and emphasized insistence on academic freedom itself. For Derrida has already shown that any worthwhile teaching (such as deconstruction, for instance), positioned in an ambivalent or equivocal relation to "classical pedagogy," neither simply frees nor binds the event or activity of (a) teaching in relation to (a) tradition. Why then might we expect that Derrida's (teaching of) deconstruction in regard to (in this essay) the teaching of Nietzsche might offer a straightforward choice to the audience or student of Derrida, between unencumbered intellectual freedom, on the one hand, or absolute bondage to pedagogical mastery, on the other? Just as Derrida, by his own admission, can neither simply take nor leave "classical pedagogy," and (for that matter) since any teaching worth the name must both take and leave it simultaneously, so those that heard Derrida speak at Montreal in 1979 would, similarly, finally be bereft of any such choice forming the basis of a conventional appeal to academic freedom. To agree with everything Derrida would have to say, to "take" deconstruction in undiluted form, would be to absolutely submit to and thereby necessarily obliterate its teaching: that is, ultimately, *to take leave of it*. On the other hand, to absolutely reject or wholly take issue with, to entirely take leave of, Derrida's discussion or approach from the outset would either necessitate, quite impossibly, a complete departure from the conventions of academic exposition, which Derrida insists constitute the minimal level of intelligibility of his (or indeed any other) learned address, or otherwise would manifest an absolute defense of "classical pedagogy" – in which case any dispute with Derrida, any supposed "taking leave" of him, could never take the form of an absolutely diametrical opposition, for reasons he himself already presupposes and makes clear. One can therefore neither "take it or leave it" in regard to Derrida's lecture, or for that matter in regard to the teaching of deconstruction, perhaps even teaching itself, in general. Thus it is not just that "classical pedagogy" and "academic freedom" as clearly identifiable categories or forms constitute contradictory or somewhat opposed elements that vie with one another, bringing an awkward tension to bear on accepted notions and norms concerning scholarly tradition and convention. Rather, it is that *both* "academic freedom" and "classical pedagogy" are themselves traversed or crosscut by differential traits that actually, paradoxically bind them together according to the logic of the supplement, of the remainder, or of the double bind.

Moreover, since one can neither simply "take it" nor "leave it" in regard to (the) teaching (of deconstruction), here again we might detect the very same constitutive problematic of "transcendental excrescence," of paradoxically inseparable a-partness, which sur-rounds and pervades the question of the anthological that is gathered up in the gathered flowers of anthologization. From this point of view deconstruction's relation to the pedagogical and its relation to the anthological might be thought to be inseparably part of . . .

Notes

1. For a discussion of the conceptual, rhetorical, grammatological (etc.) underpinnings and effects of this "and" in the interminable series – deconstruction and philosophy, deconstruction and literature, deconstruction and Marxism, deconstruction and psychoanalysis, deconstruction and feminism, deconstruction and New Historicism, deconstruction and postmodernism, et cetera, et cetera – see Jacques Derrida, "Et Cetera . . . (and so on, und so weiter, and so forth, et ainsi de suite, und so überall, etc.)," in Nicholas Royle's collection *Deconstructions: A User's Guide*.

2. Such a constitutive problematic of anthologization, imposing itself in different ways on Kamuf and Wolfreys alike at the very moment they consider anthologizing Derrida, similarly (although also differently) enters into Attridge's reflections on anthologies in his preface to the collection *Acts of Literature*. Attridge writes:

> Editors of anthologies conventionally preface their volumes with remarks on the necessary arbitrariness of selection, the inevitable violence of excerpting, the regrettable impossibility of true representativeness. All these disclaimers are as valid for this anthology as for any other, if not more so; Jacques Derrida's work seems especially ill suited, in its arguments as well as its form, to the neat compartments, the simplified headnotes, the limits on length and detail that typify the genre. . . . On the other hand, Derrida's work also helps us to appreciate the implicit, and challengeable, assumptions that underlie these conventional apologies: that there is an 'original,' 'whole,' seamless oeuvre, free from the operations of translation, that could in principle be read or represented in a nonselective, unexcerpted, nonviolent way. In large measure thanks to Derrida, we have all become aware that all reading, all memories of reading, all publi-

cation and all criticism are processes of fragmenting, anthologizing, and translating.... Perhaps Derrida's work is *more* open to anthologizing and translating than most... so long as no single anthology – such as this one – is assumed to have a transcendent or central position among all the possible representations of his writing.

3. On the loneliness of deconstruction see Derrida's "Et Cetera." He writes: "If only you knew how independent deconstruction is, how alone, so alone, all alone!... – And well, no, I believe on the contrary that nothing is less lonely and thinkable on its own" (282).

Bibliography

Attridge, Derek. "Prefaces." *Acts of Literature*. Ed. Derek Attridge. London and New York: Routledge, 1992. ix–xii.

Derrida, Jacques. "Et Cetera... (and so on, und so weiter, and so forth, et ainsi de suite, und so überall, etc.)." *Deconstructions: A User's Guide*. Ed. Nicholas Royle. Basingstoke and New York: Palgrave, 2000. 282–305.

———. *Glas*. Lincoln and London: University of Nebraska Press, 1990.

———. "Otobiographies: The Teaching of Nietzsche and the Politics of the Proper Name." *The Ear of the Other: Otobiography, Transference, Translation*. Lincoln and London: University of Nebraska Press, 1988. 1–38.

Kamuf, Peggy. "Introduction: Reading between the Blinds." *A Derrida Reader: Between the Blinds*. Ed. Peggy Kamuf. New York: Columbia University Press, 1991. xiii–xlii.

———. Preface. *A Derrida Reader: Between the Blinds*. Ed. Peggy Kamuf. New York: Columbia University Press, 1991. vii–xii.

Wolfreys, Julian. "Justifying the Unjustifiable: A Supplementary Introduction, of Sorts." *The Derrida Reader: Writing Performances*. Ed. Julian Wolfreys. Edinburgh: Edinburgh University Press, 1998. 1–49.

DAVID B. DOWNING

Theorizing the Discipline and the Disciplining of Theory

Few people who are not actually practitioners of a mature science [or English department?] realize how much mop-up work of this sort a paradigm leaves to be done or quite how fascinating such work can prove in the execution. – Thomas Kuhn, *The Structure of Scientific Revolutions*

I argue that paradigms should be seen, not as the ideal form of scientific inquiry, but rather an arrested social movement in which the natural spread of knowledge is captured by a community that gains relative advantage by forcing other communities to rely on its expertise to get what they want. – Steve Fuller, *Thomas Kuhn*

The Double Bind of Theory Anthologies

Every contemporary anthology of theory confronts an institutional double bind: they must inevitably do two things at once, both of which are mutually contradictory. On the one hand, many of the theoretical essays included in the anthology tend to challenge, cross, or disrupt disciplinary borders; on the other, anthologizing itself cannot avoid its essentially disciplinary function. Much of what counts for theoretical discourse implicitly, if not explicitly, offers a critique of traditional academic disciplines. Selecting, reproducing, and contextualizing a set of theoretical essays in an anthology serve to "discipline" those same theories. The "theory canon" supposedly represents a set of paradigmatic essays exemplifying specific schools and methods of theory. The essays themselves often resist the constraining dimensions of the methodological parameters that supposedly warrant their inclusion as representative instances of the "schools" of thought under which rubric they have been anthologized in the first place. As Barbara Johnson explains, the editors of a theory anthology are inevitably "obeying a double bind: always historicize, but always ask compared to what" (175). In short, many theories critique the normal practices of traditional disciplines while the anthologies themselves serve to discipline the theories. This disciplinary double bind is the characteristic condition of the production and dissemination of anthologies of theory.

In this essay I would like to consider the efforts to anthologize literary and cultural theory as a special instance of textbook production. When combined with textbooks in primary, secondary, and higher education, anthologies provide the institutional resources to regulate disciplinary practices by representing the objects and methods of specific subdisciplines within the field of English studies. Thus a writing handbook, or an introduction to literature textbook, or an American literature anthology, or a theory anthology, often define by default, if not by explicit articulation, the subject matter for specific specialties. Indeed, a number of recent critical studies have come to recognize the significance of textbook production as one of the principle means for creating and sustaining distinct academic disciplines.[1] As W. Ross Winterowd contends, "It is simply and undeniably the case that textbooks for English classes are massively influential, establishing the canon or reinforcing canonical traditions, instilling attitudes toward literature and language, and determining how both literature and composition will be taught" (34). The determining effect of a textbook proceeds from its positive presentation of the status and procedures of a given normal practice. David Bleich explains that "most textbooks – physical science, social science, humanities, and writing – retain one feature in common: the presentation takes place in the discourse of direct instruction. A textbook is assumed to tell students what is the case, what they should do when they have to write essays or other kinds of papers.... The 'voices' of science and writing textbooks are declarative and directive. Knowledge as textbooks represent it is not contingent on the experiences of the readership" (16).

Of course, anthologies of theory do not have the same wide circulation as do general textbooks for first- and second-year undergraduate students. But theory anthologies often serve as textbooks for upper-division undergraduate and graduate English courses in literary and cultural theory, just as literary anthologies serve as textbooks for survey courses. They therefore tend on the one hand to partake of the "declarative and directive" explication of theoretical knowledge as an identifiable disciplinary terrain with its respective methods and objects of study, while simultaneously including essays that critique and resist the "declarative and directive" modes of explication and knowledge.[2] Furthermore, some of the leading anthologies of theory explicitly present themselves as providing the resources necessary for teachers to change traditional normal practices in English studies, while at the same time the anthologies must necessarily function to consolidate and discipline innovative new directions in theoretical discourse in order to make them understandable to a wider audience of English teachers, scholars, and students.

The Kuhnification of the Humanities

I want to situate this disciplinary Catch-22 within what I will call, following Steve Fuller, the "Kuhnification of the humanities."[3] My basic premise is that Thomas Kuhn's 1962 study, *The Structure of Scientific Revolutions*, has had an enormous impact, not just on the scientific fields but also on the disciplines of the humanities. As Fuller explains, "Kuhn's 'acritical' perspective has colonized the academy" (*Thomas Kuhn* xv). And I share Fuller's recent contention that the influence of this book has been, on the whole, for the worse: "I must nevertheless conclude that the overall impact of his book has been to dull the critical sensibility of the academy" (*Thomas Kuhn* 7). Kuhn was one of the first historians of the sciences to recognize the tremendous importance of textbooks in the establishment and perpetuation of disciplinary paradigms of normal science. The socially constructed nature of the community of practitioners sharing a paradigmatic normal practice seems to de facto vindicate a healthy kind of critical pluralism. Many contemporary academics have thus celebrated this dimension of Kuhn's work insofar as it institutionalizes difference by justifying multiple paradigms and thus different kinds of textbooks and anthologies, even when they seem incommensurable with each other. The variety of paradigms is exactly the vocabulary used, either implicitly or explicitly, in the construction of theory anthologies organized into paradigmatic schools and methods.

But Fuller offers a cautionary critique of this use of Kuhn in the disciplinizing of the humanities:

> As the story of the reception of Kuhn's book is normally told, it liberated the academy from a "positivist" or "objectivist" conception of science that privileged the "hard" sciences at the expense of the other departments in the university. . . . All of these revelations induced a collective sigh of relief from practitioners of the humanities and the social sciences, who had a hard enough time making sense of each other, let alone agreeing on a common method. They quickly latched on to Kuhn's ideas and declared that they too were respectable knowledge producers laboring under paradigms. . . . Thus, the characteristic methodologies for this post-Kuhnian enterprise have involved histories and ethnographies of the research environment and deconstructions of disciplinary discourses. (Thomas Kuhn 3)[4]

Despite the apparently radical effects of Kuhn's theory, Fuller argues that exactly the opposite is the case. In short, rather than viewing *The Structure of Scientific Revolutions* as a liberating document, Fuller's recent work illustrates the essentially conservative function of Kuhn's ideas. According to Fuller, *Structure* can "be read as an exemplary document of the Cold War era. In that context, Kuhn appears as a 'normal scientist' in the Cold War political paradigm conducted by James Bryant Conant (1893–1978), president of Harvard University (1933–53), director of the National Defense Research Committee during World War II . . . and chairman of the anti-Communist Committee on the Present Danger in the 1950s – as well as the person who introduced Kuhn to this historical study of science, and through whom Kuhn acquired his first teaching post" (*Thomas Kuhn* 5). What appears to be philosophically radical (the socially constructed, community-shared paradigm) turns out to be politically conservative because paradigms serve as normalizing mechanisms that, once institutionalized, can exclude other forms of knowledge and discourse that do not adhere to the paradigm. Significant change in a scientific community occurs, according to Kuhn's theory, when anomalies or discrepancies from expected results precipitate a crisis, or period of "extraordinary" science. Scientists themselves might experience this crisis period as one of relative uncertainty about the kinds of experiments to conduct, dissatisfaction with current theory, and disorder among the results obtained. All the evidence suggests that Kuhn himself registered his own discomfort with these periods of crisis.[5] Restoration to the order of a disciplined normal practice can only happen with the arrival of a "revolutionary" new paradigm. The exemplary model of work provided by the individual or group of practitioners who successfully resolve the anomaly then serves as the basis for reestablishing a regulated course of problem-solving tasks implied, but not yet explicitly worked out, by the theory, law, or general rule guiding the new paradigm.

The conservative nature of this theory of paradigms should now be apparent. For one thing, paradigms serve to restore and to maintain order through the institutionalized mechanisms of containment: professionalization, disciplinization, normalization, standardization, exclusion. During periods of normal practice knowledge is cumulative, in contrast to the often incommensurable breaks and disjunctures occurring between different paradigms. Many academics thus appreciate the principle of closure as the defining value of disciplinary work in its ability to produce and accumulate new kinds of knowledge, but to adopt Kuhn's version of paradigms often leads to unjustified claims for disciplinary autonomy. More specifically, Kuhn's theory of scientific change based on anomalies ends up being conservative rather than revolutionary because the anomalies themselves are seen to arise *internally* among specific individual practitioners of the given "normal" science.[6]

Just how these anomalies arise in the ongoing course of a normal practice has always been the most conceptually troubling element in Kuhn's theory of paradigms. Fuller emphasizes the political consequences of this model. Namely, the notion of internally consistent academic paradigms tends to isolate a normal practice from outsiders, which means from broader social, political, and cultural arenas: "various competitors and contaminants of science – specifically religion, technology, and history – were successfully excluded from the scope of scientific inquiry" (*Thomas Kuhn* 34). Indeed, by modeling the disciplinary structure of the scientific fields, the guild function of professional disciplines as they arose in the late nineteenth century was to perform just this kind of exclusion of academic work from business and political interests. Relatively speaking, such exclusion has been the institutional basis for the "academic freedom" legitimated by the formation of the American Association of University Presses in 1915, and this doctrine has served in important cases to protect academic workers from arbitrary economic or political forces. But there are good reasons to suspect that the academic communities were never quite so isolated, nor so removed from the interests of business and capital, technology, and politics, as Kuhn's theory suggests.[7]

Despite considerable historical evidence to the contrary, Kuhn's conception of "revolutionary" change contains disciplinary innovation within the community of experts working according to a self-regulating paradigm.[8] For all practical purposes this theory therefore justifies the scientific production of knowledge in isolation from any significant public input, judgment, or assessment. This served the Cold War era well, when the direction of scientific work in both basic and applied research did not need to be questioned by outsiders: since it was self-regulating, it simply needed to be deeply funded to ensure its continuity. Paradoxically, the "disinterested" nature of the production of knowledge now had a socially constructed theorem to justify specific guilds of expertise upon which the public must rely. A disciplined academic community could now freely admit that they were working according to a normal paradigm rather than an objective reflection or representation of nature. This apparently liberating and "relativizing" turn of Kuhn's ideas is what has made his theory attractive to humanists and social scientists.

However, when educators in the humanities uncritically adopt Kuhn's notion of paradigms as liberating possibilities for new kinds of learning, it is especially important to keep Fuller's cautions in mind.

Specifically, in a Kuhnian world education becomes a process of acculturation in which dutiful students (and instructors and researchers) learn to imitate the practices authorized by the paradigm. Deeply critical, "extraneous," imaginative, innovative, speculative, postdisciplinary, nonparadigmatic kinds of work (and lore; see Harkin), to name a few, can for all practical purposes be suppressed by the Kuhnian theory of paradigms. Even as the demographics of secondary education have changed, and differences of race, class, gender, age, and ethnicity have in recent decades increased in number in the academy, underlying Kuhnian models of what counts as normal practice can be experienced by many as painful exclusions of such potentially disruptive differences. Clyde Barrow offers a vivid articulation of the "endless regulations that constitute fair warning and rules of the academic game" when played according to paradigms that "discipline behavior before the fact and, hence, legitimate the punishment of those who violate the rules of the game. Team players are rewarded with an array of quite desirable material and social incentives. The occasional renegade is still punished in a symbolic public spectacle" (254).

For the "team players" there's a great deal of joy and satisfaction that many scientists (or literary critics) experience in their professional lives through their contribution to the ongoing work of a given normal practice. As Kuhn himself puts it, we should not forget "quite how fascinating such work can prove in the execution" (24). Or how satisfying one's job security can be when one does not challenge or violate a normal practice. Indeed, the regulative nature of such practices enables the institutionalization of what Jeffrey Di Leo calls the "systems of affiliation" that "dominate our academic identity to the extent that we must define and redefine ourselves in orthodoxical terms or risk being labeled transgressive to disciplines of which we wish to be participatory members" (52). According to Kuhn, textbooks in the sciences represent "normal practice": they "mop up" the predictable results of paradigmatic problem solving once a new paradigm has been established and exemplified. Theory anthologists no doubt experience some of this satisfaction. Their "mop-up" work consists of selecting representative essays that have been written by a wide range of writers in different social, historical, and intellectual contexts, for different audiences, and for different purposes, and somehow re-presenting them as exemplary models of relatively stable schools and methods.[9] This is often not an easy task since many of the theorists resist the paradigmatic school serving to contain them. But at this stage of my argument I want to be clear that I don't believe the answer is simply to abandon the often valuable work that anthologizers perform by making such resources available. Nevertheless, theoretical reflection on the limits of the disciplinary function of anthologies should lead us to amend certain characteristics of their production and significantly modify their use in the classroom. In short, anthologizing is an enabling as well as constraining activity, which is the basic virtue and vice of disciplinary work in general. Without a clear sense of how to negotiate both dimensions of this double bind, we are much more likely, even if inadvertently or unconsciously, to enact the constraining limits and thus to intensify the socially deleterious effects of the most "innovative" theoretical models. For social and political reasons, then, I have chosen to focus on the constraining dimensions of Kuhn's theory as it has so often played itself out in the humanities.

Centripetal Paradigms and Centrifugal Theories

When we turn to the production and consumption of theory anthologies, we can specify at least two overlapping levels at which paradigms can be seen to work as disciplinizing forces. First, at the level of the organization of the anthology itself, chronological, historical paradigms, on the one hand, or paradigms of specific schools of theory, on the other, often justify sectional headings and groupings.[10] Second, at the curricular level, theory anthologies provide the objects and the methods and thus the disciplinary space required for the normal practice of teaching literary theory as a subdiscipline within English departments. In many instances anthologies also extend the range of possible practices by making new resources readily available. In this section I will focus primarily on the first, organizational level, since the function of anthologies at the curricular level follows logically from the former.

Although the editors of the anthologies may never use the word *paradigm*, my contention is that the "Kuhnification" of the humanities operates implicitly in the paradigmatic presuppositions that justify the organizing principles for these books. That is, just as most English curricula retain the basic structuring principles of period and genre as a disciplinary normal practice, theory anthologies generally use one or both of these principles (see Williams). The periodizing paradigm leads to the chronological arrangement of essays. Almost all anthologies that provide a historical overview of criticism and theory, beginning, say, with Plato and Aristotle, use some version of chronological structuring, sometimes naming periods (classical, medieval, Renaissance, neoclassical, Romantic, etc.), much as a literary anthology might do. These can be valuable resources, but again, it all depends on how they are used within the classroom. As I have argued elsewhere, it can be a sterile and futile exercise to try in a single-semester course to survey twenty-four hundred years of critical theory by following the historical paradigm structuring the anthology (see Downing). The construction of a historical sequence of highly selective or representative essays seems so "natural" that it can conceal the arbitrariness of the selection process itself. Decontextualized from their social and historical situations, brief excerpts from various philosophers and critics will often seem quaint, archaic, and irrelevant to many students. We have to intervene by using alternative goals and practices in teaching to avoid this kind of disciplinary deadliness. I will return to the question of how and whether to use these anthologies in the classroom in the final section of this essay.

When it comes to contemporary theory, the anthologists have, with some notable exceptions (e.g., Leitch; Adams and Searle), abandoned the chronological paradigm. Instead the common practice is to divide the text into sections on the basis of paradigmatic schools and methods, although sometimes the sections are designated as themes and issues (e.g., "Politics, Ideology, Cultural History" [Lodge viii]). Thus there are sections on structuralism, psychoanalysis, deconstruction, New Historicism, postcolonialism, gay and lesbian studies, and so on. The "liberating" plurality of Kuhnian paradigms seems ideally suited to justify exactly this diversity of theoretical models. Thus an anthology may appear clearly organized by the sections divided into specific schools and methods, even though a given essay captured, say, under the "reader-response" heading, might equally seem to exemplify a feminist and/or New Historicist perspective.[11]

Indeed, in their introductory and supporting frameworks the anthologizers themselves tend to perform, contrapuntally if not simultaneously, the two seemingly contradictory tasks in order to negotiate the double bind of disciplinary containment on the one hand and cross-disciplinary dispersion on the other. The editors must first perform the centripetal functions of inventing the definitional terms with sufficient scope to contain all the material in the volume. They must also perform the centrifugal, dispersive function by implementing some kind of conversational model of "putting in dialogue" the differences between the paradigms so as to emphasize exactly their plurality and diversity.[12]

A brief example drawn from one of the most well-informed theory anthologies, the fourth edition of *Contemporary Literary Criticism: Literary and Cultural Studies*, by Robert Con Davis and Ronald Schleifer, should help us to see how these tensions are negotiated in practice. One of the many virtues of this book is its consistent emphasis that "the way we understand and interpret texts and even the assessing of our emotions in this process exist in bounded and defining contexts of culture, history, and social relations" (1). This contextualizing gesture theoretically allows for social and historical differences even when the inclusion of any essay necessarily decontextualizes it from its original context. Davis and Schleifer aim for their anthology to promulgate innovative new models of cultural studies, especially the kind of "cultural critique" they describe and exemplify in their own writing.[13] I share many of their stated aims and intentions, so what follows is intended not as a refutation of their work but as a call to further qualify their claims so as to enhance the rhetorical consequences of their anthology. Without such qualifications, I believe, it is far less likely that the volume actually achieves the critical goals they aim for among their intended audience of students and nontheorists. Some of these less desirable rhetorical effects arise because of the limitations that operate implicitly through the underlying disciplinary presumptions sustained by the "Kuhnification of the humanities." For instance, even in their contextualizing efforts in the above passage, the inclusion of the words "bounded and defining" registers the self-regulating and inclusive nature of Kuhn's notion of paradigms. Paradigmatic theoretical models operate then to bind and define the possibilities for theory, and they often do so by moving away from the lived experiences and actual theorizing activities of students and other nonspecialists where multiple and overlapping contexts often yield ideological contradictions more than bound and defined paradigms. But on the scale of theory anthologies Davis and Schleifer are among the most self-reflective, so it is necessary to take a closer look at some of the critical moves they make in framing their anthology.

In their centripital rhetoric of containment they begin their "General Introduction" to the section entitled "The Nature of Literary Study" by explaining that "literary study . . . must be approached as a body of knowledge and as a discipline of inquiry, the 'disciplinary' practice of literary criticism" (1). From the perspective of anyone studying the discipline of English studies, this seems unobjectionable, but the theorists they include in the anthology refuse to do just that: they refuse, that is, to understand literary study on its own terms, and it is this tension between intrinsic definitions and extrinsic theories that their version of cultural critique seeks to negotiate. Indeed, many of the theorists in the volume are "extrinsic" to the field of English: Jacques Derrida, Michel Foucault, Jacques Lacan, Donna Haraway, James Clifford, and so on. Once it became a recognized department in the late nineteenth century, English studies strained to define itself "in its own terms" so that it could compete equally with the scientific paradigms for its rightful place in the university. New Critics like John Crowe Ransom, Cleanth Brooks, René Wellek, and Austin Warren were adamant about their concern for intrinsic criteria, and thus the New Critics enjoyed a period of relative stability, or normal practice, prior to the age of theory.[14] In our post-Kuhnian age, however, most English practitioners have abandoned the hope that there might be a single intrinsic definition suitable for everyone in an English department. Nevertheless, Kuhn's theory of paradigms has often served to rescue the otherwise improbable intellectual status and nebulous departmental justification for "English" as a field.

To simplify the case, a Kuhnian paradigm can be described so as to emphasize either its object or its method, and by shifting the emphasis to methodology one can provide relative stability to an otherwise chaotic field by narrowing its practice to a set of recognizable theoretical schools, systems, or paradigms.[15] Even if a theory arrives from outside the field of English (as is usually the case), under the rubric of paradigms it becomes possible to conceive of a school or method as relatively autonomous, like a paradigm, and thus possible to study it "in its own terms." By thus emphasizing method over object, various "interpretive communities" could be distinguished that applied their methods to a wide range of literary, cultural, and rhetorical objects. In short, the specificity of method made up for the lost specificity of the "aesthetic" object. The tolerant diversity of such subspecialities based on theoretical paradigms could be added on to the basic period and genre organization of English departments, and to this extent the Kuhnification of the humanities may have aided the departmental survival of English by containing theoretical innovation under the "field coverage" principle of disciplinary labor (Graff).

Davis and Schleifer wisely avoid any attempt to define the entire field of English, so they focus on delimiting the broad subfield of literary studies and, within that, the even narrower arena of literary criticism. They thus begin their introduction to the section "What Is Literary Studies?" in the centripetal mode by drawing on the work of one of the great synthesizers of the field, Northrup Frye: "A necessary component of criticism as the study of literature and other forms of discourse and language involves giving attention to the methods of understanding. Literary criticism, as opposed to the more general and, as Northrop Frye says, the more 'philosophical' study of aesthetics, aims at developing, as we noted in the General Introduction to this book, definitions of 'literature' and methods of 'reading'" (21). This assertion is supposed to be so general as to "contain" virtually all viable forms of what can be called "literary criticism." And since the openness of this claim doesn't specify which definition of literature or which method of reading, it seems plural and tolerant. Within this general framework the anthologizers can thereby organize the volume according to numerous different schools, methods, and paradigms.

Davis and Schleifer offer a sophisticated model of performance theory as a method for how students might encounter the dizzying array and centrifugal forces represented in the volume. The task of students is to "try on" one theory or paradigm after another, by seeing the theory they encounter in its performative dimension. Warning against the possibility of regarding the sometimes esoteric theories "as simply a body of knowledge to be learned, in which failure is always lurking," Davis and Schleifer draw on Shoshana Felman's "'performative' version of learning that encourages students to view a course in criticism as a tour on which they will explore a number of worlds from the 'inside'" (xi). That there is an identifiable "inside" to these theoretical "worlds" suggests the kind of logic Kuhn uses to identify the internal consistency of socially constructed paradigms. Such consistency becomes especially problematical when referring to schools of theory. Nevertheless, Davis and Schleifer suggest that "becoming a 'member' of the critical school we are studying constitutes a methodological wager that valuable insight can be gained from a sympathetic entry into a critical system, as opposed to an 'objective' scrutiny of a foreign object" (xi). While it certainly seems worthwhile to advocate a "sympathetic entry" into whatever one is studying, the problem is that these "schools" are less homogenized, less paradigmatically enclosed, than the benign word "school" would indicate (see Sosnoski, "Theory Junkyard"). To suggest that there are "critical systems" even further stretches the degree of methodological consistency within a given "school" – many schools are simply not systematic, especially if you examine in any detail the work of specific critics. If this is the case, it explains why it is so hard to become a "member" of a critical school, even when we put *membership* in quotation marks.

As seen from a non-Kuhnian perspective, to perform as if within the disciplinary paradigm of a theoretical "school" may be more a question of adopting the "arrested social movement" of the disciplined community of theorists occupying relatively privileged places in the academic hierarchy. In this light, as Sosnoski and Wiederhold argue, "we must question . . . the normalizing impulses that govern our critical habits, especially when we remember their cruel effects" (82). That normalizing effects can be "cruel" might seem overstated to some, but Kuhn's use of the term *community* tends to gloss the elements of fear and anxiety that often operate to constrain even the best of scientific inquiry. As Fuller puts it, "On closer inspection, a mafia mentality turns out to be at work, itself another by-product of the liberalization of science. Thus, in good Hobbesian fashion, the supposed 'community' of science refers to little more than the fact that everyone equally suffers under the same threat" (*Governance* 21). One may wish to discount these expressions as paranoid versions of the profession, but it is difficult to discredit the fact that many persons do experience the exclusive nature of theoretical schools as if they were self-selective cults.

While Davis and Schleifer counsel wisely that work in theory is often "an articulation of value, and a call to action," that "criticism may become something that one tries out, tries on, lives in, and lives through," and that "it is an experience that one actively engages in rather than a difficulty that one avoids or fends off" (xii), it is also crucial to recognize that avoiding and fending off can often be vital acts of resistance and theorizing. To "live in" and to "live through" a paradigm can be literally impossible for most students, whose backgrounds, education, life experiences, and access to material resources may be so different from the master critics they are asked to emulate that they can only perform a kind of subservient imitation in hopes that they might eventually be disciplined into the guild after a sufficient period of obedience to the paradigmatic models. Establishing disciplinary affiliation with those models is a more difficult process than merely joining a scholarly society or proclaiming a methodological allegiance, however necessary those professional steps may be. Pedagogically speaking, however, there are alternatives to the disciplined presentation of master critics exemplifying theoretical schools, and that calls for the modification of the uses of anthologies in the classroom.

Getting beyond the Magister in the Paradigm

Thus far I have been focusing primarily on the organizational level of theory anthologies insofar as historical and methodological paradigms can be said to structure most of these volumes. When we turn to the curricular level and the actual uses of these books in the classroom, there will be tremendous variation depending on different institutional settings, curricular designs and requirements, and changing student populations. In my own situation, teaching doctoral seminars in the history and theory of criticism at Indiana University of Pennsylvania (IUP), I have found the disciplinary double bind perhaps more pronounced than might be the case at a different kind of university. In what follows I will briefly outline a few of my own practical alternatives, if only to suggest the necessity of making local, ad hoc, situational adjustments to whatever anthologized resources one might wish to use.

At IUP most of our doctoral students are already teachers at various two-year and four-year colleges, so they are already colleagues in the profession, with a good bit of practical experience and knowledge of the discipline. Their ages range from early twenties to early sixties. Since most of the positions they occupy, or the ones they will be seeking once they graduate, are of a generalist nature, they typically have less need to affiliate strongly with a specialized discipline when identifying themselves on the job market. We also have a wide range of international students, so all of our classes are de facto multicultural. Even with this bare sketch, it should be apparent that most of these students do not expect careers teaching one or two graduate seminars per semester at an elite university. In such a context to design a syllabus by following the contours of a traditional theory anthology is to ensure that they are not, literally speaking, the audience for whom the anthology was designed. That is, they become situated, as James Sosnoski has configured this problem, as "token professionals" trying to emulate the master critics whom they will never become.

Now there are those who will object at this point that there are many virtues to be gained from exposure to these master critics, to new ways of thinking, to the rigors of the discipline. Stanley Fish, for example, wishes to reinforce the gates to the discipline as a necessary way of screening out those who don't pass muster: as he puts it, citing Milton's famous disclaimer of the limits of tolerance in the *Areopagitica*, "Them We Burn." Fish argues that our jobs will disappear if we don't define the discipline and police the boundaries with all the rigor we can: "independently of the potent social fact of disciplinary organization we would have nothing to say" (165). In much the same spirit David Shumway acknowledges that given the unavoidable constraints of disciplinary work, we cannot expect dynamism everywhere: "It should go without saying that much of this production is ultimately sterile, and that much is produced that is of little use to anyone beyond the discipline" (106).

But for most of my students accepting that sterility means swallowing a good bit of pain and frustration as they work diligently to emulate what Sosnoski calls the Magister – "a personification of the institution's ideally orthodox professor" (*Token Professionals* 74). Of course, for the small percentage of graduate students who will be moving into tenure-track jobs in specialized disciplinary areas, it will be necessary to emulate the paradigmatic models and affiliate as strongly as possible with the leading figures in those areas. Otherwise they will risk being "disaffiliated," as Jeffrey Di Leo puts it: "those whose affiliations do not mesh with any dominant systems of affiliation" (62). But, even so, the profession is changing so rapidly in some areas that multiple affiliations will be necessary. For the large percentage of current doctoral students the Magister remains an idealized impossibility, a kind of mythical hero who perfectly represents the exemplary figure behind a Kuhnian paradigm. It's not always a good idea to try to perform as if one could become the Magister. The effort to reproduce an impossibility can in practice lead exactly to a deadly sterility.[16] From my perspective the Kuhnification of the humanities has justified our tolerance for just this kind of sterility in our "normal practices," when reading and writing so often get reduced to mimicry of conventional forms. More than that, many whom Shumway must mean by those "beyond the discipline" are well within the everyday practices and effects of English studies. When we are accused of academic sterility and esoteric jargon by those outside the university, we have a problem with public perception and accountability for what we do. But too often the sterility is a problem experienced not just by outsiders but by those with varying degrees of investment in the discipline itself: graduate students, undergraduate students, teachers in other subdisciplines.

As an alternative, rather than starting with disciplinary definitions that seek to contain the content of the course, I often ask students to begin their coursework with institutional autobiographies, locating themselves in the profession and in their cross-cultural contexts.[17] These inevitably lead to inquiries into the changing social and political circumstances of the modern university and the changing history of the profession: how it got to be where it is and what's happening now. By thus focusing first on the students' own problems acquiring allegiances with particular and often conflicting disciplines and methodologies, a somewhat different set of institutionally self-reflective concerns typically arises. In the space I have here I will mention three interrelated issues that my students repeatedly express concern about, although these are also areas that the traditional anthologies tend not to address: the increasing corporatization and bureaucratization of the university as we enter the twenty-first century and their effects on the general mission of English studies, including the kinds of skills students will need for a changing job market; the historically painful splits among literature, composition, creative writing, and technical writing; and the shift from print to electronic environments and the impact of technology on teaching the humanities.

Most obviously, the locus of these concerns is the institutionalization of English studies. I take this to be an indication that we would be wise to focus a good bit of our theorizing and teaching in these areas rather than limit our work to the concern for theories of reading literature and/or culture that has guided most traditional anthologies. Taken together, these three areas of inquiry open some challenging questions about the relevance of what Steven North has called "College English Teaching, Inc."[18] North adapts Sosnoski's figure of the Magister to argue that graduate studies in English has historically prepared students by training them in the "Magisterial Curriculum."

Simply put, this curriculum was designed to perpetuate the discipline in a series of courses where students could be taught to imitate the reading practices of master critics in the interpretation of the historical coverage of canonized writers in different periods and genres. Up to about 1972 this model tended to function pretty well, even as critics trained in this tradition had to adapt as best they could to teaching composition courses when they had to, but generally, the idea of the Magister was to rise above the concerns of writing and pedagogy by teaching graduate seminars in one's specialty. During the post–Second World War expansion of the university new fields could simply be added to the basic model, as if adding a new paradigm for a new subdiscipline, whether theory, women's studies, or postcolonialism. But in the period of "contraction," after 1972, the job market for English Ph.D.'s crashed as the economy shifted toward what David Harvey has called the "post-Fordist 'regime of flexible accumulation'" (qtd. in Berlin 41), and funding practices for higher education shifted significantly from public to private means. The Magisterial tradition no longer serves the needs of most students in a changing work force under new forms of academic capitalism, bureaucratic restraint, fiscal "downsizing," multimedia technologies, and changing demographics. The disciplinary double binds are intensified when there is, on the one hand, an apparent loss of disciplinary authority and a questioning of borders but, on the other hand, an intensification of institutional and disciplinary boundary disputes as budgets tighten up.

Under these conditions graduate students often find themselves preparing for careers that will not likely resemble those of their teachers. Although the rise of composition and rhetoric Ph.D. programs in the past twenty-five years has often led to an alternative kind of training, the underlying problem of the disciplinary splits among literature, composition, creative writing, and technical writing persistently foregrounds unresolved problems in the profession. Yet most anthologies of theory don't ever address these concerns. This is true even if one adopts a less traditional anthology such as David Richter's *Falling into Theory*, which explicitly concerns itself with disciplinary issues. What is particularly interesting about this book is that one of its major premises is that "radical changes are afoot in the structure and method of professing literature, along with new ways of organizing traditional disciplines" (12). And Richter uses Kuhn to reassure us that things are not as bad as some say they are: "If philosopher Thomas Kuhn is right (and if his ideas about the history of science are applicable to the humanities), there should be nothing too dreadful in the long run about the state of theory into which the field of literary study has fallen.... And if the humanities are like the sciences, some new set of professional norms will sooner or later establish itself in the community of literary scholars and teachers, everyone will once more agree on which questions are worth pursuing and how to go about pursuing them, and theoretical discourse will again become optional rather than necessary" (12).

Although Richter acknowledges that such a consensual model of literary study may never arrive, using Kuhn to reassure us of the limits of disciplinary change is another consequence of the Kuhnification of the humanities. It leads us to believe that we can, perhaps sometime in the future, resettle on a more comfortable paradigm of literary study. To entertain hopes of a more self-enclosed vision of the discipline of literary study prevents us from seeing that the future might not involve a paradigm for literature at all, at least not in the traditional sense, and that, in more ways than one, the humanities might not be quite so much "like the sciences" as advocates of Kuhnian paradigms would have us believe. That is, although Richter's collection does not employ the traditional historical paradigm nor the schools paradigm, its principles of organization and selection are based on questions of "reading": why, what, and how we read. In this context the selections are very provocative, but what doesn't get theorized is that the focus on reading has left *writing* off the theoretical map and thus outside the disciplinary paradigm of literary study, even though the writing of critical essays is exactly the mechanism of evaluation and grading in literature courses. Indeed, other than Richard Ohmann, there aren't any among the many well-known contributors who might be identified as representatives of the fields of composition, rhetoric, or creative writing. One could justifiably argue that such a broader focus was not the intention of the anthology, but I think that answer only defers the pressing fact that these splits between composition and literature are among the most deeply in need of theorizing and reforming. Graduate programs in English studies must be concerned with teaching a new breed of teacher-scholars to meet new kinds of educational, curricular, and social needs in a rapidly changing culture.

Which brings us to the question of technology in relation to the resources in an anthology. Given reasonable access to on-line computers, any anthology can then be viewed as the tip of multiple archives that stretch through electronic access to a potentially limitless source of academic and nonacademic resources. The sheer availability of these resources casts anthologies in a new light: their selective principles of representation are always more visibly in tension with "virtually" the entire set of interrelated archives constituting what we call theory, literature, cultural studies, and the humanities. Richter's *Falling into Theory* includes a useful appendix listing various Web sites, but it seems to me future editions and anthologies will need their own Web sites as well since the list of theory sites is growing so rapidly that the on-line extensions become necessary. As a caution, I would not want to be misunderstood as a kind of "cyber-utopian" who sees new forms of anarchy and democracy as inevitable in on-line communities. Indeed, exactly the opposite is often the case: the fact that technology and cyberspace is being colonized by powerful economic forces that are often detrimental to educational needs is exactly why it is an area in need of theory and investigation.

Accordingly, the electronic opening of borders of theory necessarily becomes an in-class activity of theorizing how to do it, partly because there are no clear markers, no clear road maps on how to get there once you leave the printed page of a theoretical essay. Every act of theorizing by a person takes place in a living situation, but theory anthologies tend to remove theory from the lives of students and teachers in the act of representing its paradigmatic methods and practices within a relatively closed professional community of experts. Again, the risk for graduate students will depend on their specific situations: for many of my students strong or narrow affiliations with a paradigmatic practice can be a liability in a changing job market, whereas for others the liability will be in failing to identify with a dominant model. As Jeffrey Di Leo puts it, "The nature of disciplinary configurations is such that if a young scholar does not affiliate with the mainstream scholars, there is a strong possibility that he or she will fail to become affiliated with that discipline" (52). Those "strong possibilities" are precisely the consequences of our deeply Kuhnified disciplinary identities. In these instances it is self-defensively necessary to protect one's interests, particularly for graduate students, who are in the most vulnerable of professional positions. Nevertheless, our job as teachers is to put the activity of theorizing back into the lives of students as they work to read, write, and alter the discipline and the culture they will be creating and sustaining. Whatever degree of autonomy we have in our local institutions, it seems to me we ought to make our teaching a place where knowledge and theory about that knowledge spread and proliferate rapidly when freed of many of their "Kuhnified" disciplinary constraints.

Not only are paradigms more porous than Kuhn described them as, but the various kinds of work and labor practices we perform as practitioners of English studies cannot all be made accountable by traditional paradigms. Often, of course, we do perform the normal tasks assigned by reigning paradigms, which is why my argument is not meant to put an end to anthologizing, even if that were possible, nor to suggest that we can simply disavow the disciplinary function. Nor should we stop reading the theory canon, any more than we should stop reading the literary canon: that's one often quite large but for some practitioners in the field relatively small arena of the everyday labor and work we perform as English teachers, writers, and researchers. I agree with Bill Readings, who argues: "What I am calling for, then, is not a generalized interdisciplinary space but a certain rhythm of disciplinary attachment and detachment, which is designed so as not to let the question of disciplinarity disappear" (176). Ironically, the Kuhnification of the humanities has led less to a questioning "of the disciplinary form that can be given to knowledge" (177) than to reassertions of the paradigmatic forms of disciplinary knowledge. Getting over Kuhn with respect to the business of anthologizing means that we must be even more critical of the kinds of decontextualization that happen when theory is removed from its context of production and dissemination. An inquiry into the spectrum of disciplinarity, cross-, inter-, and postdisciplinary practices actually carried out in our professional lives, brings acts of theorizing out of the models and paradigms provided for us in the anthologies and into the messy, complex, daily lives of our students and ourselves, where we actually struggle with the politico-institutional realities that we both suffer and enjoy. It also means that in our scholarly work we need more professional avenues such as journals, organizations, conferences that, as Jeffrey Di Leo explains, can "serve as affiliation-free zones in an increasingly over-affiliated academic world" (61).

In the end what I'm suggesting is that the kinds of changes now needed in the profession are not merely a matter of shifting paradigms or of establishing new normal practices, however inevitable such disciplinary constraints might continue to be. Although it's beyond the scope of this essay, I am further suggesting that the roughly 125-year-old experiment with using the "ecosystem" of disciplinary models for the production of knowledge as the dominant structuring principle for higher education may be ready for significant alteration (see Hoskins). If this is true, "we must be prepared to reorganize the institutions of our profession to account for the negative effects of affiliation" (Di Leo 62) with Kuhnified normal practices. Since disciplinary paradigms tend to work better under the reign of various manifestations of positivism, they have generally worked more successfully for the sciences, and the humanities have struggled to compete using "paradigmatic" models that are not always appropriate for evaluating the range of practices we actually perform. Strictly speaking, nondisciplinary and postdisciplinary practices often already comprise the larger part of our working lives. Consequently, when disciplinary work is valorized as inherently superior to postdisciplinary kinds of teaching and learning, we may not always be preparing students for the culture and the profession they will enter. But there's no reason we can't begin to imagine a wider range of valuable practices, not so much as existing in rigidly hierarchical ways but rather as operating across variable continuums of disciplinary and postdisciplinary forms of work. We will, of course, have to invent new criteria, but that's what institutional and cultural change has always been about. Thus literacy projects, curriculum design initiatives, outreach programs, service learning, Web site and software development, collaborative teaching and research projects, and other kinds of emerging practices often draw upon and work in tension with disciplinary forms of knowing. This kind of work needs to be more fully represented in theory anthologies. To find ways that we can function as English professionals within the rapidly changing domains of postsecondary education, we'll have to be as imaginative, creative, and inventive as we can be about how to teach the reading and writing of cultures.

Notes

1. James Sosnoski puts it this way: "Textbooks are the apparatuses of orthodoxy. And orthodox textbooks are the principle means by which institutions control their subjects" (*Token Professionals* 75).

2. In *Critical Theory since 1965* Hazard Adams and Leroy Searle articulate this double bind on the first page of their introduction: "An anthology must establish boundaries, rough as they may be. . . . We recognize at the same time the broader range of theory now thought important and even the view that there can be no firm boundaries established for such concerns or for literature itself" (1).

3. *Kuhnification* is the term Steve Fuller coins, especially in chapter 7, "Kuhnification as Ritualized Political Impotence" (*Thomas Kuhn* 318). In contrast to my focus on English studies and the humanities, Fuller focuses on the impact of Kuhn on science studies: "The science studies community currently suffers from self-inflicted Kuhnification" (318).

4. For an instance of the placing of Kuhn in relation to deconstruction, see Schultz: "Kuhn has an idea of the 'reconstruction' of previous science that positions his work closer to deconstruction than to other views by philosophers of science" (32).

5. As Fuller explains: "The record also clearly shows that Kuhn disavowed every one of these [radical] appropriations of his work" (*Thomas Kuhn* 3). And later: "Thus, whenever his name was linked with that of Herbert Marcuse as gurus of the worldwide student revolutionary movement, Kuhn would point

out, quite rightly, that his view of science was very conservative, basically an extended exercise in showing how innovation could result from a highly disciplined, perhaps even authoritarian, social system" (Thomas Kuhn 74).

6. Upon occasion Kuhn does discuss forces external to the community, especially in historically extended scientific crises, such as the Copernican revolution. In these instances, as he explains, "an extended treatment would also discuss the social pressure for calendar reform, . . . [the] medieval criticism of Aristotle, the rise of Renaissance Neoplatonism, and other significant elements besides" (69). In such major social/scientific revolutions there would be no way to dismiss the external forces. Yet, always for Kuhn, the determining epistemological factors emerge from within the scientific community itself. Thus in the Copernican revolution "technical breakdown would still remain the core of the crises" (69). "Technical" here refers to the specific paradigmatic models of the laws of planetary motion known best by the scientists themselves. Regarding the external considerations, Kuhn asserts, "Though immensely important, issues of that sort are out of bounds for this essay" (69).

7. Indeed, there is a long line of critics who have attacked the corporatization of the modern university, perhaps beginning with John Jay Chapman and Thorstein Veblen: "Writing in 1909, Chapman declared, 'The men who stand for education and scholarship have the ideals of business men. They are in truth business men. . . .' Veblen 'detected the hand of business control dominating every aspect of the modern university'" (Aronowitz 17). For detailed studies of the increased corporatization of the university see also Barrow; Etzkowitz, Webster, and Healey; Readings; Slaughter and Leslie.

8. Fuller (Thomas Kuhn) provides significant evidence that Kuhn's apparently "historical" account of the rise of modern science is, in many ways, ahistorical. For one thing, while Kuhn derived his notion of paradigms by studying scientific work from about 1620 to 1920, his articulation of the normal practitioners of a given paradigm seems to be more of a post facto justification than a historical actuality. That is, since scientific work prior to the late nineteenth century did not take place in universities, there was no normalizing community of academic workers, and scientific discoveries often happened in very differing social and political circumstances, with different motives and different resources. In short, scientific advances often depended on more ad hoc, situational discoveries, and scientists in different countries often worked with different expectations and more widely varying sets of data than a paradigm would suggest. Such historical differences in

the rise of science suggest an even greater acknowledgment of the porous sense of the community of English professors, even when individuals are said to share theoretical approaches.

9. Kuhn is quite specific about the justifiable ways that textbooks necessarily truncate history in order to represent the stable outcomes of a scientific revolution. Textbooks "record the stable outcome of past revolutions and thus display the bases of the current normal-scientific tradition. . . . Textbooks thus begin by truncating the scientist's sense of his discipline's history and then proceed to supply a substitute for what they have eliminated" (137).

10. Davis and Schleifer distinguish between the formal and the historical study of literature. They offer, as a traditional view of humanistic study, Louis Hjelmslev's contention that since the humanities study "human events," singular objects produced by other humans, such as texts and authors, can only be studied using the "historical method" in contrast to the study of "natural phenomena" suitable to generalized laws, as in the sciences: "Since the 'objects' of humanistic study are unique, they can be cataloged only in chronological order. Because of this, the humanities have traditionally been 'historical' studies" (*Contemporary Literary Criticism* 2).

11. As Sosnoski argues, theories are not really methods, although they are commonly treated as such, partly because of the effect of the Kuhnification of the humanities, where disciplinary paradigms require specific methods. See *Token Professionals*, chapter 12, "Theories Need Not Be Methods" (159–67).

12. David Richter, for instance, in the second edition of *The Critical Tradition*, articulates the "dialogue" this way: "The study of critical theory tends to raise the ultimate questions of literature and its relation to life without establishing an ultimate order, because the clash of one principle, one method, one logic with another cannot be evaded. To the extent that these oppositions are genuinely understood, we are unlikely to end by resolving their differences into a tidy and harmonious chorus. We can, however, set the voices at play, engage them in contrapuntal dialogue with each other, and enter that dialogue ourselves" (14). Of course, it should go without saying that, for many, it is not an easy task to enter that dialogue "ourselves," since the pronoun glosses the social and intellectual differences among the "we" imagined as audience for the book.

13. See especially their book *Criticism and Culture: The Role of Critique in Modern Literary Theory*.

14. Wellek and Warren contrast one section, "The Extrinsic Approach to the Study of Literature," to another entitled "The Intrinsic Study of Literature," thus privileging the latter over the former. As might be expected, more than half of the book is devoted to the concluding fourth section on intrinsic methods of analysis, which begins with the statement: "The natural and sensible starting point for work in literary scholarship is the interpretation and analysis of the works of literature themselves" (127). In the third section they briefly review the apparent benefits of the extrinsic methods of relating literature to biography, psychology, society, ideas, and the other arts with the intent in each case of showing how such extrinsic methods are not as reliable as the "natural and sensible" focus on intrinsic methods of analysis.

15. For my argument to make sense it is necessary to understand that the terms *school*, *system*, and *paradigm* often function in similar if not identical ways. Kuhn himself recognized that he used the term *paradigm* in at least two ways in *Structure*, and in his 1969 "Postscript" he offered the related terms *exemplars* and *disciplinary matrices*. For our purposes here these refinements and differences of usage do not significantly alter my argument. In short, the presumed attributes of "schools" and critical "systems" derive their explanatory force in contemporary theoretical debates from the implicit functioning of what I have been calling the Kuhnification of the humanities: a theoretical school functions like a Kuhnian paradigm insofar as it designates a relatively autonomous, identifiable, and self-enclosed community based on "normal practices." Although virtually all anthologizers argue that the schools are always contentious and in debate with each other, it is also the case that many of the arguments depend upon reductive representations of opposing "schools," as if they were paradigms. "Critique" then means that academic competitors proceed by trying to refute or falsify the claims of their rivals. (See Sosnoski, *Token Professionals* and *Modern Skeletons*.) As Sosnoski contends, these kinds of arguments are quarrelsome and endless, especially in the absence of any shared criteria by which to make final judgments, a condition that characterizes humanistic inquiry far more than the relative commensurability of scientific communities. Besides, when examined closely, even the most "model" individual theorists are typically more eclectic and adaptive in actual practice when confronting specific problems in specific historical contexts. Under these conditions the effort to get "inside" the theoretical model can often mean ignoring or getting outside the specific circumstances that provided the need for and vitality of the theory under consideration.

16. Shumway has configured the problem of disciplinary emulation as a

reproduction in academia of the "Star System," whereby taking the celebrated master critics "as models implies our desire to outshine them." In this scenario "the disciple practices the same discipline as the star and so is structurally competitive with the luminary" (100–01). This may be relatively true if you happen to be teaching at a Research I university, but for the majority of English professors material differences in circumstances suggest strongly that only in an idealized world of equal opportunities are they in the "same discipline," or "structurally competitive," since any implied desire to outshine, say, Derrida, for someone teaching four or five courses in a regional university is likely to be a self-destructive internalized image. Shumway's justification of disciplinarity allows for resistance, and he concludes that disciplinary "realities can be changed, but we cannot live without them" (107). Whereas Shumway stresses the benefits of disciplinary knowledge, my emphasis is on theorizing not only how we can resist the dysfunctional components of contemporary English studies but, more important, how they can be changed.

17. Discussion of these institutional autobiographies can often be fruitful in the process of having students themselves design and construct sets of readings and problems using an expanded archive of on-line as well as print resources. Groups of students determine problems and content to be accessed by the entire class. For this to work we have to abandon the notion that we can "cover" all the theories or paradigms. Some students, however, will seek the "disciplinized" model of learning about the "Big Names" in theory, and nothing prevents them from contributing that dimension to the class.

18. North is also playing off John Crowe Ransom's famous call in *The World's Body* for the professionalization of "Criticism, Inc.": "Rather than occasional criticism by amateurs, I should think that the whole enterprise might be seriously taken in hand by professionals. Perhaps I use a distasteful figure, but I have the idea that what we need is Criticism, Inc., or Criticism Ltd." (329).

Bibliography

Adams, Hazard, and Leroy Searle, eds. *Critical Theory since 1965*. Tallahassee: Florida State University Press, 1986.

Aronowitz, Stanley. *The Knowledge Factory: Dismantling the Corporate University and Creating True Higher Learning*. Boston: Beacon Press, 2000.

Barrow, Clyde. *Universities and the Capitalist State: Corporate Liberalism and the Re-*

construction of American Higher Education, 1894–1928. Madison: University of Wisconsin Press, 1990.

Berlin, James. *Rhetorics, Poetics, and Cultures.* Urbana IL: National Council of Teachers of English, 1996.

Bleich, David. "In Case of Fire, Throw In (What to Do with Textbooks Once You Switch to Source Books." *(Re)Visioning Composition Textbooks: Conflicts of Culture, Ideology, and Pedagogy.* Ed. Xin Liu Gale and Frederic G. Gale. Albany: State University of New York Press, 1999. 15–42.

Davis, Robert Con, and Ronald Schleifer, eds. *Contemporary Literary Criticism: Literary and Cultural Studies.* 4th ed. New York: Longman, 1998.

———. *Criticism and Culture: The Role of Critique in Modern Literary Theory.* London: Longman, 1991.

Di Leo, Jeffrey R. "On Being and Becoming Affiliated." *symplokē* 7.1–2 (1999): 49–63.

Downing, David B. "Ancients and Moderns: Literary Theory and the History of Criticism." *Teaching Contemporary Theory to Undergraduates.* Ed. Dianne F. Sadoff and William E. Cain. New York: MLA, 1994. 31–44.

Etzkowitz, Henry, Andrew Webster, and Peter Healey. *Capitalizing Knowledge: New Intersections of Industry and Academia.* Albany: State University of New York Press, 1998.

Fish, Stanley. "Them We Burn: Violence and Conviction in the English Department." *English as a Discipline; Or, Is There a Plot in This Play?* Ed. James C. Raymond. Tuscaloosa: University of Alabama Press, 1996. 160–73.

Fuller, Steve. *The Governance of Science: Ideology and the Future of the Open Society.* Philadelphia: Open University Press, 2000.

———. *Thomas Kuhn: A Philosophical History for Our Times.* Chicago: University of Chicago Press, 2000.

Graff, Gerald. *Professing Literature: An Institutional History.* Chicago: University of Chicago Press, 1987.

Harkin, Patricia. "The Postdisciplinary Politics of Lore." *Contending with Words: Composition and Rhetoric in a Postmodern Age.* Ed. Patricia Harkin and John Schilb. New York: MLA, 1991. 124–38.

Harvey, David. *The Condition of Postmodernity: An Inquiry into the Origins of Cultural Change.* Oxford: Basil Blackwell, 1989.

Hoskins, Keith W. "Education and the Genesis of Disciplinarity: The Unexpected Reversal." *Knowledges: Historical and Critical Studies in Disciplinarity.* Ed. Ellen Messer-Davidow, David R. Shumway, and David J. Sylvan. Charlottesville: University of Virginia Press, 1993. 271–304.

Johnson, Barbara. "Headnotes." *College English* 66.2 (2003): 177–85. Rpt. in this volume, 384–94.

Kuhn, Thomas. *The Structure of Scientific Revolutions*. 2nd ed. Chicago: University of Chicago Press, 1970.

Leitch, Vincent B., gen. ed. *The Norton Anthology of Theory and Criticism*. Ed. William E. Cain et al. New York: W. W. Norton, 2001.

Lodge, David, with Nigel Wood, eds. *Modern Criticism and Theory: A Reader*. 2nd ed. New York: Longman, 2000.

North, Stephen. *Refiguring the Ph.D. in English Studies*. Urbana IL: National Council of Teachers of English, 2000.

Ransom, John Crowe. *The World's Body*. New York: Scribner's, 1939.

Raymond, James C., ed. *English as a Discipline; Or, Is There a Plot in This Play?* Tuscaloosa and London: University of Alabama Press, 1996.

Readings, Bill. *The University in Ruins*. Cambridge: Harvard University Press, 1996.

Richter, David H., ed. *The Critical Tradition: Classic Texts and Contemporary Trends*. Boston: Bedford, 1998.

———, ed. *Falling into Theory: Conflicting Views on Reading Literature*. 2nd ed. New York: Bedford/St. Martin's, 2000.

Schultz, William R. *Genetic Codes of Culture? The Deconstruction of Tradition by Kuhn, Bloom, and Derrida*. New York: Garland Publishing: 1994.

Shumway, David R. "Disciplinary Identities; Or, Why Is Walter Neff Telling This Story?" *symplokē* 7.1-2 (1999): 97-107.

Slaughter, Sheila, and Larry Leslie, eds. *Academic Capitalism: Politics, Policies, and the Entrepreneurial University*. Baltimore: Johns Hopkins University Press, 1997.

Sosnoski, James J. *Modern Skeletons in Postmodern Closets: A Cultural Studies Alternative*. Charlottesville: University of Virginia Press, 1995.

———. "The Theory Junkyard." *minnesota review* 41-42 (1995): 80-94.

———. *Token Professionals and Master Critics: A Critique of Orthodoxy in Literary Studies*. Buffalo: State University of New York Press, 1994.

Sosnoski, James J., and Eve Wiederhold. "Querulous Inquiries." *symplokē* 7.1-2 (1999): 64-84.

Wellek, René, and Austin Warren. *Theory of Literature*. New York: Harcourt Brace, 1947.

Williams, Jeffrey J. "Packaging Theory." *College English* 56.3 (1994): 280-99.

Winterowd, W. Ross. *The English Department: A Personal and Institutional History*. Carbondale: Southern Illinois University Press, 1998.

PART FIVE

Notes on Headnotes

VINCENT B. LEITCH

Ideology of Headnotes

In 1995 I began work as the general editor of *The Norton Anthology of Theory and Criticism*, a 2,600-page anthology published in 2001 that contains selections from 148 figures, starting with Gorgias and Plato and ending with bell hooks, Judith Butler, and Stuart Moulthrop. From start to finish this large-scale six-year project developed through a range of discrete yet overlapping tasks and stages: drafting of project description and guidelines; recruiting of editorial team; drawing up of table of contents; assigning author headnotes; early outside reviewing of both project plan and sample headnotes; composing of introduction, bibliography, alternative table of contents, and preface; writing, editing, and revising of headnotes; securing approval of copyedited manuscript and page proofs; and supervising instructor's manual and index. Two of these tasks, constructing the table of contents and compiling author headnotes, turned out to require intense collaborative work marked by unexpected problems and revealing discoveries. No Norton anthology editor has ever offered written reflection on these two matters.

Recruiting the initial four editors (later five) took several months and involved the gathering of names, talking with experts, assessing selected writing samples, contacting candidates, and signing up the final team. Several months after that we all met with our editor at the publisher's office in New York for two days in order to sketch a preliminary table of contents (TOC) and to assign headnotes, relying on a discussion and consensus approach in our sessions, then and later. While our dialogue continued over the next five years, it was, in retrospect, especially animated the first years as we faxed and then e-mailed one another back and forth about the merits and weaknesses of many dozens of potential figures and selections for our TOC. I have several fat folders stuffed with fading faxes and e-mail messages from our interchanges.

When one of our editors had to resign two years into the project, we recruited a replacement plus an additional editor to make up for lost time. This second round of recruiting, like the recruiting a year later of an author for the instructor's manual, involved the whole team making lists of candidates, asking experts, locating writing samples of candidates, and providing the publisher and general editor short lists of names to contact. The whole process resembled a job search. The two new editors proposed changes to the TOC, suggesting drops and adds as well as different selections. More dialogue and consensus-seeking ensued, especially during the few months just after the new members joined the editorial board. And even as the anthology was entering the page-proof stage two and a half years later and several months before publication, we ended up debating the entire contents as we discovered we had overshot our 2,300-page target by 600 pages, not the 250 we were expecting. At this last minute we needed to cut twenty figures, which entailed all of us making lists and arguments back and forth about those to be dropped. It was only during this last round of intense dialogue spanning two weeks that we, in fact, reached *final* agreement and established a fixed TOC. In my experience the contents are the most unstable element in anthology construction.

Dramatic and time-consuming as constructing the table of contents turned out to be, nothing was more continuously engaging and central to the work of putting together the anthology than compiling the author headnotes, requiring much more sustained research, creativity, tact, and plain labor. Each editor was responsible for drafting about thirty headnotes, with the general editor responsible for fifteen. The collaborative review process for headnotes involved several distinct steps. The general editor and the publisher's editor would separately read and mark up each drafted headnote twice, occasionally three times, infrequently only once. From time to time an outside specialist would serve as a referee (or very occasionally coauthor) to ensure scholarly accuracy. The Plato and Aristotle headnotes, for instance, were vetted by a classicist, and we had specialists look over the headnotes on Moses Maimonides, Giambattista Vico, and Martin Heidegger, to name just a few. Late in the process our copyeditor at Norton, a learned and rigorous reader, added copious refinements, corrections, and precision to the headnotes and especially to the textual annotations, which came as an unexpected and burdensome culmination. The headnotes, like the table of contents, involved intense collaborative work, and this was largely the case because the figures and selections first decided on required agreement from at least three editors, the basis of our consensus approach and the foundation of our later interactions.

Not incidentally, this key protocol of three editors agreeing on TOC items made us early in the project search high and low for the "right" selection. I read fifteen texts by Houston A. Baker Jr. and that many by György Lukács, for example, before finding what I believed to be the right ones. Sometimes the other editors would agree with my own recommendations, sometimes not. A number of my favorite theorists as well as my favorite selections did not make it into the anthology. The other editors had similar experiences.

But let me back up at this point. My very first task as general editor was to draft a project description and set of guidelines to be used in recruiting editors. The centerpiece of that early ten-page description turned out to be a one-page list titled "Protocols for Anthology Headnotes" (see the appendix). According to the protocols, which mostly codified longstanding practices, a headnote proper was to be an essay between 750 and 2,000 words, starting with the author's name; dates; and, where possible, a catchy quotation. The original protocols did not so state, but we editors quickly developed the practice of offering an introductory paragraph that summarizes the significance and relevance of the author and his or her selection(s) for our primary audience – undergraduate literature majors. The protocols thereafter required a dozen discrete tasks on the part of the editor-writer. Unexpectedly, the final protocol on bibliography – which called for one or more paragraphs of annotation covering standard editions, biographies, secondary sources, and bibliographies – added anywhere from 400 to 1,000 extra words to each headnote. As a result our headnotes range in fact from 1,200 to 3,000 words, averaging 2,200 words, a short to medium-sized essay. (A few headnotes exceed 3,000 words.) Thus very early in the process the headnote emerged for us as a regulated, intricate genre like, say, the sonnet – numerous protocols and restrictions, yet ample room for the variations and writerly pleasures characteristic of the comparatively free essay form.

The protocols did not address, and the headnotes proper do not contain, any mention of the thing most dreaded by a headnote writer – textual annotations, a neglected and invisible subgenre. In the anthology any name, title, concept, or word unknown to the average undergraduate is annotated in keeping with a longstanding tradition of textbook editing, one especially honored by the W. W. Norton Publishing Company, we discovered. If a selection from an author contains the word *dialectical*, for instance, it receives a gloss appropriate to its use in that passage: "Dialectical: reciprocal interaction." If the name Philo Judaeus happens to appear, as it does, his dates are provided and a phrase or clause explains his textual significance: "Philo Judaeus (30 BCE–45 CE), secular Jewish writer." The annotations, numbered like footnotes and located at the bottom of the page, take up a great deal of space and time, even though they are descriptive, not interpretive, and succinct, not to say clipped in style. A typical selection, say an essay by a major contemporary theorist, might receive anywhere from a dozen or two to a hundred or more annotations. The twenty-eight-page introduction to Edward W. Said's *Orientalism*, for example, required sixty glosses, taking fifteen additional manuscript pages beyond the eight-page introduction and the three-page bibliography. Throughout the project our page estimates and projections were thrown off by the unpredictability of these textual annotations.

About the annotations – a very labor-intensive element of the headnote – I want to make several rarely considered points. First, a major effect of writing annotations is to keep the audience continuously in mind, constraining the headnote writer to be committed at micro- as well as macrolevels to a relentless project of clarification. Second, each "headnote" consists, in fact, of an introductory essay, a selected prose bibliography, textual annotations, and of course a selection or selections, some of which were trimmed and shaped by the editors to save space and to ensure relevance. (In this regard consider the representative cases of Vico's *New Science* and Aristotle's *Rhetoric*, both many hundreds of pages; they required editing.) Thus when the editors for this anthology talked among ourselves about "headnotes," we almost always meant not the short to medium-sized essay on the famous figure but this essay with all the trimmings, including the edited selection(s), the evaluative bibliography, *and* the annotations. For the headnote writer an enormous amount of work was put into these ancillary elements, frequently more than that involved in the essay proper. Much graduate student labor typically went into the ancillary items as well, particularly the annotations.

One protocol for drafting headnotes turned out to be more unexpectedly revealing than all the rest: offering critiques to ensure that students studying theory would learn to look for problems as a regular aspect of reading. In contrast to the monumentalizing tendency of most headnotes, we wanted to stress that theory arises in the midst of dialogue and debate, with not everyone agreeing. We sought to alert students to the problem-oriented nature of theory as a fundamental part of doing theory, not just to prompt them to memorize key terms and concepts. One of the members of the editorial board provocatively argued, however, that nothing dates a text more than such critique and also, significantly, that critique risks undermining a main goal of the headnotes – to motivate students to read the author and her or his works. In practice this observation got turned into a simple unwritten caveat, a key rider, to the original protocol: keep critique in proportion to explanation and praise. Praise is essential in explaining why a text is included. To offer three paragraphs discussing problems and complaints about a selection and, say, only one paragraph of praise or promotion is to disincline the student to continue on to the reading. What we headnote writers discovered, in the meantime, was that combining the protocol requiring critique with the one calling for discussion of reception and progeny helped solve the problem. In recounting the reception of an author or text the writer really needed to mention hostile as well as friendly responses, dissensus as well as consensus. It works better in a headnote, for instance, to say, "Modern critics have complained that Plato is an enemy of open society," than to state flatly, "Plato is an enemy of open society." Upon reflection this "problem" with critique has to do in large part with genre: the headnote is by tradition unsigned, impartial, more or less objective, disinterested discourse. Conversely, critique typically consists of a signed, partisan, interested intervention expressed in the name of a committed point of view usually linked with a group.[1]

From everything said thus far, it is probably obvious that the headnote is an ideological form. A neighbor of the character sketch and the case study as well as the short essay, the headnote aims to set up for the uninformed reader a reading experience to come. In seeking to direct the reader it typically links the text(s)-to-come with the author (a biography), her or his other work (an oeuvre), a tradition or set of texts (canon), and a topic defining the field (a problem). The headnote tends to foreground what is common knowledge to the specialist, using a normative prose marked by accessibility, relative simplicity, and impartiality, that is, a certain kind of invisible ventriloquized style. It is part of a project of enlightenment, clarification, and demystification. As everyone knows, readers sometimes settle for the headnote, never arriving at the selection. Or readers skip headnotes altogether. Among the main ideological features of headnotes, in any case, are the following: They are rooted in personifications/authors' lives.[2] They are substitutes/"supplements" for reading.[3] They rely on constraining historical and textual contexts/frameworks. They disseminate received opinion as a part of the certification process of educational institutions.[4] These features risk shutting down rather than opening up texts. And in projecting a retrospective tone and a sense of mastery, a headnote also risks taming the conflicts characteristic of cultural productions in their time. Perennializing problems has a way of dehistoricizing and tranquilizing them. By design, anthology and textbook headnotes quickly package and contain information like a memo, valuing control, speed, organization, clarity – values preeminent in today's hurried, market-oriented societies. So while the venerable anthology headnote is a humble genre fulfilling a minor service function, it does cooperate with and further some current ideological goals.[5] And while there is no clear and simple way around these circumstances, my experience confirms that one can and should productively teach about the ideological elements of the headnote to beginning as well as advanced students of theory and criticism.

I have been asked on several occasions whether I can tell a good anthology headnote from a bad one. As an insider, my answer is yes. Common to the headnote are a number of shortcomings and disorders, some obvious, some arguable. An inadequate headnote might contain insufficient, incorrect, or excessive information; offer a weak presentation of the big picture, especially the significance and relevance of the author's work; miss key elements, innovations, and strategies of the text(s) in question; overlook important continuities/discontinuities with tradition and the author's other works; leave out reception history and/or the sociohistorical context of the selection(s); over- or under-identify with the author and his or her project; or minimize, omit, or overemphasize critique of problems and limitations in the work. Like any other essayistic writing a headnote might have shortcomings because of flaws in style, design, or argumentation. In my experience some headnotes are better than others, and some more interesting or compelling than others.

Surprisingly, I have also been asked if it is possible to write headnotes in a postmodern age. My answer is again, yes. Some of the traditional elements of the headnote genre have in recent times been reconfigured, and new features have been added. Characteristic of recent headnotes, including many of those in *The Norton Anthology of Theory and Criticism*, is forthright analysis of issues related to race, class, and gender, as well as other aspects of social history. In addition, there is a willingness in our postformalist period to critique canonical and leading contemporary figures. And with the dissemination of social constructionist viewpoints in postmodern times, writers, including headnote writers, consider history, tradition, and biography to be narrative constructs, if not factitious totalizing tales, bringing a new openness to discussions of history, tradition, biography. Given the widespread impact of deconstruction, moreover, there is now a willingness, often an eagerness, to isolate textual gaps, incoherences, and contradictions in a nonaccusatory, occasionally celebratory, manner. Such faults are regarded as inescapable and ineradicable, revealing symptoms productive for analysis. Finally, ever since the advent of reader-response theory in the 1960s and 1970s, when the reader and the intertext were born at the death of the author, a realignment has been occurring in the relations of power among the famous four elements of the critical pyramid long ago schematized by M. H. Abrams: the work, artist, audience, and universe (6). If nothing else, the matrix of conventions underlying this commonsensical scheme has come into question, complicating and loosening the grip of a whole array of standard concepts, ranging from thematic unity and author's intentions to literary imitation, autonomy, and influence. So yes, there is a postmodern headnote. Because the anthology headnote is, after all, a genre of literary criticism, it reflects the changes and trends of literary criticism: if there is a postmodern literary criticism, there is a postmodern headnote.

Let me tell a story as a way to conclude. I remember vividly as a college sophomore stumbling onto the writings of Martin Heidegger. I was supposed to be reading Robert L. Heilbroner's *The Worldly Philosophers* for an economics course. Instead I ended up wrestling with *Being and Time*, which led me to deeper and deeper inquiries into Heidegger's work, existentialism, Jean-Paul Sartre, Albert Camus, Gabriel Marcel, and back to Heidegger. This lasted for several years and was a formative experience for me. But it was all an accident. It did not start with an anthology or a headnote, and I think I am lucky for that. It turned out to be a life-enhancing extracurricular pursuit unconnected to courses, exams, requirements, notes, and clear paths of inquiry. To the extent that headnotes and anthologies close off the chances for such productive deterritorializations, they are pedagogical forms calling for a measure of wariness.[6] For me nowadays critical reading and ideology critique extend to the headnote and the anthology form and not just to the texts of influential figures. Lately I have taken to asking students to write alternative and counterhegemonic headnotes or parts of them (singly and collectively). I encourage them to search out other selections and to critique selected headnotes. Why not? Still, the best way to work against the headnote and the anthology as normative genres is by going through them, using them as material for information, for instruction, for critique, for illumination. They are by definition preludes.[7]

Appendix 1. Protocols for Anthology Headnotes

The Norton Anthology of Theory and Criticism

The headnotes for each figure will be in essay form and range between 750 and 2,000 words. The protocols below will be used flexibly so as to generate uniformity across the headnotes without them becoming predictable or perfunctory.

Protocols for Headnotes

1. Author's name; dates; and, where possible, catchy quotation by or about the author
2. Highlighting of relevant biographical details
3. Reference to author's other key theoretical or critical publications
4. Sketch of sources and forerunners
5. Inclusion of pertinent factors of social history
6. Précis of selection's/selections' main concepts, arguments, and issues, keeping in mind that selections are invariably interventions in complex arguments
7. Statement on present-day relevance, importance, or use of selection(s)
8. Comparison and contrast with selected pertinent figures in the anthology
9. Critique of problems in the selection(s)
10. Discussion of reception (friendly and hostile) and progeny
11. Information on historical trends, including especially related critical schools and movements
12. Concise explanations of key technical and theoretical terms and concepts
13. Stress on relevant perennial problems in the history of theory
14. Evaluative prose paragraphs(s) (not a list), covering (a) standard editions or texts of author; (b) biographies; (c) pertinent secondary sources on author; and (d) bibliographies of author's writings

Notes

1. See Robert Scholes's useful discussion of critique in his *Textual Power*, chapter 2.
2. See Roland Barthes, "Death of the Author"; and J. Hillis Miller, *Versions of Pygmalion* (136–37). Here I extend the scope of ideology to include such logocentric concepts as author, oeuvre, canon, supplement, and context.
3. The "dangerous/beneficial supplement" alludes to Derrida (144–57).
4. This observation is enabled by the work of Pierre Bourdieu but particularly Louis Althusser. See Althusser (127–57).
5. Anthologies, also anciently called collations, excerpts, *florilegia*, derive both from collections of epigrams first compiled around 100 BCE and from later excerpted commentaries on the Bible, as well as from medieval collections of letters, poems, recipes, and citations of authors. Put together for public circulation and for private use, early anthologies often begin with compilers' prologues (modern "headnotes"), which from late classical and early medieval times followed and developed the conventions of the well-known *prelectio* and *accessus ad auctores*, addressing systematically the life of the poet, the quality of the work, the intention of the writer, the number and order of books, and the text's meaning. Other key topics addressed include utility of the work; branch of learning; and time, place, and circumstances of composition. See Minnis, especially chapter 1.
6. On the tactic of deterritorialization see Gilles Deleuze and Félix Guattari, *Anti-Oedipus: Capitalism and Schizophrenia* (192–200, 244–62).
7. Three interviews with me about *The Norton Anthology of Theory and Criticism* have been published. "Online Colloquy Live: On *The Norton Anthology of Theory and Criticism*," *The Chronicle of Higher Education*, May 3, 2001 (available at http://www.chronicle.com/colloquylive/2001/05/norton/); "Theory, Literature, and Literary Studies Today," *Kulttuurintutkimus* (Cultural Studies) 18.1 (2001): 21–38 (in Finnish); and "Consolidating Theory," *minnesota review* 58–60 (2003): 45–61. The latter two are updated and reprinted in my *Theory Matters* (49–89). Three symposia on the anthology have appeared in print: *College English* 66.2 (2003); *Pedagogy* 3.3 (2003); and *symplokē* 11.1–2 (2003).

Bibliography

Abrams, M. H. *The Mirror and the Lamp: Romantic Theory and the Critical Tradition*. New York: Oxford University Press, 1953.

Althusser, Louis. "Ideology and Ideological State Apparatuses." *"Lenin and Philosophy" and Other Essays*. Trans. Ben Brewster. New York: Monthly Review Press, 1971. 127–57.

Barthes, Roland. "Death of the Author." *Image – Music – Text*. Ed. and trans. Stephen Heath. New York: Hill and Wang, 1977. 142–48.

Deleuze, Gilles, and Félix Guattari. *Anti-Oedipus: Capitalism and Schizophrenia*. Trans. Robert Hurley, Mark Seem, and Helen R. Lane. Minneapolis: University of Minnesota Press, 1983.

Derrida, Jacques. *Of Grammatology*. Trans. Gayatri Chakravorty Spivak. Baltimore: Johns Hopkins University Press, 1976.

Leitch, Vincent B., gen. ed. *The Norton Anthology of Theory and Criticism*. Ed. William E. Cain, et al. New York: W. W. Norton, 2001.

———. *Theory Matters*. New York: Routledge, 2003.

Miller, J. Hillis. *Versions of Pygmalion*. Cambridge: Harvard University Press, 1990.

Minnis, A. J. *Medieval Theory of Authorship*. 2nd ed. Philadelphia: University of Pennsylvania Press, 1988.

Scholes, Robert. *Textual Power: Literary Theory and the Teaching of English*. New Haven: Yale University Press, 1985.

BARBARA JOHNSON

Headnotes

The title of this essay is meant to connote several different things. It brings to mind "head games" and "headstones" as well as the literal topic, those short introductions to writers in anthologies that are conventionally called "headnotes." For the past few years I have spent a great deal of time writing those headnotes, and naturally some thoughts about them have come up along the way.

The Norton Anthology of Theory and Criticism is organized by figure, each one presented and excerpted, arranged in chronological order. Whether the reader has done or at some point plans to do something similar, everyone has certainly been a *consumer* of such work, whether as a student or as a teacher; whether viewing headnotes as grossly distorted and opinionated presentations of a more complex scholarly picture or grasping at the condensed version of what stood between oneself and total ignorance as one hastily prepared a class, or seeking to get a clear explanation of something that one had only heard about in rather mystifying tones, or wanting something slightly more sophisticated than Cliffs Notes but not a lot longer.

In all of these cases the reader of headnotes has also confronted or presupposed assumptions about what it actually means *to know*. What does an explanation explain? What does it assume? What is the relation between a life and a body of writing? Is writing organizable through individuals? What about the "spirit of the age" or "discursive initiators" or "schools"? And what should be said about historical context or causality? Wars or religions or political stances or resistances have everything to do with writings as *responses* to something. How can an anthology present its isolated selections as responses rather than as monuments? And what are headnote writers *as writers* – as writers about writers? Does one explain something as if one is inside it, an advocate for it, or outside it, a judge or mapper?

If one has a double relation to something – both passion and distance, both defense and critique – how can one put that into a discourse that will not be *signed* but will be *assigned*? With what authority does a headnote speak? Whatever you say will have a certain kind of authority. But are you therefore saying, "This is true," "This is said," or "You have heard it said, but verily I say unto you . . . "? Does knowledge have a plot or just a statement? How many turns are too many if your job is to teach first and foremost *that from which turns can be made*? This often ends up being a way of asking how much can be packed into the grammar of a sentence without messing up its clarity. My favorite of my own grammatical athletes – which, in the final analysis, ended up on the cutting-room floor, so I am resurrecting it here before it is consigned to oblivion – was in my headnote for Théophile Gautier. Contrasting him with Baudelaire (and assuming that my reader had heard of both and would relate to this sentence, which was my unjustified assumption), I wrote: "In contrast to Baudelaire – who, after one aborted voyage around Africa, spent his entire life in Paris yet acquired a reputation for a poetics of the voyage – Gautier, seen as the poet of immobility, actually traveled a lot, often on assignment from publishers." The sentence describes and then overturns a contrast that draws its energy from something that would only matter to people who already knew quite a lot, which is exactly the audience I was *not* supposed to be writing for.

The problem I thought this anthology would pose – what to include and what to exclude – remains as acute as ever and will greatly affect opinions about it. But I didn't realize how many other problems there would be, once I really started the work. The requirement to, in effect, create a canon (and with a Norton anthology one would always have to take this function seriously) is paralyzing enough to prevent anyone from wanting to undertake any anthology. What is it, then, that overrides this accurate sense of impossibility? Making annual sourcebooks, perhaps, or the desire to shape, to explain, to teach something that matters more than mere accuracy. In my case it was also a sense that this was something quite different from what I usually do, that it would be a challenge (I was certainly right about that), and that I might learn something (always a dangerous reason to do anything). If my work had in the past often been metacritical or metatheoretical – if I often put a spin on things I read and believed that *that* was what reading was – then what was I taking for granted as already in place? Could my reading strategies be of any use in the very formulation of the most basic knowledge? If the theoretical statements I had made – about warring forces of signification within the text or the necessity of encountering ignorance – *meant* anything, those frameworks should not merely operate as a critique or reading *subsequent* to basic knowledge: they should inhabit it at the root. *Especially* when what is to be "known" is theory.

The anthology's chronological organization by the date of birth of each theorist, starting with Gorgias, automatically biographizes what theory is and ties it not to intellectual dialectics or historical movements but to individual writers. The organization by birth date prevents the anthology from telling a continuous or overarching story – and is thus exactly the "raw" that prevents the anthology from getting excessively cooked in any one way, as is the fact that none of the editors knew what the others were saying. Organization by birth date does not result from any interpretation – except, of course, the massive interpretation that this is an appropriate way to organize an anthology.

Because of accidents of training and approach, I was assigned most of the French figures, plus some of the women in English, plus Edgar Allan Poe and Gotthold Ephraim Lessing. Three of the editors had to agree on the importance of a figure and a selection in order for it to be included. At the beginning of the project Vincent Leitch organized a Modern Language Association session about anthologizing theory for which I gave a paper that might stand as my starting point for what I thought I was doing. My paper was called "Exemplarity and Idiosyncrasy," and I tried to show that it was precisely a theorist's way of being idiosyncratic that was exemplary. Thus I claimed that theory is a talent for producing that for which no definite rule can be given, and not an aptitude in the way of cleverness for what can be learned according to some rule, and consequently that *originality* must be its primary property; and since there may also be original nonsense, its products must at the same time be models, that is, be *exemplary*, and consequently, though not themselves derived from imitation, serve that purpose for others.

Does anyone recognize that I have been quoting from Kant's definition of genius? (Kant was not one of my figures, thank God). Kant is speaking about genius in art rather than in theory, but I think the same paradoxical combination of exemplarity and idiosyncrasy applies. What is wonderful about texts that have really made a difference is the way in which their attention is often directed toward something else. Jakobson's study of aphasia, for example, did not set out to be the monument it later became. The juxtaposition of details of speech loss and wild speculative generalizations could have been – in fact, has been – dismissed as inadequate scholarship and unjustified theory. Yet there is something immensely suggestive about that text that draws its vitality precisely from the impossibility of sufficient justification. What is the specificity of theory, then, if it is like art, at least insofar as it is both idiosyncratic and exemplary? What follows is what I have learned from these headnotes in the form of axioms. Of course, my sample may be skewed or too small, but these were not the axioms that led me – at least not consciously – to make a case for the inclusion of these figures in the first place.

AXIOM 1: *Theory is what happens when you realize that the ways of knowing that have gotten you where you are will not be able to solve the questions that have arisen in the course of the investigation.*

My example here is Saussure. Saussure was a brilliant philologist, publishing an acclaimed book on Indo-European vowels while still a graduate student. Somehow it was all downhill from there. As he worked on historical linguistics, he had the gnawing feeling that he had to solve more basic questions about what language was. He wrote to a fellow linguist:

> I am fed up with all that, and with the general difficulty of writing even ten lines of good sense on linguistic matters. For a long time I have been above all preoccupied with the logical classification of

linguistic facts and with the classification of the points of view from which we treat them; and I am more and more aware of the immense amount of work that would be required to show the linguist *what he is doing*. . . . The utter inadequacy of current terminology, the need to reform it and, in order to do that, to demonstrate what sort of object language is, continually spoil my pleasure in philology, though I have no dearer wish than not to be made to think about the nature of language in general. This will lead, against my will, to a book in which I shall explain, without enthusiasm or passion, why there is not a single term used in linguistics which has any meaning for me. Only after this, I confess, will I be able to take up my work at the point I left off. (Qtd. in Culler 4)

He never wrote the book, of course, but after his early death his students published the *Course in General Linguistics* from class notes. Thus Saussure gave rise to structuralism by means of a book he never wrote, a book that he experienced as a spoiled pleasure in philology.

AXIOM 2. *The better you know a figure, the less likely you are to explain the figure's significance in terms of historical causality. Conversely, if you are struggling to get to know someone you don't know well, the point at which you can tell his or her story as a coherent historical picture is illuminating.*

This is an ambiguous feeling about the role of history, but more about causality. Knowing a theory from the inside makes it part of what you think with; explaining it historically is explaining it from the outside. The temptation of the fallacy of *post hoc, ergo propter hoc* is very great. Pierre de Ronsard wrote his seemingly timeless and oracular "Brief on French Poetry" not as something independent from history but as a recovery from his having been burned for taking part in partisan polemics during the wars of religion. But is his promotion of the timeless defensive or creative? If historical experience "causes" the attempt to erase history, the relation is complicated and nothing is exactly as it seems. Fully historicized, everything could end up being treated as defensive. Even if that is what we learn from history, this is a particular use of history that cannot simply be understood as a ground. It is also a critique of the ungroundedness of monuments. The debate between history and monuments cannot be solved simply by showing the history behind some monuments. What you would succeed in doing is reducing the authority of your particular monuments in the reader's mind without reducing the authority of monuments as such. The reader would simply contrast your contingent figures with the authority of the essential monuments that remain unhistoricized. You are thus obeying a double bind: always historicize but always ask *compared to what.*

Another example of problems of historical causality here is again Théophile Gautier. He wrote his praise of the uselessness of art in a preface to his novel *Mlle de Maupin*, published in 1836. He had just been attacked by the virtue police and the social visionaries – the nineteenth-century versions of the imperative from both right and left to be political – so it seemed logical to assume that his opinions arose because of those attacks. But in the course of writing the headnote I learned that some of the most striking formulas in his preface had already been published in a preface he wrote in 1830. The attacks had not directly *caused* the response, even though the presence in the air of a conflict between the utility and the uselessness of art undoubtedly overdetermined it. Another problem: in my headnote on Roland Barthes I wrote, "His father died when Roland was a year old. Thus the theorist of the death of the author grew up without a father." What was I saying there? Was I implying some causality or finessing one? Was I suggesting something I wouldn't be prepared to state?

AXIOM 3. *Just because you find something illuminating doesn't mean it will help a student understand the material.*

One of the things that happens as you investigate any figure is that your own existing inadequate knowledge gets transformed. But your ignorance might be quite different from that of your students. For you the details may be fascinating *because* the importance of the figure is in place. Your job, however, is to put in place *that knowledge.* It is hard to explain why a figure is important if you have never known an intellectual world without him or her. But even Plato has to be justified.

AXIOM 4. *Ambiguity should not be used to cover over ignorance.*

As teachers we have experience in figuring out how to say things that are not inaccurate even though they cover up something we don't know. Did he get consumption before or after this? If we don't know, we say something that doesn't hinge on the decision or could be read either way. We also teach this life-saving skill to our students. But we need to teach them to take risks, too, and not just protect their vulnerabilities. What does protecting vulnerability actually teach? All it does is avoid teaching the wrong thing. In a headnote this is a waste of space, even though in the classroom it is a lifesaver. Using ambiguity to avoid being wrong is always student behavior – it implies that someone else *does* know. But in a headnote our job is to address students, not to know everything.

One of the problems one encounters in writing headnotes is that, since we *can't* know everything, we rely heavily on the works of people who do. But sometimes this means that we don't really know what we are saying. We repeat without knowing what we have read in more than one source. When I was working on the French Renaissance, for example, I copied into my headnote for Pierre de Ronsard the fact that he had "received simple tonsure in 1543." This seemed to be a fact, but what did it mean? I could easily have assumed that I didn't need to know, but what if I could find out something by knowing this that would change what I had to say? I looked in dictionaries, other biographies, and ecclesiastical glossaries, but all I could find out was that tonsure was a haircut. I decided to look up canon law on the Internet and so searched under "canon." The first sixty sites were sites for Canon copiers. (Why *are* they called "Canon," anyway?) Then there were a few references to Harold Bloom's book on the Western canon, and then, finally, a Web site for canon law. "Simple tonsure" is a ceremony involving shaving the head and committing oneself to celibacy, which, while short of taking vows as a priest, is enough to allow the recipient to become a functionary of the church and derive a living from church properties. Thus Ronsard acquired, with his haircut, his living, his politics, and his marital status (his unmarriageability presumably made him all the more qualified to become one of France's foremost love poets). That was quite a lot not to know about him.

Second example. Writing about the fascinating life of Madame de Staël, I ended my headnote by mentioning that she and her parents were all preserved in alcohol on the grounds of their Swiss estate. Then I learned that, while her parents were indeed pickled, she herself was buried. I tried to finesse this by saying, "In death she rejoined her parents, who were floating in alcohol on the grounds of the château of Coppet." When I got back the editorial comments on my note, the editor asked, "How does this help us understand what she wrote about the French Revolution?" I cut the whole detail out.

AXIOM 5. *Follow the bouncing wife.*

This axiom was also inspired by my work on Madame de Staël. She had numerous lovers and other companions, and her intellectual itinerary is usually told as though she were a clearinghouse for the literary and political ideas of the men in her life. Her skill was to know what to borrow or steal, popularize, and promote. Her energy in making conversations happen in the first place – and her passion for them – were not in themselves anything. It was as though the ideas would have been the same whether or not they had encountered one another. Thus, even putting aside her actual originality and invention, Madame de Staël is erased by what she makes possible. And the list of her lovers eclipses and defines her life. In trying to treat her as an intellectual agent, I realized that my other headnotes seldom even mentioned the wives – not to speak of the lovers – of most male figures.

When I looked for the women in their stories, I found an interesting set of erasures. Saussure is described as a person who had nothing but an intellectual existence, yet the editors of his posthumous text thank his widow for making his notes available. In fact, one of his two sons, Raymond, became a psychiatrist and was one of the targets of Jacques Lacan's rage against psychoanalytic societies. Lacan, in effect, drew inspiration from the father to attack the son. How did this feel? Who felt what? Or consider Claude Lévi-Strauss, who had three wives, but whose biographies always treat him as a lone explorer of other cultures and who only "outs" himself as married – as not alone – when, in *Tristes Tropiques*, his wife has to be evacuated for a serious eye disease. Lévi-

Strauss's narrator's eye, too, suffers the "disease" of having pretended that fieldwork is done by lone individual European men.

The marital norm is always pronounced upon women but often neglected for men. We say, "Emily Dickinson never married," but why don't we say, in the same way, "Baudelaire never married," or, "Gautier never married," or, "Flaubert never married." A man has to be quite a character – like, say, Kant – in order for his unmarried state to seem relevant. And what about lovers, homosexual or heterosexual? With Barthes or Foucault the headnote writer might feel obliged to talk about homosexuality, but how? And what about Hélène Cixous, Adrienne Rich, or Virginia Woolf? What does marriage mean in each case? Or should Lessing's lifelong series of important male friendships be erased by his short, tragic marriage (his wife died in childbirth, along with his day-old son) – especially since he married the widow of one of his male friends? Should headnotes let show some of the stories they don't tell? Should fragmentary evidence be left for some future reader? Wouldn't this just function as noise in a headnote?

While I was working on Roman Jakobson, I noticed that very little had been said about his marital history, although his last works were edited by his widow. When I called up a scholar who had known him well – called out of the blue on Labor Day, I must add – and asked him for Jakobson's marital history, I met a wall of suspicion that I realized I would, under other circumstances, share. What did I want to know, and what for? Why was this material relevant to his work? I finally obtained information available on the public record (he married three times), but I realized that, in searching for gender equality, I had stumbled upon the whole problem of the relationship between sexuality and intellectual work. In my attempts to "out" pure minds as sexual, was I still making an invidious distinction between relationships that are recognized by the law and those that are not (even in Vermont)? How deep into what was unofficial was I trying to go, and what were my criteria? If someone called me up out of the blue and asked me whether it was true that Paul de Man had been a bigamist, wouldn't I have responded with the same wall of suspicion as Jakobson's friend? (Paul de Man, luckily, was not one of my figures either.) On the other hand, isn't it my feminist duty to investigate those domains of privacy where gender inequality is protected and perpetuated? Or would such an investigation ultimately be at the expense of women?

AXIOM 6. *If someone is famous for something, there is a good chance he or she was really also resisting it.*]

Here my two examples are Joachim du Bellay and Pierre Corneille. Du Bellay wrote one of the first defenses of a vernacular language against an imperial language. But his defense of French against Latin was also a defense against French. In arguing that French was *capable* of becoming equal to Latin, he also argued that it wasn't there yet and that only the imitation and translation of Latin culture could produce a French literature as noble as the classics. Vernacular poems and songs from popular traditions in France should not be cultivated but rather snipped off, so that the truly noble virtues of Latin could be grafted onto French roots. Poets like Clément Marot, who treated the battle of French against Latin as already won, had declared premature victory. Du Bellay was thus writing as much a defense *against* the French vernacular as *of* it.

Corneille is usually seen as the epitome of French classicism. The title of his third discourse on theater – "Of the Three Unities of Action, Time, and Place" – sets him up as a defender of rules adopted from Aristotle's *Poetics*. But Corneille was a provincial playwright who ran into classical rules the hard way: the newly created French academy attacked his popular play *Le Cid* for not conforming to the rules. He took a crash course in Aristotle, yet his discourses on theater, far from laying down the law, are really pleas for the idea that a playwright should never take the rules too literally.

AXIOM 7. *If there is a common understanding of what someone is doing, it is probably backward.*

The most obvious example of this is Derrida. In revising what is meant by wholeness, truth, speech, or text, he doesn't just change the positive terms to negative and the negative terms to positive. He analyzes and changes the understanding of the way the opposition has been constructed in the first place. If conflict and multiplicity have been seen as threats to meaning because meaning has been taken to be self-evident and whole, Derrida shows that it is the wholeness itself that is violent, created by the attempt to eradicate conflict rather than acknowledge it. His notorious sentence "There is nothing outside the text" has been taken to uphold and indeed police an inside/outside opposition that its only function is to put in question. In French "Il n'y a pas de hors-texte" – the text has no outside – in fact defines the text as having neither an inside nor an outside. Every text is structured by an attempt to reach what is outside it – the truth, the real, life, history. But since a text is *defined* by the attempt to leap out of itself into the real, there is no outside of *that* that is not also a repetition. There is no outside to the attempts to get outside. And therefore, there is no inside either, because each inside is constituted by attempts to include the outside. Derrida is trying to change the understanding of what a text is, not to draw a boundary around a reading. If Derrida warns readers that they can't simply leap into reality and leave the text behind, it is because that is what the text has already tried to do, and it might be worth taking another look at that process, not as an inside but as what is left of a failed leap.

AXIOM 8. *Headnotes are what is left of a failed leap.*

In the final analysis a headnote has to explain something difficult in simple terms, but it has to convey the difficulty within the simplicity, not just explain it away. Maybe, after all, the same could be said of *all* teaching.

Bibliography

Culler, Jonathan. *Ferdinand de Saussure*. Harmondsworth: Penguin, 1976.

LAURIE FINKE

The Hidden Curriculum

I began thinking about my own discomfort with the pedagogical genre of the headnote while contemplating a collection of brief biographies of illustrious women called *Herstory: Women Who Changed the World*. This book, edited by Ruth Ashby and Deborah Gore Ohrn and aimed at an audience of "young women," contains biographical "sketches" of some 120 women ranging from Sappho to Evita Perón, from Sultana Razia in thirteenth-century India to the 1991 Nobel Peace Prize winner, Aung San Suu Kyi. It was, in fact, an entire volume of headnotes, each a page or two in length, designed to introduce both the exotic and the familiar accomplishments of famous women to junior or senior high school students, to show them that women could "change the world." Immersed as I was at the time in writing my own headnotes for the Norton anthology, I was struck by the "hidden curriculum" that this innocent volume so blatantly revealed and that the sophistication of our own scholarly enterprise often conceals. The volume presents history (or herstory) as a series of fragmented snapshots of individuals who have achieved "greatness," defined abstractly, though never explicitly, as a quality inhering in the individual rather than as a set of actions within a particular historical context. The uniformity of the selections suggests that the entries are more or less equivalent, more or less the same, and hence interchangeable. The enormous cultural gulf between an eleventh-century Japanese writer like Murasaki Shikibu and a twentieth-century political leader like Indira Gandhi or an athlete like Babe Didrikson is subordinated to the uniformity of the entries. As such, these biographical sketches end up reinforcing the dominant ideology of our culture, the ideology and politics of liberal individualism, not so much through their content as through their form.

Perhaps the liberal ideologies of individual achievement conveyed by the headnote form are not so terrible if my goal as a teacher is to convince students that women have been as illustrious, as accomplished, as men, certainly not an unworthy goal. However, what if there are other kinds of questions that I want my students to ask that this form occludes, questions such as *how* these women managed to overcome whatever obstacles their cultures set up for women and "change the world"? The only answer the biographical headnote can yield is "because they were exceptional women." For me this shortcoming is not just hypothetical. When I ask my students in, say, a feminist theory class to write about the ways in which various social and cultural theories explain *how* specific social changes have happened, I find that they invariably fall back on explanations that posit a hero for the narrative; change happened because one or more exceptional individuals effected the change. So thoroughly have they been imbued with a hidden curriculum of liberal individualism that other possible accounts – accounts that posit structural forces, for instance – do not even occur to them; they cannot even find a language in which to articulate alternative explanations.

This real classroom struggle got me thinking about the headnotes I was writing and the way they function within the anthology's apparatus, as well as the ways in which the anthology itself functions as an apparatus of literary education. My focus is not so much on what the text says – on the "heresy of paraphrase" that necessarily troubles headnotes – but on what headnotes cannot or do not say – on the "orthodoxies of form" that are never spoken in the headnote or in the classroom. Educators have long understood that schools do more than simply transmit culturally approved knowledge – in our discipline "literature" or perhaps now "theory." They use the term *hidden curriculum* to describe the mechanisms through which education also transmits norms and values through practices that have become so routinized as to appear all but invisible (see Apple, for instance). The hidden curriculum consists of those things students learn through the practices of schooling – through its forms – rather than its stated educational objectives. As such, the hidden curriculum is taught by educational institutions, not by any individual teacher. And central to the institution of higher education are the textbooks through which we transmit knowledge in our classrooms. In literary classrooms those textbooks are primarily anthologies.

Anthologies are powerful ghosts that haunt both the organization of literature courses and the relations between teachers and students in these classes. What hidden curriculum does an anthology like *The Norton Anthology of Theory and Criticism* present to students? What values does it instantiate? The anthology form is an important method of packaging education in a consumer society, and I wonder to what extent it packages a uniquely American form of education. In American universities students are expected to purchase the books for their classes. While it seems almost obvious to say it, we must remember that the hidden curriculum works because its practices are so routinized as to seem unremarkable, hardly worth mentioning. The consequences of even this expectation, however, are significant. Through it students are taught that the knowledge they will receive in their courses is understood as a form of property – a commodity – that can be exchanged, bought and sold (the college ritual that includes the twice-yearly buying of books at the beginning of the term and their selling, usually at a fraction of their original cost, at the end is only the most visible representation of this attitude).

The anthology represents a convenient form of packaging for the intellectual property on offer in a particular literature course. Its ostensible – and even laudable – purpose is to provide a relatively inexpensive collection of texts that might be used in a particular course. Beyond that, and more problematically, it instantiates Matthew Arnold's "best which has been thought and said"; it creates the "great monuments." In doing so it reifies a series of cultural ideas about texts, so that one understands a particular text, let's say Plato's "Allegory of the Cave" or Dryden's "Essay of Dramatic Poesy," quite differently if one encounters it as an excerpt in an anthology than if one were to read the whole of *Republic* or Dryden's essay in his *Complete Works*, having borrowed them from the library. The anthology collects a series of discrete, individual, and essentially atomistic entries seen as the intellectual property of their creators. They are organized according to some principle, often chronologically, sometimes topically. The relationships among these discrete entities – all more or less equal and more or less interchangeable (as suggested by a table of contents in which individual entries are uniformly presented; see Williams) – are purely formal ones. They exist entirely outside of the human institutions and practices that make up literary studies (publishing, teaching, tenure, promotion, going to conferences). These texts are furthermore seen as the private property of the individuals credited with creating them, the fruits of their labor and their genius, seen as a quality that inheres entirely within the individual rather than in the social relations structured by particular institutions. This format alone makes these documents seem disembodied, outside of human history and politics. Instructors and their students, similarly atomized and interchangeable as consumers, pick and choose from the various entries according to individual tastes. The excerpts are offered devoid of any context, stripped of the environment that formed their horizon of reception – their relations to the author's larger body of work, allied or competing figures, the institutional context that produced the work, the sociological and historical pressures that formed it. The entries become disembodied markers to be moved around on a grid, in this case the calendar that forms the syllabus for a particular course. (The instructor's manual for *The Norton Anthology of Theory and Criticism* illustrates this point even better, since it offers sample syllabi for different kinds of courses, each made up of a different menu of texts from the anthology.)

The anthology as a genre relies on several formal features to make its contents more accessible (by which I mean able to be taught in ways that validate the hidden curriculum). These include tables of contents, headnotes, footnotes, biographies, excerpts, paraphrases, and summaries. These features are not a matter of choice for individual editors. They are dictated by the needs of the institution (education) the anthology serves; they are all part of the hidden curriculum. A particular editor might choose to deviate from one or more of these features, but in doing so he or she always runs the risk that the form will not be recognized within the genre and the anthology will not sell.

The formal features of the headnote are undoubtedly quite obvious and unremarkable (in the literal sense of that term, not worth remarking on). Yet it is precisely their inconspicuousness that we must focus on if we are to uncover the hidden curriculum they teach. Observable features of the headnote include the following:

- It precedes an individual selection (comes at the "head"). Along with the text and its annotations, it packages the entry as an atomistic, isolated, and autonomous object of study, interchangeable with all the other similarly packaged entries, separating a text from the one that came before, contributing to the sense of the anthology as a series of discrete, autonomous, and interchangeable entries.
- It provides brief explanatory material for the excerpt that will follow and so must distill a large amount of information to a few key points. The principle of selection for inclusion of information favors universality (information that abstracts the selection from its time) over particularity (information that locates the selection in its time).
- It includes biographical information, a brief account of the major events in an author's life, suggesting that the life and accomplishments of the author are the only historical information (particularity) deemed important enough to include.
- It lists the accomplishments of the individual, which are always seen as the product – and property – of the individual's genius.
- Insofar as it makes connections between a particular text and its writer and other texts or writers in the anthology, these connections are limited to connections of influence, response, or critical reception. Headnotes, for instance, are more likely to tell us about the influence of Horace's *Art of Poetry* on Sir Philip Sidney's literary criticism than to describe how his participation in various court patronage circles influenced his writing.

What the formal apparatus of the headnote conveys, unsurprisingly, is not all that far from T. S. Eliot's discussion of the work of art in "Tradition and the Individual Talent." Eliot could in fact be describing the form of an anthology: "The existing monuments form an ideal order among themselves, which is modified by the introduction of the new (the really new) work of art among them. The existing order is complete before the new work arrives; for order to persist after the supervention of novelty, the whole existing order must be, if ever so slightly, altered; and so the relations, proportions, values of each work of art toward the whole are readjusted; and this is conformity between the old and the new" (5). This is precisely what we teach about the literary tradition through the *form* of the headnote – that it exists as a series of discrete, individual, and atomistic entries – for Eliot works of art – seen as the product of individual genius. Writes John Stuart Mill in *On Liberty*, "the initiation of all wise or noble things comes and must come from individuals; generally at first some one individual" (81). For Mill works of art are the private property – the intellectual property – of the individuals credited with creating them, the fruits of their labor and of their genius. This perspective, however, makes these monuments seem disembodied, outside of human history and politics.

What the headnote teaches by this form – effortlessly and invisibly – are the values and norms of liberal humanism: independence, equality of opportunity, individualism, respect for private property, and competition. Liberalism, understood as a political philosophy that grew out of the Enlightenment and not as a particular partisan politics, preserves a view of the individual as atomized and disconnected from the social relations and institutions that affect his or her options and choices. I am not arguing that this philosophy in itself is a bad thing. My criticism is not that anthologies inculcate liberal humanist values or a particular kind of political philosophy, only that they do so in ways that naturalize it, that make it appear not as an ideology but as simply the way things are. I would maintain that in American universities at least every course we teach in every discipline teaches these liberal values (hence the term *liberal arts education*) but does so much more effectively at the level of the hidden curriculum than at the level of course content. Teaching liberalism as one ideology among others, one kind of "language game," is actually extremely difficult for these reasons; hence my students' inability to produce theoretical accounts of social change that contradict liberal individualism. They have so thoroughly absorbed its major doctrines through the *form* of their education that they are like the proverbial fish who don't realize their environment is water.

Central to the atomistic view of the individual carried by the headnote form is the liberal analysis of private property. Literary texts are always conceived of as the intellectual property of their authors. Liberalism conceives of property as the reflection of the individual's personality and the control he or she has over his or her life and activities. According to Paschal Larkin, John Locke describes property as "the outcome of human personality; . . . founded on the domination which man [sic] has over his own exertions; it represents the fruits of his labor" (1). Property asserts one's individuality because it expresses one's personality as individualism frees one from dependencies forged by social relations. The liberal ideology carried by the apparatus of teaching – in forms like the headnote – contrasts the needs of individuals with the needs of the social collectivity, individual identity with social identity, individual autonomy with the authority of the social community, always coming down on the side of the individual. "Genius," writes Mill, "can only breathe freely in an atmosphere of freedom" (79). And freedom, in this ideology, means freedom from others, freedom from social interference.

What does this ideology foreclose? What perspectives are our students going to have difficulty articulating? Eliot's description of the monuments of the literary tradition leaves out the social and cultural work that must go into the creation of a "work of art." Liberalism is capable of appreciating the individual labor (the five hundred pounds and a room of one's own Virginia Woolf argues are essential to literary production) but not the collective work – the institutions, practices, and discourses that create, preserve, and circulate "works of art" (the ways, for instance, marriage, in late nineteenth- and early twentieth-century England, was structured as a middle- and upper-class institution in which women were unlikely to have either a room of their own or an independent income). It discourages us, whether for lack of time or of expertise, from asking how the publishing industry and the university as institutions, how editors, printers, professors, librarians, information technologies, bookstores, and even students, perpetuate the "existing order of monuments." It discourages us from investigating how those monuments emerge from and participate in the debates and controversies of their time, especially when those debates involve minor or even unknown artists and writers. It artificially seals off the literary text from participation in other social spheres – politics or economics, for instance. It prevents us from asking questions about the gender or class biases of the "canon." Why are there so few women involved in the history of literary criticism? The simple (and liberal individualist answer) is that no critical or theoretical works by women, for whatever reasons, live up to the Arnoldian standard of "the best which has been thought and said." Finally, the "hidden curriculum" of liberal ideology frequently works against the stated objectives of our teaching. In literary theory, for instance, we can explicitly point out to our students that certain strains of contemporary theory proclaim the death of the author and that this position derives from an antihumanist, antiliberal philosophy, but the point is lost on them given the fetishized celebrity accorded to those individuals credited with this philosophy – Derrida, Foucault, Barthes: the names alone become synecdoches for the ideas.

Does my critique mean that I think that we shouldn't be using the anthology or the headnotes that I spent two years editing? Obviously not. In the first place, anthologies represent liberal values that we might wish to promote – like egalitarianism. Undoubtedly, anthologies, as Jeffrey J. Williams argues, "make theory readily accessible, portable, and eminently teachable" (283). Because they are relatively inexpensive, anthologies, like libraries, make texts – and information – accessible to a larger number of people. Literary theory, for instance, in the 1970s entered this country under the auspices of a few elite institutions; it was the province of the "Yale School," disseminated through conferences promoted by institutions like Johns Hopkins and by academic institutions that could afford to offer continental philosophers cushy half-year positions. What happens when these ideas are as accessible in Peoria as in Berkeley? Undoubtedly, some of the disdain anthologies come in for is the result of their democratizing of literary theory.

We are left with the problem of how to teach antiliberal "theories" like, say, poststructuralism using textbooks whose very form tailors and tames them to conform to the ideals of liberalism. If we look at this situation only from a structuralist perspective, we would seem to be doomed to repeating inadvertently the same lesson – the same hidden curriculum with each anthology, each class, each discontinuous and fragmented headnote. I would insist, however, on a more interactionist framework, one that recognizes that teachers and students, textbook editors and educational institutions, while the objects of such ideological agendas, are not simply their passive recipients. Teachers especially are the nexus where the values of liberal society meet the potential forms of resistance. Actively involving students in the classroom in a conscious effort to uncover and understand the hidden curriculum embodied in their textbooks may be the first step in engaging them in the dialogic interanimation that marks the conversation we call literary theory. Two recent books offer what strike me as exemplary practices that might point the way to making the hidden curriculum visible for our students. In *Science in Action* Bruno Latour contrasts the finished, already made science of the textbook with the process of "science in the making," calling upon teachers to engage students in the controversies, struggles, conflicts, debates, alliances, negotiations, and trials of strength that went into the making of a particular piece of science. Gerald Graff makes much the same call to English teachers in *Beyond the Culture Wars: How Teaching the Conflicts Can Revitalize American Education*. Through such pedagogical practices we begin to uncover the interactions between the free play of signification valorized by poststructuralist ideas about language and the institutional forces – including headnotes and anthologies – that enable and limit that free play. And are these not the very interactions that drew us in and made theory seem so interesting in the first place?

Bibliography

Ashby, Ruth, and Deborah Gore Ohrn. *Herstory: Women Who Changed the World*. New York: Viking, 1995.

Apple, Michael. *Teachers and Texts: A Political Economy of Class and Gender Relations in Education*. New York: Routledge and Kegan Paul, 1986.

Eliot, T. S. "Tradition and the Individual Talent." *Selected Essays*. New York: Harcourt, Brace and World, 1950. 3-11.

Graff, Gerald. *Beyond the Culture Wars: How Teaching the Conflicts Can Revitalize American Education.* New York: W. W. Norton, 1992.

Larkin, Paschal. *Property in the Eighteenth Century with Special Reference to England and Locke.* Cork: Cork University Press, 1930.

Latour, Bruno. *Science in Action.* Cambridge: Harvard University Press, 1987.

Mill, John Stuart. *On Liberty.* Indianapolis: Bobbs-Merrill, 1956.

Williams, Jeffrey J. "Packaging Theory." *College English* 56.3 (1994): 280–99.

JOHN MCGOWAN

Headnotes, Headmasters, and the Pedagogical Imaginary

It is hard not to be rueful when the talk turns to headnotes. They epitomize everything that renders teachers figures of comic ineptitude. Most humiliating, perhaps, is the familiar wheedling tone, the coaxing and pleading that begs for some response, any response, from the torpid student body. A headnote is more like an advertisement than any other known form. It must awaken desire, not satiate it. The teacher is a mediator, standing between the student and the object that is offered as a source of fulfillment, of betterment, of self-development. But even more than a mediator, the teacher is a carnival barker, holding the fold of the tent slightly open and eager to pull it all the way back and usher the student inside. The headnote is the barker's spiel, the teaser. And the good barker is the one who can suppress all intimations of desperation.

The flip side to the hysterical energy of desperation is the nonenergy of boredom, of an indifference adopted to mirror the indifference of those to whom the pitch is made. The salesperson must supply all the energy – at least at the outset – and it has to be the right kind of energy, a naive enthusiasm for the product itself. The barker must obscure the object's function in the transaction, its role in the larger cash or educational economy that has brought us, barker and gull, together. The goods themselves must be seen as motivating the connection between student and teacher.

So the headnote trumpets the quality of the main attraction. After all, an anthology has combed the field for the best, which is here, now, on display. A claim to singularity, even genius, is the first note to be sung. You won't be wasting your time spending it with this writer. But that note cannot be held. Unlike Walter Pater, the teacher/huckster cannot extol experience alone and repudiate its fruits. From singularity the headnote moves to talk of "importance" and "significance." The material is brought back into the larger economy of the discipline or of knowledge. The focus becomes what the student has to acquire in order to be a player, an educated person, or a practitioner in the field. The headnote becomes a repository of received knowledge, of the standard "line" by which this writer is known. The material is located on the map, placed in relation to other luminaries, connected to some -ism or some "school of thought." The anthologized writer is fixed into his or her place in the firmament, although exact calculations of magnitude are still fuzzy since the anthology can only admit to including the brightest stars.

The mediating headnote writer must combine reverence, even awe, with knowingness, the sure-handed placement of the anthologized writer in exactly the right spot. The trick is summing up the standard line without suggesting that this is all you need to know. How are we to entice the students into the tent if the headnote gives them everything they need to know to pass the exam? How, in other words, do we persuade them to have the experience after detailing its fruits for them ahead of time? The headnote, like a teacher, requires strategies of self-abnegation. It must imply its own inadequacies. It must humble itself before the wonders of the object it tries to sell.

Yet, paradoxically, the headnote must also be memorable. And it must be memorable in contradictory ways. It has to strain for the mnemonic. It wants to present information in a way that will stick. It has to impress, in the most literal sense of the word. The teacher is trying to imprint something as he or she imparts it. There are various ways to be memorable, but professors of literature are most likely to believe that distinction in style is the key. What is more forgettable than pedestrian prose and the clichés of received wisdom? The textbook, with its monotonous rendition of "normal science," epitomizes everything that makes education deadly – and unsuccessful. If the students we face are bored, are a hard audience to sell, that's because education has favored styles so anonymous that they drain the life from everything they touch. Our desperation stems, at least in part, from prevailing practices of the institutions we inhabit, institutions that are afraid of students and their vitality. If the headnote is the barker's spiel, it remains haunted – and is tempered – by its relationship to the textbook as damper, as the wet blanket schools try to throw over their students' animal spirits. The textbook takes its authority and the institution's authority, the hold that school has over students, as sufficient for attaining and retaining their attention. It is hard for anyone who actually teaches to trust that authority alone will do the trick – hence the likelihood that the headnote will lean more toward the rhetoric of ads.

So pity the poor headnote writer, especially the professor of literature, who comes from a field that worships the idiosyncratic, that has prided itself since the days of Oscar Wilde and George Bernard Shaw on witty contempt for received knowledge and established authorities. The constant temptation is irony, the presentation of the standard line in a voice that dissociates the writer from that line. But ironic headnotes, like an ironic teaching style, while certainly possible, are, I think, more about preserving the purity of the writer, his or her self-respect, than about serving the needs of the reader. Such an approach smacks too much of kicking away the ladder by which one has risen, thereby denying others a chance for a similar climb.

What is to be done? Faced with my distaste for the form and the ways that it makes me think about my teaching, I decided I better set myself the task of defining a good headnote. And that quickly led me to think about the teacher's relation to the conventional and the authoritative. The problem with the headnote is that it must convey the conventional in a recognizably conventional context. And it does so in a context where authority continually hovers to ensure that the material is taken seriously by the audience. That we teachers believe in its intrinsic importance just indicates that we are dupes, we are the cherished students who have fully internalized the goods school is selling. We (literary professors) wrestle with the goody-two-shoes stigma through a (second-order) conventionalized rule-breaking. We associate vitality, originality, and distinction with the unconventional, while perfecting an ironic style for those moments when we must perform within conventions, must take up our authoritative position. Straightforward justifications of our work as teachers, as part of a massive educational system, are embarrassing because so conventional. What could be more predictable than the litany of reasons the humanist will offer for the good that enforced study of the humanities can provide? There are no new arguments to add to the timeworn ones about teaching students how to think, preparing them to be citizens, providing a means for economic and social mobility, and enabling them to join an ongoing intellectual discourse. Of course, these different aims of education are not fully compatible with one another; the university is a complex, even contradictory, place. But its finite set of multiple aims is pretty well set, as is the subset associated with the humanities. The teacher knows what his or her task is, and the question is how best to accomplish it.

In other words, the problem is exactly the problem of writing in a conventional form. The outlines of the genre are clear; the trick is to take the conventional and breathe some life into it, to make it convincing on its own, without needing the props supplied by authority. The preferred strategy of literature professors for breathing life into things is to make them new. But that is not the only possible means – and certainly not always the best one. In some cases revivifying the conventional form is more about showing how it works in this place and with this project to get the job done. The meaning of a convention is its use (to paraphrase Wittgenstein). The convention justifies itself through what it enables us to accomplish.

So I will end with an unsurprising account of what a good headnote might strive to accomplish. Forgive me if the wheedling tone rears its whiny head here as I move back into teacherly persuasive mode. The headnote has two main tasks: to provide information that will help the student comprehend and appreciate the passage that follows and to enable the student to engage the material on somewhat equal terms. The first task is hardly simple, but it is straightforward. Its success depends on how fully we can imagine what the student needs to know. I had originally conceived of this essay as a portrait of the bizarre picture of students that we could derive from reading headnotes. I have no intention of underestimating how fully teachers misunderstand the needs of their students. Headnotes can miss spectacularly – by being too fussy, too pedantic, too "relevant," or too folksy. Eighteen-year-olds are an amazing mixture of sophistication and naiveté; what they don't know can be charming, infuriating, and alarming by turns. We don't know what our students don't know. Getting it right – both in assuming what they know and in adopting the right tone for presenting what they don't know – is a daunting, but recognizable, rhetorical undertaking.

Enabling student engagement is harder. It requires not exactly irreverence toward the anthologized figures, although a dash of irreverence won't hurt, since the anthology as form tends to worship. Better to say that the desired tone is matter-of-fact egalitarianism. We want to address the writer as a peer; we want to be an interlocutor unconscious of any difference in status, a full participant in the conversation in which we are both engaged. That's hard. The conventions of the form work against this approach, and readers will be hypersensitive to studied casualness or hints of *ressentiment* since they will react to the absence of expected reverence. But it is a tone worth striving for because our massive educational system – and our role as functionaries within it – is only justified, I believe, if it brings students to participate in the ongoing production and contestation of knowledge.

In writing the headnotes I found myself increasingly troubled by Wordsworth's ideal of "a man speaking to men." The very phrasing of the ideal reminds us of all the good reasons we have for resisting its easy assumption of abstraction from all the particulars that differentiate the writer from his or her audience. Wordsworth himself cannot state his ideal without immediately qualifying it. The Poet (Wordsworth's capitalization) is "a man speaking to men: a man, it is true, endowed with more lively sensibility, more enthusiasm and tenderness, who has a greater knowledge of human nature, and more comprehensive soul." Does Wordsworth's falling so comically short of his own standard entail that standard's inevitable irrelevance? Would it merely be a kind of bad faith to write headnotes that tried to abstract away from the authority of the anthologized figure and the authority of the teacherly headnote writer to gesture toward a place where figure, teacher, and student slugged it out on roughly equal terms? Could the sales pitch that offers a finished product shift to an invitation to an ongoing process of creation? And could the headnote make an end run around the authorities that put the "don't touch" sign on the displayed objects? I don't see how we can even begin to answer the last two questions in the affirmative if the headnote (and the teacher it represents) does not project an equality that is more than half-fictional now but may be less fictional in the future because we wrote today as if it were true.

Contributors

Lynn Z. Bloom, Board of Trustees Distinguished Professor and Aetna Chair of Writing at the University of Connecticut, has published a number of related works on anthologies, including "The Essay Canon" (1999) and "Writing Textbooks in/for Times of Trauma" (forthcoming). Her creative nonfiction includes "Teaching College English as a Woman" (1992) and "Living to Tell the Tale" (2003). *The Essay Canon* is forthcoming.

Terry Caesar was most recently a professor of American literature at Mukogawa Women's University in Japan. His last book, coedited with Eva Bueno, is *I Wouldn't Want Anybody to Know: Native English Teaching in Japan* (2003).

Nancy Cirillo is an associate professor of English at the University of Illinois at Chicago and curator of the H. D. Carberry Collection of Caribbean Studies. She is currently engaged in writing an annotated bibliography of these largely unavailable and out-of-print works, as well as with a preservation and access project with the jackets of about two-thirds of the thousand-volume collection.

David Damrosch is a professor of English and comparative literature at Columbia University. He is the author of *What Is World Literature?* (2003) and general editor of *The Longman Anthology of World Literature* (2004). He was president of the American Comparative Literature Association for 2001–03.

Jeffrey R. Di Leo is an assistant professor of English and philosophy at the University of Houston–Victoria. He is editor and founder of the journal *symplokē* and series editor for Class in America, published by the University of Nebraska Press. His publications include *Morality Matters: Race, Class, and Gender in Applied Ethics* (2002), *Affiliations: Identity in Academic Culture* (2003), and, with Walter Jacobs, *If Classrooms Matter: Progressive Visions of Educational Environments* (2004).

David B. Downing teaches in the Department of English at Indiana University of Pennsylvania. He is the founding editor of the journal *Works and*

Days, and his most recent book is the coedited collection, with Claude Mark Hulbert and Paula Mathieu, *Beyond English, Inc.: Curricular Reform in a Global Economy* (2002).

Laurie Finke is professor and director of women's and gender studies at Kenyon College. She is the author of *Women's Writing in England: Medieval England* (1999) and *Feminist Theory, Women's Writing* (1992) and coauthor, with Martin Shichtman, of *King Arthur and the Myth of History* (2004). She is one of the editors of *The Norton Anthology of Theory and Criticism* (2001) and, with Martin Shichtman, of *Medieval Texts and Contemporary Readers* (1987).

Gerald Graff is a professor of English and education at the University of Illinois at Chicago. His latest book, *Clueless in Academe: How Schooling Obscures the Life of the Mind*, was published in 2003.

Barbara Johnson, who teaches in the departments of English and comparative literature at Harvard University, is the Fredric Wertham Professor of Law and Society there. She is author of *The Critical Difference* (1981), *A World of Difference* (1987), *The Wake of Deconstruction* (1994), *The Feminist Difference* (1998), and *Mother Tongues* (2003). She is translator of Jacques Derrida's *Dissemination* (1981) and agonized about *The Norton Anthology of Theory and Criticism* (2001) for about three years.

Karen L. Kilcup is a professor of American literature at the University of North Carolina at Greensboro. Her recent books include *Native American Women's Writing, c. 1800–1924: An Anthology* (2000), *Soft Canons: American Women Writers and Masculine Tradition* (1999), and *Robert Frost and Feminine Literary Tradition* (1998).

Sarah Lawall is a professor emerita of comparative literature at the University of the Massachusetts, Amherst, and general editor of *The Norton Anthology of World Literature*. Her interests combine literary phenomenology, poetry and poetics from surrealism, and the concept and practice of world literature. Publications include *Critics of Consciousness: The Existential Structures of Literature* (1968), *Reading World Literature: Theory, History, Practice* (1994), and articles on literary theory and modern French poetry.

Vincent B. Leitch is the Paul and Carol Daube Sutton Chair in English at the University of Oklahoma. He has served as general editor of *The Norton Anthology of Theory and Criticism* (2001), and he has published five books, among which are *American Literary Criticism from the 1930s to the 1980s* (1988), *Cultural Criticism, Literary Theory, Poststructuralism* (1992), and *Theory Matters* (2003).

Cris Mazza's most recent books are a memoir entitled *Indigenous/Growing Up Californian* (2003) and *Homeland* (2004), a novel. Among her other notable titles are the PEN/Nelson Algren–winning *How to Leave a Country* (1992) and the critically acclaimed *Is It Sexual Harassment Yet?* (1991). She is a professor in the Program for Writers at the University of Illinois at Chicago.

John McGowan is a professor of English and comparative literature at the University of North Carolina, Chapel Hill. In addition to being one of the editors of *The Norton Anthology of Theory and Criticism* (2001), he is the author of, among other books, *Hannah Arendt: An Introduction* (1998) and *Democracy's Children: Intellectuals and the Rise of Cultural Politics* (2002).

Robert L. McLaughlin is an associate professor of English at Illinois State University. He edited *Innovations: An Anthology of Modern and Contemporary Fiction* (1998) and is senior editor of the *Review of Contemporary Fiction*. His work has appeared in *Critique*, *Pynchon Notes*, *symplokē*, and many other journals and collections.

Cary Nelson is Jubilee Professor of Liberal Arts and Sciences at the University of Illinois at Urbana-Champaign. His recent books include *Academic Keywords: A Devil's Dictionary for Higher Education* (1999), coauthored with Stephen Watt; *Revolutionary Memory: Recovering the Poetry of the American Left* (2001); and *The Wound and the Dream: Sixty Years of American Poems about the Spanish Civil War* (2002).

Angeline O'Neill has published in the areas of Australian literature, Indigenous literature, and comparative literature and recently coedited an anthology of Australian Aboriginal writing, *Those Who Remain Will Always Remember* (2000). She teaches courses in comparative Indigenous literature, Australian literature, and world literatures at the University of Notre Dame, Australia.

Richard S. Pressman is a professor of English at St. Mary's University in San Antonio, Texas. In 1990 he encouraged his department to adopt the first *Heath Anthology of American Literature*, which is still used there. He has authored some fifteen articles on American literature.

Contributors

Alan D. Schrift is a professor of philosophy and director of the Center for the Humanities at Grinnell College. In addition to editing the four anthologies mentioned in his essay, he is the author of *Nietzsche's French Legacy: A Genealogy of Poststructuralism* (1995) and *Nietzsche and the Question of Interpretation: Between Hermeneutics and Deconstruction* (1990). He is currently completing a work on the history of philosophy in France in the twentieth century that attends to the unique features of intellectual formation in France and is editing an anthology of new essays entitled *Modernity and the Problem of Evil*.

Jeffrey J. Williams has published, most recently, the edited collections *The Institution of Literature* (2002) and *Critics at Work: Interviews 1993–2003* (2003), along with *The Theory Market: Criticism and the Institution* (2004). He is also an editor of *The Norton Anthology of Theory and Criticism* (2001), editor of the journal the *minnesota review*, and a professor of English at Carnegie Mellon University.

Simon Morgan Wortham is a principal lecturer in English literature at the University of Portsmouth, England, and author of *Rethinking the University: Leverage and Deconstruction* (1999) and *Samuel Weber: Acts of Reading* (2003). He is currently editing a collection of essays on technology and deconstruction and preparing a new book on obsessional writing.

Index

Abelard, Peter, 38
Aboriginal and Torres Strait Islander Commission, 257, 261n4
aboriginal literature. *See* literature: Indigenous
About, Edmond, 37–38
Abrams, Alexander, 210
academia, 5, 10, 18, 19, 80, 92, 256, 363, 368n16; Japanese, 311
academic, 208, 209, 229; affect, 18, 208; anthologist, 53; audience, 116, 238; capitalism, 359; community, 10; competition, 367n15; criticism, 284; culture, 4, 6, 11, 24; departments, 321; disciplines, 96, 342, 343n2; discourse, 96, 339; environment, 208, 223; freedom, 338–39, 347; game, 348; hierarchy, 355; identity, 348; institutions, 128, 271, 402; jargon, 254; profession, 131; professionals, 18, 100, 122–23, 207, 220n3, 237, 247, 248, 251, 254, 260, 344; publishing, 10; resources, 361; specialty, 102; studies, 93; talk, 287; tenure, 10, 11, 126, 128, 132n8, 133n13, 143, 208, 213, 357, 398
Accadian-Babylonian literature. *See* literature: Accadian-Babylonian
Achebe, Chinua, 73
Achilles, 45n4
Acker, Kathy, 145, 146, 169
Adachi, Nobuhiro, 299, 320n1
Adams, Abigail, 54
Adams, Alice, 303
Adams, Hazard, 364n2
Adler, Mortimer J., 59
Adventures of Huckleberry Finn, 3, 21, 268
Aeschylus, 39, 54
aesthetic. *See* anthologies: aesthetic dimensions of

aesthetic criticism, 85
African American literature. *See* literature: African American
African American studies, 236, 243
African orature. *See* literature: African orature
Agee, James, 103
Alain, 194, 195, 196
Alden, John, 50–53, 55, 82
Alden's Cyclopedia of Universal Literature, 50, 52, 82
Alfau, Felipe, 144, 149
Alighieri, Dante, 39, 40, 60
Allison, David B., 193
Althusser, Louis, 194, 198, 382n4
Altieri, Charles, 11, 91
American Anthology, An, 113
American literature. *See* literature: American
American Medical Association, 161
American Poetry and Prose, 266
American studies, 323n12
American Studies Association, 323n12, 324
American Tradition in Literature, 266
Amerika, Mark, 164
Ancient Greece, 2, 42–43
Angelou, Maya, 95, 102
Anglophone Caribbean literature. *See* literature: Anglophone Caribbean
anthologia, 2–3
anthologies: academic, 14, 48, 49, 55–56, 59, 80, 115, 120, 210, 237; aesthetic dimensions of, 9, 14, 44, 48, 49, 65, 67, 74, 85, 101, 106, 113–16, 123, 127, 129, 143, 145–48, 150–52, 178, 185, 209, 229, 240, 266, 268–70, 302, 312, 353; ambivalence toward, 207–10, 212, 215; analysis of, 7; and

415

anthologies (continued)
  canon expansion, 31, 116, 249–50, 273, 296; and canon formation, 2, 9, 11, 14–15, 21, 90, 92, 106, 113, 122–23, 131, 147, 152, 193, 199, 228, 249–50, 261n2, 273, 284, 308, 343, 385; vs. collections, 4; and copyright law, 171, 176, 177; and corporate control, 7, 15, 70, 112, 130, 270, 271; cosmopolitan vs. nativist view of, 33, 34, 35; and cost, 8; and coverage, 7, 8, 47, 66, 82, 150, 152; cultural context of, 12, 31, 33, 43; and cultural evolution, 52, 53, 55, 57, 67; cultural implications of, 2, 19, 21; and cultural studies, 2, 6, 7, 23, 124; definition of, 3, 301; and democracy, 35, 275n12; disdain of, 7, 9, 10, 18, 207–21; and distribution, 8; and editorial intelligence, 186, 193; and essays (see essays); and foreign instruction, 298–325; and graduate education, 22, 357; and headnotes (see headnotes); history of, 4, 6, 14, 31–46, 47–89, 90–111; market, 1, 4, 8, 11, 14, 16, 17, 32, 63, 68, 70, 86, 94, 104, 113, 115, 118, 120, 121, 149, 155, 156, 157, 160, 161, 168, 170, 171, 172, 173, 175, 176, 182, 186, 192, 197, 207, 209, 210, 217, 224, 225, 227, 229, 231, 233, 235, 236, 237, 240, 243, 255, 329, 378; and novels, 9, 16, 38, 94, 98, 114, 117, 232, 240, 301; on-line, 5, 6; organizational structure of, 3, 8, 41, 53; orthodoxy and authority of, 1; and paraphrase, 208, 215–19, 295, 396, 398; pedagogical implications of, 1, 2, 4–5, 16, 20, 22, 186, 270, 279, 337, 347; and political correctness, 5, 12; political implications of, 1, 2, 4, 14, 16, 17, 19, 219n2, 256; print-on-demand, 5–6, 14, 90, 104–6, 109n3; and print publication, 4, 7, 157, 166, 167, 170, 235, 247, 401; and production, 8; and public sphere, 5–6; and quotation, 327, 332; as readers, 4, 94, 193; and recovery work, 14–15, 112–38; and repackaging, 9, 122; reviews of, 7; role in literary studies of, 279;

and summary, 35, 36, 45n1, 65, 194, 217, 295, 375, 398; textual apparatus of, 8, 22–24, 48, 54, 55, 67, 84, 104, 233, 302, 399; theory, 22, 207, 219n2, 343, 345, 349–52, 356, 359, 361, 364; and translation (see translation); and undergraduate students, 130; value of, 4, 9–11, 15, 150, 397, 400; and women writers, 15, 16, 51, 71, 91, 102, 112, 116, 117, 119, 121, 123, 124, 127, 128, 132n6, 155–58, 161, 168, 169, 252; work-centered, 48–49, 65, 72, 76, 85
Anthology of Canadian Native Literature in English, 248, 252–54, 259, 260
Anthology of World Literature, 60
anthropology, 96
anti-Muslim, 222
Appadurai, Arjun, 313
Apuleius, 143
Archilochus, 3
Ariss, Robert, 257, 258
Aristophanes, 37
Aristotle, 218, 350, 365n6, 374, 377, 393
Arnold, Matthew, 12, 33, 62, 79, 91, 97, 109n2, 113, 397, 402
Arnold, Thomas, 52
Aron, Raymond, 194, 199
Aronowitz, Stanley, 365n7
Ashbery, John, 184
Asian American literature. See literature: Asian American
Asian-American Literature, 315, 316–18, 320
Asian literature. See literature: Asian
Asoka Emperor of India, 61
Assyrian literature. See literature: Assyrian
Ast, Friedrich, 187
Atwan, Robert, 94, 103–4
auctores, 51
Audubon Society, 93
Auerbach, Eric, 283
Aurelius, Marcus, 35
Austen, Jane, 299, 316
Auster, Paul, 2, 310
Australian literature. See literature: Australian

416

Index

Avant-Pop: Fiction for a Daydreaming Nation, 3
Aztec literature. *See* literature: Aztec

Bachelard, Gaston, 194, 195, 199
Bacon, Francis, 35, 95, 101
Badiou, Alain, 194, 196, 202n3
Baker, Houston, 11, 375
Baldwin, James, 102
Balibar, Etienne, 194, 272
Banta, Martha, 117
Baraka, Amiri, 182
Barnes, Djuna, 144, 149
Barnes and Noble, 153
Barnstone, Toby, 40
Barnstone, Willis, 40
Barrow, Clyde, 348, 365n7
Barth, John, 144, 149
Barthelme, Donald, 144, 149
Barthes, Roland, 194, 281, 382n2, 389, 392, 402
Barzun, Jacques, 103
Bataille, Georges, 189, 190, 194, 199, 201n2
Baucom, Ian, 47, 85
Baudelaire, Charles, 385, 392
Baudrillard, Jean, 194
Bauer, Dale M., 125
Baym, Nina, 114, 267
Beach, Rex, 37, 38
Beats, 298
Beattie, Ann, 303
Beauvoir, Simone de, 194, 196, 198, 199, 200
Beckett, Jeremy, 255
Bedford, 104; and *Bedford Anthology of World Literature*, 83; Case Studies in Contemporary Criticism series, 21, 279, 285
Bedford/St. Martin's, 3, 104
Bellay, Joachim du, 393
belles-lettres, 14, 52, 90, 92, 93, 96–97, 99, 102
Belsey, Catherine, 150
Bennett, Hazel, 244n2
Bennett, Paula, 118, 134n19
Benveniste, Émile, 189, 190

Berbineau, Lorenza Stevens, 124, 130, 133n15
Bergson, Henri, 194, 198, 202n4
Bernasconi, Robert, 3, 190
Berossus, 43
Best American Essays, 94, 103
Best of the World's Classics, The, 32, 34
Betti, Emilio, 187
Beverley, John, 271
Bible, 7, 42, 64
Bierhorst, John, 74
Bird, Gloria, 247, 251, 252, 253, 255, 256
Bishop, Elizabeth, 172, 178
Bizzell, Patricia, 97–98
Black Arts movement, 181
Blaeser, Kimberly, 250–51, 252
Blair, Hugh, 97, 99
Blake, William, 306
Blanchot, Maurice, 193, 194
Bleich, David, 343
Blondel, Eric, 188, 193
Bloom, Harold, 90, 102, 390
Bloom, Lynn Z., 14, 100
Boas, Franz, 38
Boccaccio, Giovanni, 60, 144, 146
Boethius, 40
Bondanella, Peter, 3
Borges, Jorge Luis, 72, 144, 146, 148
Bourdieu, Pierre, 190, 194, 199, 214, 300, 382n4
Bouveresse, Jacques, 194, 196, 202n3
Boxer, Sarah, 5
Bradley, A. C., 306
Brady, Judy, 101
Brathwaite, Kamau, 226, 241
Brecht, Bertolt, 72
Breton, Andre, 194
Brewster, Anne, 248, 254
British literature. *See* literature: British
Broadway, 174
Brockway, George, 64
Brodhead, Richard H., 132n7
Brooks, Cleanth, 211, 215, 352
Bropho, Robert, 257–58, 261n6
Brown, Sterling, 183
Browning, Elizabeth Barrett, 128
Brunner, Edward, 179
Brunschvicg, Leon, 194, 199, 202n4

Index

Buck, Pearl, 36
Buck, Philo M., 60, 61, 79
Buell, Lawrence, 134n19
Burgard, Peter J., 201n1
Burns, Robert, 35
Butler, Judith, 373
Byzantine, 3

Caesar, Julius, 38
Caesar, Terry, 1, 21
Cahan, Abraham, 265
Cain, Kathleen Shine, 104
Calderón, Pedro, 58
Cambridge Companion to Levinas, 3, 4
Camfield, Gregg, 134n19
Campbell, George, 97
Camus, Albert, 72, 194, 200, 202n5, 380
Canguilhem, Georges, 194, 195, 199
Cannadine, David, 244n4
canon, 7, 11–15, 67, 75, 90–92, 264, 284, 296, 309, 312, 316–17, 378, 390; calcification of, 125; and class, 402; cultural, 56; and cultural studies, 284; essay, 90–111; and ideology, 311; Indigenous, 261n2; literary, 249, 300; literary and cultural theory, 342, 362; as logocentric concept, 382n2; male, 156; and master critics, 359; and mini-canons, 75; modernist, 72; new, 120, 128; and New Critics, 283; poetry, 184; reliance on *auctores*, 51; and syllabus, 307; theory, 14, 90, 106, 307; Western, 79–80, 247, 249, 260; and women, 266. *See also* anthologies: canon expansion; anthologies: canon formation; pedagogy
capitalism, 170, 176, 271, 359
Caribbean Literary Studies conference, 230
Caribbean literature. *See* literature: Caribbean
Caribbean Literature and the Environment: Between Nature and Culture, 244n13
Caribbean Rhythms: The Emerging English Literature of the West Indies, 233–35
Caribbean studies, 233, 236, 243
Caribbean theory, 239
Caribbean Writer, The, 237

Carlyle, Thomas, 96, 101, 144, 146
Carmichael, Stokely, 102
Carroll, Lewis, 144
Carson, Rachel, 102
Carter, Angela, 145, 148
Carter, Paul, 247
Cary, Alice, 121
Castoriadis, Cornelius, 194
Catton, Bruce, 96
Cavendish, Margaret, 144, 147
Celebi, Evliya, 41
Cervantes, Miguel de, 144, 146
Césaire, Aimé, 194, 196, 232, 235, 241
Chamoiseau, Patrick, 237
Chapman, John Jay, 365n7
Chase, Richard, 274n5
Chaucer, Geoffrey, 39
Chevrel, Yves, 250
Chick-Lit: Postfeminist Fiction, 3–4, 16, 155–69
Child, Lydia Maria, 131
Childers, Joseph, 23
Chinese literature. *See* literature: Chinese
Ciardi, John, 102
Cicero, 33
Cirillo, Nancy, 18
Cisneros, Sandra, 103
City Lights, 153
Civil War, 127, 264, 265, 268
Cixous, Hélène, 189, 190, 194, 199, 201n1, 392
class, 19, 114, 210, 212–14, 242, 270, 271; and anxiety, 213; and editors, 122, 123, 124; elite, 38, 39, 97, 100, 120, 122, 123, 130, 132n9, 133n13, 208, 212, 213, 214, 301, 321n2, 356, 402; middle, 100, 123, 133n14, 208, 213, 273; upper, 401; working, 123–24, 133n14, 185, 213, 272
classical studies, 32
classicism, 76; French, 393
classics, 31, 36, 37, 52, 55, 65, 98, 100, 120, 327, 393
Cliff, Michelle, 237
Clifford, James, 352
Cliffs Notes, 23, 207, 217
Clinton, Jerome, 74
Cold War, 211, 230, 265, 345, 347

418

Index

Coleridge, Samuel Taylor, 96, 97, 98
Collège de France, 195, 202n3
colonialism, 196, 229, 231, 235–36, 240, 242
Columbus, Christopher, 40
comparative literature, 33, 65, 66, 69, 191
composition. *See* writing: and composition
composition studies, 93
Conant, James Bryant, 345
Condé, Maryse, 237
Confucius, 40
Connors, Robert J., 98
Conrad, Joseph, 285
conservativism, 101
Contemporary American Women Writers, 303
Coover, Robert, 145, 149
Copernican revolution, 365n6
Corneille, Pierre, 393
Cornell University, 134n17, 245n13
Coser, Lewis A., 7
Cousins, Norman, 102
Crane, Hart, 174, 176, 184
Creeley, Robert, 172
Critchley, Simon, 3
critical studies, 85, 93, 288, 343
critical theory, 2, 24, 189, 239, 242, 285–87, 326, 350, 366n12
Crummell, Alexander, 219
cultural capital, 19, 79, 214–15, 270, 300–301, 312–13, 322n7
cultural criticism, 70, 285
cultural history, 52, 53, 63, 67, 69, 77, 78, 274n3
cultural studies, 284, 288, 351, 361
Cultural Studies Reader, 3
cultural theory, 343, 344
cummings, e. e., 175
Cyclopaedia of American Literature, 114

Dada-Surrealist, 78
Dalkey Archive Press, 142, 143
Damasio, Antonio, 219, 220n5
Damm, Kateri, 249
Damon, Maria, 322n10
Damrosch, David, 12, 13, 81, 83–84, 86n2

Dana, Richard Henry, 38
Dance, Daryl Cumber, 237
Danly, Robert, 74
Darío, Rubén, 47
Darwin, Charles, 38, 57
Davidman, Joy, 174
Dawa, Zhaxi, 31
Dawes, Kwame, 228
Dawes, Neville, 228
Day, Henry, 97
de Certeau, Michel, 194
Debord, Guy, 194
deconstruction, 21, 85, 142, 198, 215–16, 279, 285, 326–40, 341n3, 345, 350, 364n4, 379
Deleuze, Gilles, 193, 194, 196, 199, 382n6
DeLillo, Don, 141
DeLoughrey, Elizabeth, 244n13
De Quincey, Thomas, 96
Derrida, Jacques, 21, 187, 189, 190, 193, 194, 196, 197, 198, 202n4, 294, 295, 326–39, 340n2, 341n3, 352, 368n16, 382n3, 393–94, 402
Descombes, Vincent, 194
DeShell, Jeffrey, 3, 158, 160, 164
Dickens, Charles, 37
Dickie, Margaret, 134n19
Dickinson, Emily, 115, 125, 128, 265, 392
Dickinson, Susan Gilbert, 115
Diderot, Denis, 52, 144, 146
Didion, Joan, 102
Di Leo, Jeffrey R., 80, 81, 86n2, 348, 357, 362, 363
Dillard, Annie, 102
Disney World, 224
Dodge, Mary Mapes, 127
Doherty, Amy, 126
Donne, John, 102
Donnell, Alison, 237, 239, 240
Dostoevsky, Fyodor, 39, 51
Douglas, Kenneth, 64, 67
Douglas, Lloyd, 37
Douglass, Frederick, 95, 101
Dover Books, 119, 120
Downing, David B., 22, 350
Doyle, Arthur Conan, 36, 38
Dresner, Zita, 115

Dryden, John, 397
Dublin, Thomas, 133n14
Dufrenne, Mikel, 194, 199
Dumézil, Georges, 195
During, Simon, 3
Dusable Museum, 244n9
Duyckinck, Evart A., 114
Duyckinck, George L., 114

Eastman, Arthur, 104
ecocriticism, 243
École Normale Supérieure, 202n3
economics (as a discipline), 93
Edgell, Zee, 237
editors, 24, 62, 67–69, 113, 116, 179, 269, 340n2; and civil rights, 102; and class, 122–24; and formal features of anthologies, 398; and gender, 266, 267; and Norton, 43, 45n4, 63, 67, 104, 373–75; and race (Indigenous), 247–48, 252–54, 256, 259, 260; of textbook anthologies, 103; of theory anthologies, 343; white, 126
Edmundson, Mark, 269
Ehrenreich, Barbara, 213
Eisler, Benita, 123, 133n14
Eliot, Charles W., 32–35, 36, 44, 56–59, 70, 72, 83, 86n1, 148
Eliot, George, 5, 7
Eliot, T. S., 66, 71, 176, 179, 180, 181, 184, 399, 401
Elliott, Sarah Barnwell, 127
Ellison, Ralph, 144
Emerson, Ralph Waldo, 35, 72, 94, 96, 109n2, 134n19, 189, 190
English (as a discipline), 21, 59, 65, 69, 97, 100, 101, 121, 163, 191, 212, 218, 219n1, 283, 299, 304, 306, 317, 323n12, 342, 343, 344, 349, 352, 353, 362, 368n16, 403
English, Tony, 182
English Institute, 11
English literature. *See* literature: English
English Short Stories 1900 to the Present, 308
English studies, 352, 357–58, 361, 362, 364n3
Enlightenment, 70, 400
epic, 42–43, 58, 290

Epictetus, 35
Epstein, Jason, 9
Epstein, Joseph, 93
Equiano, Olaudah, 109n2
Erasmus, 52
Erdrich, Louise, 103, 172
Essay Connection: Readings for Writers, 14, 105
essays, 14, 90, 92–96, 99, 100–104, 106, 109n2
Etzkowitz, Henry, 365n7
Euripides, 39
Euro-American literature. *See* literature: Euro-American
Eurocentrism, 314
existentialism, 194, 196, 199, 200, 202n4, 380; black, 196, 199

Factory Girls: A Collection of Writings on Life and Struggles in the New England Factories of the 1840s, 123
Fadiman, Anne, 93
Fadiman, Clifton, 36, 37
Fanon, Frantz, 194, 196, 226, 232, 241, 244n5
Far, Sui Sin, 115
Faulkner, William, 38
Female Poets of America, The, 113, 131
feminism, 155–69, 266, 279, 291, 304, 305, 326, 340n1
Fern, Fanny, 130, 134n19
Ferry, Anne, 7, 84
Fetterley, Judith, 71, 121, 124, 128, 274n5
Fiedelson, Charles, 274n5
Fiedler, Leslie, 11
Fielding, Henry, 144, 145
Finke, Laurie, 23, 219n2
Fiske, John, 259, 261n7, 312, 313, 322n6
Fitzgerald, F. Scott, 299
Fliegelman, Jay, 132n9, 269, 274n3
Foerster, Norman, 266
Foner, Phillip, 123, 133n14
Ford, Karen, 182
Forester, C. S., 38
Forster, E. M., 102
Foster, Sesshu, 173
Foucault, Michel, 187, 194, 195, 196, 198, 202n3, 247, 252, 257, 352, 392, 402

Index

Frank, Manfred, 188
Franklin, Benjamin, 35
Freeman, Mary Wilkins, 117
Fremantle Arts Centre Press, 258
French literature. *See* literature: French
Freud, Sigmund, 38, 40, 187, 198
From the Green Antilles: Writings from the Caribbean, 233
Frost, Robert, 171, 172, 176, 178, 179, 184
Fuller, Steve, 344, 355, 364n3, 365n8
Fulton, Maurice Garland, 98, 99
Funk and Wagnalls, 32

Gadamer, Hans-Georg, 187, 291–94
Gaddis, William, 145, 149
Gansberg, Martin, 96
Garland, 3
Garvey, Marcus Mosiah, 232
Gates, Henry Louis, 11, 15, 179, 218
Gautier, Théophile, 385, 389, 392
gay and lesbian studies, 350
gender studies, 243
Genesis, 41, 42
Genet, Jean, 332, 335
German (as a discipline), 192
Germano, William, 3, 4, 7
Gide, André, 69
Gilgamesh, 42, 43
Gilman, Charlotte Perkins, 117, 127, 144
Gilroy, Paul, 244n10
Gilson, Etienne, 202n3
Gless, Darryl J., 25n1
global literary studies, 47
Global Voices, 82
Godine, David, 119
Goethe, Johann Wolfgang von, 5, 36, 39, 47, 51
Goldie, Terry, 248, 252, 253, 254, 256, 258
Golding, Alan C., 91, 92, 131n1
Goodman, Ellen, 102
Gosson, Renee, 245n13
Gould, Stephen Jay, 96
Graff, Gerald, 3, 20–21, 81, 86n2, 217, 310, 322n8, 353, 403
Granger, Gilles-Gaston, 194
Graulich, Melody, 128

Gray, Janet, 132n3
Great Books of the Western World, 51, 59, 62
Greek gods, 42, 43
Greek poets, 3
Gresham, William, 174
Griswold, Rufus, 113, 117, 131
Groden, Michael, 24
Guattari, Felix, 194, 382n6
Guéroult, Martial, 202n3
Guillén, Martí, 241
Guillén, Nicholás, 241
Guillory, John, 7, 11–12, 33, 79, 300, 307, 308, 317, 318, 321n3, 322n7, 323n15

Habermas, Jürgen, 187
Hadot, Pierre, 194
Hall, Stuart, 314
Hamacher, Werner, 188
Haraway, Donna, 352
Harcourt Brace, 63
Hardison, O. B., 94, 95
Harjo, Joy, 247, 251–56, 259
Harlem Renaissance, 180, 184
Harper, Frances, 128, 130, 131
Harper, Michael, 173
HarperCollins, 40, 44; and *The Harper American Literature*, 267; and the *Harper Anthology of American Literature*, 306; and the *HarperCollins World Reader*, 13, 40, 41
Harris, Susan, 134n19
Harris, Wendell V., 95
Harris, Wilson, 235, 244n12
Hartford Courant, 54
Harvard Classics, The, 32, 35, 56, 59
Harvard University, 32, 56, 98, 345
Hassan, Waïl S., 311, 312
Hawthorne, Nathaniel, 274n5, 306
Hayakawa, S. I., 96
Hazlitt, William, 96
headnotes, 20, 23–24, 71, 76, 218, 281, 283, 284, 374–83, 383–94, 395–404, 405–10
Healey, Peter, 365n7
Heath, 5, 19–20; and the *Heath Anthology of American Literature*, 5, 91, 113, 116, 219n2, 264, 267, 275n11, 306
Heath, D. C., 275n11

421

Hegel, George Wilhelm Friedrich, 195, 198, 326, 332
Heidegger, Martin, 187, 188, 190, 195, 198, 202n4, 293, 326, 374, 380
Heilbroner, Robert L., 380
Helms, Jesse, 157
Hemingway, Ernest, 174, 304, 305, 321n5
Hemingway's Youth in Michigan, 304
Hentz, Caroline Lee, 134n18
Hentzi, Gary, 23
Hermeneutic Tradition: From Ast to Ricoeur, 188
hermeneutics, 71, 187–88, 193, 216, 291, 302
Herstory: Women Who Changed the World, 395
Herzberg, Bruce, 97, 98
heteroglossia, 51, 321n3
higher education, 2, 32, 119, 211, 343, 359, 363, 396
Highet, Gilbert, 102
Hillis Miller, J., 211, 382n2
Hirsch, E. D., 293–95
Hispanic literature. *See* literature: Hispanic
history (as a discipline), 58, 65, 94, 96, 134n17, 229, 347
Hittite Empire, 43
Hogan, Linda, 103
Holmes, Oliver Wendell, 94, 97, 274n5
Holocaust Museum, 244n3
Homer, 36, 39, 40, 41, 42, 43, 45n4, 51
Hongo, Garrett, 103
Horace, 399
Houghton Mifflin, 274n7
Howes, Barbara, 233
Hughes, Langston, 177, 183
Hugo, Howard, 64, 70
humanities, 6, 10, 11, 66, 120, 121, 129, 130, 211, 323n12, 343, 344, 345, 347, 349, 350, 352, 353, 357–58, 360–63, 364n3, 366n10, 366n11, 367n15, 408
Hurt, James, 3, 39, 40, 41
Husserl, Edmund, 195, 202n4, 293, 326
Hutchins, Robert, 51, 59, 62, 87
Hyppolite, Jean, 194, 195, 199, 202

identity politics. *See* politics: identity
ideology, 2, 4, 6, 8, 80, 84, 90, 150, 219n2, 222, 223, 249, 258, 282, 283, 300, 301, 306, 307, 311, 312, 319, 321n3, 323n13, 352, 378, 379, 380, 382n5, 395, 400–403
Illinois State University, 142
Illinois University Press, 173
Indiana University of Pennsylvania, 356
Indiana University Press, 201
Indian literature. *See* literature: Indian
Indigenous literature. *See* literature: Indigenous
individualism, 219n2, 395–96, 400, 401
innovative literature. *See* literature: innovative
Innovations: An Anthology of Modern and Contemporary Fiction, 16, 139, 141, 149–53
institutionalism, 279, 348, 358
Intellectual Life of the British Working Classes, 49
International Association for Philosophy and Literature, 191
Irele, Abiola, 74
Irigaray, Luce, 190, 194, 196, 199
Irving, Washington, 96
Isaiah, 41

Jackson, Shirley, 322n6
Jacobs, Carol, 215
Jacobs, Harriet, 133n14
Jakobson, Roman, 387, 392
James, C. L. R., 232, 236, 241
James, Heather, 70, 77
Jankélévich, Vladimir, 194, 195, 199
Japanese Association for Language Teaching, 320n1
Japanese literature. *See* literature: Japanese
Japanese renga, 31
Jarrell, Randall, 171
Jen, Gish, 103
Jencks, Christopher, 211
Jewett, Sarah Orne, 117, 119, 132n7
Job, 42
Johanningsmeier, Charles, 117
Johns Hopkins, 402

Index

Johnson, Barbara, 23, 342
Johnson, Ben, 97
Johnson, B. S., 145
Johnson, Glen M., 273, 274n1, 274n2
Johnson, James Weldon, 235
Jonke, Gert, 144
Joyce, James, 61, 76, 144, 146
Judaeus, Philo, 376

Kadushin, Charles, 7
Kafka, Franz, 41
Kakutani, Michiko, 103
Kalidasa, 36
Kampf, Louis, 71
Kamuf, Peggy, 331, 332, 340n2
Kant, Immanuel, 209, 387, 392
Kaplan, Carey, 11
Karcher, Carolyn L., 118
Kaufmann, Walter, 192
Keats, John, 282, 307
Kelley, Mary, 118, 323n12
Kelly, Curtis, 299
Kennedy, X. J., 103
Kermode, Frank, 91
Kilcup, Karen L., 14–15, 81, 86n2, 117, 134n19
Kincaid, Jamaica, 101, 244n1
King, Martin Luther, Jr., 96, 101, 105
Kingston, Maxine Hong, 102
Kittler, Friedrich A., 7
Klossowski, Pierre, 193, 194
Knight, Franklin W., 244n2
Knox, Bernard, 64
Kofman, Sarah, 193, 194
Kogawa, Joy, 316
Kojève, Alexander, 194, 195, 199
Kozol, Jonathan, 96, 101
Kreiswirth, Martin, 24
Kristeva, Julia, 188, 194, 196, 199
Krutch, Joseph Wood, 102
Kuhn, Thomas, 342, 344–49, 352–55, 360, 362–63, 364n3, 365n8, 366n9, 367n15

labor: academic, 5, 130, 210, 212, 213, 275n10, 347, 353, 356, 358, 359, 362, 365n8; and graduate students, 133n12, 377

Lacan, Jacques, 194, 196, 198, 199, 352, 391
Laclau, Ernesto, 271
Lacoue-Labarthe, Philippe, 194
LaFlesche, Susette, 115
Lakoff, Robin, 102
Lamb, Charles, 96, 109n2
Lamming, George, 226, 230, 241, 244n11
Langer, Susanne, 102
Larcom, Lucy, 128, 133n14
Larkin, Paschal, 401
Larson, Magali Sarfatti, 209
Latin American studies, 223, 236
Latin literature. See literature: Latin
Latour, Bruno, 403
Lauter, Paul, 5, 7, 71, 91, 102, 132n2, 134n19, 267, 268, 269, 272, 274n6
Lawall, Sarah, 9, 13–14, 20, 65, 77, 80
Lawrence, D. H., 41
Lê, Thi Diem Thúy, 103
League of Nations, 34
Leavis, F. R., 142, 147
Le Doeuff, Michele, 194
Lefebvre, Georges, 194
Lefevere, Andre, 248–49, 250, 251
Lefort, Claude, 194
Le Guin, Ursula, 303
Leitch, Vincent, 3, 23
Leithauser, Brad, 310
Leslie, Larry, 365n7
Levin, Harry, 51, 274n5
Levinas, Emmanuel, 190, 194, 198
Levine, George, 117, 123, 210, 212
Lévi-Strauss, Claude, 189, 190, 194, 198, 199, 391–92
Lewis, C. S., 174
Lewis, Edwin H., 98
Lewis, Gordon, 244n2
Lewontin, R. C., 211
liberalism, 12, 400, 401, 402
Library of America, 119, 180
Library of American Literature, 265
Library of the World's Best Literature, Ancient and Modern, 50, 53–54
Lim, Shirley Geok-lin, 315
Lincoln, Abraham, 96, 101
Lindsay, Vachel, 185

Index

linguistic capital, 300, 308, 321n3, 322n7
linguistics, 96, 308, 387, 388
Lipsky, David, 210
literary history, 75, 114, 142, 217, 266, 267
Literary History of America, 274n5
literary studies, 12, 31, 39, 117, 120, 121, 124, 125, 127, 135n19, 279–80, 282, 283, 296, 353, 398
literary theory, 69, 250, 252, 260, 279, 296, 349, 402, 403; and dictionaries, 23, 285
literature: Aboriginal Australian, 19, 228, 248, 249, 257, 259; Accadian-Babylonian literature, 54; African American, 85, 151, 219, 223, 227, 235, 236, 243, 310, 316; African orature, 31, 40; American, 59, 60, 71, 91, 109n2, 113, 126–27, 132n9, 142, 149, 174, 235, 267, 272, 273, 298, 299, 306, 308, 309, 311, 313, 315, 319, 343; Anglophone Caribbean, 225, 232, 236–38; Asian, 61, 74; Asian American, 316–17; Assyrian, 54; Australian, 228; Aztec, 41, 314; British, 60 (*see also* literature: English); Caribbean, 18, 74, 222, 223, 226–29, 231, 233–35, 237–38, 241–43; Chinese, 60; English, 59, 67, 71, 234, 235, 299, 306, 307, 308, 309, 311, 313, 321n4; Euro-American, 38–39; French, 67, 69, 393; as "good," 247, 256, 260; Hispanic, 125, 267, 272, 311; Indian, 60; Indigenous, 19, 247–50, 253, 258–60; innovative, 15, 17, 133n13, 142, 148, 150, 152; Japanese, 60; Latin, 300; Mayan, 41; metafictional, 156; multicultural, 5, 49, 51, 70, 74, 78, 91, 120, 125; Native American, 19, 40, 74, 248–52, 254, 257, 268, 316; Oriental, 36, 63; postcolonial, 126, 237; Prakrit, 76; rationales for professing, 209; self-reflexive, 48, 85, 156, 254; Slavic, 67; women's, 123, 127; working-class, 124; world, 3, 12–14, 31, 32–33, 35, 37–41, 44, 47–51, 59, 61–64, 66–71, 74, 75, 78, 80, 81, 82, 84, 86, 149. *See also* paraliterature

Literature of the Western World, 3, 39, 41
Literatures of Asia, Africa, and Latin America, 40, 41
Lively, Penelope, 302, 303
Livingston, James T., 235–36
Locke, John, 401
Lodge, David, 350
Lodge, Henry Cabot, 32–36, 44
Logan, William, 180
Logghe, Joan, 275n13
Logic of the Gift: Toward an Ethic of Generosity, 189
Longfellow, Henry Wadsworth, 128, 274n5
Longman Publishing Company, 2, 70, 219n2; and the *Longman Anthology of British Literature*, 13; and the *Longman Anthology of World Literature*, 13, 83
Louis, Adrian, 184
Lowell Offering: Writings by New England Mill Women (1840–1845), 123, 133n14
Lowell, Amy, 185
Lowell, James Russell, 274n5
Lowell, Robert, 179
Lubbock, John, 49
Lukács, György, 375
Lyotard, Jean Francois, 194, 196, 199

Macaulay, Thomas Babington, 96
Mack, Maynard, 64, 65, 66, 67, 68, 69, 72, 73, 74, 79
MacLochlainn, Alf, 145
Macmillan Publishing Company, 119, 233; and the *Anthology of American Literature*, 267
Magaballa Books, 259
Magill, Frank, 35, 36, 37, 38, 39, 45n1
Mahfouz, Naguib, 73
Mailer, Norman, 103
Maimonides, Moses, 374
Mais, Roger, 237, 240
Malcolm X, 102
Man, Paul de, 211, 215–16, 218, 321n4, 392
Mann, Thomas, 61
Marcel, Gabriel, 380
Margaret of Navarre, 144, 146
market. *See* anthologies: market

Index

Marot, Clément, 393
Marshall, Paule, 226, 227
Marson, Una, 237
Martí, José, 232
Martin, Robert K., 132n4
Marxism, 170, 196, 199, 326, 340n1
Mason, Bobbie Ann, 303
Masterpieces of The World's Literature, Ancient and Modern, 50
Masterpieces of World Literature in Digest Form, 35
Masterplots, 35
Mauss, Marcel, 189, 190, 194, 196, 197
Mayan literature. *See* literature: Mayan
Mazza, Cris, 3, 16, 17, 149
McCaffery, Larry, 3
McCarthyism, 265
McGalliard, John, 64
McGowan, John, 23
McKay, Claude, 185
McKay, Nelly, 125
McLaughlin, Robert L., 15–16, 17
McQuade, Donald M., 97, 98, 99, 100
McVeigh, Brian, 320n1
Mead, Margaret, 96, 102
medicine (as a discipline), 77, 93, 96
medieval, 78, 350, 365n6, 382n5
Meleager, 3
Mellon Fellowship, 124
Mellon Foundation, 134n17
Melville, Herman, 274n5
Memmi, Albert, 194, 196
Mena, Maria Cristina, 126
Merleau-Ponty, Maurice, 194, 196, 198, 199
Merrill, James, 172
metafiction. *See* literature: metafiction
Metzger, Walter, 220n3
Michigan Quarterly Review, 92
Milgram, Stanley, 96
Mill, John Stuart, 400, 401
Millay, Edna St. Vincent, 183
Miller, Barbara Stoler, 74
Miller, Casey, 102
Milton, John, 35, 282, 357
Mishima, Yukio, 73
modernism, 71–72, 117, 150, 176, 180, 181, 184, 185

Monarch notes, 23
Montaigne, Michel de, 39, 95
Moore, Marianne, 179, 184
Moore, Steven, 142
Mori, Kyoko, 316
Morris, Timothy, 132n2
Morrison, Toni, 282
Moses, Daniel David, 248, 252–53, 254
Mosley, Nicholas, 144
Mouffe, Chantal, 271
Moulthrop, Stuart, 373
Moulton, Richard, 59
Mounier, Emmanuel, 194, 196, 202n4
Mount Olympus, 42
Moyne Report, 225
Mozarabic kharjas, 31
Mukarovsky, Jan, 85, 89
Mukherjee, Bharati, 103
multiculturalism, 114, 264, 265, 271, 272, 273, 315, 356
multicultural literature. *See* literature: multicultural
Mumford, Lewis, 103
Murfin, Ross, 285
Musa, Mark, 3

Naipaul, V. S., 18, 222, 223, 227, 228, 230, 236, 240, 243
Nancy, Jean-Luc, 188, 194
Narayan, R. K., 73
National Book Award for Distinguished Service to American Letters, 9
National Defense Research Committee, 345
nationalism, 225, 226, 322n10
Native American literature. *See* literature: Native American
Native American Women's Writing, c. 1800–1924, 14, 115, 122
naturalism, 41, 65
Neal, Larry, 182
Negritude, 235
Neilson, William A., 56, 57, 58
Nelson, Cary, 17, 130, 133n12, 275n10
neoclassicism, 65, 350
neocolonialism, 223, 229, 231
neo-Kantianism, 199, 202n4
neoliberalism, 19, 270

425

Neoplatonism, Renaissance, 365n6
New Criticism, 64-65, 71, 211, 215, 217, 282-83, 289, 294, 352
New Directions, 171
New England Journal of Medicine, 93
New Historicism, 285, 326, 340n1, 350
New Nietzsche: Contemporary Styles of Interpretation, 193
New Writing from the Caribbean, 237
New York Times, 5, 142, 143, 165
Newman, John Henry, 97
Nietzsche, Friedrich, 186, 187, 189, 191-93, 195, 198, 201n1, 339
Nineteenth-Century American Women Poets, 118
Nineteenth-Century American Women Writers: An Anthology, 14, 114, 115, 127
Nobel Prize, 222-23, 227, 236, 244n12
Noonuccal, Oodgeroo, 258, 261n5
Norbu, Jamyang, 31
North, Stephen, 93
Norton. See W. W. Norton and Co., Inc.

Oates, Joyce Carol, 144
O'Brien, Flann, 144
O'Brien, John, 142, 146, 148, 152
Ohmann, Richard, 360
Olson, Charles, 172
Ondaatje, Michael, 227
O'Neill, Angeline, 19
One World of Literature, 82
Oriental literature. *See* literature: Oriental
Ormiston, Gayle L., 187
Orwell, George, 95, 102, 105
Ottoman Empire, 41
Our Heritage of World Literature, 62
Out of the Kumbla, 237
Ovid, 36, 78
Owen, Catherine, 115
Owen, Stephen, 74
Oxford University Press, 2, 17, 119, 170, 171, 172, 174, 176, 177, 179, 182-84, 259; and the Anthology of Modern American Poetry, 17, 170, 171
Ozick, Cynthia, 93

Paine, Thomas, 52
Paley, Grace, 145, 147

paradigm, 48, 59, 342, 345-48, 350, 353-55, 357, 359, 360, 365n8, 367n15
paraliterature, 250
Parker, Hershel, 323n14
Pascal, Blaise, 58
Pasinetti, Pier, 64
Passeron, Jean-Claude, 214
Pater, Walter, 97, 101
Patterns of Exposition, 103
Patterson, Lee, 70, 77
Peck, Harry Thurston, 50, 51, 53, 54, 55
pedagogy, 60, 62, 64, 66, 68, 69, 74-75, 81, 84, 98, 106, 118, 141, 145, 149, 189, 198, 216-18, 283, 293, 303, 315, 320, 328, 337, 340, 359; apparatus of, 151-52, 207, 211; atomistic approaches to, 74; and the canon, 47, 91, 103, 147; classical, 337-39; and communication, 214; and composition, 98; democratic, 105; and essays, 99; and headnotes, 380, 395; and the imaginary, 405-10; and intertextuality, 146; literary, 282-83; and marketability, 186; and master critics, 355; modes of, 218-19; and organization, 57; packages, 73; and poststructuralism, 403; and procedures, 337; and tradition, 337-38; and utilitarianism, 14, 90; and world literature, 70. *See also* anthologies: pedagogical implications of
Pemmican Publications, 259
Penguin Book of American Short Stories, 308
Penn, William, 35
Perez, Eulalia, 125
Peterson, Indira Viswanathan, 74
Peterson, Linda, 104
Petrarch, Francesco, 31, 60
Petronius, 143
Petrunkevich, Alexander, 101
P. F. Collier and Son, 32, 56
Phelan, Jim, 3, 285, 287, 296
phenomenology, 65, 199, 326
Philips, Caryl, 226, 227, 244n9
philosophy, 58, 94, 192; continental, 21, 197, 402; and deconstruction, 340n1; French, 187, 194-201, 202n5; German, 187, 195; Greco-Roman, 35; political, 400

Index

Piatt, Sarah, 128
Pickering, Sam, 93
Pirandello, Luigi, 61
Pittsburgh University Press, 173
Plato, 35, 41, 188, 216, 350, 373, 374, 377, 389, 397
Platonism, 289
Plautus, 61
Pocket Books, 233
poetry, 79, 92, 96, 97, 131; American, 170–85; anthologies, 3, 17, 39, 68, 96, 123, 131n1; Egyptian, 42; English, 84; and epigrams, 3; Inuit, 41; Jewish, 273; lyric, 58, 60, 61, 68; narrative, 38; political, 170, 183, 185; punk, 173; Sumerian, 31; women's, 124
political science (as a discipline), 58, 93, 94, 192
political theory (as a discipline), 64, 192
politics: capitalist, 170, 176, 271, 359; colonial, 77, 79, 132n4, 196, 199, 222–46, 249, 257, 258, 314; communist, 345; conservative, 71, 101; democratic, 35, 215, 264, 270–74, 361, 402; egalitarian, 270, 402, 409; fourth world, 247–63; global, 47, 75; hegemony, 250, 300, 321n3; identity, 125–28, 271; imperialist, 225, 231, 300, 308, 393; liberal, 12, 400–403; Marxist, 170, 196, 199, 326, 340n1; nationalist, 225–26, 322n10; Nazi, 174; neocolonial, 223, 229, 231; neoliberal, 19, 270; postcolonial, 222–46, 314; third world, 18, 244. *See also* anthologies: political implications of; ideology; value: political
Politics of Literature: Dissenting Essays on the Teaching of English, 71
Pope, Alexander, 97
Portable Machiavelli, The, 3
postcolonial: studies, 236, 241, 243; theory, 239, 242. *See also* literature: postcolonial
postfeminism, 156, 158–59, 163, 165, 167–68
postmodernism, 21, 142, 150, 308, 315–16, 318–19, 326, 328, 340n1; Tibetan, 31

poststructuralism, 194–95, 217, 239, 326, 402–3
Pound, Ezra, 180, 184, 306, 311
Powell, Walter W., 7
Prakrit literature. *See* literature: Prakrit
Prentice-Hall, 40, 63, 70, 308; and the *Concise Anthology of American Literature*, 308
Pressman, Richard S., 19, 47, 49, 86n2
Price, Leah, 7
professionalism, 209–13, 279
Proust, Marcel, 61, 193, 203
Pryse, Marjorie, 128
Psalms, 42
psychoanalysis, 188, 326, 340n1, 350, 391
psychology (as a discipline), 96, 134n17, 367n14
publishers, 2, 32, 103–4, 116, 118, 125, 126, 151, 168, 171–78, 200, 259
Purdue University, 186
Pynchon, Thomas, 145, 316

Rabelais, 144
racism, 270, 287, 291
Random House, 9, 119, 171, 181; and the *Random House Book of Twentieth Century French Poetry*, 310
Ransom, John Crowe, 352, 368n18
Reader in Caribbean Literature, 237, 240
reader-response theory, 380
Readings, Bill, 362, 365n7
realism, 41, 65, 142–43, 145, 150
Reconstructing American Literature: Courses, Syllabi, Issues, 71
Redressing the Balance: American Women's Literary Humor from Colonial Times to the 1980s, 115
Reed, Ishmael, 144
Reichert, John, 296, 297
Reid, V. S., 237, 240
Reinventing the Enemy's Language: Contemporary Native Women's Writings of North America, 247, 251–54, 258–60
Reisman, David, 211
religion, 58, 77, 96, 134n17, 347, 384, 388
Renaissance, 41, 65, 70, 77, 121, 350, 365n6, 390

Renza, Louis A., 132n7
research models: pragmatic, 10–11, 60, 72, 75, 97, 101; solipsistic, 10
Resisting Reader: A Feminist Approach to American Fiction, 71
rewriting, 216
Rexroth, Kenneth, 298
Reynolds, David S., 128, 134n19
rhetoric (as a discipline), 192
rhetorical theory, 98
Rich, Adrienne, 173, 175, 178, 181, 392
Richards, I. A., 5, 38
Richie, Donald, 314
Richter, David, 359–61, 366n12
Ricoeur, Paul, 187, 194
Rilke, Rainer Maria, 40
Rintoul, Stuart, 261n3
Rivera, Tomás, 267
Robbins, Bruce, 209
Robinson, Jackie, 264
Robinson, Lillian, 212, 213, 268
Rockefeller, John D., 218
Rodney, Walter, 225
Rodriguez, Richard, 95, 101
Rogozinski, Jan, 244n2
Rolfe, Edwin, 179
romanticism, 41, 65, 70, 78, 306, 350
Rome, 33, 41
Ronsard, Pierre de, 388, 390
Rorty, Richard, 5, 217
Rose, Ellen Cronan, 11
Rose, Jonathan, 49
Rosset, Clément, 194, 196
Rosten, Leo, 103
Rousseau, Jean Jacques, 5, 39, 69, 78
Routledge, 4, 190
Rowlandson, Mary, 109n2
Royle, Nicholas, 340n1
Ruffo, Armand, 259, 261n7
Rukeyser, Muriel, 180, 181
Ruland, Richard, 269, 275n11
Runes, Dagobert D., 62
Rushdie, Salman, 145, 147
Ruskin, John, 97, 101
Russell, Bertrand, 96

Sagan, Miriam, 275n13
Said, Edward W., 376
Saint Augustine, Bishop of Hippo, 39
Salzman, Mark, 322n6
Sandburg, Carl, 185
Sanders, Scott Russell, 95
Sartre, Jean-Paul, 194, 196, 197, 198, 199, 200, 202n4, 281–82, 332, 380
Saussure, Ferdinand de, 194, 198, 199, 387–88, 391, 394
Scholes, Robert, 99, 100, 382n1
Schriber, Mary Suzanne, 115
Schrift, Alan D., 17, 21
Schultz, Joan, 274n5
science (as a discipline), 58, 93, 94, 96, 134n17, 343, 345, 360, 364n3, 365n6, 366n10
science fiction, 115
Searle, Leroy, 350, 364n2
Sedgwick, Catharine Maria, 118, 130
self-reflexive literature. *See* literature: self-reflexive
Seneca, 33
Senghor, Léopold Sédar, 235
Serres, Michel, 194
Shakespeare, William, 21, 36, 39, 54, 60, 121, 127, 285, 291, 299, 306, 308
Shapiro, Gary, 190
Shaw, George Bernard, 103, 407
Sheffield, Elisabeth, 160, 164
Shelley, Percy, 307
Sherlock, Philip, 244n2
Shikibu, Murasaki, 76, 144, 147, 395
Showalter, Elaine, 5, 150, 153n2
Shumway, David, 116, 138, 357, 367n16, 368n16, 370
Sidney, Philip, 399
Silko, Leslie Marmon, 248
Slaughter, Sheila, 365n7
Slavic literature. *See* literature: Slavic
Smith College, 56
Smith, Barbara Herrnstein, 25n1, 90, 91, 132n2
Smith, Louise Z., 104
Smith, Patricia, 173
Smith, Paul A., 275n11
Smith, Stevie, 144, 147
Smith, Welton, 181
Snows of Kilimanjaro and Other Stories, 305
Snyder, Gary, 298

Index

social history, 51, 59, 134n17, 150, 219n2, 379, 381
social science (as a discipline), 343, 345
sociological studies, 7
Socrates, 33
Sollors, Werner, 71
Sontag, Susan, 93
Sophocles, 39
Sorrentino, Gilbert, 144, 149
Sosnoski, James, 1, 132n2, 354, 355, 356, 357, 358, 364n1, 366n11, 367n15
Soto, Gary, 103
Soyinka, Wole, 73
Spacks, Patricia Meyer, 70
Spanish Civil War, 174
Staël, Madame de, 391
Staples, Brent, 101
Stedman, E. C., 113
Stein, Gertrude, 144, 149, 179, 181
Steinbeck, John, 103
Sterne, Laurence, 144
Stevens, Wallace, 31, 184
St. Martin's Custom Reader, 104
St. Mary's University of Texas, 272
Stoekl, Allan, 190
Straus, Farrar, 171, 172, 178, 181
structuralism, 65, 194, 195, 196, 197, 350, 388, 403
Strunk, W., 306
Swan Valley Nyoongar community, 257
Swift, Jonathan, 96, 97, 101, 102, 105
Swift, Kate, 102
Symbolist, 78
symplokē, 80, 382n7

Tan, Amy, 103
Teahouse of the August Moon, 303
Teilhard de Chardin, Pierre, 194, 202n4
Telling Travels: Selected Writings by Nineteenth-Century American Women Abroad, 115
Tennyson, Alfred Lord, 307
tenure. *See* academic: tenure
textbooks, 1, 2, 4, 10, 14, 70, 90, 91, 94–95, 96, 98, 99, 101–5, 106, 109n2, 120, 175, 184, 201, 208, 271, 279, 281, 285, 287, 301, 311, 315, 327, 343–44, 348, 364n1, 366n9, 369, 376, 378, 396–97, 402, 403, 406–7

Thalmann, William G., 70, 77
Theytus Books, 254, 259
Thomas, Clarence, 166
Thomas, Lewis, 96
Thompson, Stith, 62
Thoreau, Henry David, 109n2, 134n19, 274n5
Those Who Remain Will Always Remember: An Anthology of Aboriginal Writing, 19, 248, 253, 254, 255, 257, 258, 260, 261n4
Through a Glass Darkly: Ethnic Semiosis in American Literature, 273
Thurber, James, 102
Tolson, Melvin B., 15, 173, 179, 180–81
Tran, Duc Thao, 194
Transforming the Hermeneutic Context: From Nietzsche to Nancy, 188
translation, 58, 64, 67, 70, 81, 90, 187–90, 193, 196, 201n2, 219, 321, 393; and Derrida, 326, 328, 338, 340n2, 341n3; of Francophone writers, 237; and Japanese, 299, 302–3, 305; objections to, 34, 216; of oral tradition, 251; of poetry, 60, 61, 68; as redescription, 217
Treasury of World Literature, 62
Trilling, Lionel, 51
Truth, Sojourner, 101
Twain, Mark, 21, 54, 102, 127, 285–87, 290–93

Understanding Poetry, 99, 211
University of California Press, 172, 173
University of Chicago, 286
University of Hull, 124
University of Illinois at Chicago, 156, 164
University of Illinois at Urbana-Champaign, 174
University of Iowa, 67
University of Michigan, 97, 134n17
University of Minnesota Press, 201n2
University of New York Press, 188
University of the Virgin Islands, 237
University of the West Indies at Cave Hill, 226

value, 208, 211, 239, 256, 259, 311, 322n7, 329; and anthologies, 4, 9–11,

value (continued)
  15, 150, 397; buyback, 209; canonical, 179; cultural, 4, 34, 37, 49, 102, 208, 215, 300; disciplinary, 346; economic, 300; family, 157; and genres, 123; and headnotes, 23, 400; humanistic, 79, 90; ideological, 90; intellectual, 192; literary, 19, 123, 132n2, 282, 297; market, 176, 378; multicultural, 125, 131; pedagogical, 54, 74, 91, 211, 396; political, 17, 35, 269, 400, 402–3; research, 10–11; of textual apparatus, 24; and theory, 355; and translation, 34
van den Berg, Rosemary, 248, 254
Veblen, Thorstein, 365n7
Verghese, Abraham, 103, 319
vernacular language, 97, 216, 393
Vico, Giambattista, 374, 377
Vietnam War, 266
Villon, Francois, 61
vitalism, 199
Voices from Afar: Modern Chinese Writers on Oppressed Peoples and Their Literature, 51
Voices from an Empire: A History of Afro-Portuguese Literature, 51
Voices: Canadian Writers of African Descent, 51

W. W. Norton and Co., Inc., 16, 48, 63–64, 68–70, 72–74, 79–81, 119, 155, 174–76, 181, 193, 219n2, 259; anthologies, 16, 155, 193, 219n2; and the Norton Anthology of African American Literature, 15, 179; and the Norton Anthology of American Literature, 113, 174, 266; and the Norton Anthology of English Literature, 308; and the Norton Anthology of Modern American and British Poetry, 176; and the Norton Anthology of Postmodern American Fiction, 168; and the Norton Anthology of Theory and Criticism, 3, 5, 23, 25n2, 218, 373, 379, 381, 382n7, 384, 397, 398; and the Norton Anthology of Women's Literature, 212; and the Norton Anthology of World Literature, 13, 69, 78, 80, 85; and the Norton Anthology of World Masterpieces, 13, 39, 40, 42, 44, 63–80, 311; and the Norton

Reader, 103; and *Postmodern American Literature: A Norton Anthology*, 153n1
Wade, Barry, 73
Wahl, Jean, 194, 196
Walcott, Derek, 223, 226, 227, 235, 236, 240, 244n12
Walker, Alice, 95, 102
Walker, Nancy A., 115
Wallace, David Foster, 16, 141, 149, 153
Wall Street Journal, 166
Warner, Charles D., 50, 51, 53–55, 59
Warren, Austin, 352, 367n14
Warren, Kenneth, 113, 119, 122, 134n19
Warren, Robert Penn, 211
Washington Post, 157
Watanna, Onoto, 15, 112
Watkins, Evan, 220n2
Watt, Ian, 142
Webster, Andrew, 365n7
Weil, Simone, 194
Wellek, René, 64, 65, 67, 88, 352, 367n14
Wells-Barnett, Ida B., 131
Welsh, Sarah Lawson, 78, 237–40
Welty, Eudora, 102
Wesleyan University Press, 173
Western Canon, The, 90, 102
White, E. B., 95, 102, 105
Whittier, John Greenleaf, 128
Why Nietzsche Still? Reflections on Drama, Culture, and Politics, 190
Wideman, John Edgar, 145, 149
Wiederhold, Eve, 132n2, 355
Wiesel, Elie, 244n3
Wilkie, Brian, 3, 39, 40, 41
Williams, Eric, 244n2
Williams, Jeffrey J., 18, 25n2, 398, 402
Williams, Patricia, 101
Williams, William Carlos, 144, 171, 181
Wilson, Woodrow, 34
Winfrey, Oprah, 93
Winger, Debra, 174
Winterowd, W. Ross, 343
Wittgenstein, Ludwig, 202n3, 408
Wittig, Monique, 194
Wolfenstein, Martha, 15, 112, 131
Wolfreys, Julian, 328–29, 331, 332, 340n2

women's literature. *See* literature: women's
women's studies, 163, 168, 192, 359
Woolf, Virginia, 40, 102, 105, 392, 401
Woolman, John, 35
Wordell, Charles, 299
Wordsworth, Dorothy, 78
Wordsworth, William, 299, 409
working-class literature. *See* literature: working-class
Working Men's College, 49
world literature. *See* literature: world
World's Great Masterpieces, 50, 54
World War I, 34
World War II, 142, 197, 224, 241, 264, 265, 345, 359

Wortham, Simon Morgan, 21, 22
Wright, Richard, 102
writing: and composition, 98–100, 358, 359, 360; creative, 150, 256, 358, 359, 360; expository, 93, 98; technical, 358, 359; utilitarian, 14, 90, 97, 98
Wu, Duncan, 113, 118, 119, 120

Yale, 67, 210, 218, 402
Yale University Press, 181
Yeats, W. B., 40
Yellow Trains and Other Stories, 302–3
Young-Ing, Greg, 254
Yumi Press, 304

Zinsser, William, 102

www.ingramcontent.com/pod-product-compliance
Lightning Source LLC
Chambersburg PA
CBHW071235300426
44116CB00008B/1045